Microsoft® Excel 2010: Level 3 of 3

SANDRA RITTMAN
Long Beach City College

El Sobrante, CA

Microsoft Excel 2010: Level 3
by Sandra Rittman

Labyrinth Learning
P.O. Box 20818
El Sobrante, California 24820
800.522.9746
On the web at lablearning.com

President:
Brian Favro

Product Development Manager:
Jason Favro

Managing Editor:
Laura A. Lionello

Production Manager:
Rad Proctor

eLearning Production Manager:
Arl S. Nadel

Editorial/Production Team:
Pamela Beveridge, Belinda Breyer, Everett Cowan, Alec Fehl, Sandy Jones, PMG Media

Indexing: Joanne Sprott

Interior Design:
Mark Ong, Side-by-Side Studios

Cover Design:
Words At Work

ITEM: 1-59136-315-2
ISBN-13: 978-1-59136-315-6

Manufactured in the United States of America.

10 9 8 7 6 5 4 3 2

Table of Contents

LESSON 15: USING ADVANCED FORMATTING AND ANALYSIS TOOLS 584

LESSON 16: COLLABORATING IN EXCEL 626

LESSON 17: SHARING WORKBOOKS ON NETWORKS AND THE INTERNET 670

LESSON 18: INTEGRATING EXCEL WITH OTHER PROGRAMS 696

Quick Reference Tables

COMMENT AND TRACK CHANGES TASKS

CONVERSION AND COMPATIBILITY TASKS

DATA ANALYSIS TASKS

FORMULA TASKS

INTEGRATION TASKS

MACRO TASKS

MULTIPLE-SHEET WORKBOOK TASKS

PIVOTTABLE AND PIVOTCHART TASKS

PROTECTION AND SHARING TASKS

Preface

Microsoft® Excel 2010: Level 3 provides thorough training of Excel 2010 advanced skills. This course is supported with comprehensive instructor resources and our eLab assessment and learning management tool. And, our new work-readiness exercises ensure students have the critical thinking skills necessary to succeed in today's world.

Visual Conventions

This book uses many visual and typographic cues to guide students through the lessons. This page provides examples and describes the function of each cue.

`Type this text`	Anything you should type at the keyboard is printed in this typeface.
	Tips, Notes, and Warnings are used throughout the text to draw attention to certain topics.
Command→ Command→ Command, etc.	This convention indicates how to give a command from the Ribbon. The commands are written: Ribbon Tab→Command Group→Command→ Subcommand.
FROM THE KEYBOARD Ctrl+S to save	These margin notes indicate shortcut keys for executing a task described in the text.

Exercise Progression

The exercises in this book build in complexity as students work through a lesson toward mastery of the skills taught.

- **Develop Your Skills** exercises are introduced immediately after concept discussions. They provide detailed, step-by-step tutorials.
- **Reinforce Your Skills** exercises provide additional hands-on practice with moderate assistance.
- **Apply Your Skills** exercises test students' skills by describing the correct results without providing specific instructions on how to achieve them.
- **Critical Thinking and Work-Readiness Skills** exercises are the most challenging. They provide generic instructions, allowing students to use their skills and creativity to achieve the results they envision.

A Note About Lesson and Page Numbering

You will notice that this book does not begin with Lesson 1 on page 1. This is not an error! The lessons in this book are part of a larger text. We have repackaged the large book into smaller books – while retaining the original lesson and page numbering – to accommodate classes of varying lengths and course hours.

All content in this book is presented in the proper, intended order.

Creating PivotTables and Macros

LESSON OUTLINE

LEARNING OBJECTIVES

After studying this lesson, you will be able to:

- Create PivotTables and change their fields
- Create PivotCharts from PivotTable or worksheet data
- Set macro security to protect workbook data
- Record and run macros to automate tasks
- Add custom task buttons to worksheets

Excel has many features to help you perform sophisticated data analyses, including the PivotTable and the PivotChart. PivotTables let you summarize worksheet data dynamically to view them in various ways. In this lesson, you will arrange your data with simple drag-and-drop commands and have Excel automatically create summary formulas in the rows and columns. You also will create PivotCharts to achieve the same power and flexibility for charting data. Many Excel workbooks are used on a recurring basis. Examples include monthly expense accounts, sales forecasts, and lists of various types. Often, the same tasks are performed in these workbooks over and over. Excel allows you to create macros to automate repetitive tasks. In addition, Excel lets you assign macros to shortcut keys, buttons on the Quick Access toolbar, and custom buttons or other graphics in a worksheet. In this lesson, you will create macros and custom buttons in an Excel workbook.

Student Resources labyrinthelab.com/excel10

CASE STUDY

Simplifying Repetitive Tasks

Raritan Clinic East, an incorporated medical practice that serves a patient community ranging in ages from newborn to 18 years, is planning to construct a pediatric oncology facility. In addition, a companion facility will provide temporary housing to physicians specializing in ground-breaking cancer treatments and long-term housing for family members of the children who are receiving treatments. Sandra Chavez-Hall is the chief development officer for the clinic's foundation. She coordinates a fundraising campaign to solicit contributions from private donors, charitable organizations, industry sources, and government grants to build the two facilities. Sandra will use PivotTables and PivotCharts to analyze the contributions by various criteria.

	Row Labels	Sum of Year 1	Sum of Year 2
4	**⊟Level 1**	**117,267,482**	**118,272,625**
5	Corporate Sponsorship	17,460,000	20,300,000
6	Federal Government Grant	49,899,591	47,894,948
7	Individual Sponsorship	12,500,000	15,000,000
8	State Government Grant	37,407,891	35,077,677
9	**⊟Level 2**	**6,254,063**	**7,511,682**
10	Corporate Grant	1,250,000	1,425,000
11	Corporate Sponsorship	250,000	200,000
12	Individual Sponsorship	2,500,000	2,500,000
13	Medical Center/Large Facility	100,000	90,250
14	Medical Ctr Contribution	654,063	596,432
15	Organized Labor/Union Contribution	750,000	700,000
16	Private Grant	750,000	2,000,000
17	**⊞Level 3**	**1,317,583**	**1,204,419**
18	**⊞Level 4**	**202,100**	**85,500**
19	**⊞Level 5**	**58,287**	**109,509**
20	**⊞Level 6**	**15,186**	**6,827**
21	**Grand Total**	**125,114,701**	**127,190,562**

Levels 3–6 are collapsed to display only the subtotals.

The PivotTable shows the contributions organized by sponsor categories within each pledge level. You can easily rearrange the design to view the data in other ways.

Sandra also maintains a contributions-to-date summary report. She uses macros to record the steps used in sorting the data. By attaching each macro to a button on a worksheet, she can sort the report with one click.

	A	B	C	D	E	F	G
1	Raritan Clinic East Pediatric Diagnostic Specialists		Capital Campaign	Insert Sponsor	Sort by Leader		
2							
3	Pledge	Team Leader	Sponsor Category	Sponsor Name	Year 1	Year 2	To Date
4	Level 3	Abbott	Organization Contribution	Child Advocate Society	50,000	50,000	100,000
5	Level 3	Abbott	Organization Contribution	Kelsey Foundation	0	50,000	50,000
6	Level 4	Abbott	Organization Contribution	Hands Across Foundation	20,000	15,500	35,500
7	Level 4	Abbott	Organization Contribution	Chamber of Commerce	10,000	12,500	22,500
8	Level 5	Abbott	Organization Contribution	Accountancy Association	0	15,000	15,000
9	Level 5	Abbott	Organization Contribution	Business Roundtable	0	15,000	15,000

Macros were created to perform repetitive tasks; then they were assigned to buttons in row 1.

12.1 Creating PivotTables

Video Lesson labyrinthelab.com/videos

PivotTables are powerful data analysis tools. They let you summarize data in various ways and instantly change the view you use. You can create normal Excel lists and tables to sort and filter data and produce subtotals. A PivotTable not only subtotals groups of related data, but also goes a step further and compares one group to another. Compared with performing similar data analyses on a standard worksheet, PivotTables offer tremendous speed and flexibility.

Arranging the Source Data

You create PivotTables from columns or from a table in an Excel worksheet. The data should contain no blank rows or columns. Converting a list to a table is recommended when records will be added after the PivotTable is created. The additional table data are included automatically when the PivotTable is refreshed or updated. Data in a list are not included automatically. The following examples explain two PivotTables based on the same worksheet list.

	A	B	C	D	E	F
3	Pledge Level	Team Leader	Sponsor Category	Sponsor Name	Year 1	Year 2
4	Level 5	Abbott	Organization Contribution	Accountancy Association	0	15,000
5	Level 4	Faber	Corporate Sponsorship	Accurate Biomedical	10,000	10,000
6	Level 1	Lemus	Federal Government Grant	Admin for Children & Fam	5,129,874	8,075,333
7	Level 3	Faber	Corporate Sponsorship	Alpha Supplies Corp.	125,000	50,000
8	Level 6	Nguyen	Individual Contribution	Andres Padilla	0	500

The worksheet data on which the sample PivotTables are based

PivotTable Example 1

You could sort the preceding table by pledge level or sponsor category; however, you could not easily compare totals for the various pledge levels in each sponsor category. This is where the PivotTable comes into use. A PivotTable can summarize some or all of the data in any number of ways, and it creates grand totals for you. Each column in a PivotTable is a *field*. Examine the PivotTable and notice that the Sponsor Category field from the table is used for the row labels, the Pledge Level field for the column labels, and the Year 2 field for the data area and grand totals. Each row displays the amount given by each sponsor group in the various pledge levels.

This PivotTable summarizes contributions from all sponsor groups.

Sum of Year 2	Column Labels						
Row Labels	**Level 1**	**Level 2**	**Level 3**	**Level 4**	**Level 5**	**Level 6**	**Grand Total**
Corporate Grant		1,425,000.00		0.00			1,425,000.00
Corporate Sponsorship	20,300,000.00	250,000.00	350,000.00	22,500.00	28,750.00		20,951,250.00
Federal Government Grant	47,894,948.00						47,894,948.00
Individual Contribution					4,100.00	2,080.00	6,180.00
Individual Sponsorship	15,000,000.00	2,500,000.00	413,579.00	15,000.00	4,475.00	595.00	17,933,649.00
Local Business Contribution					2,634.00	992.00	3,626.00
Local Government Grant			243,500.00				243,500.00
Medical Center/Large Facility		90,250.00					90,250.00
Medical Ctr Contribution		596,432.00	122,340.00				718,772.00
Organization Contribution			50,000.00	28,000.00	39,050.00	3,160.00	120,210.00
Organized Labor/Union Contribution		700,000.00					700,000.00
Physician Office Contribution			25,000.00	20,000.00	30,500.00		75,500.00
Private Grant		2,000,000.00	0.00				2,000,000.00
State Government Grant	35,077,677.00						35,077,677.00
Grand Total	**118,272,625.00**	**7,561,682.00**	**1,204,419.00**	**85,500.00**	**109,509.00**	**6,827.00**	**127,240,562.00**

The amount given by each sponsor group is displayed by pledge level.

Filter buttons allow you to sort and filter the sponsor groups and pledge levels.

PivotTables automatically total the rows and columns and calculate a grand total.

PivotTable Example 2

Using the same table data, you may view the data differently—in this case, summarized first by pledge level and then by sponsor category. To create this type of view, the PivotTable layout shown in the following illustration contains the Pledge Level and then Sponsor Category fields for row labels, no column labels, and the Year 2 field for the data area and totals.

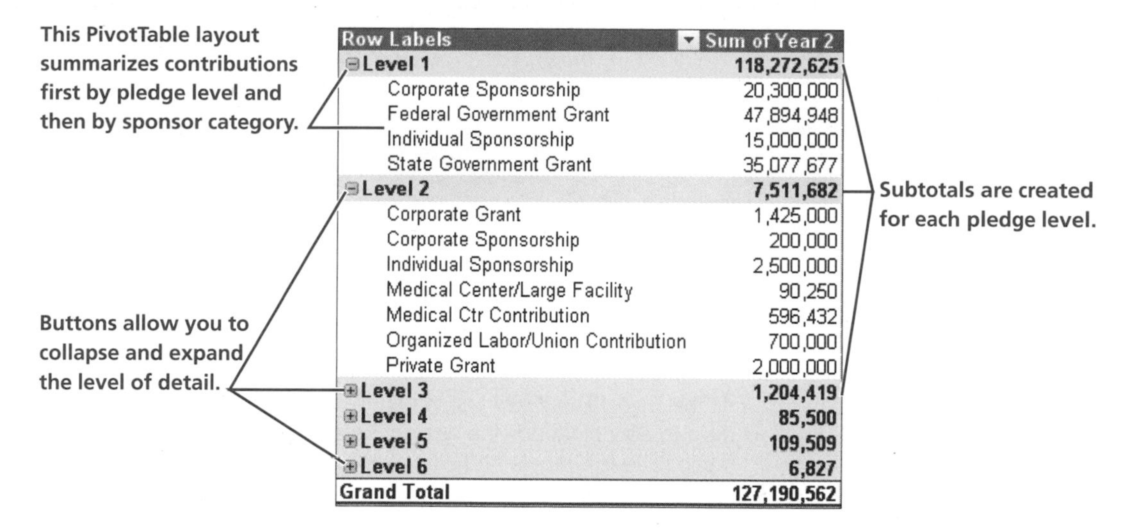
This PivotTable layout summarizes contributions first by pledge level and then by sponsor category.
Buttons allow you to collapse and expand the level of detail.
Subtotals are created for each pledge level.

Row Labels	Sum of Year 2
Level 1	118,272,625
Corporate Sponsorship	20,300,000
Federal Government Grant	47,894,948
Individual Sponsorship	15,000,000
State Government Grant	35,077,677
Level 2	7,511,682
Corporate Grant	1,425,000
Corporate Sponsorship	200,000
Individual Sponsorship	2,500,000
Medical Center/Large Facility	90,250
Medical Ctr Contribution	596,432
Organized Labor/Union Contribution	700,000
Private Grant	2,000,000
Level 3	1,204,419
Level 4	85,500
Level 5	109,509
Level 6	6,827
Grand Total	127,190,562

In this lesson, you will learn how to lay out both of these types of PivotTables and much more.

How PivotTables Work

Each area of the PivotTable plays a role in data organization. The PivotTable Field List task pane displays after you define the worksheet range to be used. The areas of the task pane are explained in the following illustration showing the settings for the preceding PivotTable Example 1.

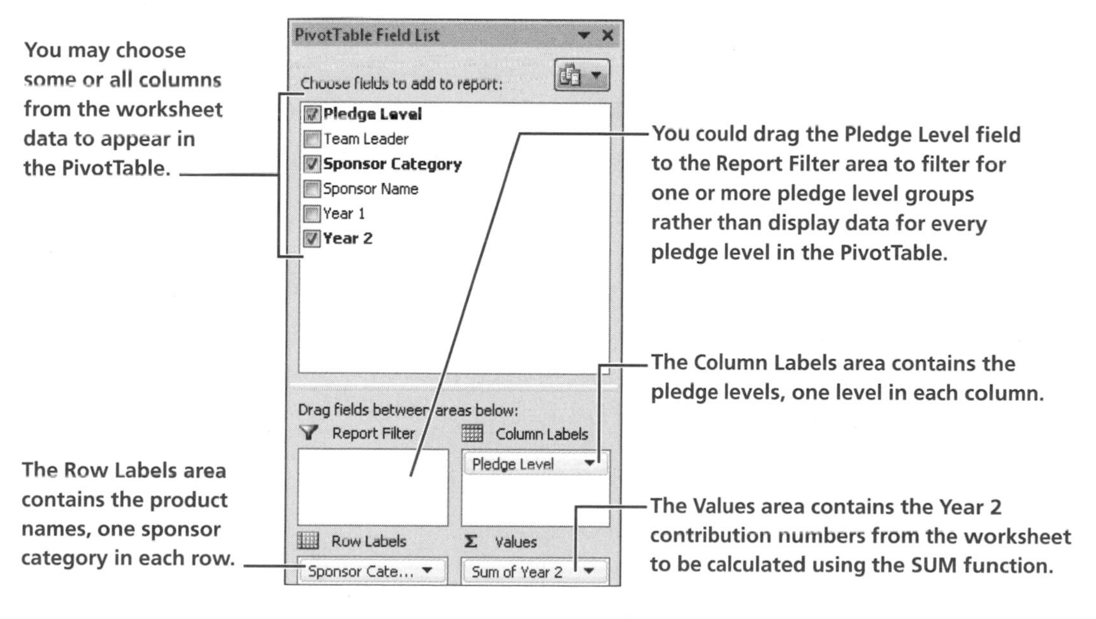
You may choose some or all columns from the worksheet data to appear in the PivotTable.
PivotTable Field List
Choose fields to add to report:
Pledge Level
Team Leader
Sponsor Category
Sponsor Name
Year 1
Year 2
You could drag the Pledge Level field to the Report Filter area to filter for one or more pledge level groups rather than display data for every pledge level in the PivotTable.
The Column Labels area contains the pledge levels, one level in each column.
Drag fields between areas below:
Report Filter
Column Labels
Pledge Level
Row Labels
Values
Sponsor Cate...
Sum of Year 2
The Row Labels area contains the product names, one sponsor category in each row.
The Values area contains the Year 2 contribution numbers from the worksheet to be calculated using the SUM function.

NOTE

You must select a cell in the PivotTable to display the PivotTable Field List task pane.

You design a PivotTable by choosing the columns (fields) to be included from the worksheet. Excel initially places all text columns that you choose into the Row Labels area and all selected number columns into the Values area for summing. If this is not your desired layout, you can drag and drop various fields into the correct areas of the task pane. Where you place fields determines how the PivotTable summarizes the data. By choosing different fields or dragging and dropping a field, you may quickly compare data in various ways. You may choose from several functions—such as SUM, COUNT, and AVERAGE—to calculate fields containing values.

QUICK REFERENCE **CREATING A PIVOTTABLE**

Task	Procedure
Create a PivotTable from a worksheet range or table	■ Select a cell in the worksheet range or table. ■ Choose Insert→Tables→PivotTable from the Ribbon. ■ Verify the worksheet range or table name in the Create PivotTable dialog box and click OK to place the PivotTable on a new worksheet. ■ In the PivotTable Field List task pane, place a checkmark by each worksheet field to be included in the design, selecting the fields in the order they should appear as row labels and values columns. ■ If necessary, drag and drop a field name to the correct area: Report Filter, Row Labels, Column Labels, or Values.
Name a PivotTable	■ Choose Options→PivotTable, type the name in the PivotTable name text box (spaces are allowed), and tap Enter.
Display the PivotTable Field List task pane	■ Select any cell within the PivotTable. ■ If the task pane is turned off, choose Options→Show→Field List from the Ribbon.

DEVELOP YOUR SKILLS 12.1.1

Create PivotTables

The best way to understand the dynamic capabilities of a PivotTable is to create one. In this exercise, you will create PivotTables from a worksheet range and a table.

Review the Worksheet Data

1. Start **Excel** and **open** the Sponsors workbook from the Lesson 12 folder in your file storage location.
2. **Maximize** the window.
   The Sponsors Sheet worksheet contains the data you will use to create two PivotTables. Look at the column headings and the various records in the rows. Each record contains data for a specific donor or government grant for the building project. Notice the dollar amounts contained in the Year 1 and Year 2 columns.

Create a PivotTable from a Worksheet Range

You will create a PivotTable that summarizes Year 2 by pledge level with subtotals for each sponsor category (corporation, individual, organization, state government agency, and so on).

3. Select **cell B4**.
   You should select a cell within the worksheet range or table before you create the PivotTable. The range should contain no blank rows or columns.

4. Choose **Insert→Tables→PivotTable** from the Ribbon.
   The Create PivotTable dialog box appears.

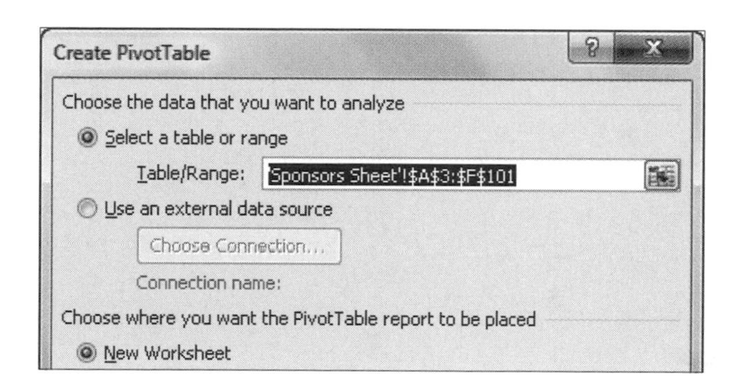

5. Verify the suggested range as shown, notice that the default is to place the PivotTable on a new worksheet, and click **OK**.
   A new worksheet appears and contains an empty PivotTable placeholder. The PivotTable Field List task pane also displays. If the task pane is turned off, choose Options→Show→Field List from the Ribbon.

6. **Rename** Sheet1 as **`PivotTable by Sponsor Category`**.

7. Select **cell A1**, which is outside the boundary of the PivotTable outline.
   Notice that the PivotTable Field List task pane disappears. You must select a cell within the PivotTable placeholder to display the task pane.

8. Select **cell A3** within the PivotTable placeholder to restore the task pane.
   Notice that the PivotTable Field List task pane contains a list of all the data fields in the worksheet range. You will choose only some of them.

9. Follow these steps to define the PivotTable in the task pane:

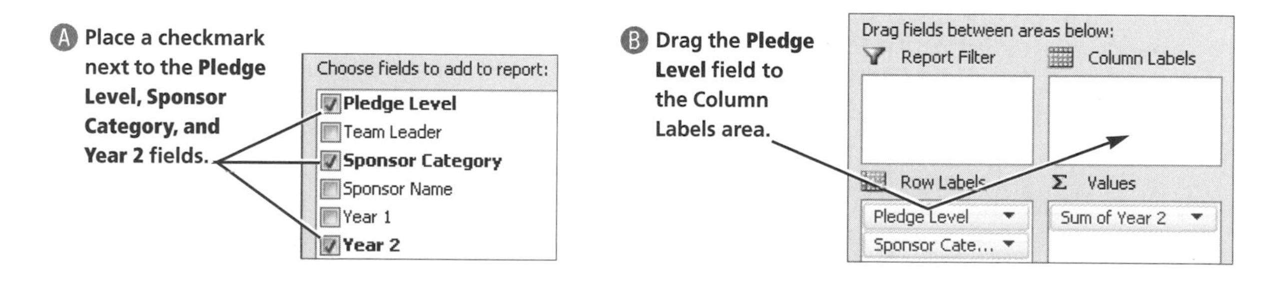

In the resulting PivotTable, notice that the sponsor categories are displayed one per row, the six pledge levels are displayed one per column, and the Year 2 contributions data are summarized with totals for each sponsor category in column H and each pledge level in row 19. The Level 1 label is not aligned over its numbers in cell B4, and you will fix this in a later exercise.

	A	B	C	D	E	F	G	H
3	**Sum of Year 2**	**Column Labels**						
4	**Row Labels**	**Level 1**	**Level 2**	**Level 3**	**Level 4**	**Level 5**	**Level 6**	**Grand Total**
5	Corporate Grant		1425000		0			1425000
6	Corporate Sponsorship	20300000	250000	350000	22500	28750		20951250
7	Federal Government Grant	47894948						47894948
8	Individual Contribution					4100	2080	6180
9	Individual Sponsorship	15000000	2500000	413579	15000	4475	595	17933649
10	Local Business Contribution					2634	992	3626
11	Local Government Grant			243500				243500
12	Medical Center/Large Facility		90250					90250
13	Medical Ctr Contribution		596432	122340				718772
14	Organization Contribution			50000	28000	39050	3160	120210
15	Organized Labor/Union Contribution		700000					700000
16	Physician Office Contribution			25000	20000	30500		75500
17	Private Grant		2000000	0				2000000
18	State Government Grant	35077677						35077677
19	**Grand Total**	**118272625**	**7561682**	**1204419**	**85500**	**109509**	**6827**	**127240562**

Name the PivotTable

10. Choose **Options→PivotTable** from the Ribbon, type **`BySponsorCategory`** in the PivotTable name text box, and **tap** [Enter].

Create a PivotTable from a Worksheet Table

The steps for creating a PivotTable from a worksheet table are the same as for a worksheet range. This time your PivotTable will group the data by pledge level with the sponsor categories in alphabetical order within each pledge level.

11. Display the **Sponsors Table** worksheet in the Sponsors workbook.
12. With any table cell selected, choose **Insert→Tables→PivotTable** from the Ribbon.
13. Verify that the suggested range is the **Sponsors_Table** and click **OK**.
14. **Rename** the new sheet as **`PivotTable by Pledge Level`**.
15. In the PivotTable Field List task pane, place a checkmark next to field names *in this order:* **Pledge Level, Sponsor Category, Year 2**.
    The task pane and the PivotTable results should display as shown. The records are grouped by pledge level with the sponsor categories in alphabetical order within each pledge level. The Year 2 subtotal displays for each pledge level, and a grand total appears at the bottom of the column. With this layout, you did not need to create any column labels.

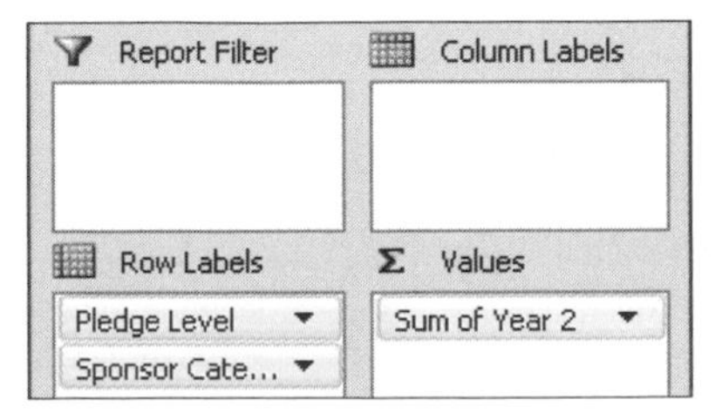

	Row Labels	Sum of Year 2
4	**⊟Level 1**	**118,272,625**
5	Corporate Sponsorship	20,300,000
6	Federal Government Grant	47,894,948
7	Individual Sponsorship	15,000,000
8	State Government Grant	35,077,677
9	**⊟Level 2**	**7,511,682**
10	Corporate Grant	1,425,000
11	Corporate Sponsorship	200,000

Name the PivotTable

16. Choose **Options→PivotTable** from the Ribbon, type **By Pledge Level** in the Pivot-Table name text box, and **tap** [Enter].
    Notice that you can type a PivotTable name with or without spaces.
17. **Save** the changes to your workbook.

Formatting a PivotTable

Video Lesson labyrinthelab.com/videos

Values and subtotals in the PivotTable do not automatically display the formatting from the original worksheet cells. You may set number formatting for a value field. You also may select and format one or more specific cells in the PivotTable. For example, you may align the column labels using commands on the Home tab of the Ribbon. The PivotTable Tools Design contextual tab contains a large selection of PivotTable styles to apply color, shading, and gridlines with one mouse click. The report layout displays in Compact Form by default, or you may choose from two other layouts. The subtotals may be displayed at the top or bottom of each group or hidden.

	A	B
3	**Row Labels**	**Sum of Year 2**
4	**⊟Level 1**	**118,272,625**
5	Faber	20,300,000
6	Lemus	82,972,625
7	Weinstein	15,000,000
8	**⊟Level 2**	**7,561,682**
9	Debowski	700,000

The Compact Form report layout with a PivotTable style applied

	A	B	C
3	**Pledge Leve**	**Team Leader**	**Sum of Year 2**
4	⊟Level 1	Faber	20,300,000
5		Lemus	82,972,625
6		Weinstein	15,000,000
7	**Level 1 Total**		**118,272,625**
8	⊟Level 2	Debowski	700,000
9		Faber	200,000

The Tabular Form report layout with filter buttons for each row label field

QUICK REFERENCE FORMATTING A PIVOTTABLE

Task	Procedure
Apply number formatting to a field	Right-click a column cell in the PivotTable, choose Number Format from the pop-up (context) menu, and choose options from the Format Cells dialog box. (Do not choose the Format Cells command from the context menu, which formats the selection rather than entire columns.)
Change the subtotals or grand totals display	Choose Design→Layout→Subtotals or Grand Totals and choose an option from the Ribbon.
Apply a PivotTable style	Choose Design→PivotTable Styles and choose a style from the Ribbon.
Apply a report layout	Choose Design→Layout→Report Layout and choose the Compact (default), Outline, or Tabular layout from the Ribbon.

DEVELOP YOUR SKILLS 12.1.2

Format a PivotTable

In this exercise, you will format the PivotTables that you created in the previous exercise. You will format selected cells, apply number formatting to values columns, choose a PivotTable style, and explore the report layout choices.

Format PivotTable Data

1. Display the **PivotTable by Sponsor Category** worksheet in the Sponsors workbook.
   You may need to use the navigation buttons at the left of the worksheet tabs to bring the desired tab into view.
2. Select the **range B4:H4** and **right-align** the labels to match the number alignment in their columns.
3. Choose **Design→Layout→Grand Totals menu ▾** from the Ribbon. Experiment by choosing each option and observe its result. Choose **On for Rows and Columns** when you are finished.
4. If necessary, **select** any cell in the PivotTable to redisplay the PivotTable Field List task pane.
5. Follow these steps to format the Year 2 contribution numbers in the PivotTable:

Ⓐ **Right-click** any number in the **range B5:H19**, and choose **Number Format** from the context menu.

Copy
Format Cells...
Number Format...

Ⓑ Choose the **Number** category, set **0** decimal places, and place a checkmark in the **Use 1000 Separator (,)** box.

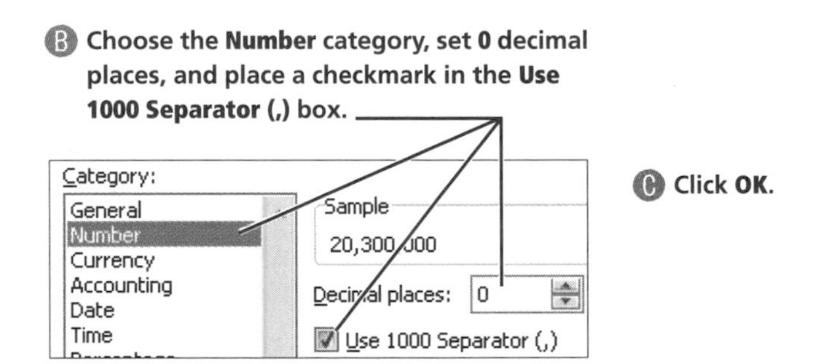

Ⓒ Click **OK**.

All number columns are displayed with the formatting that you chose because they all are part of the Sum of Year 2 field.

	A	B	C	D
3	**Sum of Year 2**	**Column Labels**		
4	**Row Labels**	**Level 1**	**Level 2**	**Level 3**
5	Corporate Grant		1,425,000	
6	Corporate Sponsorship	20,300,000	250,000	350,000
7	Federal Government Grant	47,894,948		

Apply a PivotTable Style

6. Display the **PivotTable by Pledge Level** worksheet.
7. Choose the **Design→PivotTable Styles→More** button, scroll through the available styles, and choose **PivotStyle Medium 9**.
   This style shades the subtotal rows.

Explore Report Layouts

8. Choose **Design→Layout→Report Layout→Show in Outline Form** from the Ribbon.
   This layout divides the Pledge Level and Sponsor Category fields into separate columns. Both column headings display a filter button.
9. Choose **Design→Layout→Report Layout→Show in Tabular Form** from the Ribbon.
   This layout displays a subtotal row below its detail rows.
10. Choose **Design→Layout→Report Layout→Show in Compact Form** to return to the original layout.
11. **Save** the changes to your workbook.

Changing PivotTable Fields

Video Lesson labyrinthelab.com/videos

You may add or remove fields on a PivotTable simply by adding or removing the checkmark next to the field name in the PivotTable Field List task pane. The PivotTable will automatically reconfigure to display the new data. You also may change the order of fields within the row and column areas. One of the most powerful ways of manipulating data is to move a field from the row area to the column area or vice versa. This is called *pivoting the field* (thus the name PivotTable). The display of the data field rotates to give you an entirely different view of your data, as illustrated in the two PivotTables you created in the previous exercise. There, you positioned the Region field to display as columns in the first PivotTable and as rows in the second.

DEVELOP YOUR SKILLS 12.1.3

Change PivotTable Fields

In this exercise, you will add fields to the PivotTable and reorder the display of fields. You also will pivot the view.

Add a Values Field

1. Display the **PivotTable by Pledge Level** worksheet, if necessary.
   The PivotTable contains data only for Year 2. Now you will add Year 1.
2. Place a checkmark next to **Year 1** in the task pane to add this field to the PivotTable.
   The Year 1 values are summed with subtotals and a grand total. Notice that Excel automatically added a Σ Values entry in the task pane Column Labels area because the PivotTable now contains two Sum columns.

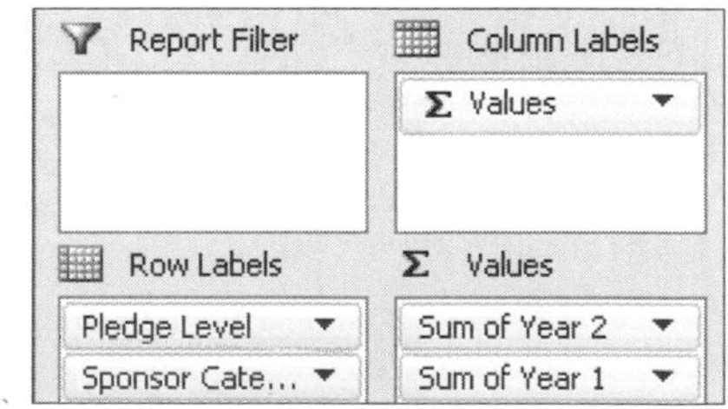

3. **Right-click** any cell in the **Sum of Year 1** column of the PivotTable, and choose **Number Format** from the context menu.
4. In the Format Cells dialog box, choose the **Number** category, set **0** decimal places, place a checkmark in the **Use 1000 Separator (,)** box, and click **OK**.
5. Repeat **steps 3 and 4** to format the **Sum of Year 2** column.

Reorder Fields

6. **Drag** Sum of Year 2 below Sum of Year 1 in the Values area.

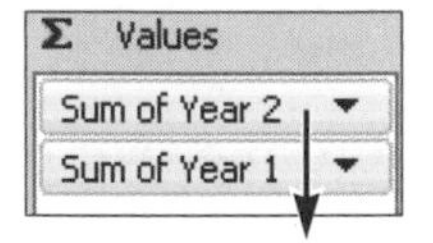

3	Row Labels	Sum of Year 1	Sum of Year 2
4	**⊟Level 1**	**117,267,482**	**118,272,625**
5	Corporate Sponsorship	17,460,000	20,300,000
6	Federal Government Grant	49,899,591	47,894,948
7	Individual Sponsorship	12,500,000	15,000,000
8	State Government Grant	37,407,891	35,077,677
9	**⊟Level 2**	**6,254,063**	**7,561,682**
10	Corporate Grant	1,250,000	1,425,000
11	Corporate Sponsorship	250,000	250,000

The PivotTable now displays the columns for both years in the order listed in the Values area of the task pane.

Add and Then Remove a Labels Field

7. Place a checkmark by the **Sponsor Name** field in the top section of the PivotTable Field List task pane.
   Notice the order of the fields in the Row Labels area. Now the sponsors and their contribution amounts are displayed within each sponsor category. Adding or deleting row labels allows you to control the level of detail displayed in a PivotTable.

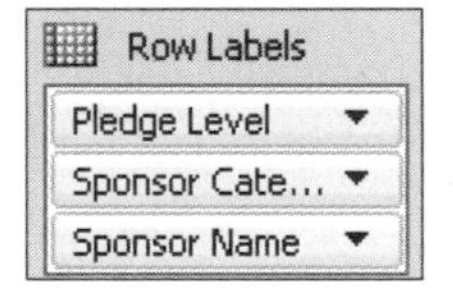

4	Row Labels	Sum of Year 1	Sum of Year 2
5	**⊟Level 1**	**117,267,482**	**118,272,625**
6	**⊟Corporate Sponsorship**	**17,460,000**	**20,300,000**
7	Jensen Pharmaceutical	7,500,000	10,000,000
8	Medical Solutions Corp.	5,460,000	4,300,000
9	Open Systems	4,500,000	6,000,000
10	**⊟Federal Government Grant**	**49,899,591**	**47,894,948**
11	Admin for Children & Fam	5,129,874	8,075,333

8. Remove the checkmark by the **Sponsor Category** field and **Sponsor Name** field in the PivotTable Field List task pane.

9. Add a checkmark by the **Team Leader** field.
   The team leader totals appear within each pledge level. Notice that some team leaders appear in multiple pledge levels. This view makes it easy to compare Year 1 and Year 2 data.

Pivot the View

10. Drag the **Team Leader** field from the Row Labels area to the Column Labels area below the Σ Values field.

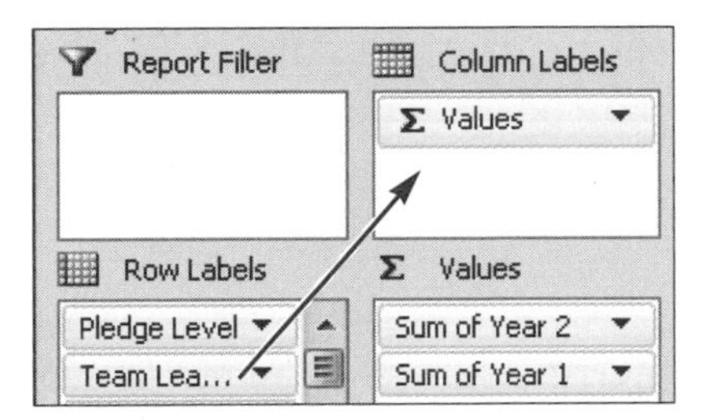

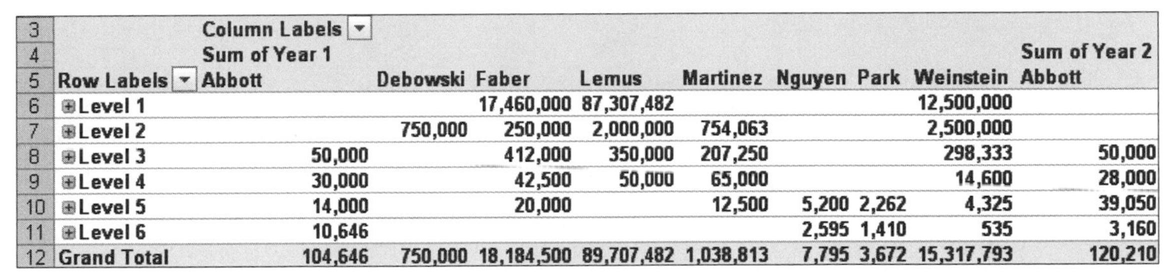

		Column Labels								
		Sum of Year 1								Sum of Year 2
	Row Labels	Abbott	Debowski	Faber	Lemus	Martinez	Nguyen	Park	Weinstein	Abbott
6	Level 1			17,460,000	87,307,482				12,500,000	
7	Level 2		750,000	250,000	2,000,000	754,063			2,500,000	
8	Level 3	50,000		412,000	350,000	207,250			298,333	50,000
9	Level 4	30,000		42,500	50,000	65,000			14,600	28,000
10	Level 5	14,000		20,000		12,500	5,200	2,262	4,325	39,050
11	Level 6	10,646					2,595	1,410	535	3,160
12	Grand Total	104,646	750,000	18,184,500	89,707,482	1,038,813	7,795	3,672	15,317,793	120,210

You just pivoted the team leader field to be displayed in columns rather than rows. This view allows you to compare each team leader's overall performance among the various pledge levels, but comparing Year 1 to Year 2 is more difficult than in the previous view.

11. **Undo** the pivot you performed in the previous step.
12. **Save** the changes to your workbook.

Filtering a PivotTable with AutoFilter

Video Lesson labyrinthelab.com/videos

You may set the PivotTable to filter, or include, specific items in the data summaries. The totals and subtotals are recalculated for the selected items. The Row Labels and Column Labels headings have an AutoFilter button that displays the same sorting and filtering options that are available on the columns of worksheet lists and tables.

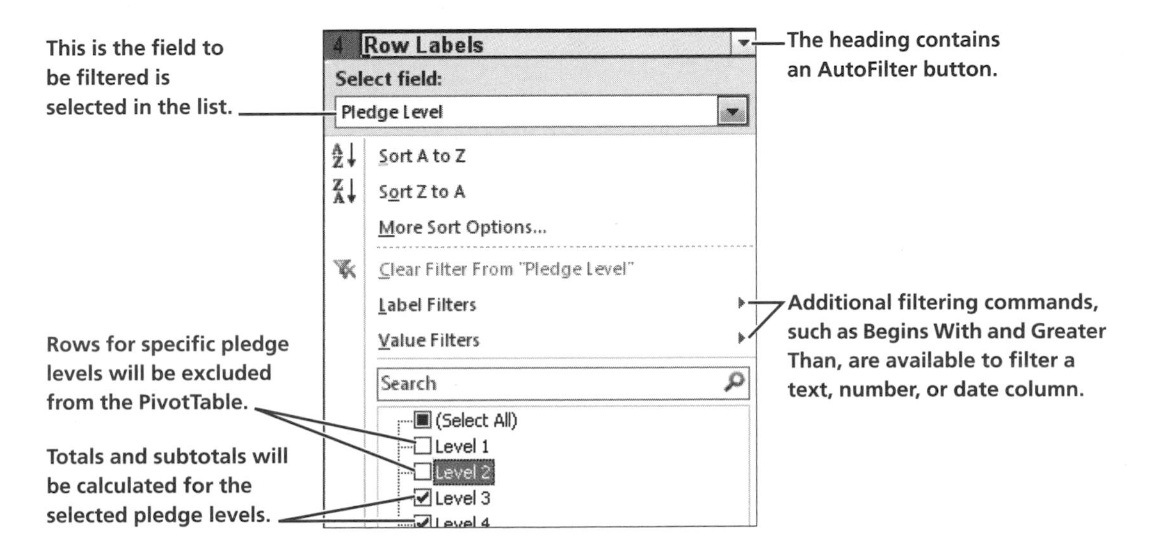

Filtering PivotTables with Slicers

New to Excel 2010, slicers are menu frames displayed on the worksheet that contain all filtering choices in one field. You can choose items or clear a filter without having to drop down a list. Selected items are highlighted in slicers, making it easy to see which criteria have been applied to the PivotTable filter. Slicer frames may be resized, moved, and formatted with styles for a consistent appearance. Slicers also may be shared in other worksheets of the same workbook for use with multiple PivotTables based on the same data set. Changing the filtering selections in a shared slicer causes all connected PivotTables to update automatically.

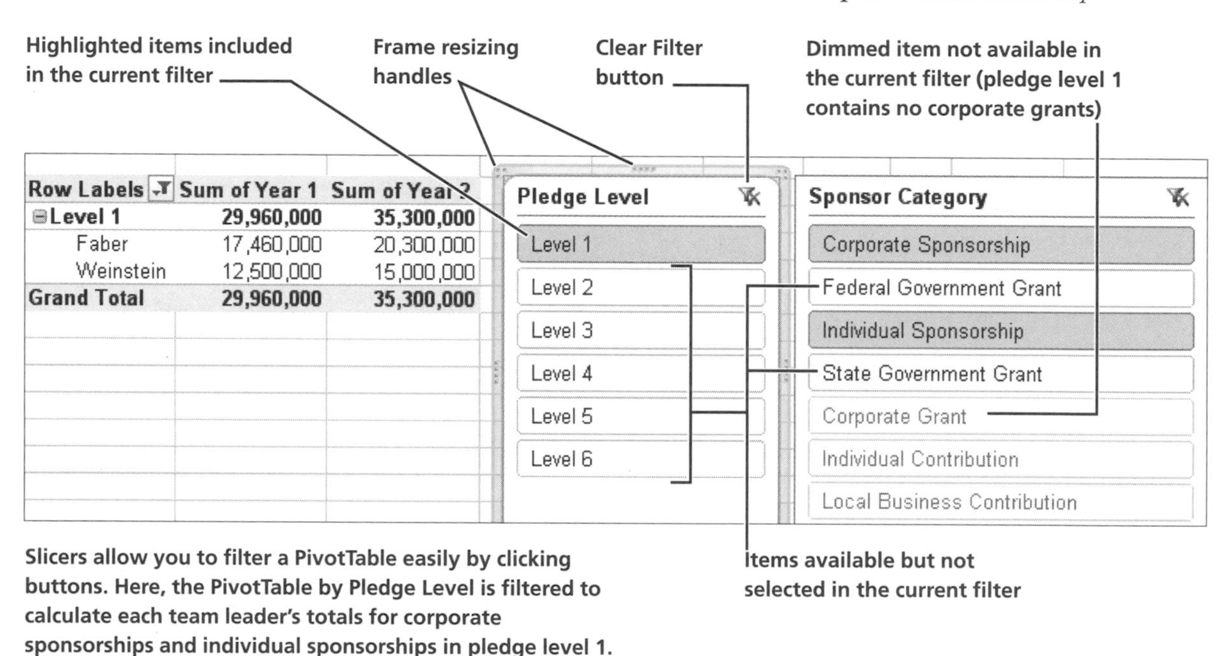

Slicers allow you to filter a PivotTable easily by clicking buttons. Here, the PivotTable by Pledge Level is filtered to calculate each team leader's totals for corporate sponsorships and individual sponsorships in pledge level 1.

QUICK REFERENCE — CHANGING PIVOTTABLE FIELD ORDER AND FILTERING A PIVOTTABLE USING AUTOFILTER AND SLICERS

Task	Procedure
Change the field order in rows or columns	■ Drag a field name above or below another field in an area list at the bottom of the PivotTable Field List task pane.
Remove a field	■ Uncheck the field name from the PivotTable Field List task pane.
Filter for specific items using AutoFilter	■ Click the AutoFilter button next to Row Labels, Column Labels, or a specific column label, if available, in the PivotTable. ■ Choose a field from the fields available in the filtering list. ■ Remove the checkmark form the desired item(s), or choose Label Filters, Value Filters, or Date Filters, depending on the type of data in the column.
Filter for specific items using slicers	■ Select any cell in the PivotTable. ■ Choose Options→Sort & Filter→Insert Slicer from the Ribbon. (Or, choose Design→Filter→Slicer.) ■ Place a checkmark next to the desired fields in the Insert Slicers dialog box, and click OK. ■ Choose one or more items in slicers, as desired. To select additional items in a slicer, hold down [Ctrl] while clicking each item. To remove items from a multiple selection, hold down [Ctrl] while clicking each item.

QUICK REFERENCE	CHANGING PIVOTTABLE FIELD ORDER AND FILTERING A PIVOTTABLE USING AUTOFILTER AND SLICERS
Task	**Procedure**
Clear a filter from a slicer	■ Choose the Clear Filter button in the upper-right corner of the desired slicer.
Move and resize a slicer	■ Point to a slicer's frame or title bar and drag to the desired location on the worksheet. ■ Drag a corner or side handle on the slicer frame to resize the slicer.
Display slicer buttons in multiple columns	■ Select the slicer. ■ Choose Options→Buttons→Columns, and choose the number of columns from the Ribbon.
Apply a style to a slicer	■ Select the slicer. ■ Choose Options→Slicer Styles, and choose a style from the Ribbon.
Connect a slicer to additional PivotTables based on the same data set in the workbook	■ Select the slicer. ■ Choose Options→Slicer→PivotTable Connections from the Ribbon. ■ Place a checkmark by the PivotTable name(s) to which you wish to connect the slicer.

DEVELOP YOUR SKILLS 12.1.4

Filter a PivotTable with Slicers

In this exercise, you will display slicers on a PivotTable worksheet. You will move, resize, and format the slicers to fit around the PivotTable. Then, you will select items from the slicers to filter the PivotTable to look at the data in various ways.

Insert Slicers

1. Display the **PivotTable with Slicers** worksheet in the Sponsors workbook. (**Scroll** to the right in the worksheet tabs to locate the tab, if necessary.)
   The PivotTable displays the Sponsor Categories field as rows and the Sum of Year 1 and Sum of Year 2 fields as columns.
2. **Select** any cell in the PivotTable to display the PivotTable Tools in the Ribbon, if necessary.
3. Choose **Options→Sort & Filter→Insert Slicer** from the Ribbon.
4. Place a checkmark next to the **Pledge Level, Team Leader,** and **Sponsor Category** fields in the Insert Slicers dialog box; click **OK**.

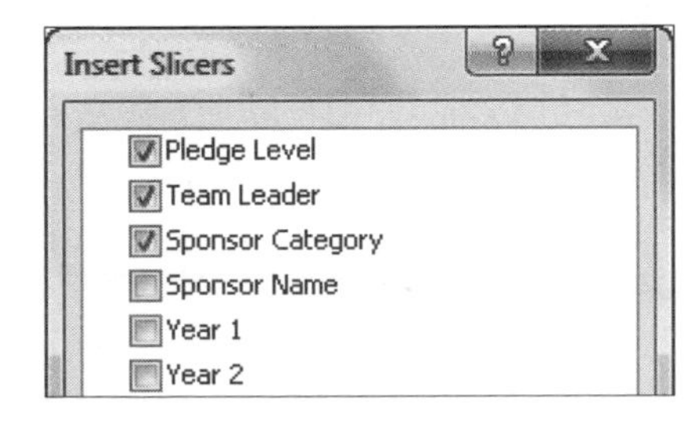

5. Select **cell A1** to hide the PivotTable Field List task pane, if still displayed.

Move and Resize Slicers

6. Follow thesc steps to move and resize the Sponsor Category slicer:

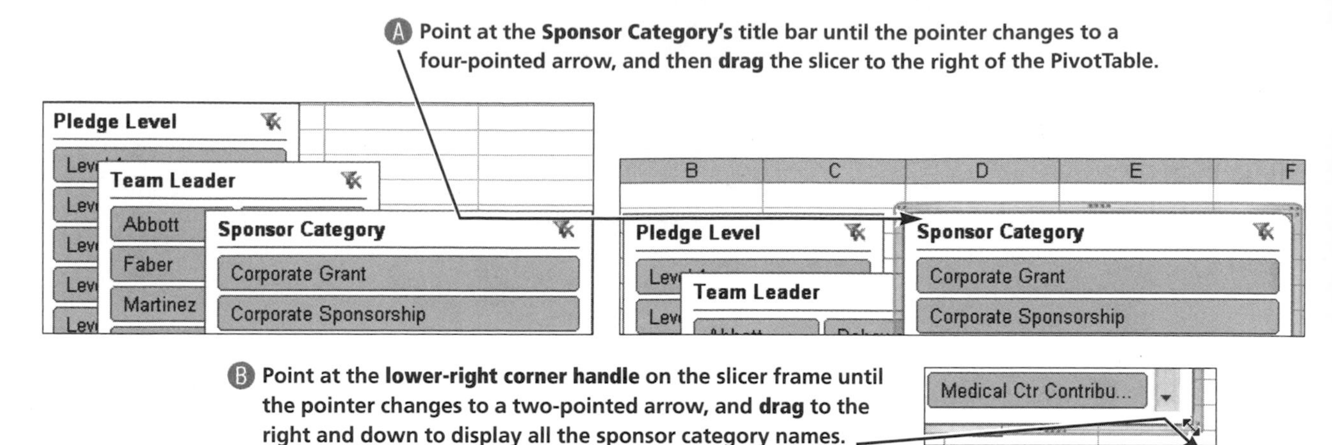

Ⓐ Point at the **Sponsor Category's** title bar until the pointer changes to a four-pointed arrow, and then **drag** the slicer to the right of the PivotTable.
Pledge Level
Team Leader
Abbott
Faber
Martinez
Sponsor Category
Corporate Grant
Corporate Sponsorship
B
C
D
E
F
Ⓑ Point at the **lower-right corner handle** on the slicer frame until the pointer changes to a two-pointed arrow, and **drag** to the right and down to display all the sponsor category names.
Medical Ctr Contribu...

7. Drag the **Pledge Level** slicer and **Team Leader** slicer to **row 20** as shown.

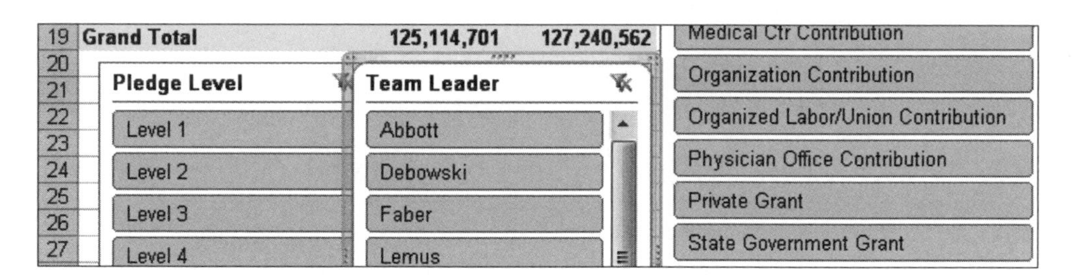

8. Click the **Pledge Level** title to display the slicer's frame, and then **hold down** Shift and click on the **Team Leader** title.

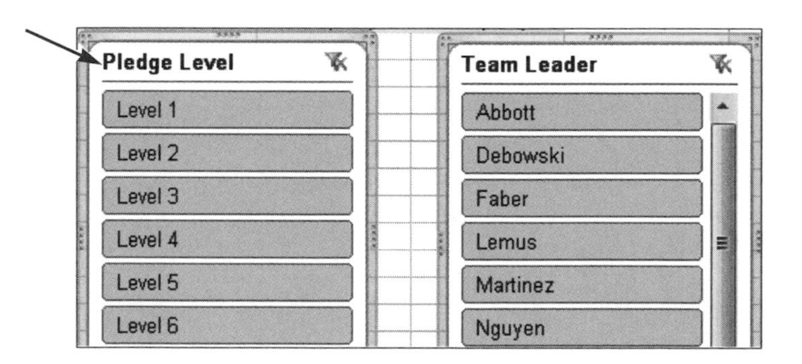

Frames appear around the two slicers to indicate both are selected. If you click a slicer button by mistake, click the Clear Filter button in the upper-right corner of the slicer and repeat step 8.

9. Choose **Options→Buttons→Columns** from the Ribbon, and change the number of columns from 1 to **2**.

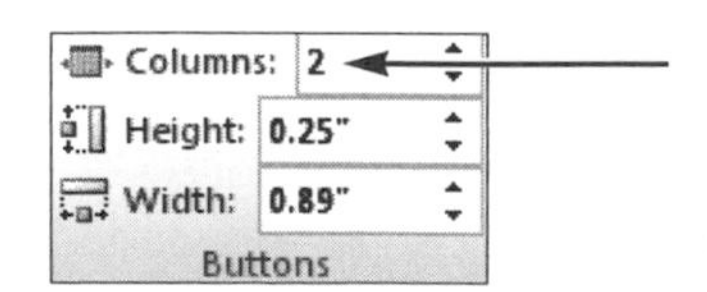

Apply Slicer Styles

10. Click the **Sponsor Category** title in the slicer at the right of the PivotTable, choose **Options→Slicer Styles,** and choose any style from the Ribbon.
11. Repeat **step 10** to apply styles of your choice to the **Pledge Level** slicer and **Team Leader** slicer.

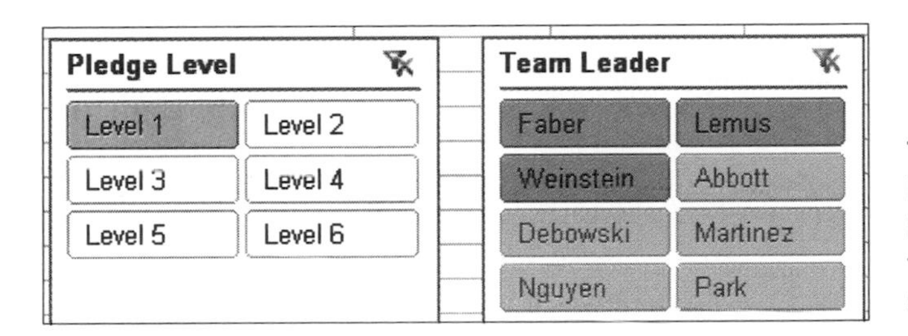

Filter the PivotTable

12. Choose **Level 1** in the Pledge Level slicer.

Pledge Level: Level 1, Level 2, Level 3, Level 4, Level 5, Level 6

Team Leader: Faber, Lemus, Weinstein, Abbott, Debowski, Martinez, Nguyen, Park

The Team Leader slicer shows that Faber, Lemus, and Weinstein are included in the PivotTable totals. The buttons are dimmed for the other team leaders because they did not solicit any contributions at pledge level 1.

Row Labels	Sum of Year 1	Sum of Year 2
Corporate Sponsorship	17,460,000	20,300,000
Federal Government Grant	49,899,591	47,894,948
Individual Sponsorship	12,500,000	15,000,000
State Government Grant	37,407,891	35,077,677
Grand Total	**117,267,482**	**118,272,625**

Sponsor Category: Corporate Sponsorship, Federal Government Grant, Individual Sponsorship, State Government Grant, Corporate Grant

Four sponsor categories are displayed in the PivotTable, matching the four highlighted buttons in the Sponsor Category slicer. These are the only types of sponsors to contribute at level 1, the highest dollar level.

13. Click the **Clear Filter** button on the Pledge level slicer to restore all data in the PivotTable.
14. Select **Corporate Sponsorship** in the Sponsor Category slicer.
    The Sum of Year 2 total in the PivotTable is 20,951,250. The slicers show that Pledge Levels 1–5 and team leader Faber are included.
15. **Hold down** Ctrl and select **Individual Sponsorship**.
    The PivotTable and slicers reflect the additional category. You can use Ctrl*+click to select additional items or deselect them in a slicer.*
16. Experiment by **selecting** and **deselecting** various criteria in the slicers; **clear filters** from all slicers when you are finished.
17. **Save** the changes to the workbook.

Editing PivotTable Calculations

Video Lesson labyrinthelab.com/videos

You are not limited to summing values in a PivotTable, and you may create additional formulas.

Changing the Function for a Values Area Item

By default, the subtotals and grand totals in a PivotTable sum the values in a field. You may use the Summarize Values By command to change the SUM function to a different function, such as AVERAGE, MAX, or COUNT. Not all Excel functions are available by using this command.

If the Values area of the PivotTable Field List task pane contains only one entry, all Sum columns will change to the function you selected. If multiple entries exist in the Values area, you may change the function for one entry at a time.

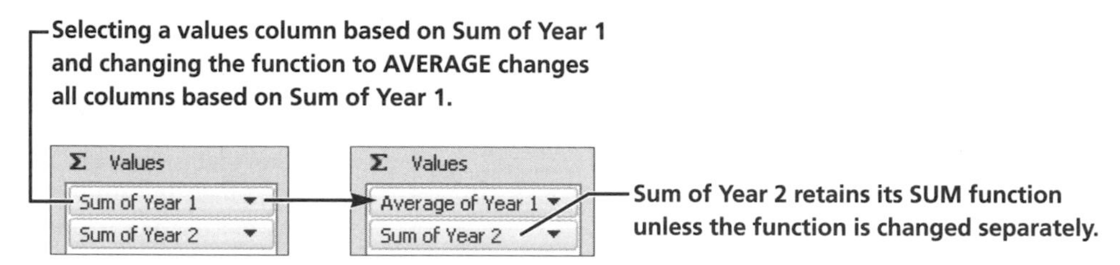
Selecting a values column based on Sum of Year 1 and changing the function to AVERAGE changes all columns based on Sum of Year 1.
Σ Values
Sum of Year 1
Sum of Year 2
Σ Values
Average of Year 1
Sum of Year 2
Sum of Year 2 retains its SUM function unless the function is changed separately.

Creating a Calculated Field

Some functions not available with the Summarize Values By command described previously may be typed in the Insert Calculated Field dialog box. A calculated field is a column that you create manually in the PivotTable. This field contains a formula using values from one or more existing fields. For example, the formula could subtract the value in one field from another to find the difference, as shown in the following illustration. You enter the formula once, and Excel displays the formula result in every record of the PivotTable. For accuracy, you should select field names from the list rather than type their names in creating the formula for a calculated field.

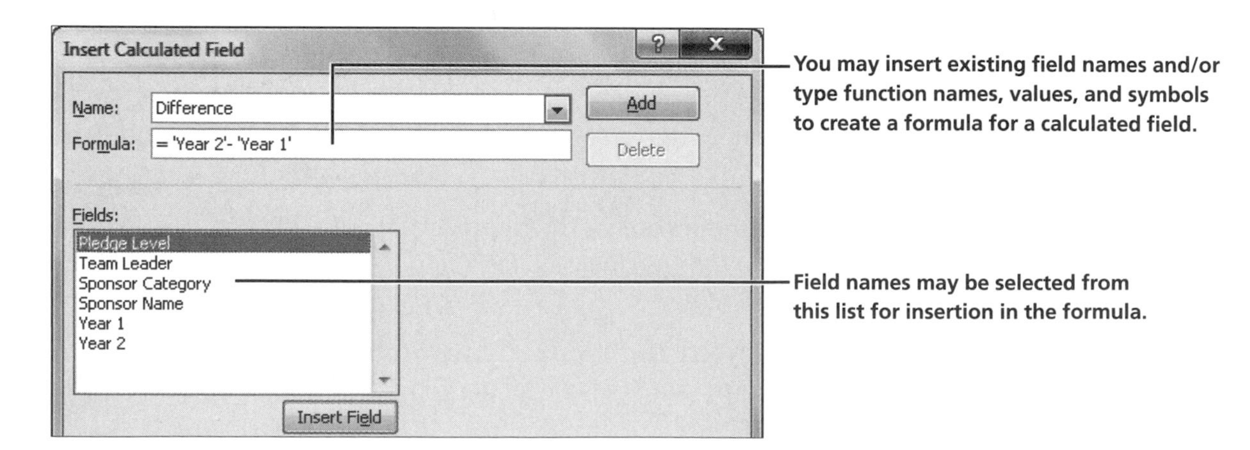
Insert Calculated Field
Name: Difference
Formula: = 'Year 2'- 'Year 1'
Add
Delete
Fields:
Pledge Level
Team Leader
Sponsor Category
Sponsor Name
Year 1
Year 2
Insert Field
You may insert existing field names and/or type function names, values, and symbols to create a formula for a calculated field.
Field names may be selected from this list for insertion in the formula.

Converting Column Data to a Calculation

The Show Values As command creates formulas using preset options. For example, you can calculate percentages of a total, the difference between values in two columns, a running total, or a ranked order. If you want to display the original column data along with the converted data, simply drag and drop the field name from the field list to the Values area to create a duplicate field.

Refreshing PivotTable Data

PivotTables do not automatically update after the source data is changed.

FROM THE KEYBOARD
[Ctrl]+[Alt]+[F5] to refresh all data sources

PivotTables often are created with data from sources external to the Excel workbook containing the PivotTables. For example, the source data may be in another Excel workbook or an Access database. After you change the source data—even if in a worksheet range or table within the same workbook—you must refresh the PivotTables manually. Using the Ribbon, you may refresh just the active PivotTable or all PivotTables in the workbook. You also may set a PivotTable option to refresh data from external sources when the workbook is opened.

QUICK REFERENCE — EDITING PIVOTTABLE CALCULATIONS AND REFRESHING DATA

Task	Procedure
Change the function used to calculate subtotals and grand total(s)	■ Select a number cell in any column of the PivotTable that contains the existing calculation. ■ Choose Options→Calculations-→Summarize Values By menu ▼, and choose a different function from the Ribbon. ■ If desired, repeat for any other calculation listed separately in the Values area of the PivotTable Field List task pane.
Create a calculated field to the right of existing PivotTable columns	■ Select any cell within the PivotTable. ■ Choose Options→Calculations→Fields, Items, & Sets menu ▼→Calculated Field from the Ribbon. ■ Type a name in the Name box of the Insert Calculated Field dialog box. ■ Edit the formula =0 to the desired formula by double-clicking field names and typing other parts of the formula, including math symbols (such as + or *).
Modify a formula in a calculated field	■ Choose Options→Calculations→Fields, Items, & Sets menu ▼→Calculated Field from the Ribbon. ■ Choose the calculated field name in the Name drop-down list (not the Field list) of the Insert Calculated Field dialog box. ■ Edit the formula and click Modify.

QUICK REFERENCE **EDITING PIVOTTABLE CALCULATIONS AND REFRESHING DATA (continued)**

Task	Procedure
Delete a calculated field	■ Choose Options→Calculations→Fields, Items, & Sets menu ▾→Calculated Field from the Ribbon. ■ Choose the calculated field name in the Name drop-down list (not the Field list) of the Insert Calculated Field dialog box. ■ Click Delete.
Convert all data in a field to percentages of a total or calculate a difference, running total, or ranked order	■ If a duplicate field is desired to retain the original column data, drag and drop the field name from the upper part of the PivotTable Field List into the Values area. ■ Choose a number cell in the desired column of the PivotTable where you want to convert data. ■ Choose Options→Calculations→Show Values As menu ▾, and choose the desired preset option from the Ribbon to convert all data in the field.
Refresh PivotTables after changing source data	■ Choose Options→Data→Refresh menu ▾ from the Ribbon and choose one of the following: ◆ Refresh to update the active PivotTable. ◆ Refresh All (or use [Ctrl]+[Alt]+[F5]) to update all PivotTables in the workbook.

DEVELOP YOUR SKILLS 12.1.5

Change PivotTable Calculations

In this exercise, you will change the default SUM to a different function. You will create a calculated field to set a 110 percent contributions goal for each team leader. You also will change a value in the original source table and observe the effect upon PivotTables.

1. Display the **PivotTable by Pledge Level** worksheet.

Change a Function

2. Select a number cell in **column B** of the PivotTable. Then, choose **Options→Calculations→Summarize Values By menu ▾→Average** from the Ribbon.
   The column heading changes to Average of Year 1 in the PivotTable and the Values area of the task pane. The subtotals and grand total now calculate averages. Notice that the Sum of Year 2 column did not change. You must edit the function separately for each calculation listed in the Values area of the task pane. You will leave Sum of Year 2 as is.

Create a Calculated Field

Assume that you set a goal for all team leaders to increase contributions by 110 percent in Year 3.

3. Choose **Options→Calculations→Fields, Items, & Sets menu ▾→Calculated Field** from the Ribbon.

4. Follow these steps to create a calculated field in the Insert Calculated Field dialog box:

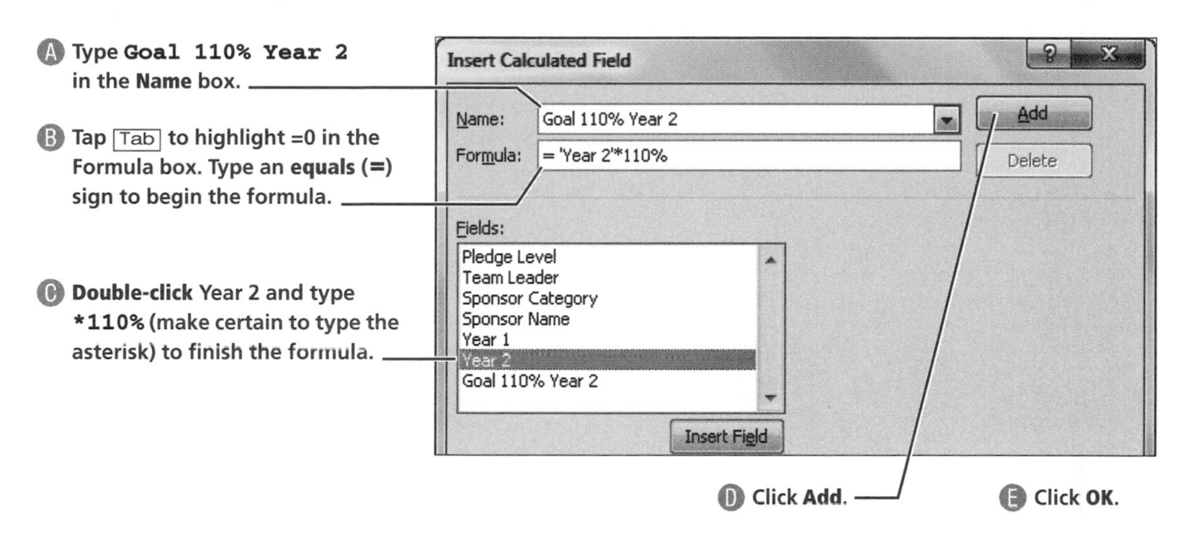

The calculated field displays as the last column of the PivotTable.

3	Row Labels	Average of Year 1	Sum of Year 2	Sum of Goal 110% Year 2
4	⊟**Level 1**	**13,029,720**	**118,272,625**	**130,099,888**
5	Faber	5,820,000	20,300,000	22,330,000
6	Lemus	17,461,496	82,972,625	91,269,888
7	Weinstein	12,500,000	15,000,000	16,500,000

Change Worksheet Data

Cell C10 of the PivotTable shows that team leader Faber is responsible for $250,000 of Level 2 contributions in Year 2. Next, you will change a value in the table upon which the PivotTable is based.

5. Display the **Sponsors Table** worksheet. (Do not select the Sponsors Sheet tab.)

6. In **cell F98** for Year 2, change 250,000 to **200000**.

7. Display the **PivotTable by Pledge Level** worksheet.
   Notice that Faber's level 2 amount in Year 2 still appears as 250,000 in cell C10. Changes to the source data do not *automatically update in the PivotTables.*

Refresh PivotTables

8. Choose **Options→Data→Refresh menu ▾→Refresh All** from the Ribbon.
   Faber's amount now appears as 200,000, and the goal was recalculated in cell D10. Any other PivotTables or PivotCharts based on the same source data would also be updated.

9. **Save** the changes to your workbook.

12.2 Creating PivotCharts

Video Lesson labyrinthelab.com/videos

A PivotChart presents data from a PivotTable. There are two ways to create a PivotChart.

1. You may chart an existing PivotTable by choosing a chart type from the Insert ribbon as for a normal Excel chart.
2. You may use the PivotChart command to create a PivotTable and PivotChart from the source data at the same time. The chart builds as you choose fields in the PivotTable Field List task pane.

The field(s) in the values area of the PivotTable are displayed as data series in the chart. The row labels in the PivotTable are used as the axis labels in the chart, and the column labels are the data series in the chart legend.

Filtering PivotCharts

The PivotChart may be filtered using the AutoFilter buttons on the chart, AutoFilter buttons on the PivotTable, or slicers added to the worksheet. (See the previous filtering topics in this lesson.) The filtering is applied to the related PivotTable as well.

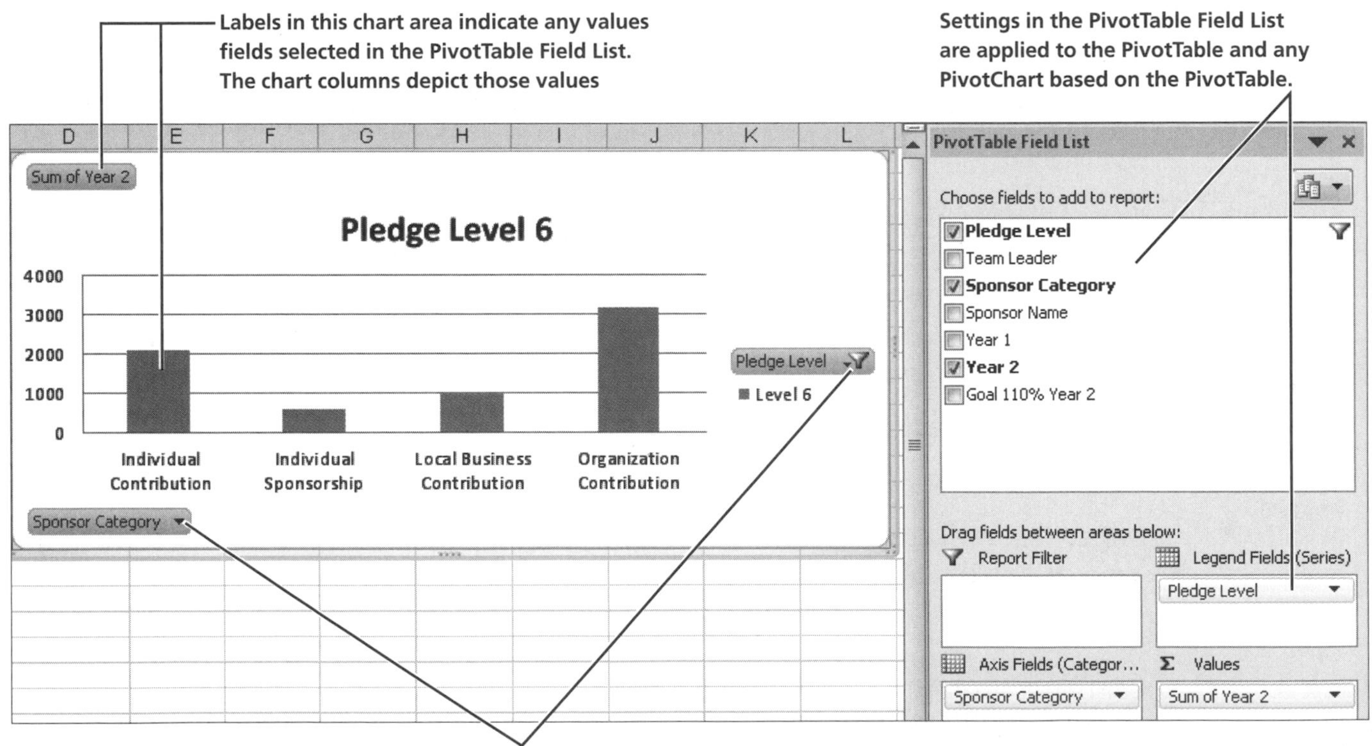

A PivotChart

Copy a PivotTable before creating a PivotChart. Any changes to the chart update in the PivotTable copy. The design in the original PivotTable will be preserved for further analysis.

Formatting and Printing PivotCharts

You format PivotCharts using the same Ribbon commands as for normal Excel charts. You choose from the same variety of chart styles, including column, line, and pie. You format chart objects just as you would on a normal Excel chart. Some chart formatting, such as data labels, is not preserved after a PivotChart is refreshed. When a PivotChart is selected, the Print command will print only the chart. By first selecting a worksheet cell, you can print both the PivotTable and PivotChart as displayed on the worksheet.

QUICK REFERENCE **WORKING WITH PIVOTCHARTS**

Task	Procedure
Create a PivotChart from an existing PivotTable	■ Select any cell within the PivotTable. ■ Choose Insert→Charts, and choose a chart type from the Ribbon. The chart is created next to the PivotTable.
Create a PivotTable and PivotChart concurrently from a worksheet range or table	■ Select any cell in the worksheet range or table. ■ Choose Insert→Tables→PivotTable menu ▼→PivotChart from the Ribbon. ■ Verify the worksheet range or table name in the Create PivotTable with PivotChart dialog box and click OK to place the PivotTable and PivotChart placeholders on a new worksheet. ■ Choose options for the PivotTable in the PivotTable Field List task pane. These options also create a column PivotChart automatically.
Modify PivotChart format	■ Select the chart and choose from the Design, Layout, and Format Ribbons as for a normal Excel chart.
Filter data in a PivotChart	■ Choose the AutoFilter button on the PivotChart for the desired field, and choose filtering options from the drop-down list. *or* ■ Choose Analyze→Data→Insert Slicer, choose the desired slicer(s), and click OK. ■ Choose the desired filtering criteria from the slicer(s).

DEVELOP YOUR SKILLS 12.2.1

Create a PivotChart

In this exercise, you will create a PivotChart from an existing PivotTable.

1. Display the **PivotChart** worksheet of the Sponsors workbook. (**Scroll** to the **right** in the worksheet tabs to locate the tab, if necessary.)

Create a PivotChart

2. **Select** any cell within the PivotTable and choose **Insert→Charts→Column.** Below 2-D Column in the chart types menu, choose **Clustered Column.**
A new column chart is created immediately from the settings in the PivotTable Field List.

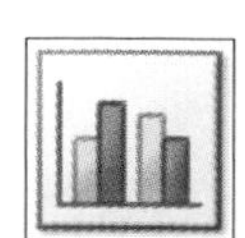

Notice that while the PivotChart is selected, the Column Labels area of the PivotTable Field list task pane is labeled Legend Fields (Series). The Row Labels area is labeled Axis Fields (Categories).

3. **Point** at the chart frame and **drag** the chart just below the PivotTable.

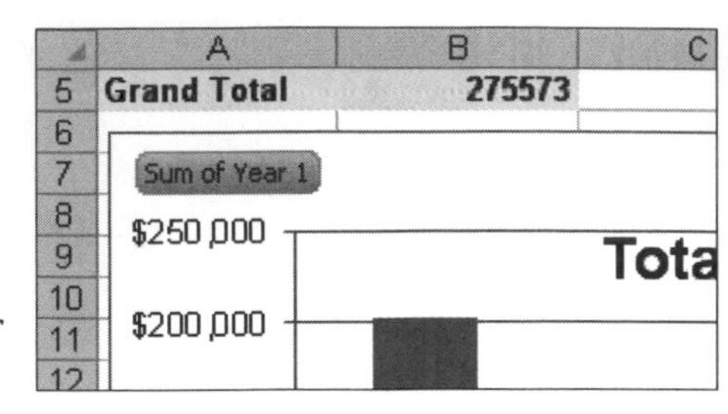

4. Place a checkmark next to **Year 2** in the PivotTable Field List.
   The Sum of Year 2 column displays in the PivotTable, and the PivotChart displays an additional column for the Sum of Year 2 series.

Filter the PivotTable and PivotChart

Notice that the PivotTable has been filtered to display pledge Levels 4–6. The PivotChart matches this filtering. You will use the AutoFilter button on the chart to remove pledge level 4. You could also use the Row Labels AutoFilter button on the PivotTable.

5. Follow these steps to filter the PivotChart:

(A) Choose the **Pledge Level AutoFilter** button at the lower-left corner of the PivotChart.

Pledge Level

(B) **Scroll** down the list.

(C) Remove the checkmark next to **Level 4**.

☐ Level 3
☐ Level 4
☑ Level 5
☑ Level 6

(D) Click **OK**.

Format the PivotChart

6. **Select** the chart, if necessary.

7. Choose **Design→Type→Change Chart Type→Column→Clustered Cylinder** from the Ribbon and click **OK**.
   The chart is reconfigured to the new chart type. You may use chart formatting commands on any PivotChart.

8. Choose **Layout→Labels→Chart Title→Centered Overlay Title** from the Ribbon, type **Levels 5 and 6** (your text appears in the Formula Bar), and **tap** [Enter].

9. Feel free to add other formatting to the chart. For example, the values labels on the vertical axis could be formatted as Currency with no decimals, as shown here.

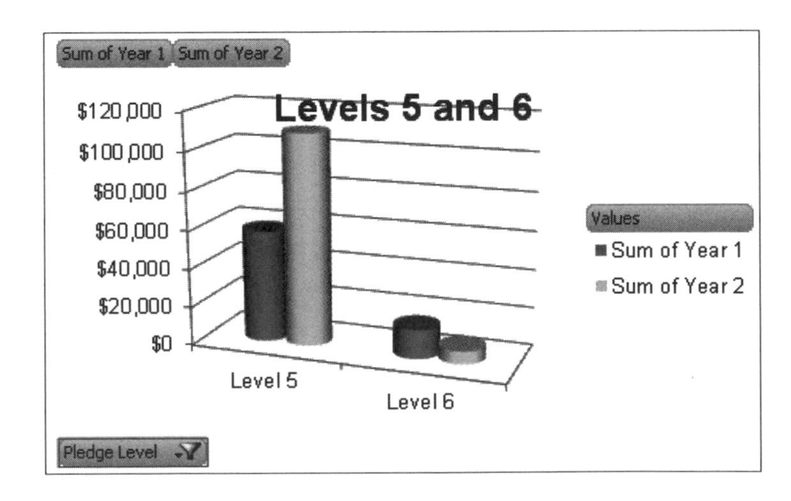

10. **Save** the changes.
11. Use [Ctrl]+[W] or the **Close** button shown to close the workbook but leave Excel **open**.

12.3 Changing Macro Security

Video Lesson labyrinthelab.com/videos

A macro is a recorded set of mouse and keyboard actions that can be played back at any time. Macros are useful for automating routine tasks, especially if those tasks are lengthy. Though macros are a huge timesaver for your frequently used procedures, they also are a prime way to pass viruses to computers. Therefore, be cautious about opening workbooks containing macros that you receive from others.

Security Levels

You change macro security in the Trust Center section within Excel Options. Your setting there is in effect for all Excel workbooks that you open on your computer. The setting is not embedded in any workbooks that you save and share with others. You may choose among four different levels of security in Excel that control whether macros in an opened workbook are available or disabled:

- **Enable all macros**—You are not protected from potentially unsafe macros. This option is not recommended for general use.
- **Disable all macros except digitally signed macros**—This option automatically disables unsigned macros and enables macros from publishers you previously added to the trusted publishers list in the Trust Center. An invisible digital signature or visible signature line may be added to an Excel workbook.
- **Disable all macros with notification**—This is the default option, and it displays a message allowing you to enable macros in the specified workbook if you wish or use the workbook without enabling the macros.
- **Disable all macros without notification**—Only macros in workbooks that you placed in a trusted location of the Trust Center are allowed to run. All other digitally signed and unsigned macros are disabled.

If you have antivirus software installed, the file will be scanned for viruses before it is opened regardless of the security level you set.

Your network system administrator may set macro security and prevent users from changing it.

QUICK REFERENCE **CHANGING MACRO SECURITY**

Task	Procedure
Change macro security	Choose File→Options →Trust Center→Trust Center Settings button→Macro Settings, and choose a macro security option.

DEVELOP YOUR SKILLS 12.3.1

Verify Macro Security

In this exercise, you will verify the macro security setting on your computer. Then you will open a workbook and enable its macros.

1. Choose **File→Options** →**Trust Center**. Click the **Trust Center Settings** button and choose the **Macro Settings** category from the left side of the window. Choose **Disable All Macros with Notification** if not already selected.

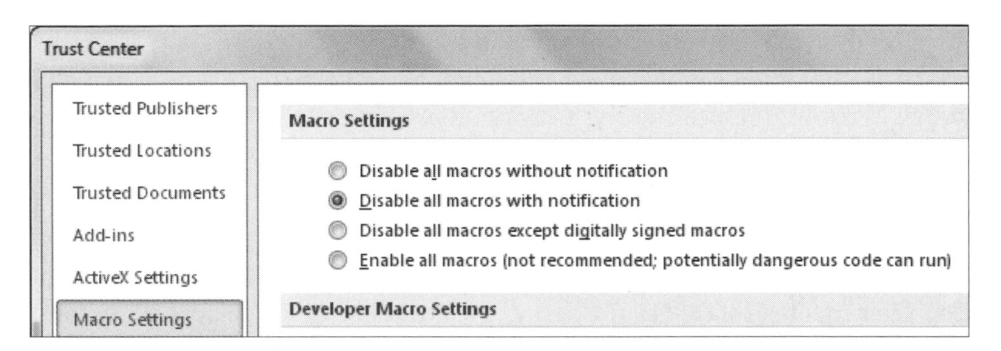

2. Choose the **Message Bar** category from the left side of the window. Verify that the following option is selected: **Show the Message Bar in All Applications When Content, Such As ActiveX and Macros, Has Been Blocked**.
3. Click **OK** twice to exit the Excel Options window.
4. **Open** the Macro Test workbook from the Lesson 12 folder in your file storage location.
   A Security Warning message displays below the Ribbon to alert you that macros are disabled. If you do not respond, the message will disappear after you begin working in the workbook.

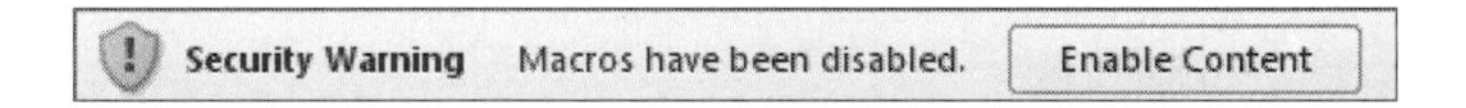

5. Click the **Enable Content** button next to the Security Warning.
   The macros are enabled.
6. Click the **Sort by Leader** button.
   The worksheet list should sort in order by team leader, indicating that the macro worked successfully.
7. **Close** the workbook without saving changes.

12.4 Recording Macros

Video Lesson labyrinthelab.com/videos

Excel's macro recording feature saves your keystrokes and the commands you issue for a task. For example, you may record steps to choose page layout options and print a document by clicking the appropriate commands in the Ribbon. You then may play back a recorded macro at a later time. This is similar to using a video camera. You turn it on, press the record button, and stop recording when finished. You may replay the recording as many times as you want. Similarly, macros play back recorded keystrokes and mouse actions.

 **After the Record Macro button is clicked in the Status Bar, the Stop Recording button appears.** 

Naming a Macro

You should name your macros. If you do not, Excel names them Macro1, Macro2, and so on. Name your macros following the same rules that are used for defined names for ranges. Macro names may not contain spaces but may include capital letters or underscores to separate words. For example, you may name a macro FormatTitle or Format_Title.

Recording Macro Steps

Most actions you perform are recorded in the macro. These include mouse actions, choosing Ribbon commands, selecting options in dialog boxes, using cursor keys to navigate the worksheet, and typing text. Any mistakes and corrections you make during recording also are saved in the macro. You may decide not to rerecord the macro, however, if the final result is correct.

You should practice the procedure you wish to automate before you actually record the macro. This will help you avoid mistakes during the recording process.

Storing Macros

Macros are available only in the workbook in which you create them unless you assign them to the Personal Macro Workbook.

Current Workbook

Some macros are useful only in a particular workbook. For example, you may develop a macro to sort worksheet rows in a specific manner. The macro is useful only in the workbook in which it is created, so you would choose the storage option This Workbook.

Personal Macro Workbook

The Personal.xlsb file is a hidden file that makes its macros available in all open workbooks on your computer system. For example, you may create a macro to format headings with a consistent style to be used in various workbooks. You will assign a macro to the Personal Macro Workbook and delete macros from it in a Skill Builder exercise of this lesson.

Saving a Workbook Containing Macros

If you attempt to save a workbook containing macros using the normal Excel Workbook file format, Excel displays the message "The following features cannot be saved in macro-free workbooks: VB Project." Clicking No in the message box displays the Save As dialog box, where you should choose the Excel Macro-Enabled Workbook file format. The file is saved with the extension .xlsm in the file name to indicate that it contains a macro.

File name: Contributions with Macros
Save as type: Excel Macro-Enabled Workbook

QUICK REFERENCE — RECORDING A MACRO

Task	Procedure
Record a macro	■ Create the worksheet and prepare to record the macro. ■ Click the Record Macro button on the Status Bar in the lower-left corner of the window. ■ Right-click the Status Bar and choose Macro Recording in the context menu if the button does not display. Tap [Esc] to hide the context menu.) ■ Type a descriptive name in the Macro Name box (spaces are not allowed) and fill in other options as desired. ■ Click OK to begin recording. ■ Execute the commands and actions you want the macro to record. ■ Click the Stop Recording button on the Status Bar when you have finished recording.
Delete a macro	■ Choose View→Macros→View Macros (the top part of the button) from the Ribbon or use [Alt]+[F8]. ■ Choose the desired macro name and click Delete.
Save a workbook containing macros	■ Choose Save and click No in the message box or choose Save As. ■ Choose Excel Macro-Enabled Workbook from the Save as Type list in the Save As dialog box.

DEVELOP YOUR SKILLS 12.4.1

Record a Macro

In this exercise, you will record a macro to sort a table first by team leader and then by the contributions to date. You will save the workbook in the macro-enabled file format.

Before You Begin: *Macro security should be set to Disable All Macros with Notification from Develop Your Skills 12.3.1.*

Open the Workbook

1. **Open** the Contributions workbook.
   Take a moment to review the worksheet. Notice that it contains a table of sponsors and that each sponsor has been assigned to a team leader. Also notice that the list is sorted in order by sponsor name, and the table's AutoFilter column heading buttons are turned off. The goal of the next few exercises is to sort the table and add new sponsors to the table. You will record macros to automate the sorting process.

Record the Sort_by_Leader Macro

2. Click the **Record Macro** button on the Status Bar at the bottom-left corner of the window. (**Right-click** the Status Bar and choose **Macro Recording** in the context menu if the button does not display. **Tap** [Esc] to hide the context menu.)
   The Record Macro dialog box appears.

3. Follow these steps to name the macro and begin the recording process:

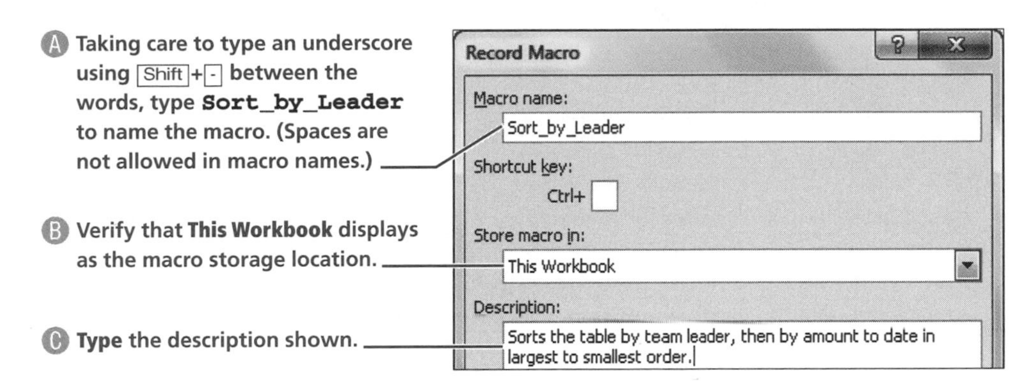

A Taking care to type an underscore using [Shift]+[-] between the words, type **Sort_by_Leader** to name the macro. (Spaces are not allowed in macro names.)
B Verify that **This Workbook** displays as the macro storage location.
C **Type** the description shown.
Record Macro
Macro name:
Sort_by_Leader
Shortcut key:
Ctrl+
Store macro in:
This Workbook
Description:
Sorts the table by team leader, then by amount to date in largest to smallest order.

4. Click **OK**, and the macro will begin recording your actions.
   If you make any mistakes, just correct the errors as you would normally. Major errors may be fixed either by stopping the recording and starting over or by editing the macro in the Visual Basic Editor (not covered in this lesson).

5. Select **cell B4** in the table.
   This step ensures that the proper data is selected prior to sorting whenever the macro is run.

6. Choose **Data→Sort & Filter→Sort** from the Ribbon.

7. Follow these steps to set the Sort parameters and initiate the Sort:

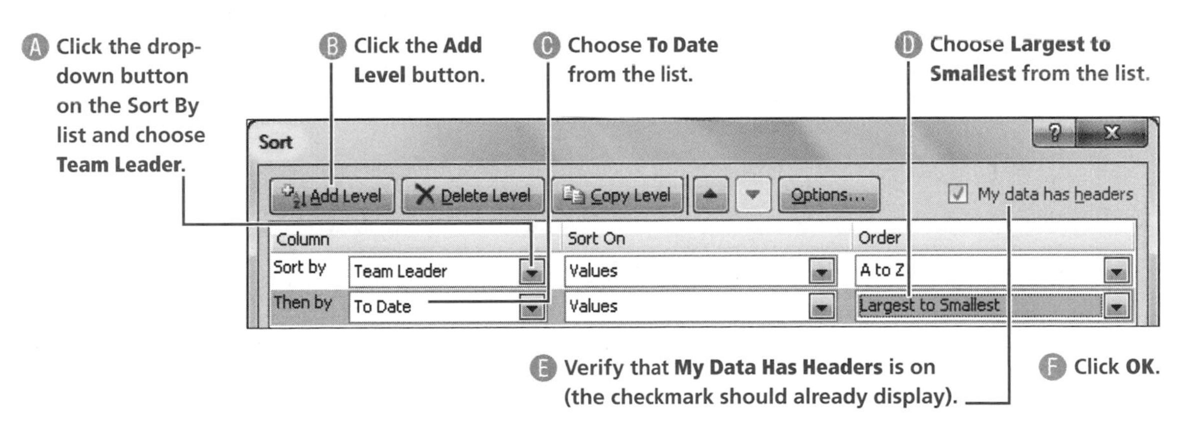

A Click the drop-down button on the Sort By list and choose **Team Leader**.
B Click the **Add Level** button.
C Choose **To Date** from the list.
D Choose **Largest to Smallest** from the list.
Sort
Add Level
Delete Level
Copy Level
Options...
My data has headers
Column
Sort On
Order
Sort by
Team Leader
Values
A to Z
Then by
To Date
Values
Largest to Smallest
E Verify that **My Data Has Headers** is on (the checkmark should already display).
F Click **OK**.

8. Click the **Stop Recording** button on the Status Bar at the bottom-left corner of the window.

Your actions have been saved in the macro. The list is sorted as shown in the following illustration. Keep in mind that the macro recorded this sort sequence.

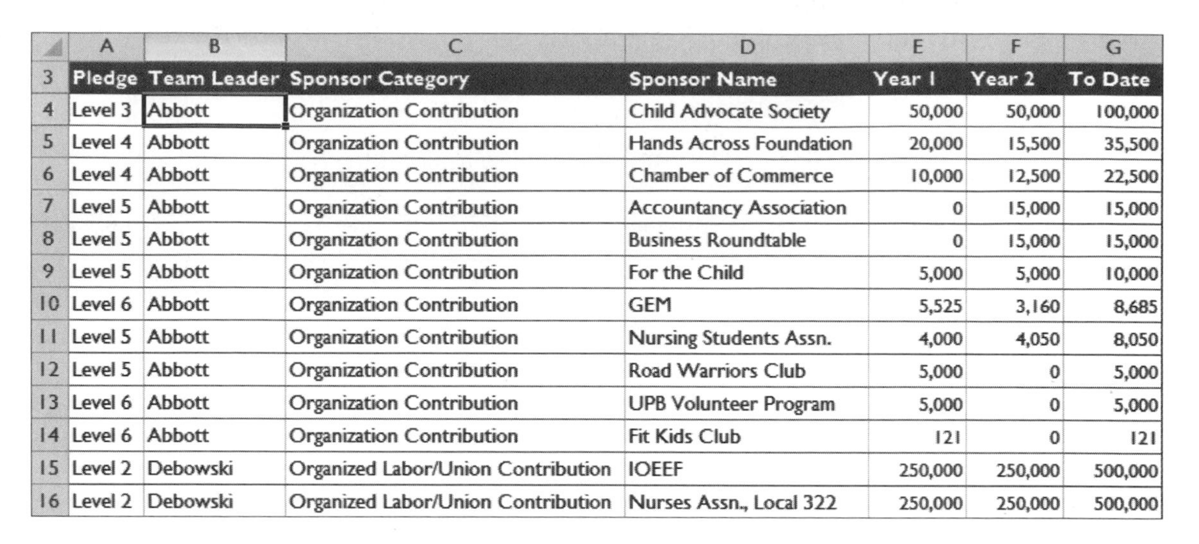

	A	B	C	D	E	F	G
3	Pledge	Team Leader	Sponsor Category	Sponsor Name	Year 1	Year 2	To Date
4	Level 3	Abbott	Organization Contribution	Child Advocate Society	50,000	50,000	100,000
5	Level 4	Abbott	Organization Contribution	Hands Across Foundation	20,000	15,500	35,500
6	Level 4	Abbott	Organization Contribution	Chamber of Commerce	10,000	12,500	22,500
7	Level 5	Abbott	Organization Contribution	Accountancy Association	0	15,000	15,000
8	Level 5	Abbott	Organization Contribution	Business Roundtable	0	15,000	15,000
9	Level 5	Abbott	Organization Contribution	For the Child	5,000	5,000	10,000
10	Level 6	Abbott	Organization Contribution	GEM	5,525	3,160	8,685
11	Level 5	Abbott	Organization Contribution	Nursing Students Assn.	4,000	4,050	8,050
12	Level 5	Abbott	Organization Contribution	Road Warriors Club	5,000	0	5,000
13	Level 6	Abbott	Organization Contribution	UPB Volunteer Program	5,000	0	5,000
14	Level 6	Abbott	Organization Contribution	Fit Kids Club	121	0	121
15	Level 2	Debowski	Organized Labor/Union Contribution	IOEEF	250,000	250,000	500,000
16	Level 2	Debowski	Organized Labor/Union Contribution	Nurses Assn., Local 322	250,000	250,000	500,000

Save the Workbook as Macro-Enabled

9. Click **Save**.
   A message displays as shown. The VB Project indicated is a Visual Basic Project module containing your macro.

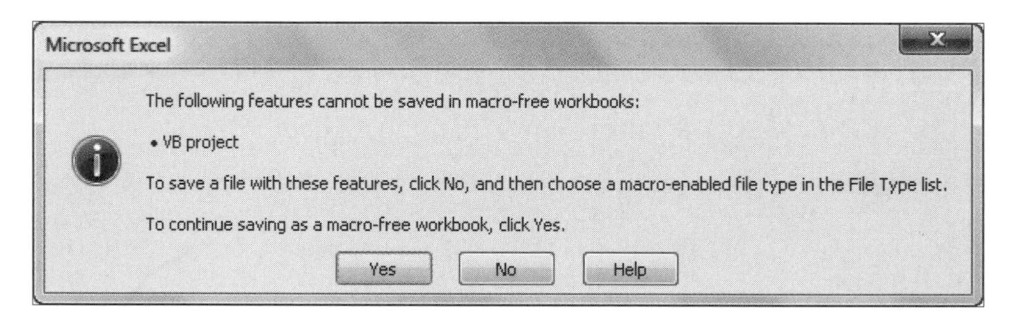
Microsoft Excel
The following features cannot be saved in macro-free workbooks:
• VB project
To save a file with these features, click No, and then choose a macro-enabled file type in the File Type list.
To continue saving as a macro-free workbook, click Yes.
Yes
No
Help

10. Click **No** to display the Save As dialog box.
11. Edit the **File Name** to **`Contributions with Macros`**.
12. Drop down the Save As type list, choose **Excel Macro-Enabled Workbook**, and click **Save**.

File name: Contributions with Macros
Save as type: Excel Macro-Enabled Workbook

The macro is saved as part of the workbook named Contributions with Macros.xlsm. If you were to close the workbook, the macro would be available the next time you opened the workbook. The Disable All Macros with Notification security setting is in effect, so you still can control whether macros actually are enabled in an opened workbook.

12.5 Running Macros

Video Lesson labyrinthelab.com/videos

You may run macros in a variety of ways. The method you use depends on how the macro was assigned. You may create a macro and assign it to a shortcut key, graphic, or Quick Access toolbar button. An unassigned macro must be run by using the Macros command on the Ribbon and selecting a macro. This procedure may be used to run any macro recorded in the current workbook, even if the macro was assigned. The keyboard shortcut [Alt]+[F8] may be used to display the Macro dialog box.

FROM THE KEYBOARD
[Alt]+[F8] to view macros

QUICK REFERENCE **RUNNING A MACRO**

Task	Procedure
Run an unassigned or assigned macro from the Ribbon	■ Choose View→Macros→View Macros from the Ribbon or use [Alt]+[F8]. ■ Choose the desired macro name and click Run.
Run an assigned macro	■ Use the shortcut key or click the assigned graphic, worksheet button, or Quick Access toolbar button.

DEVELOP YOUR SKILLS 12.5.1

Run an Unassigned Macro

In this exercise, you will sort the contributions table manually in a different order and then run the Sort_by_Leader macro.

Before You Begin: You must have completed Develop Your Skills 12.4.1, and the Contributions with Macros workbook should be open. Macro security should be set to Disable All Macros with Notification from Develop Your Skills 12.3.1. If you reopened the Contributions with Macros workbook and the Security Warning message appears under the Ribbon, choose Enable Macros.

1. Select **cell D4** and choose **Data→Sort & Filter→Sort A to Z** from the Ribbon.
   The contributions table is sorted alphabetically by sponsor name. Now you will run the macro you created in the previous exercise.
2. Choose **View→Macros→View Macros** from the Ribbon.
3. Choose the **Sort_by_Leader** macro and click **Run** in the Macro dialog box.
   The list is sorted by team leader, then by the To Date amount in highest to lowest order within each team leader's rows. The macro saves you time because you did not need to choose the Sort command and set options manually.
4. **Save** the changes to the workbook.

12.6 Assigning Macros

Video Lesson labyrinthelab.com/videos

You may run a macro from within the Macro dialog box. However, macros are more accessible if you assign them to shortcut keys, custom buttons or graphics on a worksheet, or buttons on the Quick Access toolbar. You then run the macro by issuing the shortcut key or clicking the object to which the macro is assigned.

Assigning Macros to Shortcut Keys

Excel lets you assign a macro to a shortcut key as you name the macro. You may run the macro simply by using the shortcut key combination. You must use [Ctrl] or [Ctrl]+[Shift] as part of the shortcut key combination. Any shortcut you assign will override an existing Excel command shortcut. For example, you may assign [Ctrl]+[B] to a macro, but that combination would no longer choose Bold from the Ribbon.

TIP

If you are in the habit of using Microsoft's command shortcuts, use [Ctrl]+[Shift] for your macro shortcuts.

DEVELOP YOUR SKILLS 12.6.1

Assign a Macro to a Shortcut Key

In this exercise, you will create a macro to add a new sponsor to the table and assign the macro to a shortcut key. You will run the macro to add a sponsor. Then you will assign a shortcut key to the macro you created in the previous exercise and use its shortcut key to sort the list.

Before You Begin: You must have completed Develop Your Skills 12.4.1 and 12.5.1, and the Contributions with Macros workbook should be open. Macro security should be set to Disable All Macros with Notification from Develop Your Skills 12.3.1. If you reopened the Contributions with Macros workbook and the Security Warning message now appears under the Ribbon, choose Enable Macros.

Assign a Shortcut Key and Record the Insert_Sponsor Macro

You will record a new macro that automates the process of inserting a new sponsor record just below the table header row.

1. Click the **Record Macro** button on the Status Bar.
   The Record Macro dialog box appears.
2. Follow these steps to name a new macro:

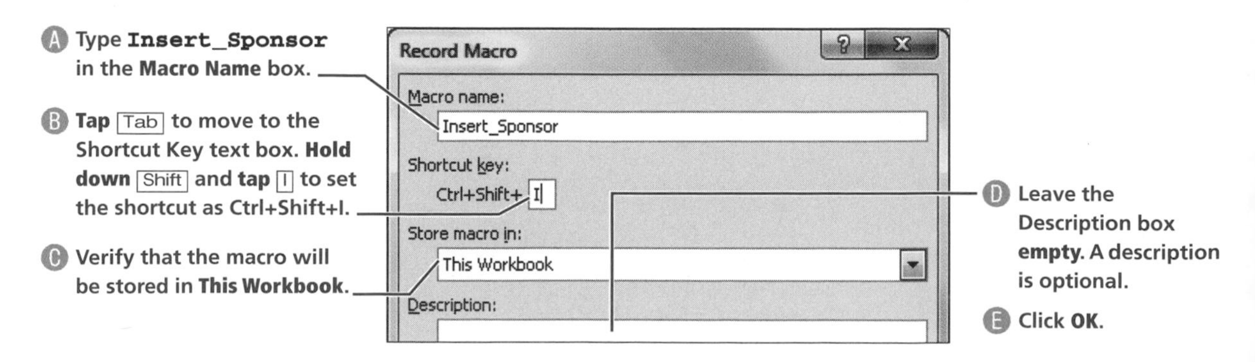

A Type Insert_Sponsor in the Macro Name box.
B Tap [Tab] to move to the Shortcut Key text box. Hold down [Shift] and tap [I] to set the shortcut as Ctrl+Shift+I.
C Verify that the macro will be stored in This Workbook.
D Leave the Description box empty. A description is optional.
E Click OK.
Record Macro
Macro name:
Insert_Sponsor
Shortcut key:
Ctrl+Shift+ I
Store macro in:
This Workbook
Description:

In the next few steps, you will perform the actions to be recorded in the macro. You will insert a blank table row below the column headings and copy cell formatting to the blank cells.

3. Select **cell A4**.
4. Taking care not to select the menu ▾ button, choose **Home→Insert** from the Ribbon.
   A blank row is inserted at row 4, and its cells are formatted like the column headings.
5. Select the **range A5:G5**, and choose **Home→Clipboard→Format Painter** from the Ribbon.
6. Select **cell A4** to apply the cell formatting from row 5 to the blank row 4.
7. Select **cell A4** again to position the pointer for data entry.
8. Click the **Stop Recording** button on the status bar.

Run the Macro to Add New Sponsors

9. Delete the blank **row 4** that you inserted while creating the macro.
10. Use [Ctrl]+[Shift]+[I] to run the Insert_Sponsor macro. (Hold down [Ctrl], then also hold down [Shift], and then tap [I]. Release [Ctrl] and [Shift].)
    The pointer moves to cell A4 and blank cells are inserted. New sponsors always will be added to a new row below the header row.

    If your macro did not work correctly, choose View→Macros→Macros→Insert_Sponsor, and then click Delete. Then repeat steps 1–10, choosing Yes when asked if you wish to replace the macro.
11. **Add** the following sponsor to the table. **Tap** [Tab] after entering the Year 2 value, and the To Date total will be calculated automatically.

4	Level 6	Weinstein	Individual Contribution	Raul T. Garcia	0	500	500

12. **Run** the Insert_Sponsor macro again and add this sponsor to the table:

4	Level 6	Weinstein	Individual Contribution	Wayne Zobe	0	300	300

Assign a Shortcut Key to the Sort_by_Leader Macro

13. Choose **View→Macros→View Macros** from the Ribbon.
14. Choose the **Sort_by_Leader** macro and click **Options** in the Macro dialog box.
15. In the Shortcut Key text box, **press** [Shift], and **tap** [L] to set the shortcut key to Ctrl+Shift+L. Click **OK**.

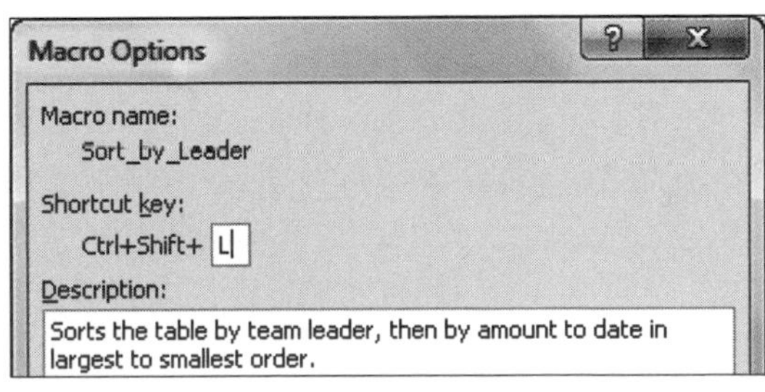

16. Click **Cancel** to exit the Macro dialog box.
17. Use [Ctrl]+[Shift]+[L] to run the macro.
    The table is sorted by team leader and then by To Date amount in highest to lowest order within each team leader group. The Raul T. Garcia record moves to row 98 in the Weinstein team leader group. The Wayne Zobe record moves to row 101.
18. **Save** the changes to the workbook.

Assigning Macros to Custom Buttons

Video Lesson labyrinthelab.com/videos

A macro assigned to a custom button is run whenever the button is clicked. The easiest way to create a custom button is to add a shape, such as a rectangle, to the worksheet. You then assign a macro to the button. You may position custom buttons anywhere in a worksheet. To avoid deleting buttons in error, do not place them in rows or columns that could be deleted in the future. A custom button may also contain a descriptive label to help identify its function or the macro that is assigned to it.

You may create custom buttons using the Button (Form Control) tool on the Developer tab. To display this tab, choose File→Options from the Ribbon, select Customize Ribbon at the left of the Excel Options dialog box, and place a checkmark next to Developer in the Main Tabs list at the right. The Developer tab contains commands for working with macros.

QUICK REFERENCE **ASSIGNING A MACRO**

Task	Procedure
Assign a macro to a shortcut key as the macro is created	■ Click the Record Macro button on the Status Bar. ■ While filling in options in the Macro dialog box, click in the Shortcut Key text box and key a single letter, or hold [Shift] and key the letter.
Assign a macro to a shortcut key after the macro is created	■ Choose View→Macros→View Macros from the Ribbon. ■ Choose the macro name and click Options in the Macro dialog box. ■ In the Macro Options dialog box, click in the Shortcut Key text box and key a single letter, or hold [Shift] and key the letter.
Assign a macro to a custom button or graphic on the worksheet	■ Record the macro. ■ Insert a shape, picture, or clip art image on the worksheet. Right-click the object and choose Assign Macro from the context menu. Choose the desired macro from the Assign Macro dialog box. ■ To display a text label in a shape used as a custom button, select the button in the worksheet and type the desired text in the button. ■ If necessary, resize the button or graphic, drag it to the desired worksheet location, and align multiple buttons.

DEVELOP YOUR SKILLS 12.6.2

Assign Macros to Custom Buttons

In this exercise, you will create buttons and assign the Insert_Sponsor and Sort_by_Leader macros to them.

Before You Begin: Macro security should be set to Disable All Macros with Notification from Develop Your Skills 12.3.1. If you reopened the Contributions with Macros workbook and the Security Warning message appears under the Ribbon, choose Enable Macros.

Create Buttons

1. Choose **Insert→Illustrations→Shapes→Rectangles→Rectangle** shape tool from the Ribbon.
2. Drag the mouse to draw a button on **cell D1**.
3. Copy and paste the button to cell **E1**.

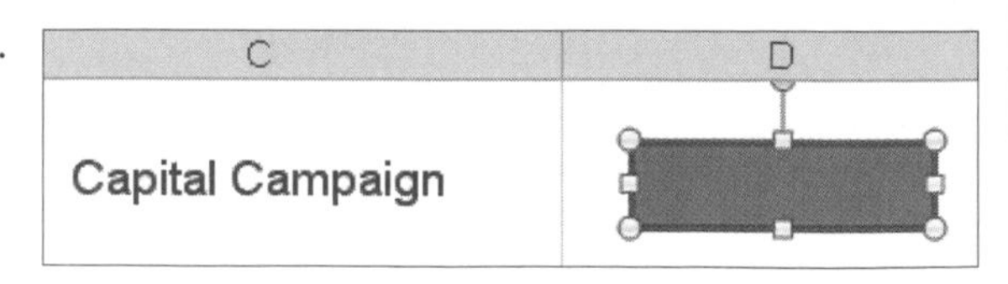

Name Buttons

4. Select the **first button** and type **`Insert Sponsor`**; do *not* tap Enter.
5. Select the **second button** and type **`Sort by Leader`**.
   Button text may contain spaces because it is only a label.
6. **Click** outside the button to deselect it.

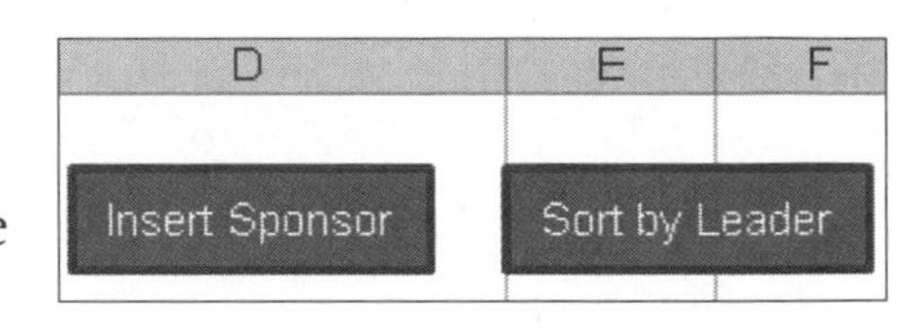

7. If necessary, **align** the buttons: Select the first button, use Shift+click to select the second button, and choose **Format→Arrange→Align→ Align Top** from the Ribbon.
   Formatting the buttons is easier if completed before you assign macros to the buttons. If you wish, you may change the colors and outline in custom buttons.

Assign Macros to Buttons

8. **Deselect** the two buttons.
9. **Right-click** the Insert Sponsor button and choose **Assign Macro** from the context menu.
10. In the Assign Macro dialog box, choose **Insert_Sponsor** from the list and click **OK**.
11. Use the preceding steps to assign the **Sort_by_Leader** macro to its button.

Run Macros Using the Buttons

12. **Deselect** the button.
13. Click the **Insert Sponsor** button to run the Insert_Sponsor macro. (Deselect the button and select again if the pointer does not display as a hand as you select the button.)
   A new row appears just below the header row.

14. Add this sponsor to the new row:

4	Level 3	Abbott	Organization Contribution	Kelsey Foundation	0	50,000	50,000

15. Click the **Sort by Leader** button to run the Sort_by_Leader macro.
   The new row is sorted into the worksheet as row 5.
16. **Save** the changes and **close** the workbook.
   Now you have learned to create simple macros to automate routine tasks. You ran macros using the Ribbon, shortcut keys, and custom buttons on the worksheet.

12.7 Concepts Review

Concepts Review labyrinthelab.com/excel10

To check your knowledge of the key concepts introduced in this lesson, complete the Concepts Review quiz by going to the URL listed above. If your classroom is using Labyrinth eLab, you may complete the Concepts Review quiz from within your eLab course.

Reinforce Your Skills

REINFORCE YOUR SKILLS 12.1

Create a PivotTable and a PivotChart

In this exercise, you will create a PivotTable and PivotChart simultaneously from a worksheet table. You will practice placing and pivoting fields to change your view of the data.

1. **Start** Excel and **open** the rs-Jan Sales PivotTable workbook from the Lesson 12 folder.
   The January Sales worksheet displays one month's activity at Avery Internet Auto Sales. Before you create a PivotTable, take a moment to look over the layout of the data fields and records. For example, notice that there is just one field for numeric data in this table.

Create the PivotTable and PivotChart

2. Select **cell A4**.
   This tells Excel to use the table data when you create the PivotTable.
3. Choose **Insert→Tables→PivotTable** **menu ▾→PivotChart** from the Ribbon, verify **JanSales** as the table data to be used, and click **OK** to create a PivotTable and PivotChart in a new worksheet.
4. **Rename** the Sheet1 sheet tab to **`PivotTable`**.
   The PivotTable Field List task pane is displayed. If it does not and you made certain the chart is selected, choose Analyze→Show/Hide→Field List. You may turn on/off the pane as needed.
5. In the PivotTable Field List task pane, place a checkmark in the **Sold By** and **Price** checkboxes.
   The PivotTable displays the total sales for each salesperson using the Sum of Price field in the values area of the PivotTable Field List task pane. The chart is selected, so the task pane displays Axis Fields (Categories) and Legend Field areas.
6. **Select** a cell in the PivotTable, and the same areas now are titled Row Labels and Column Labels to reflect those items in the PivotTable.

Add a Field

Since you may need to know which types of cars each salesperson sold during January, you will place a new field in the row field's area.

7. Place a checkmark in the **Type** box on the task pane to add the field to the Row Labels area.

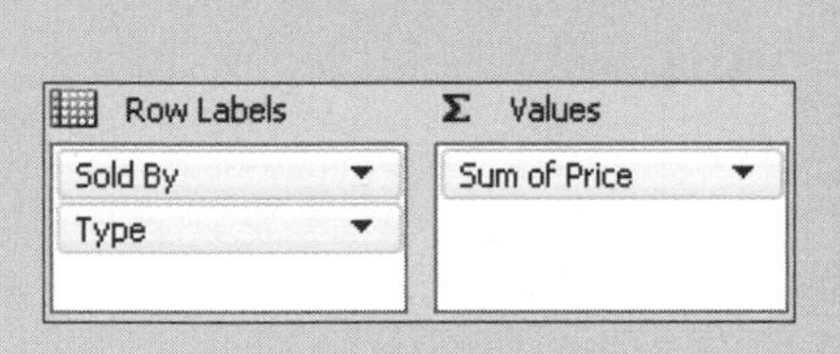

	A	B
1	Row Labels	Sum of Price
2	⊟Jones	190470
3	Coupe	37950
4	SUV	152520
5	⊟Lehman	142620
6	Sedan	65445
7	SUV	54675
8	Truck	22500
9	⊟Palmas	146675
10	Sedan	98425
11	Truck	48250
12	Grand Total	479765

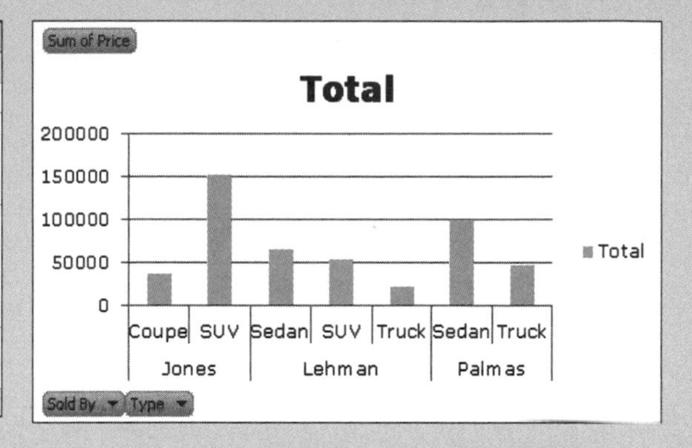

The PivotTable and PivotChart expand to display the sales of the various types of vehicles sold by each salesperson. It might also be interesting to summarize how the revenue at the dealership breaks down by vehicle type, so in the next step you will pivot the Type field from the row area to the column area.

Arrange Items in the Window

You may not see the entire PivotTable and PivotChart as items change in the window.

8. Follow these steps to maximize space:

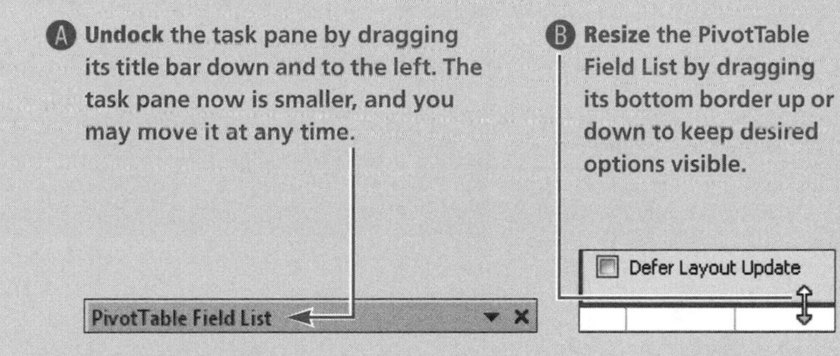

A **Undock** the task pane by dragging its title bar down and to the left. The task pane now is smaller, and you may move it at any time.
PivotTable Field List
B **Resize** the PivotTable Field List by dragging its bottom border up or down to keep desired options visible.
Defer Layout Update

C To prevent the PivotChart from covering the PivotTable in the next step, **move** the PivotChart to the right by dragging the chart frame, until the left edge of the chart is in column G.

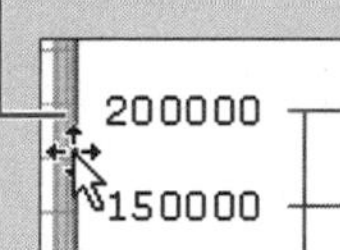

Pivot the View

9. Drag the **Type** field to the Column Labels area.

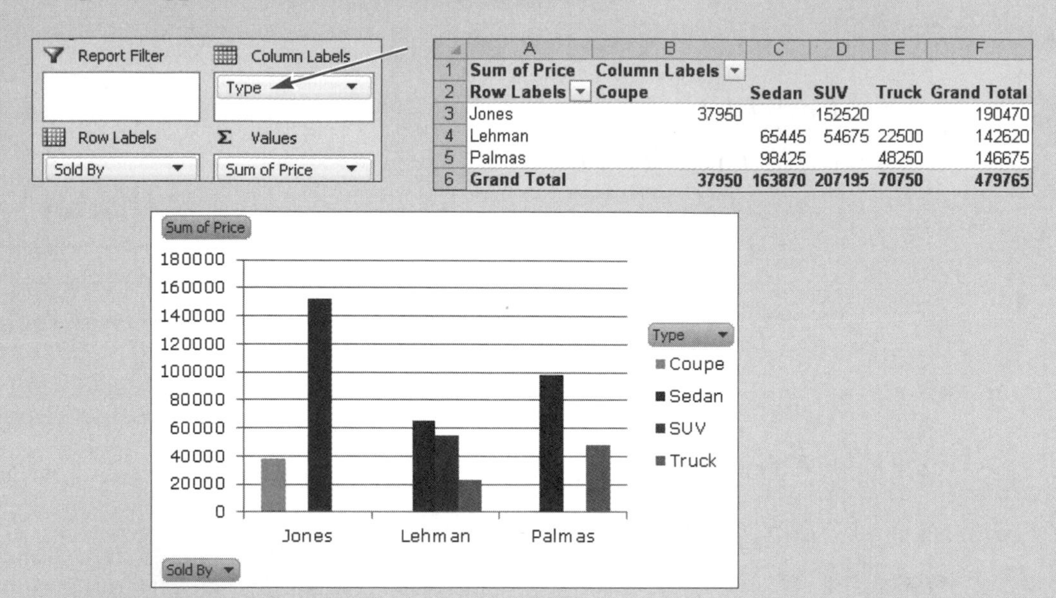

Sum of Price	Column Labels				
Row Labels	Coupe	Sedan	SUV	Truck	Grand Total
Jones	37950		152520		190470
Lehman		65445	54675	22500	142620
Palmas		98425		48250	146675
Grand Total	**37950**	**163870**	**207195**	**70750**	**479765**

The Grand Total line at the bottom of the PivotTable displays the revenue for each type of car. The chart displays columns for each car type.

Add a Field and Pivot the View

10. Place a checkmark in the **New/Preowned** box on the task pane to add the field to the Row Labels area and observe the effect in the PivotTable and the PivotChart.

11. Drag the **New/Preowned** field above Sold By in the Row Labels area of the task pane as shown.

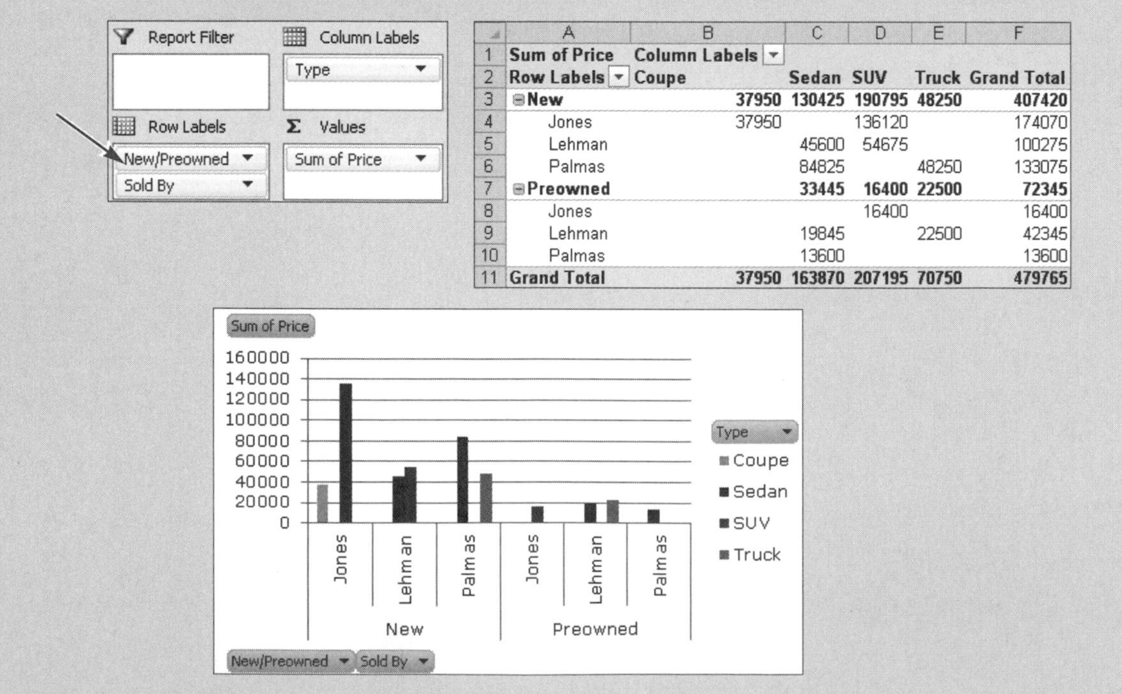

Sum of Price	Column Labels				
Row Labels	Coupe	Sedan	SUV	Truck	Grand Total
⊟New	**37950**	**130425**	**190795**	**48250**	**407420**
Jones	37950		136120		174070
Lehman		45600	54675		100275
Palmas		84825		48250	133075
⊟Preowned		**33445**	**16400**	**22500**	**72345**
Jones			16400		16400
Lehman		19845		22500	42345
Palmas		13600			13600
Grand Total	**37950**	**163870**	**207195**	**70750**	**479765**

This view clearly shows that revenue is much greater for new cars than preowned, as might be expected.

12. Move the PivotChart to below the PivotTable so both fit on **one printed page**.
13. **Drag** the PivotTable Field List task pane to the right edge of the screen, until the task pane is docked.
14. **Select** a cell in the PivotTable to deselect the PivotChart.
    Only the chart would print when the chart is selected.
15. **Save** the changes and **close** the workbook.
    As you have seen, PivotTables and PivotCharts help you display and analyze data in various ways with a minimum of setup steps.

REINFORCE YOUR SKILLS 12.2

Filter a PivotTable

In this exercise, you will filter to exclude data items from a PivotTable. You also will use a slicer to filter by a field not displayed in the PivotTable.

1. **Open** the rs-Feb Sales PivotTable workbook.
   Look at the table data in the February Sales worksheet. A PivotTable and a PivotChart were created using this data.
2. Display the **PivotTable** worksheet.
   You will not use the field buttons in the PivotChart, so they were turned off in the Analyze ribbon.
3. **Select** a cell within the PivotTable to display the PivotTable Field List task pane, if necessary.

Use AutoFilter

4. Follow these steps in the PivotTable to suppress the display of data for Walk-In sales:

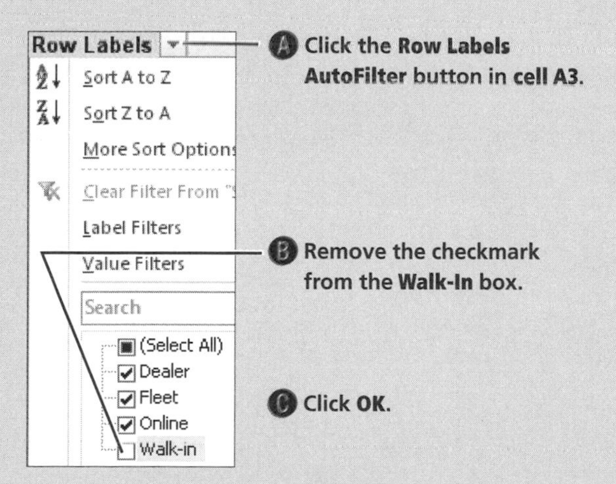

Notice that no data is displayed for Walk-In sales, and the Row Headers filter button displays a filter icon. You may use this method to switch the display of individual data items on and off for any field in the Row Labels or Column Labels.

5. Display the **Row Labels** filter list again and choose **Clear Filter from "Source."**

Delete and Add Fields in the PivotTable

6. In the PivotTable Field List task pane, remove the checkmark from the **Source** box.
7. Place a checkmark in the **Financing** box to add the field to the PivotTable.
   The pie chart displays bank/credit union financing as 46 percent, dealer financing as 42 percent, and cash as 12 percent for all vehicles sold.

Filter with a Slicer

Notice that the New/Preowned field does not have a checkmark in the PivotTable Field List, so the field does not appear in the PivotTable. At times, you may wish to maintain a simplified PivotTable and PivotChart design. You can use slicers to filter for fields that are not displayed. Next, you will filter for new and preowned vehicles.

8. Choose **Insert→Filter→Slicer** from the Ribbon.
9. In the Insert Slicers dialog box, place a checkmark next to **New/Preowned**, and click **OK**.
   The New/Preowned slicer displays on the worksheet window, and the PivotTable Filter List task pane is hidden.
10. Point to the **New/Preowned** title in the slicer, and **drag** the slicer frame so it is not covering the PivotTable or PivotChart.

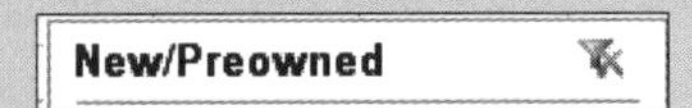

11. Choose **New** in the slicer.
    The Sum of Price column in the PivotTable and the PivotChart percentages have changed to include only new vehicles. The pie chart displays Dealer financing as 46 percent but Cash financing as only 6 percent of new vehicles sold.
12. Choose **Preowned** in the slicer.
    The values and percentages update to include only preowned vehicles. Now you can see that dealer financing is only 21 percent and the majority of preowned vehicle purchases were paid in cash.
13. **Select** the PivotChart, choose **Design→Chart Styles→More**, and choose a **chart style** that displays good contrast between the colors of the text and pie slices.
14. Change the **page orientation** or **resize** the chart, if necessary, to fit the PivotTable and PivotChart on one printed page.
15. **Save** the changes and **close** the workbook.

REINFORCE YOUR SKILLS 12.3

Create a Macro for the Personal Macro Workbook

In this exercise, you will create a macro that selects an entire worksheet, formats all cells with bold, and widens the columns. You will assign the macro to the personal macro workbook to make it available for use in other workbooks you may open.

Begin Recording the Macro

1. **Start** a new workbook.
2. Click the **Record Macro button** on the Status Bar.
3. **Type** the macro name **FormatSheet** in the Record Macro dialog box.
4. Set the Store Macro In option to **Personal Macro Workbook**.

Choose This Workbook instead if you cannot save a macro to the Personal Macro Workbook on your computer system.

5. Click **OK** (and replace the macro if it already exists) to begin the recording process.

Set Worksheet Formats

6. Use Ctrl+A to select the entire worksheet.
7. Use Ctrl+B to bold all cells.
8. Choose **Home→Cells→Format** →**Column Width** to display the Column Width dialog box, type **12**, and **tap** Enter to choose **OK**.
9. Select **cell A1** to deselect the highlighted cells.
10. Click the **Stop Recording** button on the Run the Macro status bar.
11. Choose **File→Close** and choose **not** to save when Excel asks if you want to save the workbook.

Run the Macro

12. Start a new workbook and choose **View→Macros→View Macros** (the top part of the button) to display the Macro dialog box.
    Any macro with PERSONAL.XLSB! in its name has been saved to the Personal Macro Workbook and is available to all open workbooks.
13. Choose the **PERSONAL.XLSB!FormatSheet** macro and click the **Run** button. (Choose FormatSheet rather than PERSONAL.XLSB!FormatSheet if you saved the macro to This Worksheet.)
    The column and text formats are set. Keep in mind that you may apply virtually any formatting to cells, columns, rows, text, or numbers with a macro.

Delete the Macro from the Personal Macro Workbook

Macros stored in the Personal Macro Workbook cannot be removed with the Delete button in the Macro dialog box. Just read the next steps and complete step 20 if you saved the macro to This Workbook rather than Personal Macro Workbook.

14. Choose **View→Macros→View Macros** from the Ribbon.
15. Follow these steps to delete the FormatSheet macro from the Personal Macro Workbook:

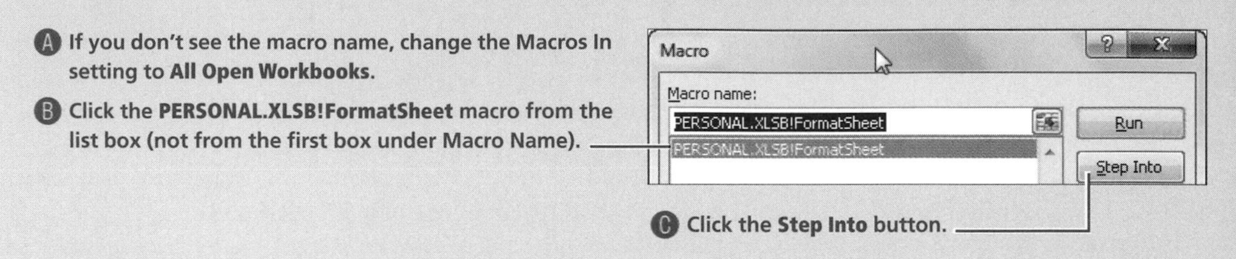

A If you don't see the macro name, change the Macros In setting to **All Open Workbooks.**
B Click the **PERSONAL.XLSB!FormatSheet** macro from the list box (not from the first box under Macro Name).
Macro
Macro name:
PERSONAL.XLSB!FormatSheet
PERSONAL.XLSB!FormatSheet
Run
Step Into
C Click the **Step Into** button.

The macro code displays in the Microsoft Visual Basic for Applications window.

16. In the Microsoft Visual Basic for Applications window, choose **Tools→Macros**.
17. In the Macros dialog box, set the Macros In option to **VBA Project (PERSONAL.XLSB)**.
18. Choose the **FormatSheet** macro, click **Delete**, and click **OK** to confirm.
19. **Close** the Microsoft Visual Basic for Applications window to reveal the Excel workbook window.
    In this exercise, you deleted the macro to keep the computer system "clean." Normally, you would leave macros stored in the personal macro workbook so they could be used in all workbooks.
20. **Close** the empty workbook without saving it.

Apply Your Skills

APPLY YOUR SKILLS 12.1

Create a PivotTable

In this exercise, you will create a PivotTable to calculate the cost of care and shelter for healthy and sick animals at Capital City Animal Shelter.

1. **Open** the as-April Expenses workbook from the Lesson 12 folder.
2. Examine the April Expense Report worksheet. Identify the fields you will use in the PivotTable.

Create the PivotTable

3. Create a **PivotTable** on a new worksheet.
4. **Rename** the new sheet with a descriptive name of your choice.
5. **Rename** the PivotTable as **`April Expenses`**.
6. Set up fields for the PivotTable so that the rows summarize the data by **cats/dogs** and then by **age**.
7. Set up fields so that the columns compare the cost of caring for **healthy** and **sick** animals.
8. Set up fields to total the cost of **care** and **shelter**.

Format the PivotTable

9. **Apply** a PivotTable style.
10. Format all numbers with **Comma Style and two decimal places.**
    When you finish, your PivotTable should match the following figure, except for field labels.

Your PivotTable displays some additional labels. They were removed from this figure because they would display a significant part of the exercise solution.

	A	B	C	D
3	**Sum of Total Costs**	**Column Labels**		
4	**Row Labels**	**Healthy**	**Sick**	**Grand Total**
5	**⊟Cat**	**349.75**	**292.25**	**642.00**
6	Adult	349.75	182.50	532.25
7	Kitten		109.75	109.75
8	**⊟Dog**	**919.50**	**448.00**	**1,367.50**
9	Adult	564.00	67.00	631.00
10	Pup	355.50	381.00	736.50
11	**Grand Total**	**1,269.25**	**740.25**	**2,009.50**

Change Worksheet Data and Update the PivotTable

11. In the April Expenses worksheet, change the cost per day in **cell F1** to **`$5.25`**.
12. Do whatever is necessary to **update** the PivotTable to reflect the change you just made.
13. **Save** the changes and **close** the workbook.

APPLY YOUR SKILLS 12.2

Create a PivotTable and PivotChart

In this exercise, you will create a PivotTable and PivotChart that display the cost of care and shelter for sick and healthy animals summarized by animal type and health. The chart will be a stacked column chart.

1. **Open** the as-May Expenses workbook.
2. Examine the May Expense Report worksheet. Identify the fields you will use to create the PivotTable and its accompanying PivotChart.

Create the PivotTable and PivotChart

3. Create a **PivotTable** and **PivotChart** together on a new worksheet.
4. **Rename** the new sheet with a descriptive name of your choice.
5. **Rename** the PivotTable as **`May Expenses`**.
6. Set up fields for the PivotTable and PivotChart so that the table and chart summarize the data by **cats/dogs** and then by **health**.
7. Set up fields so that the **shelter cost** and **veterinary cost** are calculated separately.
8. Format all numbers in the PivotTable with **Comma Style and no decimal places**.

Format the PivotChart

9. Change the chart type to **Stacked Column**.
10. Apply a PivotChart **style** and a **chart layout** of your choice.
    When you finish, your PivotTable and PivotChart should match the following figure, except for field labels.

Your PivotTable displays one additional label. It was removed from this figure because it would display a significant part of the exercise solution.

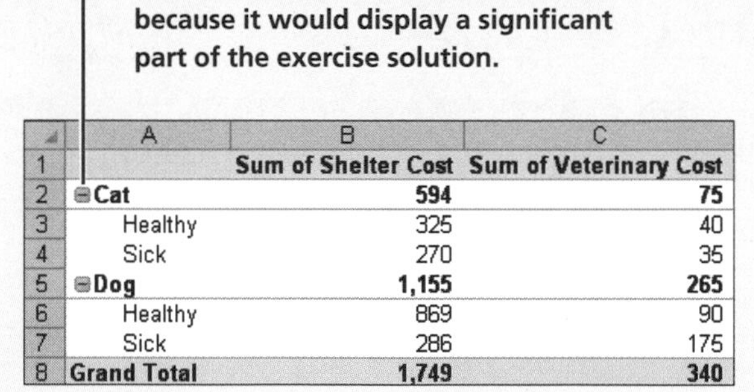

	A	B	C
1		Sum of Shelter Cost	Sum of Veterinary Cost
2	⊟Cat	594	75
3	Healthy	325	40
4	Sick	270	35
5	⊟Dog	1,155	265
6	Healthy	869	90
7	Sick	286	175
8	Grand Total	1,749	340

Your PivotChart style and layout may differ from that shown.

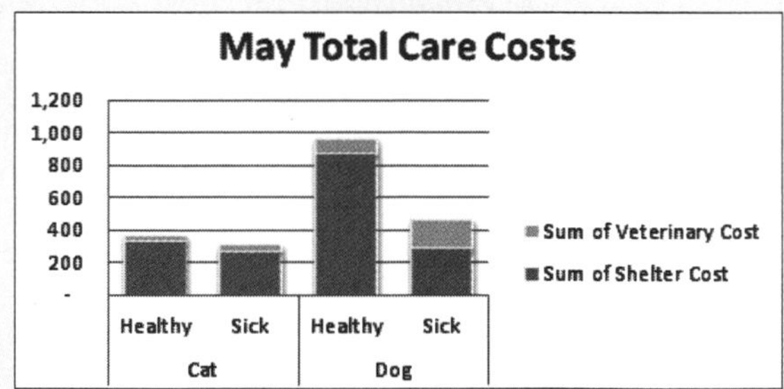

11. Change the **page orientation** and make any other adjustments necessary to fit the PivotTable and PivotChart on **one printed page**.
12. **Save** the changes and **close** the workbook.

APPLY YOUR SKILLS 12.3

Create a Macro that Inserts the Date

*In this exercise, you will create a macro that inserts the phrase **Today's Date** in cell A1 and the TODAY() function in cell A2. The macro also will format the two cells. You will assign the macro to the current workbook only.*

1. Start a **new workbook** containing three blank worksheets.
2. Select **cell A10**.

Record the Macro

3. Begin **recording** a new macro.
4. **Name** the macro **TodaysDate**, assign the shortcut keystroke **Ctrl+Shift+D** to the macro, and store it in **This Workbook**. Your macro should record all of the actions in **steps 5–11**.
5. Select **cell A1**.
6. Type **Today's Date** into **cell A1**.
7. Enter the formula **=TODAY()** in **cell B1**.
   This function displays the current date in the cell.
8. Left-align the date in **cell B1**.
9. Format **cells A1:B1** with size 12, bold, and a blue color for text.
10. Set the width of **column A** to **20**.
11. Select **cell B1**.
12. **Stop** the macro recording.
13. **Save** as a Macro-Enabled Workbook with the name **as-Today's Date** in the Lesson 12 folder in your file storage location.

Test the Macro Using the Ribbon Command

14. Display the **Sheet2** worksheet.
15. Run the macro using the **Run** command in the Macro dialog box.
    If your macro does not insert text, format the text, and widen column A as specified in steps 5–11, then delete the macro and rerecord it.

Test the Macro Shortcut Key

16. Display the **Sheet3** worksheet.
17. **Test** the macro using the [Ctrl]+[Shift]+[D] keystroke combination.
18. Have your instructor or a teaching assistant initial that you have successfully run the macro. ___________
19. **Save** as **as-Today's Date** again and **close** the workbook.

APPLY YOUR SKILLS 12.4

Create Macros and Assign Buttons

In this exercise, you will create a defined name for a list, create two macros, assign buttons to them, and finally run the macros using the buttons.

1. **Open** the as-Holiday Donations workbook.
2. Display the **November Donations** worksheet, if not already displayed.
3. **Create** two macros for use in this workbook only and **assign** them to buttons as shown in the following table. The table describes the button text, macro names, and macro functions for each button. Position the buttons above the list in rows 3:4.

Button Text	Macro Name	Macro Function
Sort by Patron	Sort_by_Patron	Sort the patron list in rows 6–16 in A to Z order based on the patron last names and first names in columns A:B.
Sort by Details	Sort_by_Details	Sort the the patron list in rows 6–16 from largest to smallest based on the donation details in column D.

4. **Save** as a Macro-Enabled Workbook in the Lesson 12 folder in your file storage location.

Test the Macros

5. Manually **sort** the list in A to Z order by the type of donation in **column C**.
6. **Test** the Sort_by_Patron macro.
7. **Test** the Sort_by_Details macro.
8. Have your instructor or a teaching assistant initial that you have successfully run the macros. __________
9. **Save** again and **close** the workbook.

Critical Thinking & Work-Readiness Skills

In the course of working through the following Microsoft Office-based Critical Thinking exercises, you will also be utilizing various work-readiness skills, some of which are listed next to each exercise. Go to labyrinthelab.com/workreadiness *to learn more about the work-readiness skills.*

12.1 Create a PivotTable and PivotChart

Dr. Edward Jackson, chief operating officer of Raritan Clinic East, would like a PivotTable and a PivotChart created from data to show a summary of patients' daily drug charges in each hospital station by doctor name. Open ct-Raritan Clinic East Patients (Lesson 12 folder). Look at the Patients worksheet. Title the list appropriately and descriptively. You will adjust column widths in a later exercise. Perform a two-column sort by Station then by Doctor. Insert both a PivotTable and PivotChart into a new worksheet and rename the worksheet `PivotChart`. Set up the PivotTable to display daily cost totals by station and then by doctor name. Format the chart for appropriate size and appearance. Save your work as **`ct-Raritan Clinic East Patients [Your Last Name]`**. Keep the file open.

WORK-READINESS SKILLS APPLIED

- Organizing and maintaining information
- Using computers to process information
- Seeing things in the mind's eye

12.2 View Details using the PivotChart

Dr. Edward Jackson would now like to see a summary of patients. Open ct-Raritan Clinic East Patients [Your Last Name], if necessary. Using options on the PivotTable Field List and the PivotChart, display the doctor specialty and doctor names, and then graph only Dr. Lawrence's patients. Resize and move the chart, if necessary. Format the PivotChart worksheet to print on one page. Save your work, and keep the file open.

WORK-READINESS SKILLS APPLIED

- Seeing things in the mind's eye
- Organizing and maintaining information
- Using computers to process information

12.3 Create Macros

You have decided to help Dr. Edward Jackson be more productive by adding macros the Patients worksheet. If necessary, open ct-Raritan Clinic East Patients [Your Last Name]. On the Patients worksheet, create a macro to automatically insert today's date in cell H1 and right align it. Create another macro to autofit the column widths. Test the macros by running them. Then, save as a macro-enabled workbook. Close your file when you are finished.

WORK-READINESS SKILLS APPLIED

- Showing responsibility
- Making decisions
- Selecting technology

Using Financial Functions and Data Analysis

LESSON OUTLINE

LEARNING OBJECTIVES

After studying this lesson, you will be able to:

- Use the PMT and FV functions to analyze loans and investments
- Adjust one or more variables using the Goal Seek and Solver tools
- Create what-if models in the Scenario Manager

Several Excel tools allow you to perform a *what-if analysis* on worksheet data. For example, you might ask, "What if our company obtained a loan for 9 percent rather than 8 percent?" By changing the interest rate used in a formula to various rates, you could see the effect on the monthly loan payment. Excel's built-in financial functions may be used for various types of calculations. In this lesson, you will use the PMT (Payment) function to determine the monthly payment for a business loan. You also will use the FV (Future Value) function to determine the future value of investments. Excel provides other tools to help you find solutions to what-if questions. In this lesson, you will use Goal Seek and Solver to answer a variety of questions. Excel also provides the Scenario Manager to view alternative scenarios with up to 32 input variables for advanced data analysis.

Student Resources labyrinthelab.com/excel10

CASE STUDY

Analyzing a Fundraising Campaign

Sandra Chavez-Hall coordinates a fundraising campaign to build two new facilities at Raritan Clinic East. The clinic will borrow an initial amount to begin the planning process, until Raritan's foundation raises enough contributions to start building. Sandra will set up an Excel worksheet that calculates the loan repayment schedule using the PMT (Payment) function and a variety of input variables. Major funding for the building projects will be provided by various grants and sponsors. One contribution plan allows corporate and individual sponsors to make monthly payments toward their pledge amounts. These payments will be invested, and Sandra will use the FV (Future Value) function to forecast the total earned. Then she will use Excel's Goal Seek and Solver tools to explore various financing scenarios. She will use the Scenario Manager to view various models comparing fundraising goals and expenses.

	A	B
1	**Loan Analysis**	
2		
3	Phase 1 Site Plan Cost	$580,473.95
4		
5	**Loan**	
6	Loan Amount	$480,473.95
7	Interest Rate	5.45%
8	Number of Months	60
9	Monthly Payment	$ 9,166.67
10	Total Interest	$ 69,525.96
11		
12	**Total Cost**	
13	Down Payment	$100,000.00
14	Total Loan Payments	$549,999.92
15	Total Financed Cost	**$649,999.92**

The Goal Seek and Solver tools help determine the maximum Phase 1 site plan cost and loan interest rate that will keep the total financed cost within budget.

Scenario Summary	Current Values:	Scenario 1	Scenario 2	Scenario 3	Scenario 4
Changing Cells:					
Cash_Contributions	2,000,000	1,000,000	1,500,000	2,000,000	3,250,000
In_Kind_Contributions	25,000	50,000	50,000	25,000	53,000
Grants	25,000	30,000	50,000	25,000	200,000
Interest_Income	25,000	20,000	20,000	25,000	80,000
Result Cells:					
Projected_Net_Income	$ 1,965,000	$ 990,000	$ 1,510,000	$ 1,965,000	$ 3,473,000
Targeted_Expenses_vs._Income	5.30%	10.00%	6.79%	5.30%	3.07%
Total_Income	$ 2,075,000	$ 1,100,000	$ 1,620,000	$ 2,075,000	$ 3,583,000

Scenario Manager compiles a report to compare the results of several scenarios.

13.1 Creating Financial Functions

Video Lesson labyrinthelab.com/videos

Excel provides more than 50 financial functions that calculate important financial numbers. For example, Excel has basic financial functions for determining monthly payments on loans, the total interest paid on loans, the future value of investments, and other such questions. Excel also has advanced financial functions for calculating depreciation of assets, internal rates of return, and other more advanced business topics.

PMT and FV Functions

The PMT (Payment) and FV (Future Value) functions are the most useful financial functions for the average Excel user. The PMT function calculates the required payment for a loan when you specify the loan amount, interest rate, and number of payments you will make. The FV function calculates the total amount you will have in an investment when you specify the deposit amount, interest rate, and number of deposits.

Financial Function Syntax

You may enter financial functions using the Insert Function dialog box or by typing them. You may use the actual values or cell references in the formulas. Keep in mind that using the cell reference offers more flexibility. For example, you may easily change the number of deposits in an FV function without having to edit the formula. Like all other functions, financial functions have a specific syntax you must follow. The generic format of the PMT and FV functions are shown in the following table.

Function	Syntax
PMT (Payment)	PMT (rate, periods, loan amount)
FV (Future Value)	FV (rate, periods, payment)

Most car loans and fixed-rate mortgages have payment amounts that remain constant throughout the term of the loan. The PMT and FV functions can be used when the payment amount remains constant. The various arguments in the PMT and FV functions are outlined in the following table.

Argument	Description
Periods	This is the number of payments made for a loan or deposits for an investment. Most loans have a monthly payment period, so you should specify the number of months instead of the number of years. For example, use 60 as the number of periods for a five-year auto loan (5 years*12 months per year).
Rate	This is the interest rate for each period of the loan or investment. Although loans are quoted as annual rates, payments usually are made monthly. Therefore, you will need to divide the interest rate by 12 in the formula. For example, a 7 percent annual rate would be expressed as 7%/12.
Payment	This is the amount invested in each period. The payment must be the same for each period.
Loan amount	This is the amount borrowed.

Argument	Description
Present value (optional)	This is the starting balance of an investment, such as the current amount in a savings account. You are not required to enter the argument if the starting balance is 0 (zero).
Future value (optional)	This is the balance you wish to have at the end of an investment. You are not required to enter the argument if the balance will be 0 (zero).
Type (optional)	This indicates when the payments are due. You are not required to enter the default argument 0 (zero) if payments are made at the end of the period, such as the last day of each month. Enter 1 if payments are due at the beginning of the period.

Converting Negative Numbers to Positive

Excel treats payments as debits (money you owe), so the PMT and FV functions display the result as a negative number. This is a convention that bankers and other financial professionals use. Placing a minus (–) sign before the cell reference for the loan amount or payment in the formula changes the result to a positive number, which may be more easily understood.

A minus (–) sign may be entered before the loan amount or payment in a PMT or FV formula. As an alternative, the minus sign may be entered just before the function name, as in =–PMT or =–FV. Placing the minus sign in either location converts the result to a positive number.

DEVELOP YOUR SKILLS 13.1.1

Use the PMT and FV Functions

In this exercise, you will set up a loan worksheet that will calculate the monthly payment on a construction loan using the PMT function. You also will use the FV function to calculate the monthly deposit required to save the $10,000 down payment.

Create a PMT Function

1. **Start** Excel and **open** the Fundraising workbook from the Lesson 13 folder in your file storage location.
2. **Maximize** the window, if necessary.
   The $700,000 site plan cost and $100,000 down payment are already entered in the Loan worksheet.
3. In the Loan worksheet, select **cell B6** and enter the formula **=B3-B13**.
   The result is $600,000. The loan amount is the site plan cost minus the down payment. The PMT function will use the loan amount as one of its arguments.
4. Select **cell B7** and enter **6%** as the interest rate.
5. Select **cell B8** and enter **60** as the number of months.
6. Select **cell B9** and enter the formula **=PMT(B7,B8,B6)**.
   The result equals ($37,125.43). Remember that the generic PMT function syntax is =PMT(rate, periods, loan amount). Notice that the B7, B8, and B6 references in the function refer to the interest rate, number of months, and loan amount in the worksheet.

   Excel formats the payment in Currency Style, red, and in parentheses. The red color and parentheses indicate a negative number. You will convert this number to a positive number in the following steps.

   Finally, notice that $37,125.43 seems a very large payment because the interest rate in cell B7 is an annual rate of 6 percent. The borrower would not pay 6 percent interest per month. The interest rate must be divided by 12 (the number of months in a year) to calculate a monthly interest rate in the function. You will do this in the following steps.

7. Select **cell B9**.
8. Click in the **Formula Bar**, position the insertion point after the equals (=) sign in the formula, and **type** a minus (–) sign.
9. Position the insertion point after **cell B7** in the formula and type **/12** to divide the **cell B7** rate by 12, and **complete** the entry.
   The completed formula is =–PMT(B7/12,B8,-B6). The new payment equals $11,599.68. This payment certainly will be more affordable. The minus sign converts the number to a positive, and the B7/12 argument establishes a 0.5 percent per month rate.
10. Format **cell B9** in Accounting format with two decimal places.
11. Select **cell B14** and enter the formula **=B9*B8**.
    Total loan payments equal $695,980.86.
12. Select **cell B10** and enter the formula **=B14-B6**.
    Total loan interest equals $95,980.86. The loan amount in cell B6 is subtracted from the total payments to determine the total interest.
13. Select **cell B15** and enter the formula **=B13+B14**.
    The total cost equals $795,980.86 to finance the phase 1 site plan. Your worksheet should match the following illustration.

	A	B
1	Loan Analysis	
2		
3	Phase 1 Site Plan Cost	$700,000.00
4		
5	Loan	
6	Loan Amount	$600,000.00
7	Interest Rate	6.00%
8	Number of Months	60
9	Monthly Payment	$ 11,599.68
10	Total Interest	$ 95,980.86
11		
12	Total Cost	
13	Down Payment	$100,000.00
14	Total Loan Payments	$695,980.86
15	Total Financed Cost	$795,980.86

14. **Save** the changes to the workbook.

Create the FV Function

Corporate and individual sponsors may make monthly payments to the capital campaign. These contributions will be invested to earn interest.

15. Display the **Investment** worksheet of the Fundraising workbook.
16. Select **cell B5**, and type **0** to indicate that the sponsor will make no initial contribution.
    The cell displays a hyphen (–) to indicate zero.
17. Select **cell B7**, and enter **2.5%** for the annual interest rate.
18. Select **cell B8**, and enter **36** for the number of monthly payments.

19. Select **cell B6**, and enter the formula **=B3/B8**.
The formula divides the $300,000 pledge amount by 36 months. The monthly contribution is $8,333.

20. Select **cell B9**.

21. Follow these steps to choose the FV (Future Value) function:

	A	B
1	Invested Contributions	
2		No initial contribution
3	Pledge Amount	$300,000.00
4		
5	Starting Balance	$ -
6	Monthly Contribution	$ 8,333
7	Interest Rate	2.5%
8	Number of Months	36
9	Total Investment	

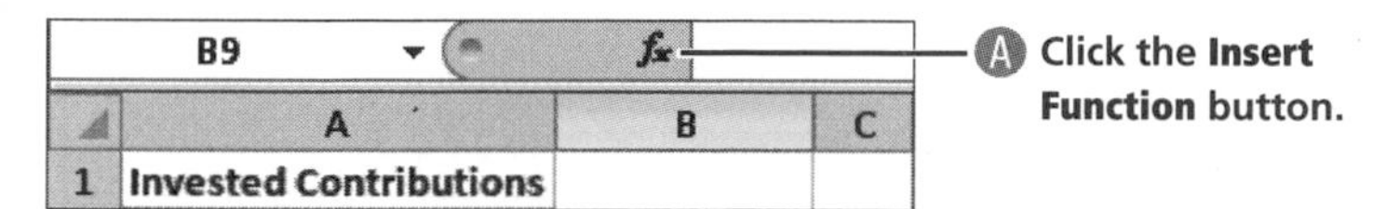

Ⓐ Click the **Insert Function** button.

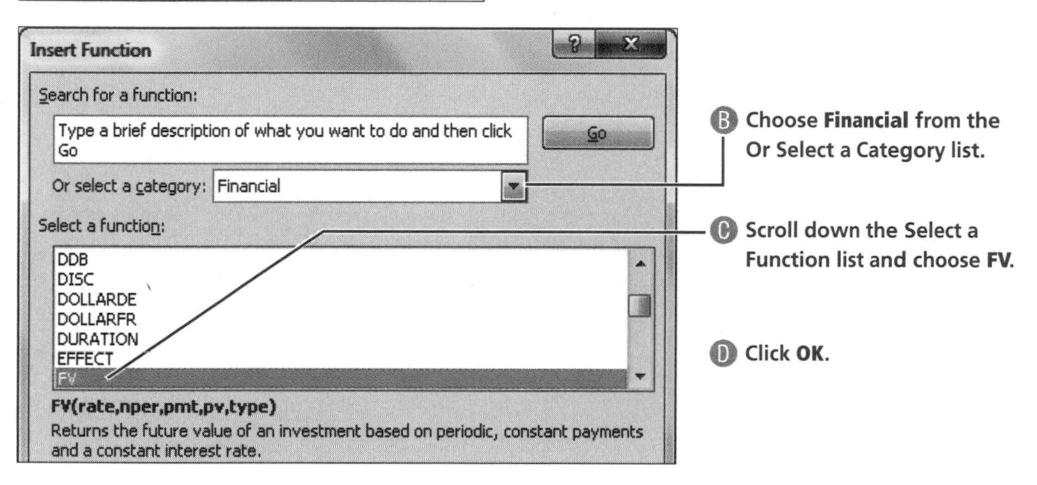

Ⓑ Choose **Financial** from the Or Select a Category list.

Ⓒ Scroll down the Select a Function list and choose **FV**.

Ⓓ Click **OK**.

22. Follow these steps to specify the function arguments:

Ⓐ If necessary, drag the **Function Arguments** dialog box aside so that the range **A1:B9** is visible.

Ⓑ Click in the **Rate** box, select **cell B7** in the worksheet, and type **/12**. This divides the annual interest rate by 12 months.

Ⓒ Click in the **Nper** box and select **cell B8** in the worksheet to set the number of payment periods.

Ⓓ Click in the **Pmt** box. Type a minus (–) sign and click **cell B6** to set the payment amount to a negative value.

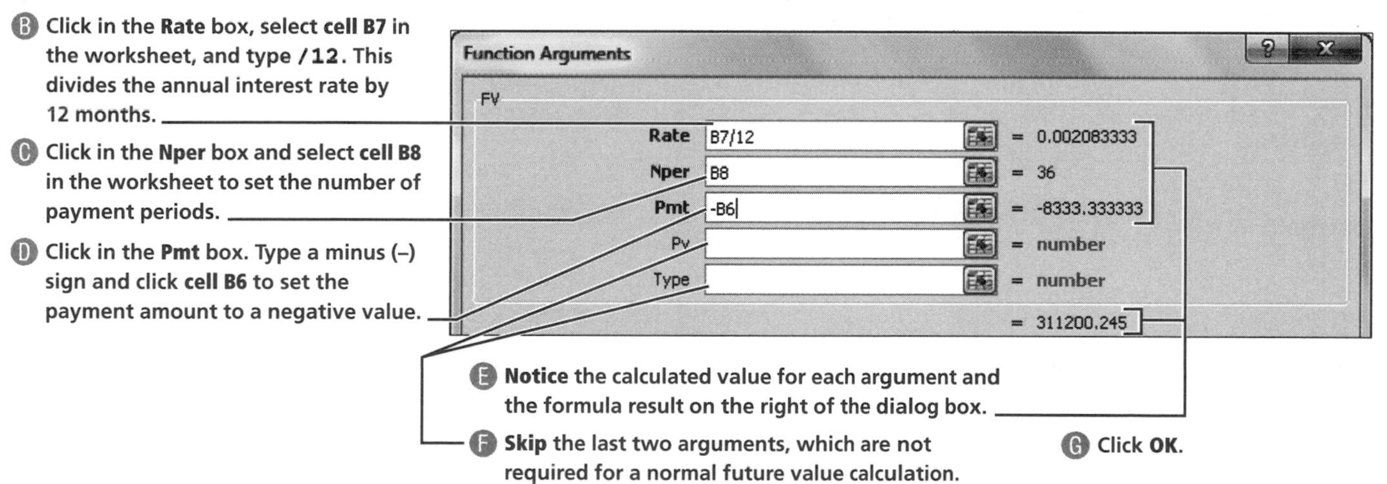

Ⓔ **Notice** the calculated value for each argument and the formula result on the right of the dialog box.

Ⓕ **Skip** the last two arguments, which are not required for a normal future value calculation.

Ⓖ Click **OK**.

The completed formula is =FV(B7/12,B8,-B6), and the result $311,200.24 appears in cell B9. With deposits of $8,333 per month in an investment fund earning 2.5 percent, the contributions would total this amount in three years.

Include Optional Arguments

What if sponsors were required to contribute an initial payment of 25 percent of the total pledge amount and make payments on the first of each month? In the next steps, you will modify the FV formula.

23. Select **cell E5**, and enter the formula **=E3*25%** for the initial contribution.
    The result is $75,000.
24. Copy the **range B6:B9** to the **range E6:E9**.
25. Select **cell E6**, and click in the **Formula Bar**.
26. Making certain to type the **parentheses**, edit the formula to **=(E3-E5)/E8**.
    The monthly contribution now is $6,250. It is based on $225,000, the remainder of the pledge amount after the sponsor makes the initial contribution.
27. Select **cell E9**, and click the **Insert Function** button at the left of the Formula Bar to display the Insert Function dialog box.
28. Follow these steps to enter optional arguments:

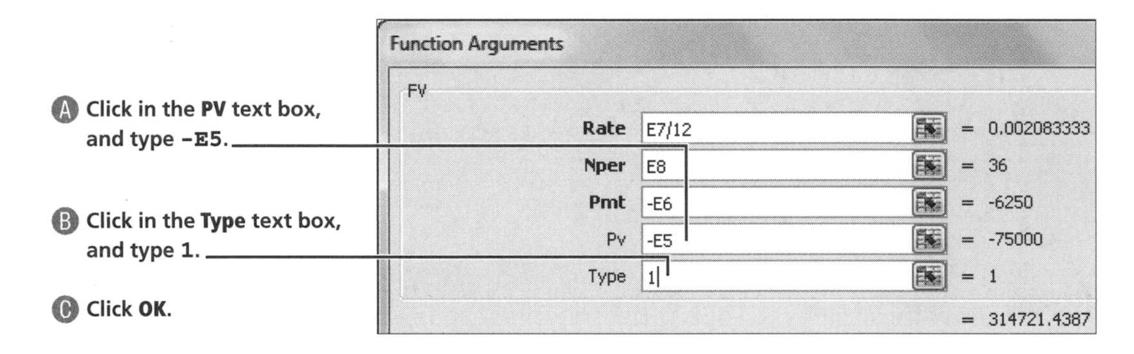

The revised formula is =FV(E7/12,E8,-E6,-E5,1). The new total investment is $314.721.44. The -E5 argument is entered as a negative number. It indicates the starting balance, or the present value of the investment before the monthly payments begin. The Type argument of 1 indicates that payments will be made at the beginning of each month. The total future value of the investment in cell E9 is larger with these two payment options as compared to cell B9.

29. Change the number of months to 24 in **cells B8** and **E8**.
    By experimenting with the values for rate, number of periods, and payment used in the FV function, you may create various plans for saving the desired amount or meeting the sponsor's budget for the monthly payment. In the next exercises, you will use Excel's tools to automate this analysis.
30. **Save** the changes, and leave the workbook **open**.

13.2 Using Data Analysis Tools

Video Lesson labyrinthelab.com/videos

Excel provides several tools to perform advanced what-if analyses. Goal Seek is best used when you know the formula answer you want but not the specific value in one cell that would achieve the answer. The Solver sets the values of multiple cells to produce the desired result that you specify for a target cell. You also may set minimum and maximum values for Solver to use in calculations. Scenario Manager saves a model worksheet with various changes to values so that you may compare the scenarios side by side.

Using Goal Seek

With Goal Seek you set a goal for a specific formula result. For example, you will set a monthly payment goal of $10,000 in the Loan worksheet. The goal cell must contain a formula, which is a PMT function in this example. You will instruct Goal Seek to adjust the down payment to achieve the desired monthly payment.

QUICK REFERENCE **USING GOAL SEEK**

Task	Procedure
Set up a Goal Seek solution	■ Test the worksheet with sample data to make certain that formulas are functioning properly. ■ Select the cell for which you want to set a goal. The cell must contain a formula. ■ Choose Data→Data Tools→What-If Analysis →Goal Seek from the Ribbon. ■ Type the desired goal value in the To Value box. ■ Click in the By Changing Cell box and choose the worksheet cell for which Goal Seek will adjust the value.

DEVELOP YOUR SKILLS 13.2.1

Use Goal Seek

In this exercise, you will use Goal Seek to adjust the down payment based on a specific monthly payment that you enter. Then you will adjust the interest rate.

Use Goal Seek to Adjust the Down Payment

Assume that you wish to see the effect on the down payment that Raritan Clinic would be required to pay if the monthly payment were $10,000 rather than $11,599.68 as previously calculated.

1. Display the **Loan** worksheet of the Fundraising workbook.
2. Select **cell B9**.
   Choosing the cell for which you wish to set a goal prior to starting Goal Seek will ensure that you set the goal for the correct cell. The currently selected cell reference displays in the Set Cell box when you open Goal Seek.
3. Choose **Data→Data Tools→What-If Analysis** →**Goal Seek** from the Ribbon.

4. Follow these steps to set the Goal Seek parameters:
   You may either type cell references or use point mode in the Goal Seek dialog box.

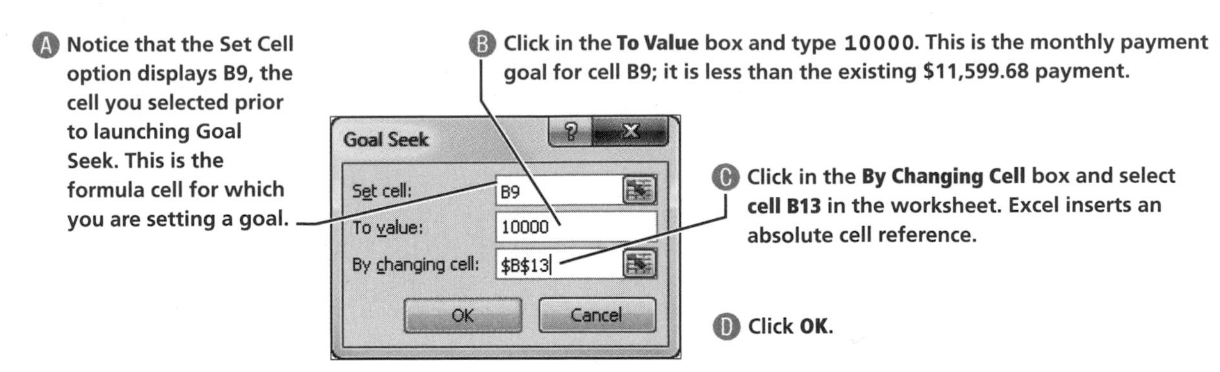

A Notice that the Set Cell option displays B9, the cell you selected prior to launching Goal Seek. This is the formula cell for which you are setting a goal.
B Click in the To Value box and type 10000. This is the monthly payment goal for cell B9; it is less than the existing $11,599.68 payment.
C Click in the By Changing Cell box and select cell B13 in the worksheet. Excel inserts an absolute cell reference.
D Click OK.
Goal Seek
Set cell:
B9
To value:
10000
By changing cell:
$B$13
OK
Cancel

   The Goal Seek Status dialog box indicates that Goal Seek found a solution for the goal. The down payment in the worksheet has been adjusted to $182,744.39. As you can see, a higher down payment is required with a $10,000 monthly payment.

5. Click **Cancel** in the Goal Seek Status dialog box to undo the change to the down payment.

Use Goal Seek to Adjust the Interest Rate

You wish to know what the loan interest rate would have to be if the monthly payment were $12,000.

6. Make certain **cell B9** is still selected and choose **Data→Data Tools→What-If Analysis→Goal Seek** from the Ribbon.
7. Type **12000** in the **To Value** box to set the monthly payment goal.
8. Click in the **By Changing Cell** box, and then select **cell B7** (the interest rate cell) in the worksheet.
9. Click **OK**, and the interest rate is changed to 7.42 percent.
10. Move the **Goal Seek Status** dialog box, if necessary, to see **cell B7**.
11. Click **OK** again to confirm the change to the interest rate.
12. **Save** the changes.

Change Values in a What-If Analysis

After seeking a goal, you also may experiment with the what-if analysis by changing the site plan cost or other values directly in the worksheet. The cells you change should contain values and not formulas.

13. Select **cell B3** and change the **site plan cost** to **$500,000**.
    What impact does this change have on the other amounts?
14. Feel free to experiment with Goal Seek. When you are finished, **close** the workbook **without** saving the changes.

Using Solver

Video Lesson labyrinthelab.com/videos

Goal Seek is easy to use but is somewhat limited. Goal Seek adjusts only one variable at a time. Excel's Solver tool can solve problems when more than one variable requires adjustment. In fact, you may specify up to two hundred variables, but all variables must appear in a formula related to the objective cell. You may specify a precise objective cell value, as with Goal Seek, or you may specify that Solver determine the Max (maximum) or Min (minimum) value. For example, you may specify a monthly payment of $300 for an auto loan. In addition, Solver lets you specify one or more constraints. Constraints give you extra control by limiting a cell's possible range of values in the suggested solution. You may not set a constraint for any cell that is used in the objective cell's formula. Instead, you must enter the desired value in the appropriate worksheet cell. The new Solver version in Excel 2010 includes a choice of three solving methods. The default GRG Nonlinear method is appropriate for many typical business problems that have a smooth nonlinear solution.

See the Excel Help for more information about the Solver's three solving methods: GRG Nonlinear, Simplex LP for linear problems, and Evolutionary for other problems.

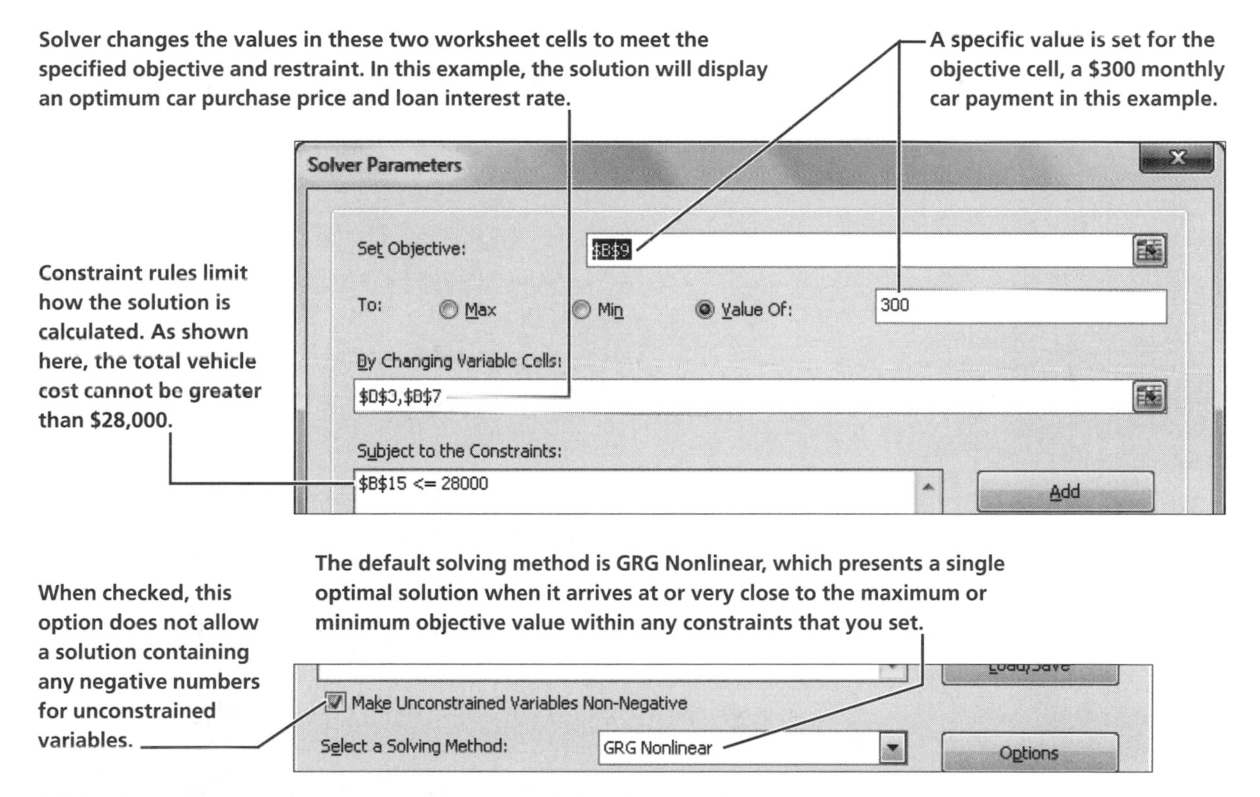

Solver changes the values in these two worksheet cells to meet the specified objective and restraint. In this example, the solution will display an optimum car purchase price and loan interest rate.
A specific value is set for the objective cell, a $300 monthly car payment in this example.
Constraint rules limit how the solution is calculated. As shown here, the total vehicle cost cannot be greater than $28,000.
Solver Parameters
Set Objective:
$B$9
To:
Max
Min
Value Of:
300
By Changing Variable Cells:
$D$3,$B$7
Subject to the Constraints:
$B$15 <= 28000
Add
The default solving method is GRG Nonlinear, which presents a single optimal solution when it arrives at or very close to the maximum or minimum objective value within any constraints that you set.
When checked, this option does not allow a solution containing any negative numbers for unconstrained variables.
Make Unconstrained Variables Non-Negative
Select a Solving Method:
GRG Nonlinear
Options

Solving for optimum values in two cells based on an objective cell value and a constraint rule

Installing Solver

Solver is not part of the typical Office 2010 installation but is an add-in program. The Solver command displays in an Analysis group on the Data ribbon after installation.

Your network administrator may not grant permission to install add-in programs.

QUICK REFERENCE — INSTALLING ADD-INS AND USING SOLVER

Task	Procedure
Install or remove an add-in tool	■ Choose File→Options →Add-Ins. ■ Choose Excel Add-Ins to the right of Manage at the bottom of the window, and click Go. ■ In the Add-Ins dialog box, place a checkmark in the box for each desired add-in. Removing checkmarks uninstalls add-ins that are currently installed.
Set up a Solver solution	■ Test the worksheet with sample data to make certain that formulas are functioning properly. ■ Choose Data→Analysis→Solver from the Ribbon. ■ If desired, click the Reset All button to clear previously set options in the Solver Parameters dialog box. ■ Click in the Set Objective box and choose the worksheet cell for which you want to set a goal. ■ Choose Max or Min; or, choose Value Of and type a desired goal value for the objective cell in the text box. ■ Click in the By Changing Variable Cells box and choose one or more worksheet cells whose values you want Solver to adjust. Type a comma between cell references. ■ If desired, click the Add button and set one or more constraint rules in the Add Constraint dialog box. ■ Place a checkmark next to Make Unconstrained Variables Non-Negative if only positive numbers are acceptable in the solution for these variables. ■ Click Solve in the Solver Parameters dialog box. ■ Read the message in the Solver Results dialog box, choosing Keep Solver Solution or Restore Original Values.
Save Solver results as a scenario to view again later	■ Click Save Scenario in the Solver Results dialog box. ■ Type a scenario name.

DEVELOP YOUR SKILLS 13.2.2

Use Solver

In this exercise, you will use Solver to determine the site plan cost and interest rate required to achieve the total financed cost that you specify.

Before You Begin: Solver must be installed using the procedure given in the preceding Quick Reference table.

Reset to Original Values

1. **Open** the Fundraising workbook from the Lesson 13 folder.
2. In the **Loan** worksheet, **reenter** the original value of **6%** in cell B7. Make certain that **cell B3** contains $700,000.00, **cell B8** contains 60, and **cell B13** contains $100,000.00. *All worksheet cells should contain the values or formulas you created in Develop Your Skills 13.1.1.*

Use Solver to Adjust the Cost and Interest Rate

3. Choose **Data→Analysis→Solver** from the Ribbon.
4. Follow these steps to set the objective cell value and specify the variable cells:

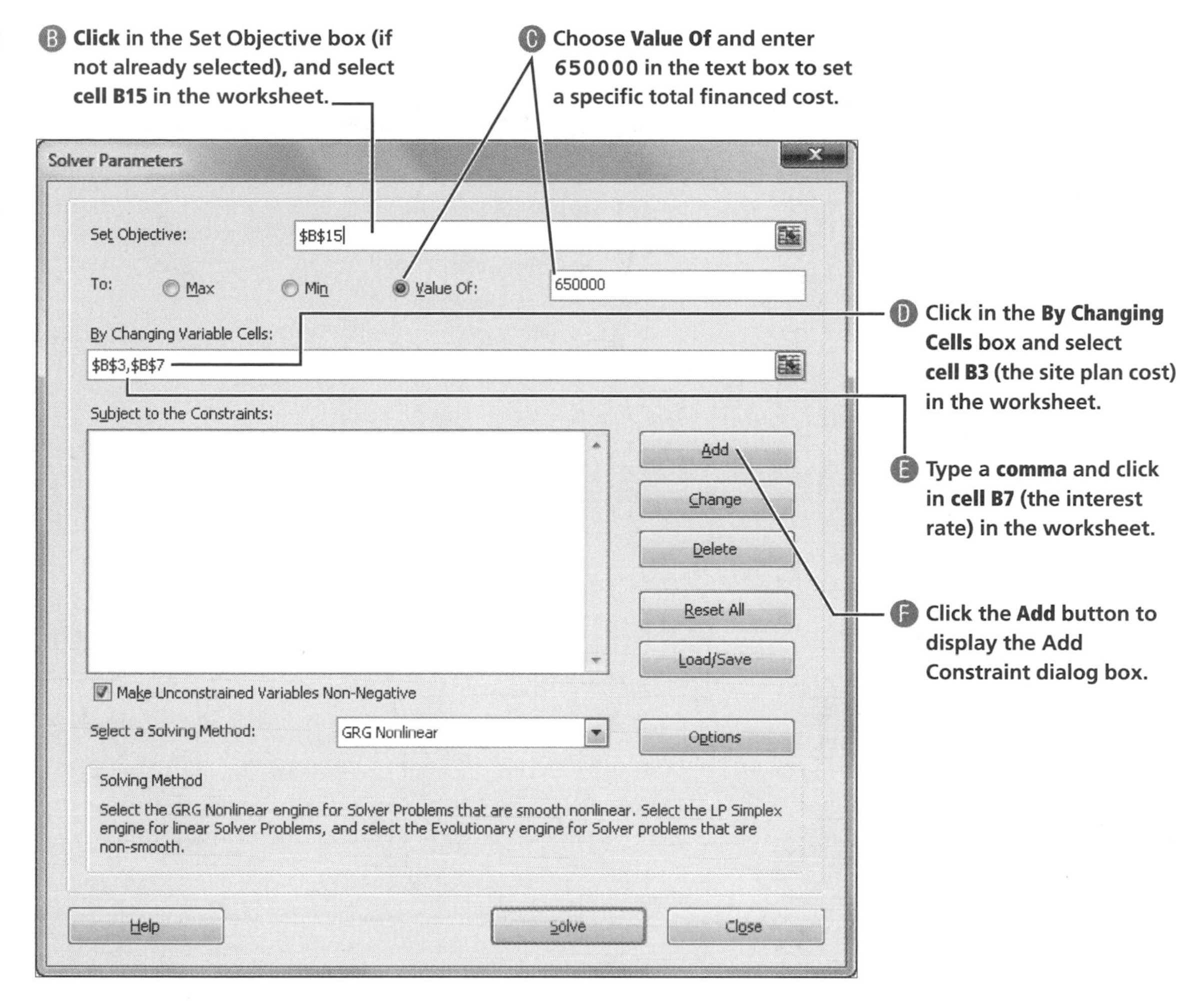

Excel converts the objective cell and variable cells to absolute cell references as you entered them in the Solver Parameters dialog box.

5. Follow these steps to specify a constraint:

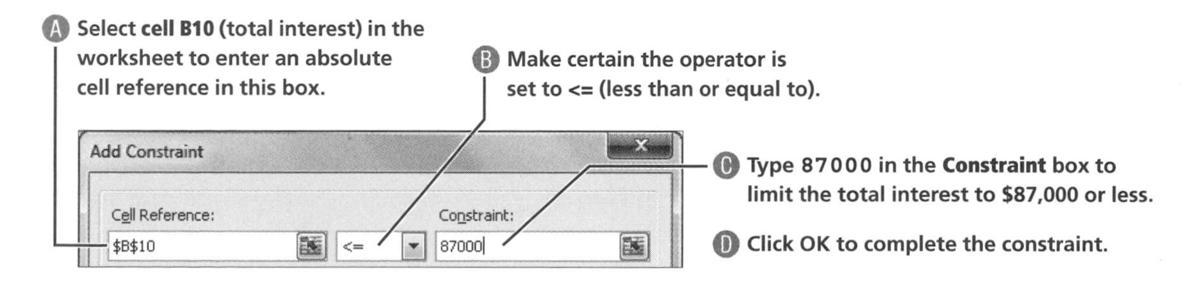

A Select **cell B10** (total interest) in the worksheet to enter an absolute cell reference in this box.
B Make certain the operator is set to <= (less than or equal to).
C Type 87000 in the **Constraint** box to limit the total interest to $87,000 or less.
D Click OK to complete the constraint.
Add Constraint
Cell Reference:
$B$10
<=
Constraint:
87000

The constraint rule appears in the Subject to the Constraints list of the Solver Parameters dialog box.

6. Take a moment to review the options you have set in the Solver Parameters dialog box.

7. Click the **Solve** button, and the Solver will go to work.
   When the Solver has completed its calculations, the Solver Results dialog box should report that a solution has been found that meets all conditions.
8. Follow these steps to accept the proposed solution:

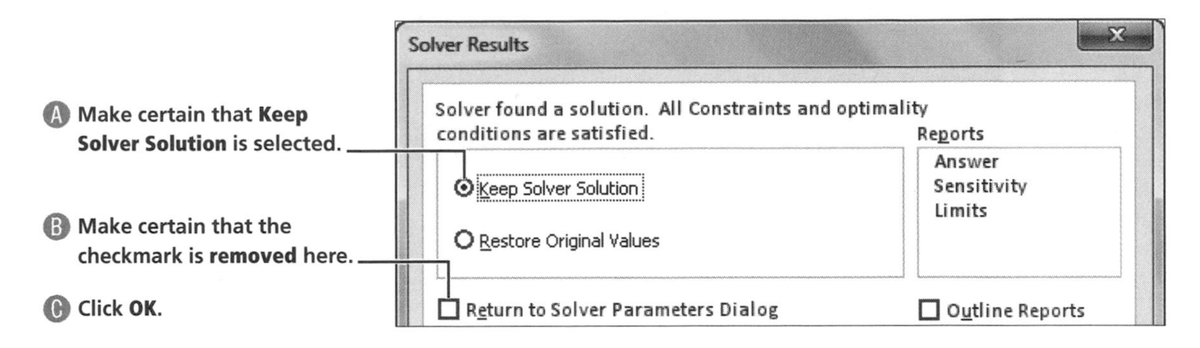

Make certain that Keep Solver Solution is selected.
Make certain that the checkmark is removed here.
Click OK.
Solver Results
Solver found a solution. All Constraints and optimality conditions are satisfied.
Reports
Answer
Sensitivity
Limits
Keep Solver Solution
Restore Original Values
Return to Solver Parameters Dialog
Outline Reports

The completed solution should match the following example.

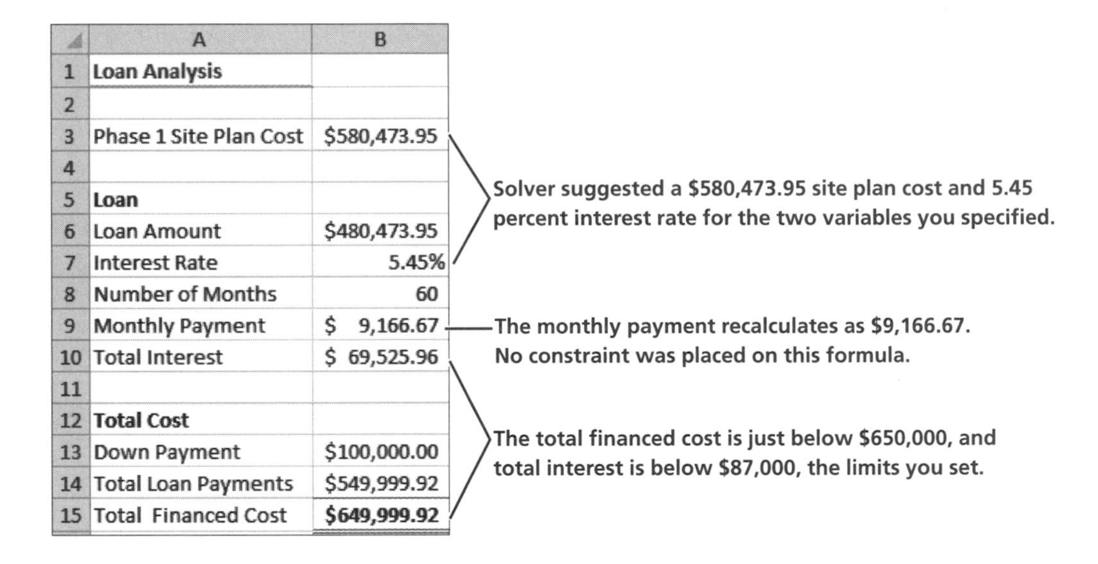

	A	B
1	Loan Analysis	
2		
3	Phase 1 Site Plan Cost	$580,473.95
4		
5	Loan	
6	Loan Amount	$480,473.95
7	Interest Rate	5.45%
8	Number of Months	60
9	Monthly Payment	$ 9,166.67
10	Total Interest	$ 69,525.96
11		
12	Total Cost	
13	Down Payment	$100,000.00
14	Total Loan Payments	$549,999.92
15	Total Financed Cost	$649,999.92

Solver suggested a $580,473.95 site plan cost and 5.45 percent interest rate for the two variables you specified.
The monthly payment recalculates as $9,166.67. No constraint was placed on this formula.
The total financed cost is just below $650,000, and total interest is below $87,000, the limits you set.

Use Solver to Adjust the Cost

You determine that a maximum $11,000 monthly payment is acceptable, and a local bank offers a 6 percent business loan. You wish to know the maximum site plan cost you can negotiate, but your research shows that $650,000 is the lowest bid you are likely to receive.

9. Choose **Data→Analysis→Solver** from the Ribbon.
10. Click **Reset All** to clear the previous options, and click **OK** to confirm.

11. Follow these guidelines to set options in the Solver Parameters dialog box:

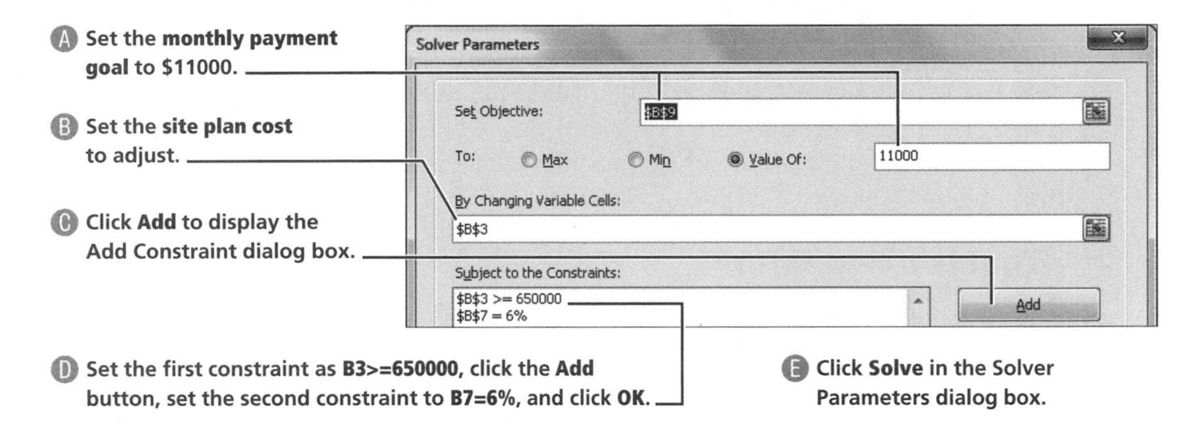

A Set the **monthly payment goal** to $11000.
B Set the **site plan cost** to adjust.
C Click **Add** to display the Add Constraint dialog box.
D Set the first constraint as **B3>=650000**, click the **Add** button, set the second constraint to **B7=6%**, and click **OK**.
E Click **Solve** in the Solver Parameters dialog box.
Solver Parameters
Set Objective:
$B$9
To:
Max
Min
Value Of:
11000
By Changing Variable Cells:
$B$3
Subject to the Constraints:
$B$3 >= 650000
$B$7 = 6%
Add

Solver reports it could not find a solution. The interest rate still is 5.45% in cell B7 because the constraint for interest rate was ignored. You may not set a constraint for any cell used in the objective cell's formula, =–PMT(B7/12,B8,B6). You must enter the desired interest rate in the worksheet.

12. Choose **Restore Original Values** make certain that the checkmark is removed next to Return to Solver Parameters Dialog, and click **OK**.
13. In **cell B7**, change the interest rate to **6%**.
14. Choose **Data→Analysis→Solver** .
15. Select the constraint rule **$B$7=6%**, and click the **Delete** button.
16. Click **Solve** to use the other options that you previously set.
    This time a solution was found. The site plan cost equals $668,981.85. This is the maximum price that you may negotiate on to meet the $11,000 monthly payment goal. Notice that the monthly payment in cell B9 is rounded up to $11,000.01, which Solver found to be the optimum solution.
17. Click **OK** to acccpt thc proposed solution.
18. **Save** the changes to the workbook.

Experiment with Solver

19. Take a few minutes to experiment with Solver.
    Depending on the variables and constraints you create, Solver may report that no solution was found or suggest a 0 (zero) or negative amount in one or more cells. If this occurs, choose Restore Original Values and solve again after editing the options.
20. When you have finished, **close** the workbook **without** saving changes.

Scenario Manager

Video Lesson labyrinthelab.com/videos

Excel provides the Scenario Manager to create and save what-if models with up to 32 variables. This allows you to model virtually any what-if scenario. Scenario Manager does not solve for a specific variable value to achieve a formula result as Goal Seek and Solver do. You may, however, save a Solver solution as a scenario.

What Is a Scenario?

A scenario is a group of values assigned to cells in a what-if model. The model calculates formula results based on the values you enter in the scenario. Scenarios are given names to identify them, and they are saved and organized using the Scenario Manager.

Managing Scenarios

You may create and manage a large number of scenarios in the Scenario Manager. This way, you may compare various scenarios and the results they achieve. The Scenario Manager also lets you display and print a summary of all scenarios. The scenario summary does not automatically update when you change any scenario values. You must create a new summary.

Adding Scenarios

Selecting the variable cells in the worksheet before issuing the Scenario Manager command is recommended. The Ctrl key is used to select noncontiguous cell ranges. The Scenario Manager has an Add button that allows you to create new scenarios. Each scenario may contain different values. The following illustration shows the Scenario Values dialog box with values entered for the variable cells. If you enter a formula for a variable, Excel will convert the result to a value.

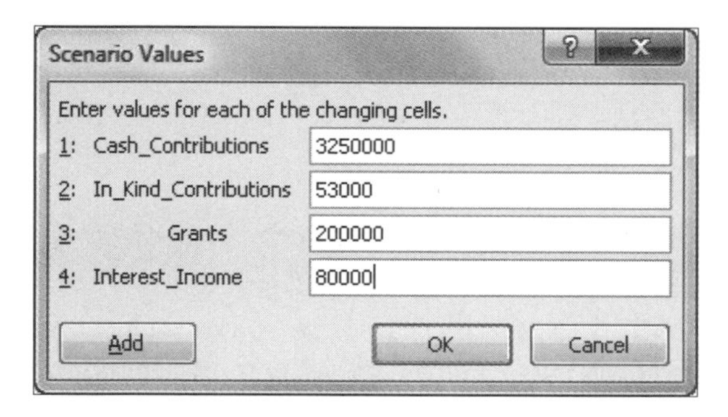

The entered values are applied to cells in the worksheet, thus forming a scenario.

QUICK REFERENCE	USING SCENARIO MANAGER
Task	**Procedure**
Create a scenario	■ Create defined names for all worksheet cells containing variables or result formulas affected by the variables. ■ Select the worksheet cells containing the desired variables but do not select any cells containing result formulas. ■ Choose Data→Data Tools→What-If Analysis→Scenario Manager from the Ribbon. ■ Click the Add button in the Scenario Manager dialog box. ■ In the Add Scenario dialog box, type a scenario name. ■ In the Scenario Values dialog box, edit values as desired.
Display a scenario in a worksheet	■ Choose the desired scenario name in the Scenario Manager dialog box. ■ Click the Show button.
Edit a scenario	■ Choose the desired scenario name in the Scenario Manager dialog box. ■ Click the Edit button. ■ In the Scenario Values dialog box, edit values as desired.
Display and print a summary of all scenarios	■ Click the Summary button in the Scenario Manager dialog box. ■ Choose Scenario Summary or Scenario PivotTable Report. ■ Click in the Result Cells box and choose one or more worksheet cells containing result formulas based on the scenario values. Type a comma between cell references. Excel places the report on a new worksheet. ■ Print the scenario report worksheet, if desired.
Remove a scenario summary worksheet	■ Right-click the Scenario Summary worksheet tab at the lower-left corner of the workbook window, and choose Delete from the context menu. ■ Click Delete to confirm deletion of the worksheet.

DEVELOP YOUR SKILLS 13.2.3

Use the Scenario Manager

In this exercise, you will use a model to analyze fundraising goals with certain budgeted expenses that are necessary to raise the funds. You understand that a lower expense-to-income percentage indicates that resources are being used more effectively. Therefore, you will take a closer look at each component of the projected income to set achievable goals. You will create a model and use Scenario Manager to set up and manage multiple scenarios.

Set Up the Model

1. **Open** the Campaign Scenarios workbook from the Lesson 13 folder.
2. In the **Campaign Analysis** worksheet, enter the model values in the **range B4:B7** as shown.
   Notice that the formula to sum the total income already has been entered in cell B8. The expenses and their sum formula have been entered in the range B11:B15.

	A	B
1	Capital Campaign Net Income Model	
2		
3	*Income Goals*	
4	Cash Contributions	1,000,000
5	In-Kind Contributions	50,000
6	Grants	30,000
7	Interest Income	20,000
8	Total Income	$ 1,100,000

3. Select **cell B17**, and review the formula =B8-B15 in the Formula Bar.
   The generic formula is Projected Net Income = Total Income – Total Expenses.

4. In **cell B18**, enter the formula **=B15/B8**.
   The result equals 0.1. Notice that this formula divides the total expenses by the total income to compare the two amounts.

5. Format **cell B18** as **bold** and **Percent Style** with **two decimal places**.
   Expenses are 10.00 percent of net income. This model is the starting point from which you will create scenarios to see the effect on the Targeted Expenses vs. Income percentage.

Name the Variable Cells and Results Cells

In the next few steps, you will name the variable cells in the model using the Create from Selection command in the Formulas ribbon. Naming the variable cells is beneficial because the names, rather than cell references, will appear in the Scenario Manager dialog box. You also will name some results cells containing formulas because they will appear in a summary report.

6. Select the **range A4:B8**, which includes the income labels and the cell values to which they refer.

7. With the **range A4:B8** still selected, **hold down** Ctrl and select the **range A17:B18**, which includes labels and formula cells.
   Both ranges should appear selected.

	A	B
1	Capital Campaign Net Income Model	
2		
3	*Income Goals*	
4	Cash Contributions	1,000,000
5	In-Kind Contributions	50,000
6	Grants	30,000
7	Interest Income	20,000
8	Total Income	$ 1,100,000
9		
10	*Targeted Expenses*	
11	Web/Social Media Development	25,000
12	Print Materials	10,000
13	Events	50,000
14	Salaries - Grant Proposals	25,000
15	Total Expenses	$ 110,000
16		
17	Projected Net Income	$ 990,000
18	Targeted Expenses vs. Income	10.00%

8. Choose **Formulas→Defined Names→Create From Selection** from the Ribbon.

9. Place a checkmark in the **Left Column box** (if not already checked) and click **OK**.

10. Choose **Formulas→Defined Names→Name Manager** to view all defined names and their Refers To entries.

11. Widen the **Name** column and **Refers To** column, if necessary, to view entire entries in the Name Manager dialog box.

12. Close the **Name Manager** dialog box.

Create the First Scenario

13. Taking care not to select cell B8, select the **range B4:B7** as shown to the right.
    Only the income variables will be adjusted in the Scenario Manager. Usually it is best to preselect the cells as you did here, though you may always select the cells once the Add Scenario dialog box is displayed.

	A	B
3	*Income Goals*	
4	Cash Contributions	1,000,000
5	In-Kind Contributions	50,000
6	Grants	30,000
7	Interest Income	20,000
8	Total Income	$ 1,100,000

14. Choose **Data→Data Tools→What-If Analysis** →**Scenario Manager** from the Ribbon.
    The dialog box should indicate that no scenarios are currently defined.
15. Click the **Add** button to add a new scenario.
16. Follow these steps to set scenario options in the Add Scenario dialog box:

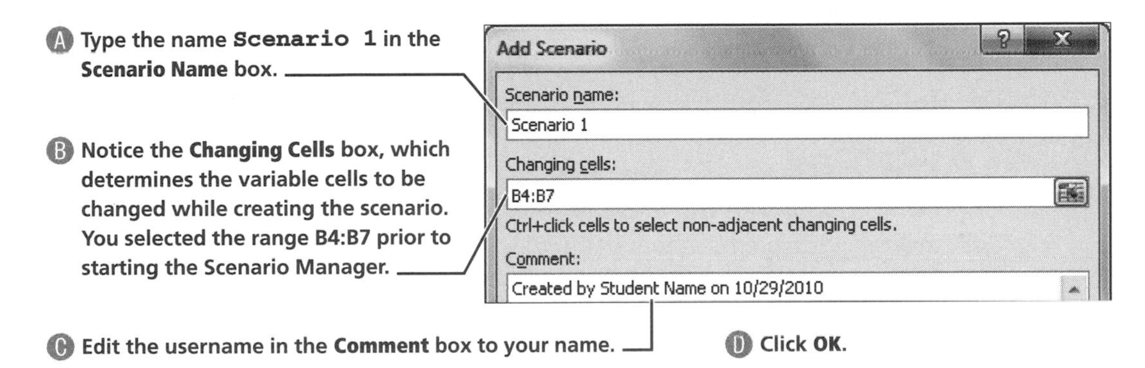

A Type the name Scenario 1 in the Scenario Name box.
B Notice the Changing Cells box, which determines the variable cells to be changed while creating the scenario. You selected the range B4:B7 prior to starting the Scenario Manager.
C Edit the username in the Comment box to your name.
D Click OK.
Add Scenario
Scenario name:
Scenario 1
Changing cells:
B4:B7
Ctrl+click cells to select non-adjacent changing cells.
Comment:
Created by Student Name on 10/29/2010

The Scenario Values dialog box appears as shown; do not make any changes in the dialog box. Review the defined names displayed to the left of the variable boxes. Notice that Excel filled in the variable boxes with the current values from the range B4:B7 that you selected in the worksheet.

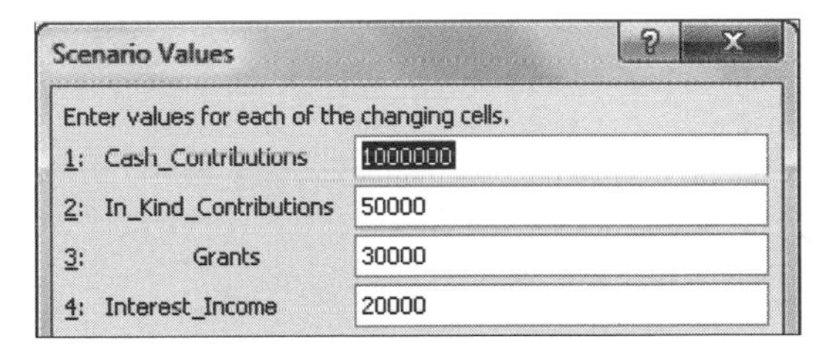

17. Click **OK** to complete the scenario.
    The Scenario Manager dialog box displays the scenario name you just created. This scenario will serve as a starting point and a comparison for other scenarios.

Add Another Scenario

18. Click the **Add** button in the Scenario Manager dialog box.
19. Enter the name **`Scenario 2`** in the **Add Scenario** dialog box, make certain the Changing Cells are **B4:B7**, edit the Comment to include your name, and click **OK**.
20. Change the variables for **Cash_Contributions** and **Grants**, as shown to the right.
21. Click **OK** in the Scenario Values box.
    Scenario 1 and Scenario 2 now appear in the Scenario Manager dialog box.

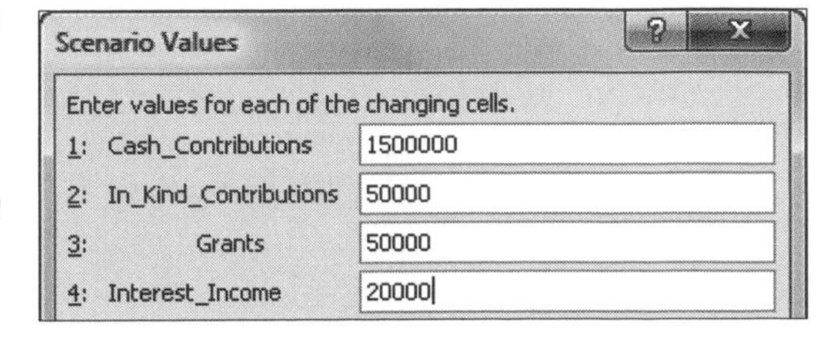

Show the Results

22. Make certain **Scenario 2** is chosen, and click the **Show** button in the Scenario Manager dialog box. (Move the dialog box to view the worksheet values, if necessary.)
    Excel substitutes the scenario values into the model. The formula in cell B18 calculates the Targeted Expenses vs. Income result, which equals 6.79 percent.

23. Choose **Scenario 1** and click the **Show** button.
    As you can see, the Scenario Manager rapidly lets you see the results of various scenarios.

24. Now add **two new scenarios** using the data in the following table:

Variable	Scenario 3 Scenario Value	Scenario 4 Scenario Value
Cash Contributions	500,000	3,250,000
In-Kind Contributions	25,000	53,000
Grants	25,000	200,000
Interest Income	25,000	80,000

25. Use the **Show** button to display the results of each scenario.

Edit a Scenario

26. Choose **Scenario 3** in the Scenario Manager dialog box and click the **Show** button.
    The Expenses vs. Net Sales equals 19.13 percent. This percentage is much too high. Fortunately, the Scenario Manager lets you adjust scenario values until a desired result is achieved.

27. With **Scenario 3** still chosen, click the **Edit** button.

28. Click **OK** in the Edit Scenario box.

29. Change the **Cash Contributions** value to **2000000** in the Scenario Values dialog box and click **OK**.

30. Click the **Show** button again, and the result equals 5.30 percent.
    You can use these scenarios to determine which income items need to be adjusted to achieve an acceptable percentage.

Display a Summary of All Scenarios

31. Click the **Summary** button in the Scenario Manager dialog box.
    Notice that you may display a scenario summary or a scenario PivotTable report.
32. Follow these steps to select Scenario Summary report options:

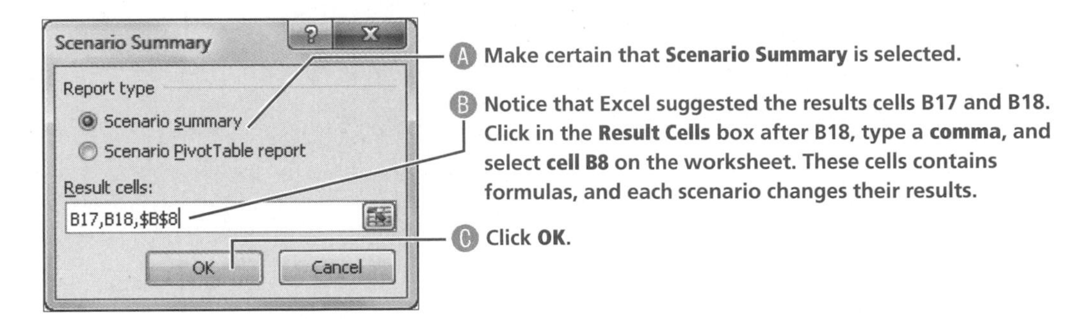
Scenario Summary
Report type
Scenario summary
Scenario PivotTable report
Result cells:
B17,B18,$B$8
OK
Cancel
A Make certain that Scenario Summary is selected.
B Notice that Excel suggested the results cells B17 and B18. Click in the Result Cells box after B18, type a comma, and select cell B8 on the worksheet. These cells contains formulas, and each scenario changes their results.
C Click OK.

Excel inserts the summary on a new worksheet named Scenario Summary. Review the summary, which displays the results data in the order you chose in the previous step. You may print a summary as you would print any other worksheet. You also may remove a summary by deleting its worksheet.

33. **Save** and **close** the workbook.

13.3 Concepts Review

Concepts Review labyrinthelab.com/excel10

To check your knowledge of the key concepts introduced in this lesson, complete the Concepts Review quiz by going to the URL listed above. If your classroom is using Labyrinth eLab, you may complete the Concepts Review quiz from within your eLab course.

Reinforce Your Skills

REINFORCE YOUR SKILLS 13.1

Use the PMT Function and Solver

In this exercise, you will use the PMT function to calculate mortgage payments for a 30-year fixed mortgage. The generic syntax of the PMT function is repeated below for your convenience. You also will use Solver to determine the purchase price and interest rate required for a specified total cost.

Payment Function Syntax =PMT(rate, periods, loan amount)

Before You Begin: The Solver add-in must be installed on your computer system to complete the last steps of this exercise.

Create a PMT Function

1. **Start** a new workbook and set up the worksheet shown to the right using a formula in **cell B5** to calculate the loan amount as **Purchase Price – Down Payment**.

	A	B
1	30-Year Mortgage Analysis	
2		
3	Purchase Price	260,000.00
4	Down Payment	25,000.00
5	Loan Amount	235,000.00
6	Interest Rate	9.00%
7	Number of Years	30
8	Monthly Payment	
9	Total Interest	
10	Total Cost of Home	

2. Select **cell B8** and enter the formula **=-PMT(B6/12,B7*12,B5)**.
   The result equals $1,890.86. Notice that the formula has a minus (–) sign after the equals (=) sign. Also, the first argument divides the interest rate in cell B6 by 12 because payments will be made monthly. Likewise, the second argument multiplies the number of years in cell B7 by 12 months in a year. Excel formats the result with the Currency Style because you used the PMT function.
3. Select **cell B9** and enter **=B8*B7*12-B5** to calculate the total interest.
   The result equals $445,710.73. Take a few moments to study the formula and notice that it calculates the total payments over the term of the loan and subtracts the loan amount. Also notice that the number of months is determined by multiplying the number of years in cell B7 by 12.
4. Select **cell B10** and enter **=B9+B3** to calculate the total cost of the home.
5. **Format** all dollar amounts in **Comma Style with two decimal places**. Format the percentage with **two decimal places**.

Create a Pie Chart

You will create a pie chart that compares the two costs—purchase price and total interest.

6. Select the noncontiguous **ranges A3:B3** and **A9:B9**, as shown.
   This selection allows the pie chart to compare the Purchase Price to the Total Interest.

	A	B
1	30-Year Mortgage Analysis	
2		
3	Purchase Price	260,000.00
4	Down Payment	25,000.00
5	Loan Amount	235,000.00
6	Interest Rate	9.00%
7	Number of Years	30
8	Monthly Payment	1,890.86
9	Total Interest	445,710.73
10	Total Cost of Home	705,710.73

7. Choose **Insert→Charts→Pie** →**Pie in 3D** and create the following embedded pie chart.

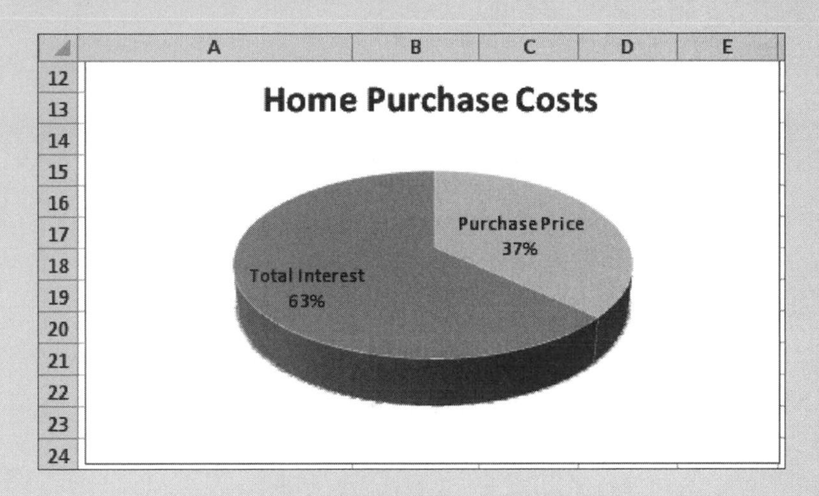

8. Use **Layout 1** and resize the chart smaller if needed. Position the pie chart in **row 12** below the data.

Use a What-If Analysis

Notice that the monthly payment in cell B8 is approximately $1,891.

9. Select **cell B6**.
10. Change the **Interest Rate** to **6%** and notice the impact on the monthly payment and the chart slices.
11. Experiment with various interest rates. Also, try changing the down payment and note the impact on the monthly payment.
12. When you are finished, make certain that the **purchase price** is **260,000** and change the **down payment** back to **25000** and the **interest rate** to **6%**.

Use Solver

What interest rate and purchase price are needed to achieve a monthly payment of $1,500, an interest rate not to exceed 7 percent, and total interest not to exceed $300,000? You will use Solver to find these values.

13. Select **cell B8** and choose **Data→Analysis→Solver** from the Ribbon.
    The Solver Parameters dialog box displays.
14. Verify that the **Set Objective**: box displays cell $B$8.
15. Choose the **Value Of** option and type **1500** for the monthly payment.
16. Click in the **By Changing Variable Cells** text box, select **cell B3** in the worksheet for the purchase price, type a **comma**, and select **cell B6** for the interest rate.
17. Click the **Add** button and create a constraint for the interest rate not to exceed **7%**.

18. Add a constraint for the **total interest** not to exceed **300000**.

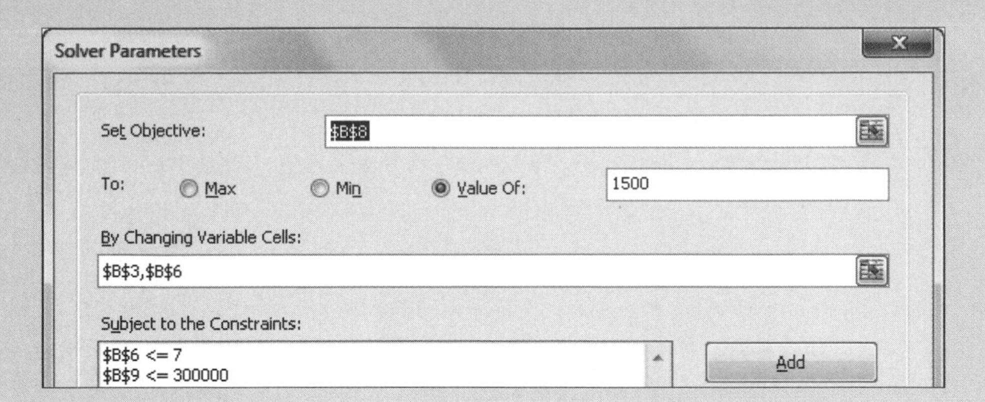

19. Click **Solve** and **OK** to accept Solver's suggested solution.
    The new purchase price should be $271,203.84 with an interest rate of 6.15 percent. Solver may suggest a different solution, but the variables should meet all the requirements that you set in the dialog box.
20. **Save** as **rs-Home Mortgage** in the Lesson 13 folder, and then **close** the workbook.

	A	B
1	**30-Year Mortgage Analysis**	
2		
3	Purchase Price	271,203.84
4	Down Payment	25,000.00
5	Loan Amount	246,203.84
6	Interest Rate	6.15%
7	Number of Years	30
8	Monthly Payment	1,500.00
9	Total Interest	293,796.12
10	Total Cost of Home	564,999.95

REINFORCE YOUR SKILLS 13.2

Use the FV Function

In this exercise, you will use the Future Value (FV) function to determine the future value of a college fund. This is important if you are saving for a college education, but the worksheet also may be used to determine the future value of nearly any investment that has consistent contributions. The generic syntax of the FV function is repeated below for your convenience.

Future Value Function Syntax =FV(rate, periods, payment)

1. **Start** a new workbook.
2. Use the **Column Width** command to set the width of **column A** to 19 and **column B** to 14.
3. **Enter** the data shown to the right.
4. Format the interest rate in **cell B3** as a **percentage** with **two decimal places**.
5. Select **cell B6** and enter the function **=FV(B3/12,B4*12,-B5)**.
   The result equals $96,017.23. Notice that the formula has a minus (–) sign between the comma and B5. Otherwise, the FV function would return a negative number. Also, notice that the interest rate in cell B3 is divided by 12 to produce a monthly rate. The number of years in cell B4 is multiplied by 12 to produce the total number of monthly payments.
6. **Save** as **rs-Original College Fund** in the Lesson 13 folder.
   You will continue to use this workbook in the next exercise.

	A	B
1	College Fund	
2		
3	Interest Rate	8.00%
4	Number of Years	18
5	Monthly Contribution	200
6	Future Value	

REINFORCE YOUR SKILLS 13.3

Use Goal Seek

In this exercise, you will use Goal Seek to determine the interest rate required to save $200,000 by contributing $300 monthly for 18 years.

Before You Begin: *You must have completed Reinforce Your Skills 13.2, and the rs-Original College Fund workbook should be open.*

Use Goal Seek

1. Choose **File→Save As**, name the new workbook **`rs-College Fund Goal`**, and **save** it in the Lesson 13 folder.
2. Select **cell B5** and change the **monthly contribution** to **`300`**.
   Notice that this increases the future value of the investment to approximately $144,000. In the next few steps, you will use Goal Seek to determine the interest rate necessary to achieve a future value of $200,000 with a monthly contribution of $300 for 18 years.
3. Select **cell B6** and choose **Data→Data Tools→What-If Analysis** →**Goal Seek** from the Ribbon.
4. Set the **To Value** option to **`200000`**.
5. Set the **By Changing Cell** option to **`B3`** (the interest rate cell).
6. Click **OK** and notice that a 10.91 percent interest rate is required.
7. Click **OK** in the Goal Seek Status dialog box to accept the change to the interest rate.
8. Use **Goal Seek** to determine the interest rate required to achieve a $275,000 future value with a $325 monthly contribution.

	A	B
1	**College Fund**	
2		
3	Interest Rate	12.92%
4	Number of Years	18
5	Monthly Contribution	325
6	Future Value	$275,000.00

=FV(B3/12, B4*12,-B5)

9. **Save** and **close** the workbook.

REINFORCE YOUR SKILLS 13.4

Use the Scenario Manager

In this exercise, you will use the Scenario Manager to project the profit for a new toy manufacturer named KidCraft. Donna Williams, the founder of KidCraft, needs to set up the model as part of her business plan. She is trying to raise funds, and a business plan and financial model are a crucial part of this process.

Create the Worksheet

1. **Start** a new workbook.
   In the next steps, you will create the worksheet shown to the right.
2. **Enter** the labels in **column A** and the values in the **range B3:B8**.
3. Use the **SUM** function in **cell B9** to calculate the expenses in the range B5:B8.
4. Calculate the **Gross Profit** in **cell B11** as the Forecasted Revenue – Total Costs.
5. Calculate the **Net Profit** in **cell B12** as the Gross Profit*70%.

	A	B
1	KidCraft FY5 Projected Income	
2		
3	Forecasted Revenue	$ 345,000
4		
5	Employee Costs	62,000
6	Capital Expenditures	75,900
7	Manufacturing	58,650
8	Marketing and Sales	55,200
9	Total Costs	$ 251,750
10		
11	Gross Profit	$ 93,250
12	Net Profit	$ 65,275

6. **Format** the values with the **Comma Style** and **Accounting** formats shown.
7. **Rename** the worksheet tab as `Projected Income`.

Name the Cells

8. Select the **range A3:B12**.
9. Choose **Formulas→Defined Names→Create from Selection** from the Ribbon.
10. Make certain that the **Left Column box** is checked, and click **OK**.
    The names are defined for the cells in column B. This will be helpful when you use the Scenario Manager.

Create the First Scenario

The first scenario will be based on existing values in the worksheet.

11. Select **cell B3**, and then **press and hold** Ctrl while you drag to select the **range B5:B8**.
    The blank cell B4 and the total cost in cell B9 should not be included in the selection. You will create scenarios by changing the selected cells.
12. Choose **Data→Data Tools→What-If Analysis** →**Scenario Manager** from the Ribbon.
    The dialog box should indicate that no scenarios are currently defined.
13. Click the **Add** button to add a new scenario.

14. Type the name **Scenario 1**, edit the **Comment** box to include your name, and click **OK**.
The Scenario Values dialog box displays.

Add Scenario

Scenario name:
Scenario 1
Changing cells:
B3,B5:B8
Ctrl+click cells to select non-adjacent changing cells.
Comment:
Created by Student Name on 10/29/2010

15. Click the **Add** button to complete Scenario 1 and display the Add Scenario dialog box.
You may create additional scenarios without returning to the initial Scenario Manager dialog box.

Add Other Scenarios

16. Type the name **Scenario 2** and click **OK**.

17. Change only the Forecasted Revenue number to **500000** and click **Add**.

18. Now add **two new scenarios** using the data in the following table, making certain that you click **OK** after entering values for Scenario 4 rather than using Add as you will do for Scenario 3.

Variable	Scenario 3 Scenario Value	Scenario 4 Scenario Value
Forecasted Revenue	700,000	700,000
Employee Costs	80,000	80,000
Capital Expenditures	35,000	42,000
Manufacturing	98,000	85,000
Marketing and Sales	85,000	70,000

19. Use the **Show** button in the Scenario Manager dialog box to show the results of each scenario.

Display a Summary of All Scenarios

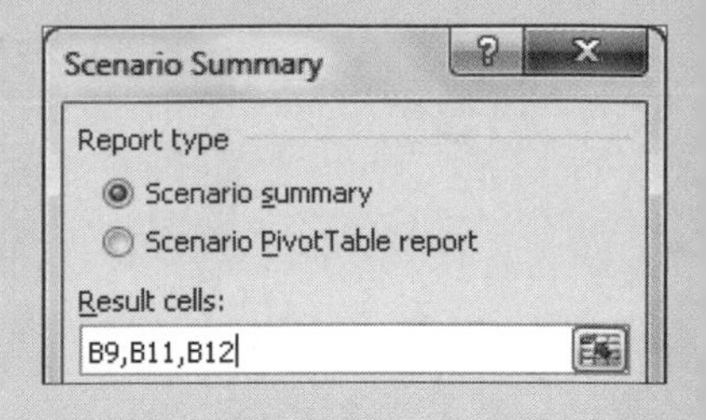

20. Click the **Summary** button in the Scenario Manager dialog box.
21. Choose the **Scenario Summary** option; set results cells for the Total Costs, Gross Profit, and Net Profit; and click **OK**.
Excel inserts the summary on a new worksheet, shown here.

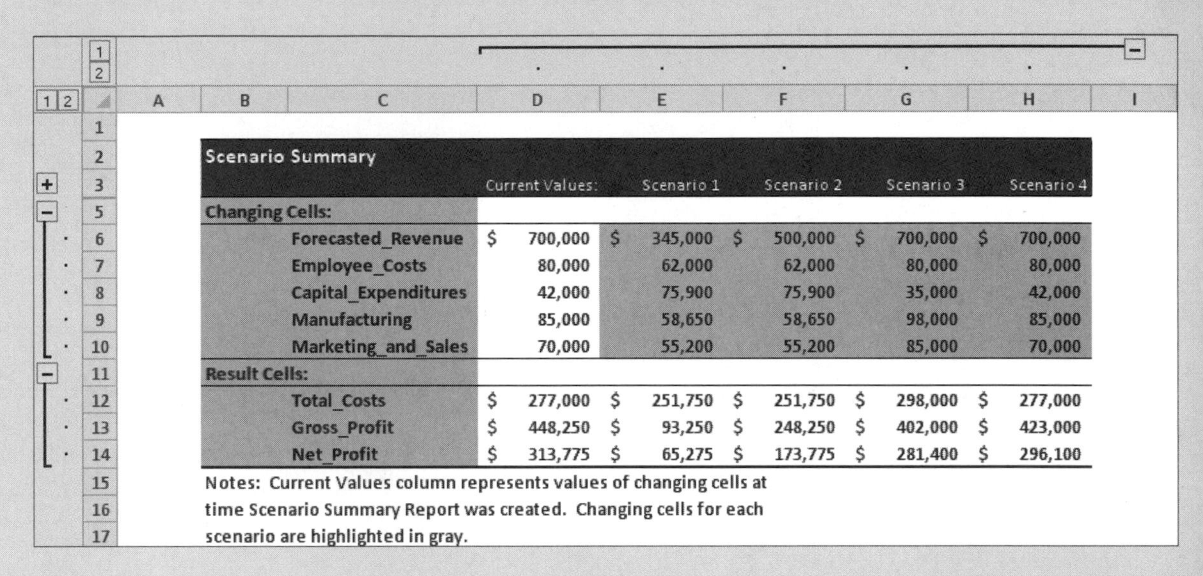

Scenario Summary	Current Values:	Scenario 1	Scenario 2	Scenario 3	Scenario 4
Changing Cells:					
Forecasted_Revenue	$ 700,000	$ 345,000	$ 500,000	$ 700,000	$ 700,000
Employee_Costs	80,000	62,000	62,000	80,000	80,000
Capital_Expenditures	42,000	75,900	75,900	35,000	42,000
Manufacturing	85,000	58,650	58,650	98,000	85,000
Marketing_and_Sales	70,000	55,200	55,200	85,000	70,000
Result Cells:					
Total_Costs	$ 277,000	$ 251,750	$ 251,750	$ 298,000	$ 277,000
Gross_Profit	$ 448,250	$ 93,250	$ 248,250	$ 402,000	$ 423,000
Net_Profit	$ 313,775	$ 65,275	$ 173,775	$ 281,400	$ 296,100

Notes: Current Values column represents values of changing cells at time Scenario Summary Report was created. Changing cells for each scenario are highlighted in gray.

22. **Save** as **`rs-Financial Scenarios`** in the Lesson 13 folder and **close** the workbook.

Apply Your Skills

APPLY YOUR SKILLS 13.1

Use the FV Function and Solver

In this exercise, you will calculate the future value of a mutual fund investment. Then you will use Solver to determine the rate of return needed to achieve a specific future value.

Before You Begin: The Solver add-in must be installed on your computer system to complete this exercise.

1. **Create** the worksheet shown at right.
2. Taking care to display the answer as a **positive** number, use the **FV** function to calculate the future value in **cell B6**.
3. **Format** all cells as shown and adjust the column widths.

	A	B
1	Investment Projections	
2		Utilities Mutual Fund
3	Projected Annual Rate of Return	11.00%
4	Number of Years	20
5	Monthly Contribution	$ 300
6	Future Value	$

4. Use **Solver** to determine the annual rate of return needed to achieve a future value of $300,000 with a monthly contribution of $400 or less. Accept Solver's suggested answer.
5. **Save** with the name **`as-Mutual Fund`** in the Lesson 13 folder of your storage location and **close** the workbook.

APPLY YOUR SKILLS 13.2

Use the PMT Function and Goal Seek

In this exercise, you will calculate the monthly payment for a home equity loan. Then you will use Goal Seek to determine the amount you could borrow with a monthly payment of $200.

1. **Create** the worksheet shown at right.
2. Taking care to display the answer as a **positive** number, use the **PMT** function to calculate the monthly payment in **cell B7**.
3. **Format** all cells as shown and adjust the column widths.

	A	B
1	Home Equity Loan Analysis	
2		Credit Union
3	Interest Rate	6.00%
4	Number of Years	10
5	Loan Amount	$15,000.00
6	Monthly Payment	

4. Use **Goal Seek** to determine what the loan amount could be if the monthly payment were $200, and accept Goal Seek's suggested answer.
5. **Save** with the name **`as-Home Equity Loan`** in the Lesson 13 folder and **close** the workbook.

APPLY YOUR SKILLS 13.3

Use Scenario Manager

In this exercise, you will use Scenario Manager to project salaries and expenses by creating three scenarios for a budget worksheet.

1. **Open** the as-Budget Scenarios workbook from the Lesson 13 folder of your storage location.
2. Create **Scenario 1** using the existing model data in the Budget worksheet. Use only the **Sales** and **Customer Support** costs as variables.
3. Create **Scenarios 2 and 3** using the data in the following table:

Variable	Scenario 2	Scenario 3
Sales	2,500,000	2,000,000
Customer Support	100,000	85,000

4. Show **Scenario 3** in the worksheet.
5. **Display** a scenario summary report to include the following results: Salaries and Wages Total, Staffing Expenses Total, Sales Staffing Ratio, and Customer Support Staffing Ratio.
6. **Save** and **close** the workbook.

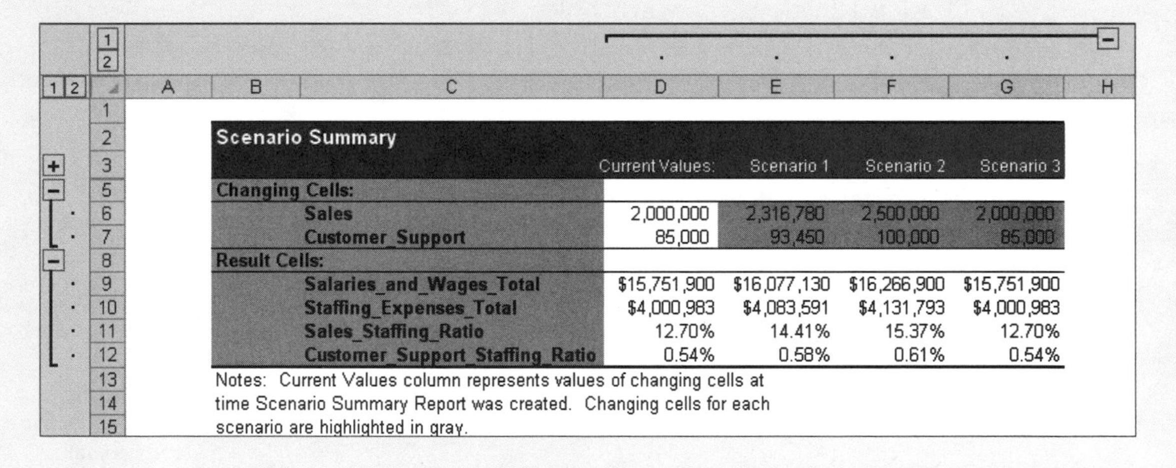

Scenario Summary	Current Values:	Scenario 1	Scenario 2	Scenario 3
Changing Cells:				
Sales	2,000,000	2,316,780	2,500,000	2,000,000
Customer_Support	85,000	93,450	100,000	85,000
Result Cells:				
Salaries_and_Wages_Total	$15,751,900	$16,077,130	$16,266,900	$15,751,900
Staffing_Expenses_Total	$4,000,983	$4,083,591	$4,131,793	$4,000,983
Sales_Staffing_Ratio	12.70%	14.41%	15.37%	12.70%
Customer_Support_Staffing_Ratio	0.54%	0.58%	0.61%	0.54%

Notes: Current Values column represents values of changing cells at time Scenario Summary Report was created. Changing cells for each scenario are highlighted in gray.

Critical Thinking & Work-Readiness Skills

In the course of working through the following Microsoft Office-based Critical Thinking exercises, you will also be utilizing various work-readiness skills, some of which are listed next to each exercise. Go to labyrinthelab.com/workreadiness *to learn more about the work-readiness skills.*

13.1 Use the PMT Function

Sandra Chavez-Hall is ready to start planning the fundraising for building Phase 2 at Raritan Clinic East. Raritan will get a business loan to help pay the startup costs. Set up a new worksheet for Sandra. Use the PMT formula to determine the monthly payment needed if the loan amount is $1,500,000, the annual interest rate is 7%, and number of years is 5. Then, create a formula to calculate the total cost of the loan. The generic formula is Total Loan Cost = Monthly Payment * Number of Payments. Save your work as **ct-Raritan Clinic Phase 2 [Your Last Name]** in the Lesson 13 folder. Keep the file open.

WORK-READINESS SKILLS APPLIED

- Arithmetic/mathematics
- Solving problems
- Using computers to process information

13.2 Use the FV Function and Goal Seek

Raritan Clinic East will solicit contributions for the total loan cost. The contributions will be invested in a fund that pays interest. Sandra wants to calculate the total investment after three years. Open ct-Raritan Clinic Phase 2 [Your Last Name], if necessary. Create an appropriate formula for Sandra. Use the FV function to show the total investment if monthly contributions are $50,000, the annual interest rate is 4%, and the number of years is 3. Then, use Goal Seek to determine the monthly contributions needed to achieve a future value equal to the total loan cost. You calculated the loan cost in the previous exercise. Save your work and keep the file open.

WORK-READINESS SKILLS APPLIED

- Arithmetic/mathematics
- Solving problems
- Using computers to process information

13.3 Use Scenario Manager

Before publicizing the fundraising goals, Sandra wants to understand the economics behind the interest rate and watch the interest as it accrues. Sandra is aware that the investment interest may vary, but she is not certain how much it affects her goals. Use the Scenario Manager to help her understand how the fluctuation of just one percentage point can influence the total investment. If necessary, open ct-Raritan Clinic Phase 2 [Your Last Name]. Use Scenario 1 to retain the present future value information. Create Scenario 2 to show what will happen if the interest rate drops to 3%. Prepare a scenario summary sheet that displays both scenarios. Save and close the file when you are finished.

WORK-READINESS SKILLS APPLIED

- Arithmetic/mathematics
- Solving problems
- Using computers to process information

Applying Advanced Functions and Auditing

LESSON OUTLINE

LEARNING OBJECTIVES

After studying this lesson, you will be able to:

- Use 3-D cell references in formulas to summarize workbook data
- Create a lookup formula to locate a value or text in a list
- Use subtotal formulas to calculate data in filtered lists
- Build formulas with criteria IF functions and logical functions to perform actions based on criteria
- Use text functions to reformat data
- Correct formula errors using the auditing tools

Complex worksheets for decision making often require advanced functions based on the values in other cells. You may set up detailed worksheets with an identical design for various categories or time periods of a project and summarize the data on a separate worksheet. In this lesson, you will use 3-D cell references in formulas to create the summary calculations. The HLOOKUP and VLOOKUP functions help to use one piece of information to find another in a list. You will use the VLOOKUP function to locate the fundraising award for each team member. With the criteria IF and SUBTOTAL functions, you may sum, average, or count values when specific criteria are satisfied. You also may use logical functions, such as AND or NOT, to specify various criteria in formulas. Excel's text functions help you to reformat data imported into an Excel workbook from another program. For example, you will use the SUBSTITUTE function to replace a misspelled job title with the correct title. In addition, you will learn how to work with formula auditing tools, which are particularly useful in locating errors in complex formulas that are dependent on other formulas.

Student Resources labyrinthelab.com/excel10

CASE STUDY

Summarizing Fundraising Performance

Sandra Chavez-Hall coordinates a fundraising campaign to build two new facilities at Raritan Clinic East. To track the performance of her team members, Sandra uses an Excel workbook with a worksheet for each month. To combine the data from the monthly worksheets into a quarterly summary worksheet, Sandra uses 3-D cell references in SUM formulas.

B5 | =SUM(October:December!B5)

	A	B	C
1	Raritan Clinic East	Capital Campaign	
2	Pediatric Diagnostic Specialists	October-December	
3			
4		Contributions	
5	Cash Contributions	$ 207,895	
6	In-Kind Contributions	$ 25,382	
7	Grants	$ 1,612,200	
8	**Total Contributions**	**$ 1,845,477**	
9			
10	**Total Direct Expenses**	**$ 43,563**	
11			

Summary | October | November | December

A worksheet formula containing a 3-D cell reference to cell B5 on three worksheets

Sandra also needs to calculate monthly contributions raised by the Raritan Clinic Foundation team members. Sandra uses the VLOOKUP function and a lookup table to determine whether team members receive an award. She also uses the lookup table to display a message that indicates each team member's goal achievement status.

	A	B	C	D	E	F	G
4	**Team Leader**	**Goal**	**Amount Raised**	**Over (Under) Goal**	**Award Rate**	**Award Points**	**Achieved Goal?**
5	Abbott	$25,000	$31,810	$6,810	5%	1,591	Above Goal
6	Debowski	$100,000	$95,350	($4,650)	1%	954	Below Goal
7	Faber	$60,000	$52,500	($7,500)	0%	-	Under Achiever
8	Lemus	$100,000	$110,350	$10,350	7%	7,725	Over Achiever

Over (Under) Goal	**Award Rate**	**Message**
($100,000)	0%	Under Achiever
($5,000)	1%	Below Goal
$0	3%	At Goal
$5,000	5%	Above Goal
$10,000	7%	Over Achiever

A worksheet using VLOOKUP and a lookup table to find the award percentage and the goal achievement status

14.1 Using 3-D Cell References in Formulas

Video Lesson labyrinthelab.com/videos

You can create a workbook containing detail worksheets and a summary worksheet. You may use a linking formula in the summary worksheet to refer to the contents of a cell in a single detail worksheet. Excel also allows you to perform calculations using the contents of the same cell address in multiple worksheets, which is called a 3-D cell reference. Contrast the following linking formula and normal summing formula with a formula containing a 3-D cell reference.

Type of Formula	Example	What It Does
Linking	=Supplies!C6	Gets the contents from cell C6 in the Supplies worksheet
Normal	=Supplies!C6 + Utilities!C6	Sums cell C6 from the Supplies and Utilities worksheets only
3-D	=SUM(Supplies:Equipment!C6)	Sums cell C6 in all worksheets from Supplies through Equipment in the workbook

Why Use a 3-D Reference?

Using a 3-D reference provides two advantages over normal cell references in a multisheet formula. First, you do not have to click the cell in each worksheet to build the formula. Also, the formula automatically includes the specified cell from additional worksheets that you insert within the worksheet range.

Deleting a worksheet or moving a worksheet tab to outside the range in the 3-D reference removes that worksheet's values from the formula result.

Creating a 3-D Reference

Functions that you may use to create 3-D references include SUM, AVERAGE, COUNT, MAX, MIN, and some statistical functions. A formula may contain a single cell or a cell range as a 3-D reference. Remember that the cells being referenced must be the identical cell addresses in all detail worksheets. You cannot, for example, use cell B2 from one worksheet and cell C3 from another. But, you may, for example, use the range B2:E2 from all the worksheets. The cell or range must also contain the same type of data, such as values.

QUICK REFERENCE	CREATING 3-D CELL REFERENCES IN FORMULAS
Task	**Procedure**
Create a 3-D reference	■ Design all worksheets so that the cell contents to be calculated are in the identical cell addresses. ■ Select the cell to contain the formula in the summary worksheet. ■ Type the function beginning, such as =SUM(. ■ Click the first sheet tab and hold down [Shift] while clicking the last sheet tab to be referenced. ■ In the sheet currently displayed, select the cell or range to be referenced, and complete the formula.

DEVELOP YOUR SKILLS 14.1.1

Create 3-D Cell References

In this exercise, you will create 3-D cell references to one cell in several worksheets. You will also create a 3-D reference to a cell range.

1. **Start** Excel and **open** the Campaign Summary workbook from the Lesson 14 folder in your file storage location.
2. **Maximize** the window.
   You will create 3-D references on the Summary worksheet to sum values from the other three worksheets.
3. Display the **October** worksheet to see that the worksheet design for **rows 1–8** is identical to that of the Summary worksheet. Display the **November** worksheet, and then display **December** to see that they contain an identical structure.
4. Display the **Summary** worksheet.

Create a 3-D Cell Reference Formula for Contributions

5. Follow these steps to create a formula that adds the values in cell B5 from each of the monthly contributions worksheets:

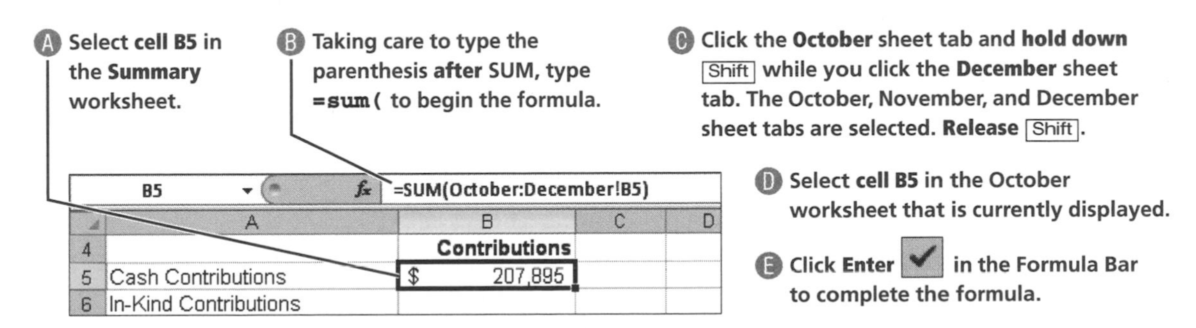

A Select cell B5 in the Summary worksheet.
B Taking care to type the parenthesis after SUM, type =sum(to begin the formula.
C Click the October sheet tab and hold down Shift while you click the December sheet tab. The October, November, and December sheet tabs are selected. Release Shift.
D Select cell B5 in the October worksheet that is currently displayed.
E Click Enter in the Formula Bar to complete the formula.
B5
=SUM(October:December!B5)
A
B
C
D
4
Contributions
5 Cash Contributions
$ 207,895
6 In-Kind Contributions

The Formula Bar displays =SUM(October:December!B5). Notice that an exclamation (!) point separates the worksheet names from the cell address. The formula result is $207,895, which is the total cash contributions from cell B5 in the October, November, and December worksheets.

6. Use **Autofill** to copy the formula in **cell B5** to the range **B6:B7**.

7. **Deselect** the highlighted range.
8. Select **cell B7** and look in the Formula Bar to see that the 3-D reference is included in the formula that you copied.

Create a 3-D Cell Range Formula for Total Direct Expenses

Now you will calculate the total direct expenses to generate the contributions and grants. You will use the SUM function for the same cell range across the three monthly worksheets.

9. Display the **October** worksheet.
   Review the expense data in rows 11–14. The other monthly worksheets are designed identically with values in the range B11:B14.
10. Display the **Summary** worksheet.
11. Select **cell B10**.
12. Choose **Home→Editing→AutoSum** [Σ] from the Ribbon.
13. Click the **October** sheet tab.
14. **Hold down** [Shift] while you click the **December** sheet tab to select all monthly sales worksheets, and then **release** the [Shift] key.
15. Drag to select **cells B11:B14** in the October worksheet.
    Although the October worksheet is displayed, you are specifying the cells to be summed in all the detail sheets that you selected.
16. Click **Enter** [✓] in the Formula Bar to complete the formula.
    The Formula Bar displays =SUM(October:December!B11:B14). The formula result is $43,563.

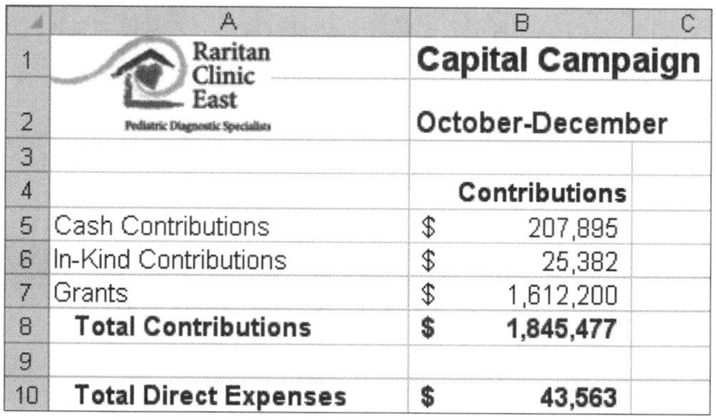

	A	B		C
1	Raritan Clinic East	Capital Campaign		
2	Pediatric Diagnostic Specialists	October-December		
3				
4			Contributions	
5	Cash Contributions	$	207,895	
6	In-Kind Contributions	$	25,382	
7	Grants	$	1,612,200	
8	**Total Contributions**	**$**	**1,845,477**	
9				
10	**Total Direct Expenses**	**$**	**43,563**	

17. **Save** the changes, **close** the workbook, and leave Excel **open**.

14.2 Introducing Lookup Functions

Video Lesson labyrinthelab.com/videos

The VLOOKUP (Vertical Lookup) and HLOOKUP (Horizontal Lookup) functions are used to retrieve a piece of data from a lookup table located somewhere in the same worksheet, a separate worksheet, or a different workbook. In this lesson, you will look up the award percentage rate, which depends on the the team leader's fundraising over or under the goal. The dollar increment values display down the first column of a vertical lookup table or across the first row of a horizontal lookup table. You may use either format and its matching function.

Take care to place a lookup table outside rows or columns that might be deleted in the future.

	E	F
15	Over (Under) Goal	Award Rate
16	($100,000)	0%
17	($5,000)	1%
18	$0	3%
19	$5,000	5%
20	$10,000	7%

A vertical lookup table containing dollar amounts under or over the fundraising goal amounts and their corresponding award rates

The same data arranged in a horizontal lookup table

	A	B	C	D	E	F
15	Over (Under) Goal	($100,000)	($5,000)	$0	$5,000	$10,000
16	Award Rate	0%	1%	3%	5%	7%

Lookup Function Syntax

The generic parts of the HLOOKUP and VLOOKUP functions are identical, as shown in the following table.

Function	Syntax
HLOOKUP (Horizontal Lookup)	HLOOKUP(lookup value, table array, column index number, range lookup)
VLOOKUP (Vertical Lookup)	VLOOKUP(lookup value, table array, column index number, range lookup)

The following table outlines the arguments of the VLOOKUP function.

Argument	Description
Lookup value	The value in the worksheet to be looked up in the first column of the table array
Table array	The cell range containing the lookup table, which may be expressed as absolute cell references or a defined name
Column index number	The column number in the table array that contains the corresponding data to be retrieved
Range lookup (optional; the default is TRUE)	A logical value that specifies a search for an exact or approximate value in the table array (TRUE) or an exact match only (FALSE)

How the VLOOKUP Function Works

The formula =VLOOKUP(D5,Award_Table,2) is used as an example to explain how the search takes place in the lookup table. Cell D5 contains the lookup value $6,810. The defined name Award_Table indicates that the search takes place in the table array located in the range $E$16:$G$20. The search is conducted down the first column of the table array until the highest value not greater than the lookup value is located. The number 2, the column index number in the formula, indicates that the corresponding award rate will be retrieved from the second column of the lookup table.

Cell E5 contains the VLOOKUP formula to find Abbott's award rate based on $6,810 in funds raised over the goal.

Excel searches for the lookup value $6,810 down the first column of the lookup table. The search stops at $5,000 on row 19 because the lookup value is at least $5,000 but not $10,000.

	A	B	C	D	E
4	Team Leader	Goal	Amount Raised	Over (Under) Goal	Award Rate
5	Abbott	$25,000	$31,810	$6,810	5%
6	Debowski	$100,000	$95,350	($4,650)	1%
7	Faber	$60,000	$52,500	($7,500)	0%

	E	F
15	Over (Under) Goal	Award Rate
16	($100,000)	0%
17	($5,000)	1%
18	$0	3%
19	$5,000	5%
20	$10,000	7%

Traveling along row 19, the search moves to column 2 of the lookup table, as specified by the column index number in the function.

The award rate 5 percent is returned to cell E5.

When a lookup formula will be copied to other cells, the cell range of the table array should be expressed in the formula as a defined name or absolute cell references, such as $E$16:$F$20.

Specifying the Range Lookup Argument

Excel uses the default range lookup argument TRUE so the search is conducted in the first column of the table array for either an exact match of $6,810 or the closest value that is not greater than $6,810. At times, you may want to search only for an exact match of the lookup value. The formula =VLOOKUP(A5,Employee_Records,2,FALSE) includes the FALSE range lookup argument, which restricts the search to an exact match. Assume that cell A5 contains the last name Abbott. A search for an exact match is conducted in the first column of the Employee_Records table array. If Abbott is not found, Excel displays #N/A in the formula cell to indicate a Value Not Available error.

Sorting a Table Array

The rows in the table array must be sorted in lowest to highest (A to Z) order in the first column when the TRUE range lookup argument is used. This way, you can be assured that VLOOKUP will stop at the proper row and return the correct value. Sorting the table array is not required when the FALSE range lookup argument is used.

DEVELOP YOUR SKILLS 14.2.1

Use VLOOKUP

In this exercise, you will set up a three-column table array and then use the VLOOKUP function to calculate award points and display messages.

Create a Table Array

1. **Open** the Awards workbook from the Lesson 14 folder, and display the **December** worksheet.
   You will create the table array in the range E16:G20 and assign a defined name to that range. The labels in row 15 are optional and not part of the table array.

2. Complete the **table array** by entering the numbers and text shown in the following illustration. Use a **minus sign** (–) to enter the negative numbers in cells E16 and E17.
   The number formatting is already applied to the blank cells.

	E	F	G
15	Over (Under) Goal	Award Rate	Message
16	($100,000)	0%	Under Achiever
17	($5,000)	1%	Below Goal
18	$0	3%	At Goal
19	$5,000	5%	Above Goal
20	$10,000	7%	Over Achiever

Assign a Range Name to the Table Array

In the next few steps, you will assign a defined name to the table array. Naming a range for a table array is optional. You would use absolute cell references in the lookup formula if you did not use a defined name.

3. Follow these steps to create the range name:

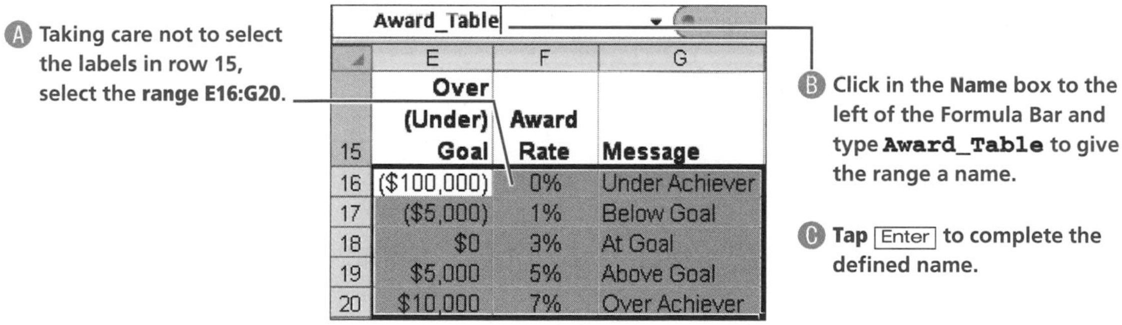

Award_Table

	E	F	G
15	Over (Under) Goal	Award Rate	Message
16	($100,000)	0%	Under Achiever
17	($5,000)	1%	Below Goal
18	$0	3%	At Goal
19	$5,000	5%	Above Goal
20	$10,000	7%	Over Achiever

Ⓐ Taking care not to select the labels in row 15, select the **range E16:G20**.

Ⓑ Click in the **Name** box to the left of the Formula Bar and type **Award_Table** to give the range a name.

Ⓒ Tap Enter to complete the defined name.

4. **Deselect** the table array.

Create a VLOOKUP Formula for the Award Rate

You will use the VLOOKUP function to calculate the award rate for each team leader in column E.

5. **Enter** the formula **`=VLOOKUP(D5,Award_Table,2)`** in **cell E5**.
   The 5 percent award rate is returned from the lookup table to cell E5.
6. Take a few moments to study the three arguments in the function you just entered and understand how the lookup works.
7. Use **Autofill** to copy the formula from **cell E5** down to the **range E6:E12**.
8. Select **cell E7** and review the formula in the Formula Bar.
   The award rate returned from the lookup table is 0 percent. Notice that all arguments are the same for this function, except that the relative cell reference tells VLOOKUP to look up the value from cell D7.

Calculate the Award Points

*The formula Over (Under) Goal * Award Rate calculates the team member's award points.*

9. **Enter** the formula **`=C5*E5`** in cell F5.
   The result equals 1,591.
10. Use **AutoFill** to copy the commission formula in **cell F5** down for the other team members.

	A	B	C	D	E	F	G
4	**Team Leader**	**Goal**	**Amount Raised**	**Over (Under) Goal**	**Award Rate**	**Award Points**	**Achieved Goal?**
5	Abbott	$25,000	$31,810	$6,810	5%	1,591	
6	Debowski	$100,000	$95,350	($4,650)	1%	954	
7	Faber	$60,000	$52,500	($7,500)	0%	-	
8	Lemus	$100,000	$110,350	$10,350	7%	7,725	
9	Martinez	$70,000	$66,000	($4,000)	1%	660	
10	Nguyen	$45,000	$48,000	$3,000	3%	1,440	
11	Park	$30,000	$31,680	$1,680	3%	950	
12	Weinstein	$70,000	$67,000	($3,000)	1%	670	

Create a VLOOKUP Formula for the Goal Achievement Messages

11. Select **cell G5** and enter the function **`=VLOOKUP(D5,Award_Table,3)`**.
    The message Above Goal is returned. Notice that you used the same arguments for this function that you did in cell E5 except that the last argument is 3 instead of 2. This instructs VLOOKUP to return the message text from column 3 of the table array.
12. Use **AutoFill** to copy the quota message formula in **cell G5** down for the other team members.
    Rows 5–20 should match the following illustration.

	A	B	C	D	E	F	G
4	**Team Leader**	**Goal**	**Amount Raised**	**Over (Under) Goal**	**Award Rate**	**Award Points**	**Achieved Goal?**
5	Abbott	$25,000	$31,810	$6,810	5%	1,591	Above Goal
6	Debowski	$100,000	$95,350	($4,650)	1%	954	Below Goal
7	Faber	$60,000	$52,500	($7,500)	0%	-	Under Achiever
8	Lemus	$100,000	$110,350	$10,350	7%	7,725	Over Achiever
9	Martinez	$70,000	$66,000	($4,000)	1%	660	Below Goal
10	Nguyen	$45,000	$48,000	$3,000	3%	1,440	At Goal
11	Park	$30,000	$31,680	$1,680	3%	950	At Goal
12	Weinstein	$70,000	$67,000	($3,000)	1%	670	Below Goal
13							
14							
15					**Over (Under) Goal**	**Award Rate**	**Message**
16					($100,000)	0%	Under Achiever
17					($5,000)	1%	Below Goal
18					$0	3%	At Goal
19					$5,000	5%	Above Goal
20					$10,000	7%	Over Achiever

13. Select **cell F16** and change the rate to **`1%`**.
    The rate in cell E7 changed from 0 percent to 1 percent, and the corresponding award points in cell F7 now is 525.
14. Click **Undo** to change the entry back to 0% in cell F16.
15. Select **cell G16** and change the message to **`Counsel`**.
    Notice that the result in cell G7 changed to Counsel because you changed the message in the lookup table.
16. Click **Undo** to change the entry back to *Under Achiever.*
17. **Save** the changes, and leave the workbook **open**.

14.3 Using the SUBTOTAL Function to Calculate Filtered Lists

Video Lesson labyrinthelab.com/videos

You can filter a worksheet list to display only the records that meet certain criteria. For example, you can filter to display records that did not meet the monthly fundraising goal. If the records are in an Excel table, formulas in the total row use the SUBTOTAL function and automatically recalculate for the filtered records. When the records have not been converted to a table, you may use the SUBTOTAL function to calculate values in the filtered list.

SUBTOTAL Function Syntax

The generic parts of the SUBTOTAL function are shown in the following table.

Function	Syntax
SUBTOTAL	SUBTOTAL(function number, range1, [range2],...)

The following table outlines the arguments of this function.

Argument	Description
Function number	The arithmetic operation that will be performed
Range1	The range containing the values to be calculated
Range2, range3, and so on	(Optional) Additional ranges, cell references, or specific values to be included in the calculation

The following table describes the basic functions you may use. See Excel Help for additional statistical functions to calculate standard deviation and variance.

Function Number	Function	Operation Performed
1	AVERAGE	Averages the range
2	COUNT	Counts cells containing numbers in the range
3	COUNTA	Counts nonblank cells in the range
4	MAX	Returns the largest number in the range
5	MIN	Returns the smallest number in the range
6	PRODUCT	Multiples all values contained in the formula arguments
9	SUM	Adds the range

How the SUBTOTAL Function Works

The formula =SUBTOTAL(9,C5:C20) is used as an example to explain the function result. The range to be calculated is C5:C20. SUBTOTAL differs from a normal SUM or AVERAGE formula because SUBTOTAL ignores any rows that are not displayed in the filter result. In this example, the argument 9 indicates that the SUM function will calculate the values in the filtered range.

A function formula may be created using the Insert Function button on the Formula Bar, Formula AutoComplete, or the Function Library on the Formulas ribbon, or by typing the formula directly in the cell or Formula Bar.

DEVELOP YOUR SKILLS 14.3.1

Use the SUBTOTAL Function

In this exercise, you will filter a list to display team leaders who achieved at least $50,000 in fundraising. Then you will use the SUBTOTAL function to sum and average the filtered values.

Sum the Entire List

1. **Open** the Awards workbook from the Lesson 14 folder, if necessary, and display the **December** worksheet.
2. Select **cell C13**, choose **Home→Editing→AutoSum** [Σ] from the Ribbon, and click **Enter** in the Formula Bar.
   The result should be $502,690, which is the total raised in December. Notice that the Formula Bar displays =SUM(C5:C12).

Filter the List

3. Select **cell A4**, and choose **Data→Sort & Filter→Filter** from the Ribbon.
   Each column heading in row 4 displays an AutoFilter button.
4. In **cell C4**, choose the Amount Raised column heading **AutoFilter** button.
5. Point to **Number Filters** in the context (or pop-up) menu, and choose **Greater Than**.
6. In the **Custom AutoFilter** dialog box, enter **50000** in the text box as shown, and **tap** [Enter] to choose **OK**.

	A	B	C
4	Team Leader	Gc	Amount Rais
6	Debowski	$100,000	$95,350
7	Faber	$60,000	$52,500
8	Lemus	$100,000	$110,350
9	Martinez	$70,000	$66,000
12	Weinstein	$70,000	$67,000

The list displays five records for team members who achieved $50,000 or more. Notice that the SUM result in cell C13 still displays $502,690 rather than the total for just the filtered records. The sum is not recalculated automatically.

Sum the Filtered List

7. Select **cell C13**, and choose **Home→Editing→AutoSum** [Σ] from the Ribbon.

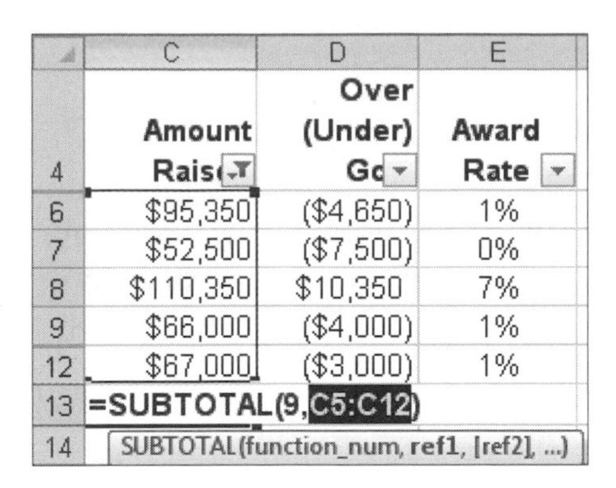

	C	D	E
4	Amount Raised	Over (Under) Goal	Award Rate
6	$95,350	($4,650)	1%
7	$52,500	($7,500)	0%
8	$110,350	$10,350	7%
9	$66,000	($4,000)	1%
12	$67,000	($3,000)	1%
13	=SUBTOTAL(9,C5:C12)		
14	SUBTOTAL(function_num, ref1, [ref2], ...)		

Now Excel recognizes that the list has been filtered. The formula =SUBTOTAL(9,C5:C12) appears in the Formula Bar. The argument 9 indicates that the filtered range will be summed.

8. Click the **AutoSum** [Σ] button again to complete the formula.
   The result should be $391,200, which is the subtotal for the five filtered records.

Average the Filtered List

9. Follow these steps to create a subtotal formula that averages the Over (Under) Goal amount for the filtered records:

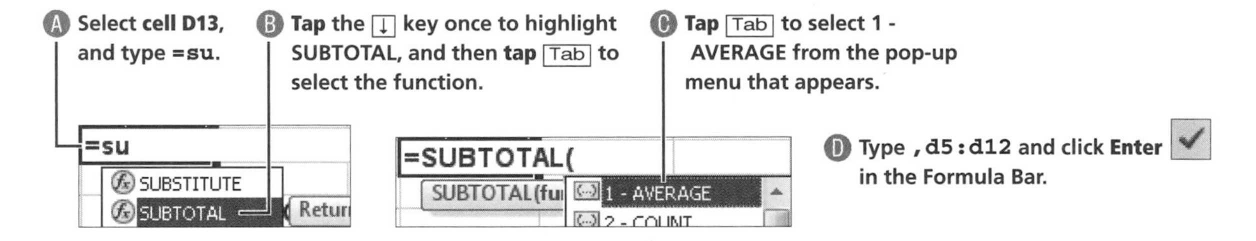

A Select cell D13, and type =su.
B Tap the ↓ key once to highlight SUBTOTAL, and then tap Tab to select the function.
C Tap Tab to select 1 - AVERAGE from the pop-up menu that appears.
D Type ,d5:d12 and click Enter in the Formula Bar.
=su
SUBSTITUTE
SUBTOTAL
=SUBTOTAL(
1 - AVERAGE

The formula =SUBTOTAL(1,D5:D12) appears in the Formula Bar. Notice that you included the entire list range D5:D12 even though the filter does not display cell D5. The result should be –1,760. Although the five team leaders raised the highest amounts, their average is below the goal.

10. Use **Format Painter** to apply the formatting from **cell D12** to **cell D13**.
    The result should appear as ($1,760).
11. Apply additional formatting of your choice to the **range C13:D13** so that the subtotals are noticeable.
12. **Save** the changes, and leave the workbook **open**.

14.4 Creating Formulas Using Criteria IF Functions

Video Lesson labyrinthelab.com/videos

Excel also provides functions that average, count, or sum cells that meet one or more criteria. The AVERAGEIF, COUNTIF, and SUMIF functions calculate using one criterion. The AVERAGEIFS, COUNTIFS, and SUMIFS functions calculate using multiple criteria that you specify. Only cells meeting all the criteria are averaged, counted, or summed.

Function Syntax

The generic parts of the two types of functions are shown in the following table.

Function	Syntax
AVERAGEIF	AVERAGEIF(range, criteria)
COUNTIF	COUNTIF(range, criteria)
SUMIF	SUMIF(range, criteria, sum range)
AVERAGEIFS	AVERAGEIFS(range1, criteria1, range2, criteria2)
COUNTIFS	COUNTIFS(range1, criteria1, range2, criteria2)
SUMIFS	SUMIFS(sum range, range1, criteria1, range2, criteria2)

The AVERAGEIFS, COUNTIFS, and SUMIFS functions may include up to 127 ranges and corresponding criteria.

The following table outlines the arguments of these functions.

Argument	Description
Range	The cells to be compared with the criteria
Criteria	Enclosed in quotation (") marks, the comparison value, text, or expression using a comparison operator, such as =, >, <, >=, <=, or <> (not equal to)
Sum range	The potential cells to be summed

How the SUMIF Function Works

The formula =SUMIF(C5:C12,">=30000",C5:C12) is used as an example to explain the function result. The range to be evaluated is C5:C12. Enclosed in quotation marks ("), the criterion is greater than or equal to 30,000. The sum range C5:C12 contains the potential cells to be summed. Excel performs the logical test C5:C12>=30000. Only the values of cells containing at least 30,000 in the range C5:C12 are summed. The formula also could be entered as =SUMIF(C5:C12,">=30000") without the last argument because the range and sum range are the same.

The range will be used both to evaluate for criteria and to calculate the result if the sum range is not specified in a SUMIF formula.

How the COUNTIFS Function Works

The formula =COUNTIFS(F5:F12,"Yes",G5:G12,"Yes") is used as an example to explain the function result. The range F5:F12 is evaluated for cells containing the text *Yes. Also, the range* G5:G12 is evaluated for *Yes*. Only records meeting both criteria are counted.

	A	B	C	D	E	F	G
4	**Team Leader**	**Nov. Goal**	**Nov. Raised**	**Dec. Goal**	**Dec. Raised**	**Achieved Nov. Goal?**	**Achieved Dec. Goal?**
5	Abbott	$25,000	$24,500	$25,000	$31,810		Yes
6	Debowski	$90,000	$92,200	$100,000	$95,350	Yes	
7	Faber	$40,000	$44,475	$60,000	$52,500	Yes	
8	Lemus	$80,000	$79,620	$100,000	$110,350		Yes
9	Martinez	$70,000	$52,170	$70,000	$66,000		
10	Nguyen	$25,000	$25,250	$45,000	$48,000	Yes	Yes
11	Park	$25,000	$27,570	$30,000	$31,680	Yes	Yes
12	Weinstein	$50,000	$45,650	$70,000	$67,000		
13						*Count:*	**2**

The COUNTIFS function finds two team leaders who meet both criteria of ***Yes in columns F and G.***

DEVELOP YOUR SKILLS 14.4.1

Create a SUMIF Function

In this exercise, you will use the SUMIF function to add cells containing $30,000 or greater in monthly fundraising.

1. Display the **November** worksheet of the Awards workbook.
2. Enter **Raised at Least $30,000** in **cell A13**.
3. Widen **column A** to fit the text in **cell A13**.
4. Use **Format Painter** to copy the number format from **cell C12 to C13**.
5. Format the **range A13:C13** as bold.
   Next you will create a formula that adds the values in cells where the amount raised is at least $30,000.
6. Select **cell C13** and click the **Insert Function** button in the Formula Bar.
7. Follow these steps to find the SUMIF function:

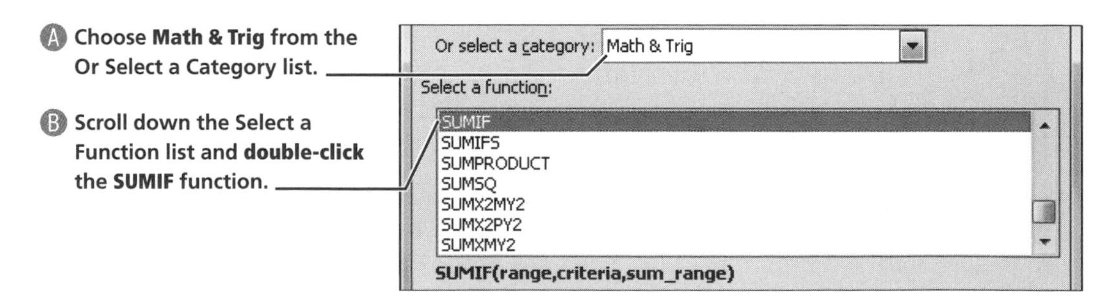

The Function Arguments dialog box appears for the SUMIF function.

8. If necessary, move the **Function Arguments** dialog box out of the way of **column C** by dragging its title bar.

9. Follow these steps to specify the SUMIF function arguments:

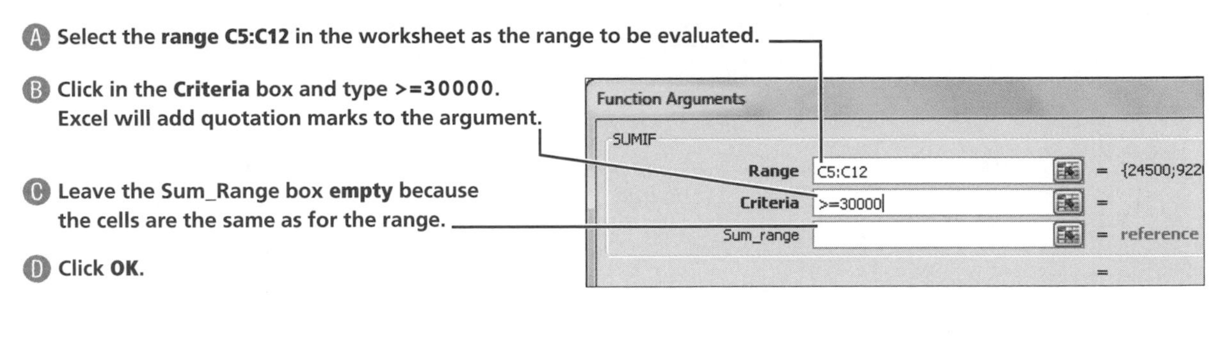

A Select the range C5:C12 in the worksheet as the range to be evaluated.
B Click in the Criteria box and type >=30000. Excel will add quotation marks to the argument.
C Leave the Sum_Range box empty because the cells are the same as for the range.
D Click OK.
Function Arguments
SUMIF
Range
C5:C12
= {24500;922
Criteria
>=30000
=
Sum_range
= reference
=

10. Review the completed formula in the Formula Bar.
The formula is =SUMIF(C5:C12, ">=30000"). The result is $314,115.

C13	=SUMIF(C5:C12,">=30000")		
A	B	C	D
12 Weinstein	$50,000	$45,650	($4,350)
13 **Raised at Least $30,000**		**$314,115**	

11. **Save** the changes, and leave the workbook **open**.

14.5 Using Logical Functions in Formulas

Video Lesson labyrinthelab.com/videos

In the preceding topic, you used the SUMIF function to sum values that met certain criteria. Excel provides several logical functions that allow you to customize your criteria when comparing data. The IF function is the basis of many formulas used for decision making. The IF function performs a logical test that you design. You can use the AND, OR, and NOT functions in IF formulas to specify one or more criteria to be checked. AND requires that all conditions be met, but OR is satisfied with any one of the conditions. Excel displays *TRUE* or performs the specified action when the criteria are met. Excel displays *FALSE* or performs a different action when the criteria are not met.

IF, AND, OR, and NOT Function Syntax

The following table describes the generic parts of the logical functions IF, AND, OR, and NOT.

Function	Syntax
IF	IF(logical test, value if true, value if false)
AND	AND(condition1, condition2,...)
OR	OR(condition1, condition2,...)
NOT	NOT(condition)

The following table outlines the arguments of these logical functions.

Argument	Description
Logical test	The condition being checked using a comparison operator, such as =, >, <, >=, <=, or <> (not equal to)
Value if true	The value, text in quotation (") marks, or calculation returned if the logical test result is found to be true
Value if false	The value, text in quotation (") marks, or calculation returned if the logical test result is found to be false
Condition	A logical expression to be evaluated as true or false; one of multiple expressions evaluated by an AND function or an OR function

How Logical Functions Work Together

The formula =IF(AND(B5>=25000,B5<=50000),D5,"") is used as an example to explain the function results shown in the following illustration.

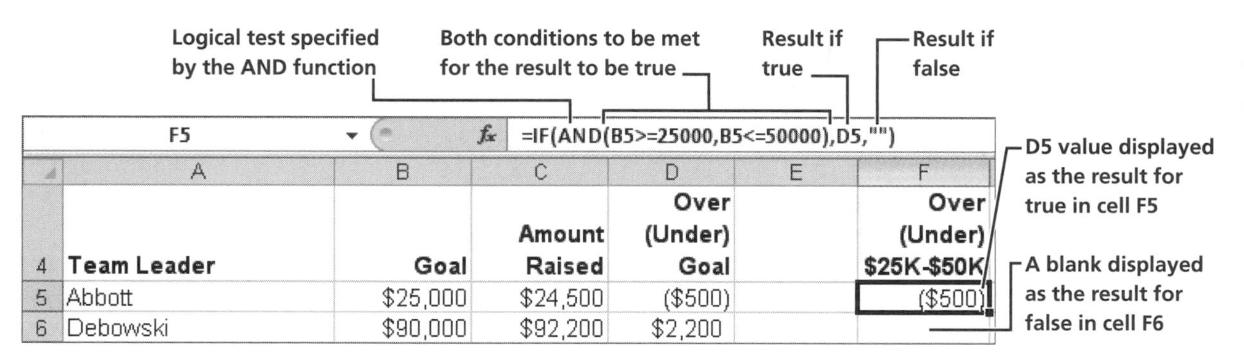

An IF function containing an AND function for the logical test

Excel performs the logical test AND(B5>=25000, B5<=50000). Parentheses surround the AND function's multiple arguments. The first argument seeks a monthly fundraising goal equal to or greater than $25,000. The second argument limits the goal to $50,000 or less. The logical test, therefore, searches for goals between $25,000 and $50,000. The AND function requires that all specified conditions be met for the result to be true. If a value is not between $25,000 and $50,000, the result of the logical test is false. D5 is the value-if-true argument in the IF function, and the contents of cell D5 will be displayed in the formula cell when true. The value-if-false argument "" (quotation marks without any text between them) indicates that the formula cell will be blank when false.

The logical test NOT(L5=M5) could be used in an IF formula to ensure that two values are not identical. If the value in L5 is not equal to the value in M5, the value-if-true action is performed. If the values are equal, the value-if-false action is performed.

IFERROR Function Syntax

The IFERROR function checks a formula for an error. The generic parts of the IFERROR logical function are shown in the following table.

Function	Syntax
IFERROR	IFERROR(value, value if error)

The following table outlines the arguments of the IFERROR function.

Argument	Description
Value	The formula being checked for an error
Value if error	The value, text in quotation (") marks, or calculation returned if the formula result is found to be an error

Excel checks formulas and returns the following error types described in the following table.

Error Type	Description	Common Cause
#DIV/0!	Value is divided by 0	Divisor cell referenced in the formula contains 0 or is empty
#N/A	Value not available	Cell referenced in the formula is empty
#NAME?	Text in a formula is not recognized	Misspelled or nonexistent range name in formula
#NULL!	Nonadjacent areas referenced in a formula	The existence of a space character instead of punctuation, such as a comma (,)
#NUM!	Invalid numeric value in a formula or function	Nonnumeric text in a function that requires a numeric argument
#REF!	Invalid cell reference	The editing or deletion of cell(s) referenced in the formula
#VALUE!	Incorrect data type used in a formula	Cell referenced in the formula contains text rather than a value

How the IFERROR Function Works

Inexperienced Excel users may not recognize Excel's error types, such as #N/A, displayed in formula result cells. Adding the IFERROR function to a formula allows you to display a descriptive message rather than the error type, as shown in the following illustration on the right. You also may define messages, such as "NA" (Not Applicable) or "0," to display when error results are acceptable.

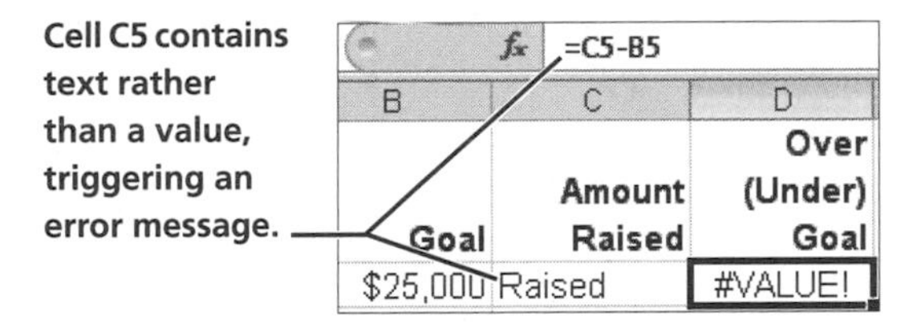

The formula result displays the normal #VALUE! error message when an error is found.

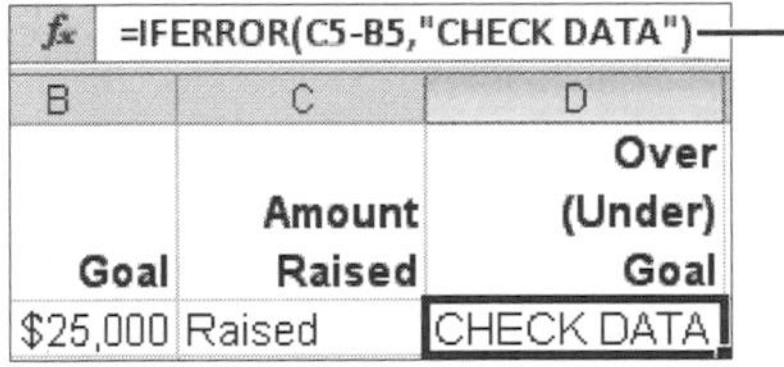

The defined error message is enclosed within quotation marks (").

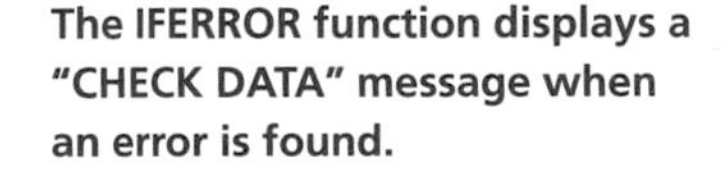

The IFERROR function displays a "CHECK DATA" message when an error is found.

The IFERROR function should not be confused with the ISERROR function. First available in Excel 2007, IFERROR requires only a value-if-error action to be specified. Earlier Excel versions require a lengthier IF(ISERROR(logical test),value-if-true, value if false) formula structure.

DEVELOP YOUR SKILLS 14.5.1

Use Logical Functions

In this exercise, you will use the IF and AND functions to create a formula. The formula result displays the difference between the goal and the amount raised for team leaders whose fundraising goals were between $25,000 and $50,000.

Use the IF Function

1. Display the **November** worksheet in the Awards workbook, if necessary.
2. Select **cell F5**, and choose **Formulas→Function Library→Logical** →**IF** from the Ribbon.
   You may use the Function Library as an alternative to the Insert Function button on the Formula Bar.
3. If necessary, move the **Function Arguments** dialog box out of the way by dragging its title bar until you can see **columns B–D**.

Specify an Argument Using the AND Function

4. Follow these steps to enter the IF function arguments:

A Taking care to type the punctuation as shown, enter **`and(B5>=25000,B5<=50000)`** in the **Logical_Test** box.

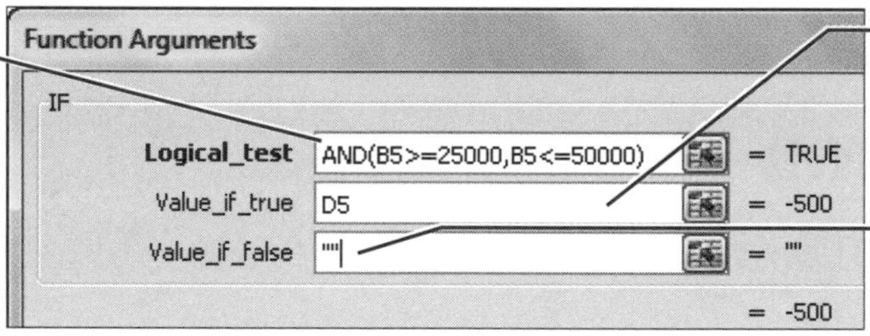

Function Arguments

IF

Logical_test	AND(B5>=25000,B5<=50000)	=	TRUE
Value_if_true	D5	=	-500
Value_if_false	""	=	""
		=	-500

B **Tap** Tab **to select the Value_If_True box, and select cell D5 in the worksheet.**

C **Tap** Tab **to select the Value_If_False box, and type "" (use** Shift**+' twice to type the quotation marks).**

In the Function Arguments dialog box, notice that the logical test evaluates as TRUE at the right of its text box. Both arguments that you specified with the AND function are true. The Value_If_True result is –500.

5. Click **OK**.
6. Use **Format Painter** to apply the formatting from **cell D5** to **cell F5**.
   The result in cell F5 should appear as ($500).

Copy the IF Formula

7. Use **AutoFill** to copy the formula in **cell F5** to the **range F6:F12**.

	A	B	C	D	E	F
4	**Team Leader**	**Goal**	**Amount Raised**	**Over (Under) Goal**		**Over (Under) $25K-$50K**
5	Abbott	$25,000	$24,500	($500)		($500)
6	Debowski	$90,000	$92,200	$2,200		
7	Faber	$40,000	$44,475	$4,475		$4,475
8	Lemus	$80,000	$79,620	($380)		
9	Martinez	$70,000	$52,170	($17,830)		
10	Nguyen	$25,000	$25,250	$250		$250
11	Park	$25,000	$27,570	$2,570		$2,570
12	Weinstein	$50,000	$45,650	($4,350)		($4,350)
13	**Raised at Least $30,000**		**$314,115**			

Values appear in column F for five records that meet both conditions you specified with the AND function. The other formula cells in column F appear blank, which you specified as the Value_If_False argument.

8. **Save** the changes, **close** the workbook, and leave Excel **open**.

14.6 Using Functions to Format Text

Video Lesson labyrinthelab.com/videos

Workbook data may be imported from sources other than Excel. These data may not be formatted as you wish. For example, employee names may be contained in one column. Sorting and filtering the names would be much easier if the names were separated into three columns for last name, first name, and middle name. Some names may not begin with a capital letter. Excel's text functions can help you clean up the data.

Creating Formulas with Text Functions

You create the formulas in a blank area of a worksheet to duplicate the data using the formats that you specify. You may use the Paste Values command to convert the formulas into values. Then you may delete the original unformatted data, if you wish. You may specify the text argument in a formula as a cell reference, another formula that results in text, or specific text surrounded by quotation marks.

If you are familiar with Excel macros and VBA (Visual Basic for Applications), you may program a macro that converts text in a range of cells or an entire worksheet rather than use functions.

Changing the Case of Text with PROPER, LOWER, and UPPER

The PROPER function changes the first letter of each word in the text to uppercase and the other letters of the word to lowercase. The LOWER function changes all text to lowercase, and UPPER converts all text to uppercase. You should check the converted text for unintended results. For example, the PROPER function converts "JAMES DENTON II" to "James Denton Ii." You may edit such cells manually. The syntax of these functions is shown in the following table.

Function	Syntax
PROPER	PROPER(text)
LOWER	LOWER(text)
UPPER	UPPER(text)

In the illustration of the three function formulas below, the original text is in column A. The PROPER, LOWER, and UPPER formulas and their results are in column B.

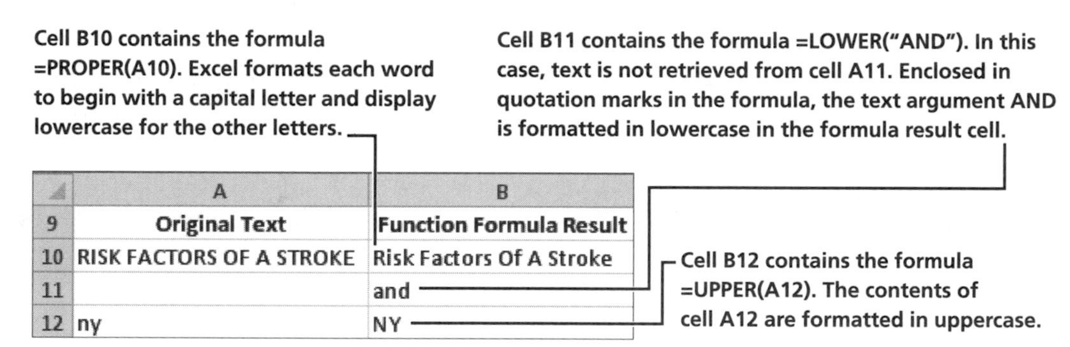

The results of the PROPER, LOWER, and UPPER functions

Using SUBSTITUTE to Replace Text

The SUBSTITUTE function changes the specified text characters to a different set of characters. The function, which is case sensitive, looks for an exact match. If an exact match is not found, the original text is displayed in the formula result cell.

The generic parts of the function are shown in the following table.

Function	Syntax
SUBSTITUTE	SUBSTITUTE(text, old text, new text, [instance number)]

The following table outlines the arguments of the SUBSTITUTE function.

Argument	Description
Text	The text to be searched
Old text	The text to be replaced, which may be in a cell, returned by a formula result, or enclosed in quotation (") marks as the function argument
New text	The text to be substituted for the old text
Instance number	(Optional) The occurrence of old text to be replaced within the full text, as in 2 to substitute only the second instance of "e" in "Indexed." All instances, if the instance number is omitted

The formula =SUBSTITUTE(I5,"Nurse Aid,""Nurse Aide") is used as an example to illustrate the function arguments and results shown below. The formula was entered in cell B5 and copied down column B. In this example, the optional instance number argument is not included because the text appears only once in the cell contents.

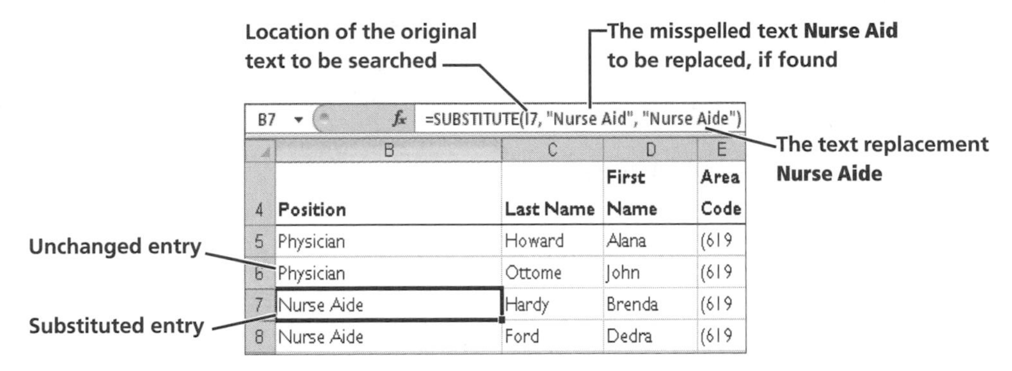

The SUBSTITUTE function only replaces text for which it finds an exact match.

Calculating the Text Length with LEN

The LEN function counts the characters, including spaces, in the specified text string, which may be in a cell, returned by a formula result, or enclosed in quotation (") marks as the function argument. The LEN function often is used with other functions to obtain a desired result. The syntax of the function is shown in the following table.

Function	Syntax
LEN	LEN(text)

You can use the LEN function to locate some input errors in cells. In the following example, the formula =LEN(F5) counts the characters in a phone number. The formula was copied down column G. Cell F8 contains the number 555-00027. The formula result is 9. Any result other than 8 indicates an input error.

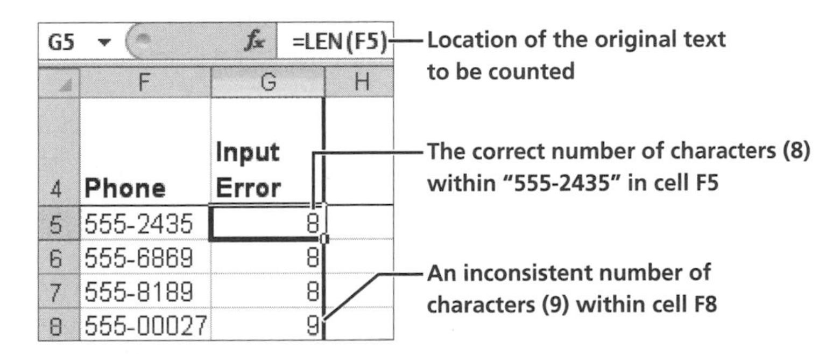

The LEN function counts the total characters in the specified text.

The Conditional Formatting command in the Home ribbon may be used to highlight cells containing abnormal results.

Using FIND to Locate Text

The FIND function locates a specific text string within text. The result returns the starting character position of the found text. You may specify an optional character number at which Excel is to start the search. Excel counts characters from the left of the text to arrive at this character. The FIND function may be used with other functions to obtain a desired result. The syntax of the FIND function is shown in the following table.

Function	Syntax
FIND	FIND(find text,within text,[character start number)]

The following table describes the arguments of the FIND function.

Argument	Description
Find text	The text to be found
Within text	The text in which the search will take place, which may be in a cell, returned by a formula result, or enclosed in quotation (") marks as the function argument
Character start number	(Optional) The starting character for the search, counted from the left in the searched text; the first character, if the start number is omitted

The function =FIND (" ",K5) is used to explain the function arguments in the following illustration. The search is performed in the contents of cell K5. A space is found at the sixth character of the text, and the function result is 6.

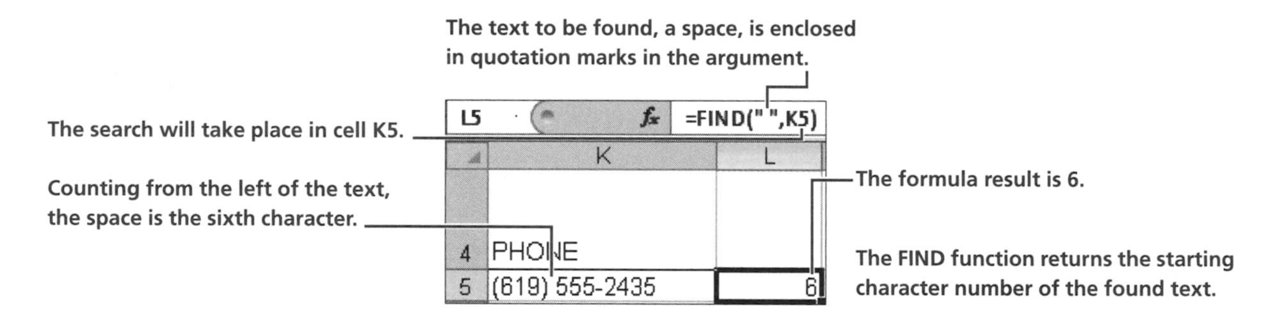
The text to be found, a space, is enclosed in quotation marks in the argument.
The search will take place in cell K5.
Counting from the left of the text, the space is the sixth character.
L5
=FIND(" ",K5)
K
L
4 PHONE
5 (619) 555-2435
6
The formula result is 6.
The FIND function returns the starting character number of the found text.

Using LEFT, MID, and RIGHT to Extract Text

Data copied into an Excel worksheet may contain extra characters that you do not want. You can use the LEFT, MID, and RIGHT functions to extract a certain number of characters, depending on their location in the text string. For example, you can use the RIGHT function to extract the last four digits of a social security number. The MID function counts the characters from the left until it arrives at the starting character number you specified. The extracted characters display in the formula result cell, and the original text is not affected. The syntax of these functions is shown in the following table.

Function	Syntax
LEFT	LEFT(text,[number of characters])
MID	MID(text,character start number, number of characters)
RIGHT	RIGHT(text,number of characters)

The arguments in the LEFT, MID, and RIGHT functions are described in the following table.

Argument	Description
Text	The text characters to be counted or extracted
Number of characters	(Optional for the LEFT and RIGHT functions) The total characters to be extracted; the first character, if this argument is omitted
Character start number	(Optional for the LEFT and RIGHT functions) The starting character to be extracted, counted from the left in the text; the first character, if the start number is omitted

The following illustration of the formula =LEFT(M5,3) explains the basic use of the LEFT function to extract text. Notice that the original text in cell M5 remains unchanged, and the result displays in the N5 formula cell.

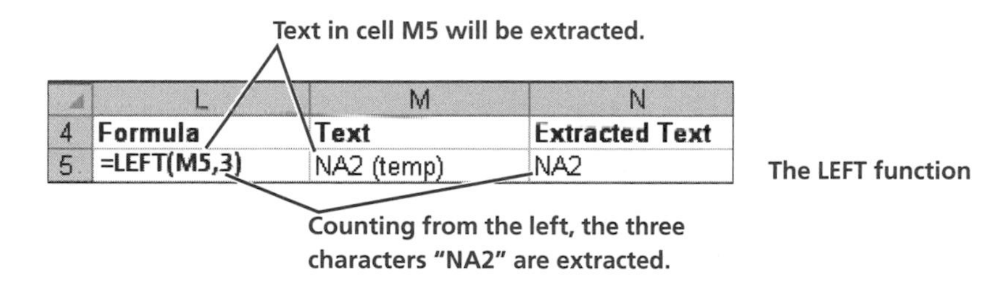

The LEFT function

The formula =RIGHT(M6,4) in cell N6 is used below to explain the basic use of the MID function to extract text.

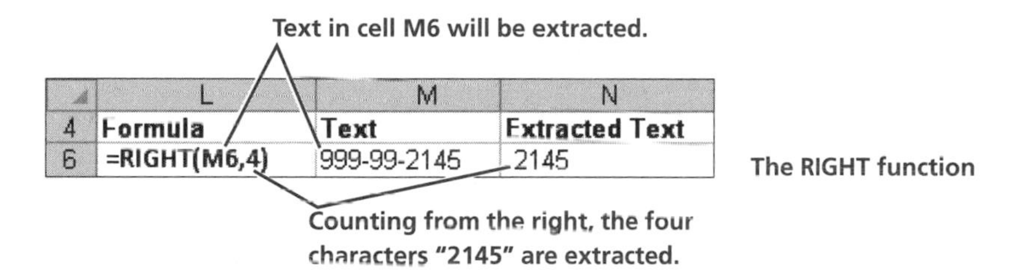

The RIGHT function

The formula =MID(M7,4,3) in cell N7 explains the basic use of the MID function to extract text. Remember that the start number and number-of-characters arguments are required for this function.

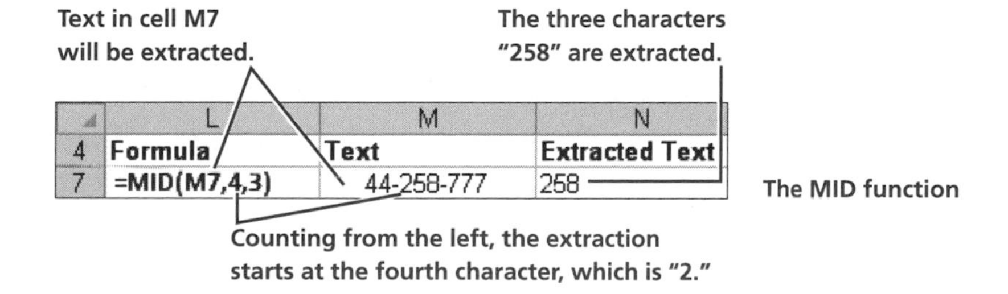

The MID function

Splitting Names

The formulas in the following table use multiple functions to extract a last name, first name, and middle name into separate columns. Function formulas work well to perform this task when the names do not have the same number of units. For example, a middle name may be included for some names, but not for others. In the following formulas, the FIND function looks for a space in the name, expressed by the argument " " as a space surrounded by quotation marks. To locate the middle name, the argument LEN(C7&D7) sums the character length of the first name and last name. Do not be concerned if you do not understand the complexity of the formulas, but you may challenge yourself to think about how they work. These formulas may be used when no spaces exist within a name unit. For example, the first name must be "LaRonda" or "Laronda" rather than "La Ronda." Any names with spaces, titles, or suffixes, such as "Dr." or "Jr.," would need to be cleaned up manually.

Formula	Text Extracted	Original Text	Result
=RIGHT(J5,LEN(J5)-FIND("#",SUBSTITUTE(J5," ","#",LEN(J5)-LEN(SUBSTITUTE(J5," ","")))))	Last name	Jose Edgar Garcia	Garcia
=LEFT(J5,FIND(" ",J5))	First name	Jose Edgar Garcia	Jose
=IF(LEN(C7&D7)+2>=LEN(J7),"", MID(J7,LEN(D7)+2,LEN(J7)-LEN(C7&D7)-2))	Middle name	Jose Edgar Garcia	Edgar

The Text to Columns command in the Data ribbon can split names into separate columns. The names, however, must all contain the same number of name units. If some names contain a middle name, then all other names must contain a blank field for the middle name unit.

DEVELOP YOUR SKILLS 14.6.1

Use Functions to Format Text

In this exercise, you will use various text functions to clean up data. You will substitute text to correct a misspelling. You will split the area codes and phone numbers into two columns. You also will check the length of the phone numbers to identify any input errors. Finally, you will examine formulas that split employee names into columns for last name and first name, as well as format the names with the proper case.

Use the SUBSTITUTE Function

1. **Open** the Data Clean Up workbook from the Lesson 14 folder.
   Take a few moments to review the data in columns H–K. "Nurse Aid" is misspelled in column I, and some names in column J do not display the correct case. You wish to split the phone numbers into two columns. You will create text formulas in columns B and E–G to reformat some of the data.
2. Select **cell B7**, and choose **Formulas→Function Library→Text** →**SUBSTITUTE** from the Ribbon.
3. If necessary, move the **Function Arguments** dialog box out of the way by dragging its title bar until you can see **row 7**.

4. Follow these steps to complete the Function Argument dialog box:

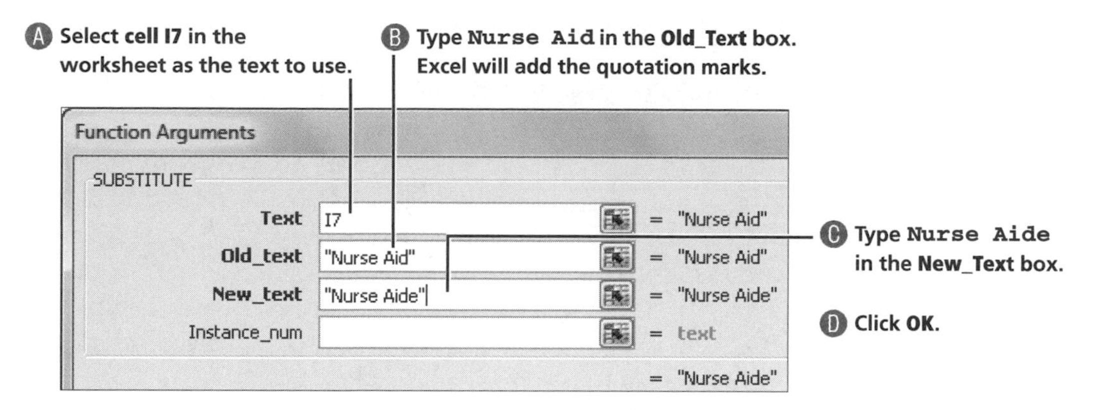

A Select cell I7 in the worksheet as the text to use.
B Type Nurse Aid in the Old_Text box. Excel will add the quotation marks.
Function Arguments
SUBSTITUTE
Text
I7
= "Nurse Aid"
Old_text
"Nurse Aid"
= "Nurse Aid"
New_text
"Nurse Aide"
= "Nurse Aide"
Instance_num
= text
= "Nurse Aide"
C Type Nurse Aide in the New_Text box.
D Click OK.

Cell B7 displays Nurse Aide. *The Formula Bar displays =SUBSTITUTE(I7,"Nurse Aid","Nurse Aide"). The SUBSTITUTE function replaced the original text. If this did not happen, make certain that you typed the text entries exactly as instructed, including the capital letter at the beginning of each word.*

5. Copy **cell B7** and paste in the **range B5:B8**.
   The original text Physician *from cells I5 and I6 displays in cells B5 and B6. The original cells did not contain* Nurse Aid, *and no replacement was necessary.*

Split the Phone Numbers

In the next steps, you will split the phone numbers so that the area code appears in column E and the remainder in column F.

6. Select **cell E5**, and choose **Formulas→Function Library→Text** →**LEFT** from the Ribbon.
7. Follow these steps to complete the Function Arguments dialog box:

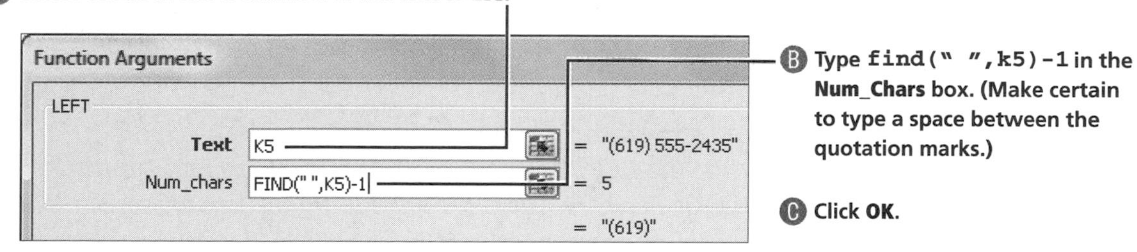

A Select cell K5 in the worksheet as the text to use.
Function Arguments
LEFT
Text
K5
= "(619) 555-2435"
Num_chars
FIND(" ",K5)-1
= 5
= "(619)"
B Type find(" ",k5)-1 in the Num_Chars box. (Make certain to type a space between the quotation marks.)
C Click OK.

The Formula Bar displays =LEFT(K5,FIND(" ",K5)-1). Cell K5 contains the text (619) 555-2435. The FIND function locates the space after the area code in cell K5. Including the space, the number of characters in (619) is six. You entered –1 to subtract the space character. The Num_Chars argument then evaluates as 5. The result in cell E5 is (619).

8. Use the **AutoFill** handle to copy **cell E5** down to the **range E6:E8**.
9. Select **cell F5**, and choose **Formulas→Function Library→Text** →**RIGHT** from the Ribbon.

10. Follow these steps to complete the Function Arguments dialog box:

Ⓐ Select **cell K5** in the worksheet as the text to use.

Function Arguments		
RIGHT		
Text	K5	= "(619) 555-2435"
Num_chars	LEN(K5)-FIND(" ",K5)	= 8
		= "555-2435"

Ⓑ Type `len(k5)-find(" ",k5)` in the **Num_Chars** box. (Make certain to type a space between the quotation marks.)

Ⓒ Click **OK**.

The Formula Bar displays =RIGHT(K5,LEN(K5)-FIND(" ",K5)). The result in cell F5 is 555-2438. The formula extracted eight characters of the phone number from the right of the entry.

This Num_Chars argument is more complex in this formula. The LEN function calculates 14 characters as the text length in cell K5. Again, the FIND function locates the space after the area code. The six characters up through the space are subtracted from fourteen. The Num_Char argument evaluates as eight characters counted from the right.

11. Use the **AutoFill** handle to copy **cell F5** down to the **range F6:F8**.
Notice that the phone number in cell F8 contains one extra digit.

Use the LEN Function

12. Select **cell G5**, and enter the formula **`=len(f5)`**.

13. Use the **AutoFill** handle to copy **cell G5** down to the **range G6:G8**.
Cell G8 displays 9 as the character length, indicating an input error. You can use the LEN function to locate some input errors based on the character length in cells.

Examine Function Formulas That Split the Names

14. Select **cell C5**, and review the formula in the Formula Bar.
The formula is =PROPER(RIGHT(J5,LEN(J5)-FIND(" ",J5))). This formula extracts the last name from the text ALANA HOWARD *in cell J5. The RIGHT, LEN, and FIND functions are similar to those you used to extract the phone numbers in column F. The PROPER function capitalizes the first letter of the result and changes the other letters to lowercase. The result in cell C5 is* Howard.

15. Select **cell D5**, and review the formula in the Formula Bar.
The formula is =PROPER(LEFT(J5,FIND(" ",J5)-1)). This formula extracts the first name from the text ALANA HOWARD *in cell J5. The LEFT and FIND functions are similar to those you used to extract the five-character area codes in column E. The PROPER function adjusts the case of the text. The result in cell D5 is* Alana.

16. **Save** the changes, **close** the workbook, and leave Excel **open**.

14.7 Tracing Formulas

Video Lesson labyrinthelab.com/videos

Excel's auditing tools are useful for analyzing complex formulas that are dependent on other formulas. The auditing tools are also quite helpful for locating errors in formulas.

The Formula Auditing Tools

The Formula Auditing tools are used primarily for displaying and hiding cell tracers. Cell tracers are arrows that identify precedent and dependent cells of formulas. The Formula Auditing group of the Formulas ribbon is shown at right.

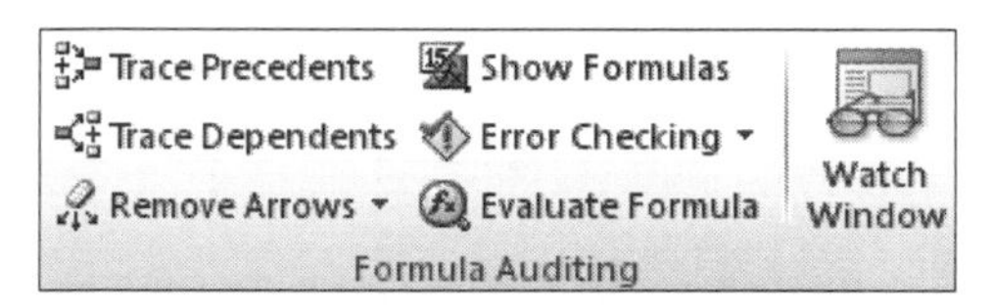

The Formula Auditing tools on the Formulas Ribbon

Tracing Precedents

The Trace Precedents command displays arrows that point from the cells referenced by a formula to the cell containing the formula. A formula may reference cells containing values and/or cells that contain other formulas. Thus, a formula may have several levels of precedents. Repeating the Trace Precedents command adds the next level to the display. The following illustrations show the Awards workbook with the precedent cell tracers (arrows) displayed for the award points formula in cell F6. The first level includes cells C6 and E6, referenced in the formula. Cell E6 contains its own formula for the award rate. The second level displays the precedent for that formula, which depends on a lookup table.

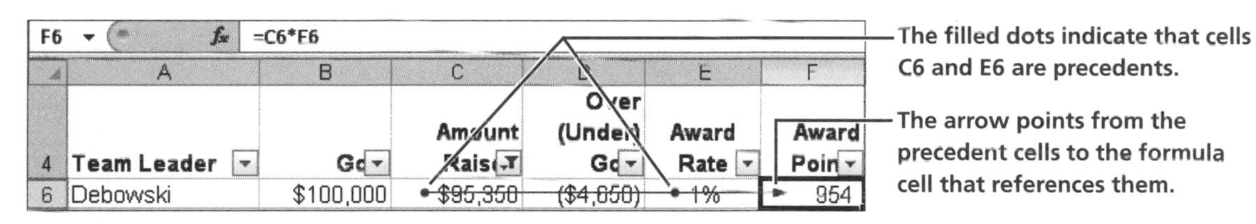

The filled dots indicate that cells C6 and E6 are precedents.

The arrow points from the precedent cells to the formula cell that references them.

The first level of precedents for the formula C6*E6

	A	B	C	D	E	F	G
4	Team Leader	Gd	Amount Rais	Over (Under) Gd	Award Rate	Award Poin	Achieved Goal?
6	Debowski	$100,000	$95,350	($4,650)	1%	954	Below Goal
7	Faber	$60,000	$52,500	($7,500)	0%	-	Under Achiever
8	Lemus	$100,000	$110,350	$10,350	7%	7,725	Over Achiever
9	Martinez	$70,000	$66,000	($4,000)	1%	660	Below Goal
12	Weinstein	$70,000	$67,000	($3,000)	1%	670	Below Goal
13			**$391,200**	**($1,760)**			
14							
15					**Over (Under) Goal**	**Award Rate**	**Message**
16					($100,000)	0%	Under Achiever
17					($5,000)	1%	Below Goal
18					$0	3%	At Goal
19					$5,000	5%	Above Goal
20					$10,000	7%	Over Achiever

The second level showing the lookup table as a precedent for the VLOOKUP formula in cell E6

DEVELOP YOUR SKILLS 14.7.1

Trace and Clear Precedent Arrows

In this exercise, you will trace to cells that make up the formula in cell F6 and then trace precedents for cell G6.

1. Select **cell F6** in the **December** worksheet of the Awards workbook.
2. Choose **Formulas→Formula Auditing→Trace Precedents** from the Ribbon.
   Tracer arrows appear, indicating that the formula in cell F6 is dependent on cells C6 and E6. Next you will look for any precedents to those two cells.
3. Choose **Formulas→Formula Auditing→Trace Precedents** again in the Ribbon.
   A tracer arrow from the table array in rows 16–20 to cell E6 appears. This shows that the formula in cell E6 depends on the table array. Cell C6 has no precedents because it does not contain a formula.
4. Choose **Formulas→Formula Auditing→Remove Arrows menu ▾→Remove Precedent Arrows** from the Ribbon to hide the second level of tracer arrows.
   Now only the first precedent level displays.
5. Choose **Formulas→Formula Auditing→Remove Arrows** to hide all tracer arrows.
   This command removes all levels at one time.
6. Select **cell G6** and choose **Formulas→Formula Auditing→Trace Precedents** from the Ribbon.
   The formula in cell G6 clearly is dependent on cell D6 and cell E16 in the table array.
7. Choose **Formulas→Formula Auditing→Remove Arrows** to hide all tracer arrows.
8. You made no changes, so just leave the workbook **open**.

Tracing Dependents

Video Lesson labyrinthelab.com/videos

The Trace Dependents command shows you the dependents for a selected cell. Dependents are formula cells that reference the selected cell. Repeating the Trace Dependents command displays an additional set of arrows that trace the next level of dependents until all dependent cells are identified.

DEVELOP YOUR SKILLS 14.7.2

Trace Dependents

In this exercise, you will trace to cells that are dependent on the value in cell C6.

Before You Begin: You must have completed Develop Your Skills 14.4.1, 14.5.1, 14.6.1, and 14.7.1.

1. **Open** the Awards workbook, display the **December** worksheet, and select **cell C6**.
2. Choose **Formulas→Formula Auditing→Trace Dependents** from the Ribbon.
   As indicated by the three arrow heads shown here, cells C13, D6, and F6 include a reference to cell C6 in their formulas. You will trace the dependents for those three cells in the next step.

	C	D	E	F	G
4	Amount Rais	Over (Under) Gc	Award Rate	Award Poin	Achieved Goal?
6	$95,350	($4,650)	1%	954	Below Goal
7	$52,500	($7,500)	0%	-	Under Achiever
8	$110,350	$10,350	7%	7,725	Over Achiever
9	$66,000	($4,000)	1%	660	Below Goal
12	$67,000	($3,000)	1%	670	Below Goal
13	**$391,200**	**($1,760)**			

3. Repeat the **Trace Dependents** command.
   Additional tracer arrows point from cell D6 to cells E6 and G6. The filled dot in cell D6 indicates that the cell is a precedent for cell E6, which has a formula dependent on cell D6. Another tracer arrow points from cell D6 to the subtotal formula in cell D13.

	C	D	E	F	
4	Amount Rais	Over (Under) Gc	Award Rate	Award Poin	Ach G
6	$95,350	($4,650)	1%	854	Below
7	$52,500	($7,500)	0%	-	Under
8	$110,350	$10,350	7%	7,725	Over A
9	$66,000	($4,000)	1%	660	Below
12	$67,000	($3,000)	1%	670	Below
13	**$391,200**	**($1,760)**			

4. Choose **Formulas→Formula Auditing→Remove Arrows** to remove the tracer arrows.
5. Select **cell G16** in the table array and choose the **Trace Dependents** command.
   A number of tracer arrows are drawn from cell G16 to cells with formulas dependent on the data in that cell.
6. Repeat the **Trace Dependents** command until all dependent cells are revealed.
7. Use the **Remove Arrows** command to remove the tracer arrows.
8. **Close** the workbook and leave Excel **open**.

14.8 Auditing Formula Errors

Video Lesson labyrinthelab.com/videos

Cells with formulas sometimes display error messages such as #VALUE!, #NAME!, or #DIV/0!. A formula may display an incorrect result rather than a message. Errors may be caused by incorrect cell entries in precedent cells, empty cells, incorrect or missing defined names, or incorrect formulas. Excel can help you identify cells that contain errors that prevent the display of correct formula results.

If error checking does not appear to be working, ensure that Enable Background Error Checking and the desired Error Checking Rules have a checkmark in the Formulas category of the Excel Options dialog box.

Auditing Single Cells

Excel continuously checks for common errors as you work, depending on the error checking options selected in the Excel Options dialog box. Excel alerts you to inconsistent formulas and other potential errors by displaying a small triangle icon in the upper left of a cell. You may handle marked cells one cell at a time. An error checking menu is available while the cell is selected to get help, show calculation steps, edit the formula, or ignore the error. The menu commands vary depending on the error type. Excel marks a SUM formula when it determines that adjacent cells are not included in the sum range. If the range is correct, you would choose the Ignore Error command from the menu.

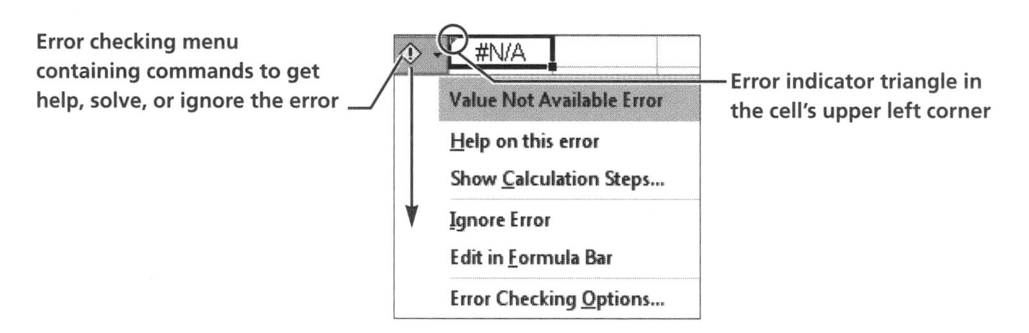

Error Checking in Multiple Cells

The Error Checking command on the Formulas ribbon allows you to navigate and respond to error messages throughout the worksheet, similar to the spell checker. The Error Checking dialog box summarizes each error and provides the same commands as the error checking menu available on a single cell.

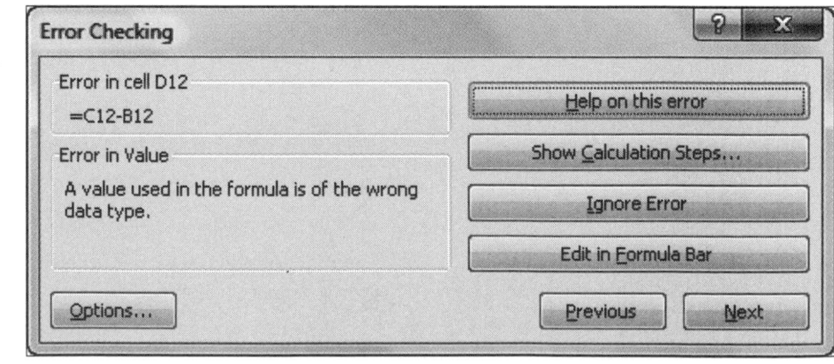

Tracing Errors

The Trace Error command on the Formulas ribbon draws arrows that point from any precedent cells to the selected cell containing the error message.

QUICK REFERENCE	AUDITING FORMULAS
Task	**Procedure**
Audit a single cell marked as containing an error	■ Select the cell containing a triangle icon in its upper-left corner. ■ Click the error checking button to the left of the cell and choose a command from the menu.
Audit all cells marked as containing an error	■ Choose Formulas→Formula Auditing→Error Checking from the Ribbon. ■ Choose a command in the Error Checking dialog box. ■ Click Resume after editing a formula to view the next error.
Trace precedents for a cell displaying an error message	■ Select the cell displaying the error message. ■ Choose Formulas→Formula Auditing→Error Checking→Trace Error from the Ribbon to display tracer arrows.
Restore triangle icons for ignored errors	■ Choose File→Options →Formulas category. ■ Under Error Checking, click Reset Ignored Errors.
Show calculation steps in any formula	■ Select a cell containing a formula. ■ Choose Formulas→Formula Auditing→Evaluate Formula from the Ribbon. ■ In the Evaluate Formula dialog box, click Step In to view more information about an underlined expression, if desired, and then click Step Out to display the result. ■ Click Evaluate to display the result of the next underlined expression. ■ Continue clicking Evaluate until all expressions are evaluated and the formula result displays.

DEVELOP YOUR SKILLS 14.8.1

Check Errors in Formulas

In this exercise, you will respond to formula error messages using Excel's error checking commands.

Enable Error Checking

1. **Open** the Error Check workbook from the Lesson 14 folder.
2. Choose **File→Options** →**Formulas** category.

3. Follow these steps to review the error checking options, but do not make any changes unless your instructor directs:

Error Checking

Enable background error checking

Indicate errors using this color:

Reset Ignored Errors

Error checking rules

Cells containing formulas that result in an error

Inconsistent calculated column formula in tables

Cells containing years represented as 2 digits

Numbers formatted as text or preceded by an apostrophe

Formulas inconsistent with other formulas in the region

Formulas which omit cells in a region

Unlocked cells containing formulas

Formulas referring to empty cells

Data entered in a table is invalid

A Make certain that the **Enable Background Error Checking** box has a checkmark.

B Review the items in the **Error Checking Rules** area of the Excel Options dialog box.

C Hover the mouse over any information icon to display a **ScreenTip** that explains the option.

4. Click **Cancel** (or **OK** if your instructor directs you to change any options).

Edit a Formula to Correct an Error

5. Notice that a #REF! error message displays in **cell G9**.
6. Select **cell G9**.
   The Formula Bar displays =VLOOKUP(D9,Award_Table,4). The formula in cell G9 is dependent on the value in cell D9 and the table array in rows 16–20.
7. Point to the **error checking menu button** to the left of the selected cell.

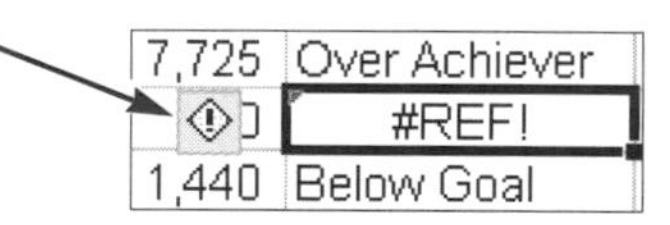

7,725
Over Achiever
#REF!
1,440
Below Goal

   A ScreenTip displays possible causes of the error, including a reference error in the function. Cell D9 and the defined name Award_Table appear to be correct in the formula. The column index number, however, refers to a nonexisting column 4 in the table array. The column index number should refer to column 3.
8. Click the **error checking menu button** to the left of **cell G9** and choose **Edit in Formula Bar** from the menu.
9. Replace **4** with **3** in the formula and **tap** Enter to complete the entry.
   Cell G9 now correctly displays Below Goal.

Check for Errors

The Error Checking command is useful for responding to multiple error messages in a worksheet.

10. Choose **Formulas→Formula Auditing→Error Checking** from the Ribbon.
    The Error Checking dialog box displays, and cell D12 is selected in the worksheet.
11. Move the dialog box, if necessary, to view **row 12** in the worksheet.
12. Click the **Help on This Error** button in the Error Checking dialog box.
13. Take a few moments to explore the help suggestions, and then **close** the Excel Help window.

14. Read the left side of the **Error Checking** dialog box.
    The dialog box displays the cell D12 formula and analyzes the problem as to an Error in Value. Notice that the a67000 entry in cell C12 is not a value.
15. Select **cell C12** in the worksheet, **delete** the letter "a" in the Formula Bar, and **complete** the entry.
16. Click **Resume in the Error Checking** dialog box.
    Correcting the error in cell C12 allowed the other formulas in row 12 to display correct results. No error messages now exist in any cells.
17. Click **OK** to respond to the message that error checking is complete.
18. **Save** the changes, **close** the workbook, and leave Excel **open**.

Evaluating Formulas

Video Lesson labyrinthelab.com/videos

The Evaluate Formula command allows you to see what each part of a formula includes. You may evaluate any formula, but this tool is particularly helpful with multiple-operator formulas. For example, in the formula =B13*(1-$F$18), the Evaluate Formula dialog box would show you the actual value of B13. The formula is easier to analyze than just looking at the cell reference. As you step through the evaluation process, you will see the actual values and calculations that make up the complete formula.

DEVELOP YOUR SKILLS 14.8.2

Evaluate a Formula

In this exercise, you will evaluate the projected contributions formula in the Calculations worksheet of a financial report.

1. **Open** the Financial Report workbook from the Lesson 14 folder.
   This workbook contains two worksheets. The Factors worksheet contains values that are used in formulas on the Calculations worksheet.
2. Select **cell B6** in the **Calculations** worksheet.
   *This cell contains the projected contributions formula =Factors!B2*Factors!B3*B5. Notice that the cell references include the Factors worksheet name because they are on a different worksheet.*
3. Choose **Formulas→Formula Auditing→Evaluate Formula** from the Ribbon.
   The Evaluate Formula dialog box displays the formula with the first expression underlined to indicate cell B2 in the Factors worksheet.
4. Click the **Evaluate** button in the Evaluate Formula dialog box.
   The first part of the formula, Factors!B2, is evaluated, and the cell's actual value of 1.05 is displayed in the dialog box.
5. Click the **Evaluate** button to evaluate the next part of the formula.
   The second expression of the formula evaluates as 10000, the actual value of cell B3 in the Factors worksheet.

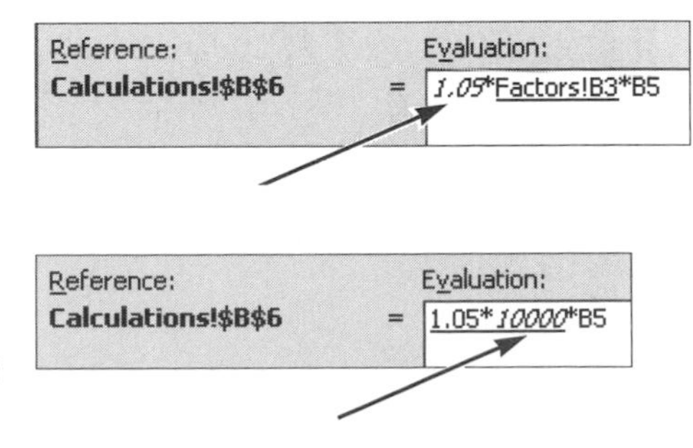

6. Click **Evaluate**.
   *The italicized result shows that the prior calculation 1.05%*10000 equals 10500. This product will be multipled by cell B5 in the Calculations worksheet.*

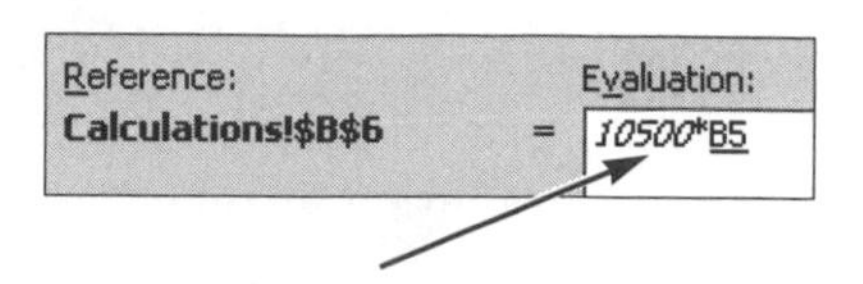

7. Continue to click the **Evaluate** button until the final answer of 2,100,000 is displayed in the Evaluate Formula dialog box.
   With every click of the Evaluate button, each part of the formula is displayed, showing you step by step how the final result of $2,100,000 is calculated.
8. Click **Restart** in the Evaluate Formula dialog box to repeat the evaluation process.
9. This time click **Step In** to preview the upcoming evaluation, and then click **Step Out** to complete the evaluation.
10. Continue using **Step In** and **Step Out** when the expression includes a cell reference, and then use **Evaluate** for the final steps of the formula evaluation.
11. When finished, close the **Evaluate Formula** dialog box.
12. **Close** the workbook **without** saving; you made no changes.

14.9 Concepts Review

Concepts Review labyrinthelab.com/excel10

To check your knowledge of the key concepts introduced in this lesson, complete the Concepts Review quiz by going to the URL listed above. If your classroom is using Labyrinth eLab, you may complete the Concepts Review quiz from within your eLab course.

Reinforce Your Skills

REINFORCE YOUR SKILLS 14.1

Create 3-D Cell References

In this exercise, you will add a new worksheet to the workbook and use a 3-D cell reference to add values from several worksheets.

Copy a Worksheet

1. **Open** the rs-Project Budget workbook from the Lesson 14 folder.
2. Display each worksheet in the workbook to see that they have an identical design.
   Cell B9 of each worksheet contains the total number of days to complete a task.
3. **Right-click** on the worksheet tab to copy the **Site Design Team** worksheet, then position the copy first in the worksheet order.
4. **Rename** the new worksheet as **`Budget`**.
5. Change the label in **cell A1** to **`Website Development Budget`**.
6. Change **cell A3** to **`Estimated Cost Per Day`** and center the label.
7. Delete the labels and values in the **range A4:B9**.
8. Type and align the entries in **cells A4 and A6** as shown in the following illustration.

	A	B
1	Website Development Budget	
2		
3	Estimated Cost Per Day	Days to Complete
4	$700	65
5		
6	Budget	

Enter a 3-D Cell Reference

You will use a 3-D cell reference to cell B9 in the four task worksheets to calculate the total number of worker-days for the entire project.

9. Select **cell B4**.
10. **Tap** [=].
11. Type **s** to display functions beginning with the letter *s* in the **Formula AutoComplete** function list. (Choose **File→Options→Formulas→Working with Formulas→ Formula AutoComplete** to turn the option on if the function list does not appear.)
12. Type **u** to display the SUM function in the **AutoComplete** list.
13. **Tap** [↓] twice to highlight SUM, and then **tap** [Tab] to select SUM.
    The function =SUM(displays in the cell and the Formula Bar.
14. Click the **Site Design Team** sheet tab.
15. **Hold down** [Shift] while you click the **Shopping Cart** sheet tab.

16. Select **cell B9** in the currently displayed worksheet.

17. Click **Enter** ✓ in the Formula Bar to complete the formula.
The result equals 63 total days. The formula totaled cell B9 from all four worksheets.

18. Examine the 3-D cell reference in the Formula Bar.
The formula displays as =SUM('Site Design Team:Shopping Cart Team'!B9). A colon (:) indicates the range of worksheet names, and an exclamation (!) point separates the worksheet reference from the cell reference. Single quotation marks (') surround the sheet name because they contain spaces.

The 3-D reference must refer to the same cell in each of the detail worksheets, but you may create the formula in any cell.

Create the Cost Formula

19. In **cell B6** of the **Budget** worksheet, enter the formula **=A4*B4** to calculate the budget needed to complete the website development project.

20. Format the budget amount as **Currency format with no decimal places**, if not already formatted so.

Test the 3-D Cell Reference

21. Display the **Site Design Team** worksheet and change the value in **cell B8** to **4**.
Take note of the new sum in cell B9.

22. Display the **Budget** worksheet, and verify that the total number of days increased to 65 in **cell B4** and the budget increased to $45,500 in **cell B6**.
3-D cell references allow you to calculate the values in several worksheets on a single summary worksheet.

23. **Save** the changes and **close** the workbook.

REINFORCE YOUR SKILLS 14.2

Create a Table Array and HLOOKUP Function

In this exercise, you will use a table array and the VLOOKUP function to assign the letter grades A–F to students based on their test scores. Then you will learn to use the Transpose command to convert the table array for use with the HLOOKUP function. You also will review how to edit properties for a defined name.

Create a Table Array

1. **Open** the rs-Test 1 Grades workbook from the Lesson 14 folder.

2. Enter the table array data in the **range F5:G9** as shown to the right.
Notice that you listed the test score values in ascending (lowest to highest) order so that the VLOOKUP function will assign the proper grade. In a moment, you will create a formula to determine the letter grades in column D.

	F	G
3	Grade Table	
4	Test Scores	Letter Grade
5	0	F
6	60	D
7	70	C
8	80	B
9	90	A

3. Taking care not to select the labels in rows 3 and 4, select the **range F5:G9**.

4. Click in the **Name** box on the left of the Formula Bar, and type **`Grade_Table`**.
5. **Tap** [Enter] to assign Grade_Table as the defined name for the table array.
   You may always use the absolute cell range for a table array and reference that range in the lookup formula. A defined name, however, usually is clearer.

Use the VLOOKUP Function

6. Select **cell D4** and click the **Insert Function** [fx] button in the Formula Bar.
7. Choose **All** from the Select a Category list in the Insert Function dialog box.
8. **Tap** [V] to jump to the functions beginning with the letter *V* in the Select a Function list.

Or select a category: All
Select a function:
VARP
VARPA
VDB
VLOOKUP
WEEKDAY
WEEKNUM
WEIBULL

9. Continue **tapping** [V] until VLOOKUP is highlighted, and then **tap** [Enter] to choose VLOOKUP.
10. Move the **Function Arguments** dialog box aside until you can see **columns D–G**.

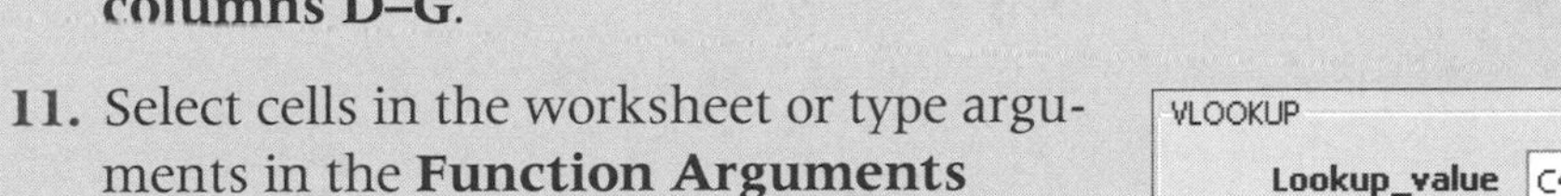

11. Select cells in the worksheet or type arguments in the **Function Arguments** dialog box as shown to the right.

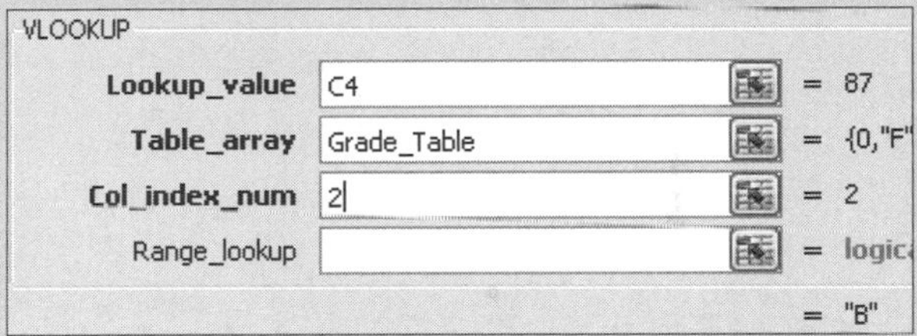

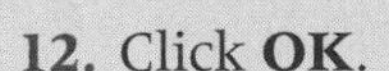

12. Click **OK**.
    The grade result should be B. Take a few moments to understand how this formula works. VLOOKUP searched down the left column of the table array for the lookup value 87 (the value in cell C4). It stopped at 80 because the lookup value is at least 80 but not 90. Traveling along row 8, the lookup proceeded to the second column in the table array and returned the letter grade B from cell G8.
13. Use **AutoFill** to copy the formula down the column for the other students.
    The worksheet should match the following illustration.

	A	B	C	D	E	F	G
3	**Last**	**First**	**Test Scores**	**Letter Grade**		**Grade Table**	
4	Espinoza	Marlo	87	B		Test Scores	Letter Grade
5	Kim	Alicia	95	A		0	F
6	Savant	Susan	34	F		60	D
7	Warren	Reed	67	D		70	C
8	Lee	Jimmy	82	B		80	B
9	Soth	Ashley	91	A		90	A
10	Sulai	Raj	94	A			
11	Brown	Bernice	78	C			

14. **Save** the changes.

Sort the List and Delete a Record

Notice that the lookup table is located in the same rows as the student data. In the next steps, you will see how this may cause a problem.

15. Select **cell A4** and choose **Data→Sort & Filter→Sort A to Z** from the Ribbon.
    The student records are sorted in alphabetical order by last name, and Excel protected the table array from being included in the sort. Notice that two students have a B grade.
16. **Right-click** row 8 and choose **Delete** from the context menu to remove Susan Savant's record.

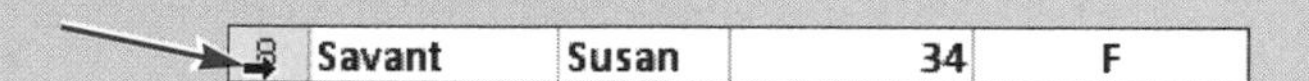

As you can see, row 8 included the table array data for the B grade. The formula now returns a C grade instead of B for two students.

17. Click **Undo** to restore row 8.

Convert the Table Array from Vertical to Horizontal

Rows 1 and 2 would not likely be deleted, so they are a safer location for the lookup table. You will convert the vertical array to horizontal to fit in these two rows.

18. Select the **range F4:G9** (including the labels) and use Ctrl+C to copy.
19. Select **cell E1** and choose **Home→Paste menu ▾→Transpose** from the Ribbon.
    The copied cells are pasted in a horizontal orientation rather than vertical. Transpose *means "to switch or reverse." The command is available if you copy cells but not if you cut them.*
20. Center the test scores in the **range F1:J1** so that they align with their matching grades.
21. Widen **column E** so that the labels display completely.
22. Select the **range F4:G9** and **tap** Delete.
    The grade formulas in column D display the #N/A error message because cells F5:G9 now are empty. You will rebuild the formula using the HLOOKUP function.

Edit the Defined Name

Next you will display the Name Manager dialog box and update the Refers To range for one of the defined names.

23. Choose **Formulas→Defined Names→Name Manager** from the Ribbon.
24. Select **Grade_Table**.
25. Click the **Collapse** button next to Refers To in the bottom right of the dialog box.
26. Taking care not to select the labels in column E, select the **range F1:J2**.
27. Click the **Expand** button to display Name Manager.
28. Click **Close**, and then click **Yes** to confirm.
    The grade formulas currently return the value 60.

Use the HLOOKUP Function

29. Select **cell D4**, edit the first letter to **H** so the function name reads *HLOOKUP,* and **complete** the formula.
    The formula now is =HLOOKUP(C4,Grade_Table,2). The only difference between VLOOKUP and HLOOKUP is the orientation of the table array. Occasionally you may decide to use a horizontal table array for a better worksheet design.
30. Use **AutoFill** to copy the **D4** formula down for the other students.

	A	B	C	D	E	F	G	H	I	J
1	**Test 1 Grade Calculations**				Test Scores	**0**	**60**	**70**	**80**	**90**
2					Letter Grade	F	D	C	B	A
3	**Last**	**First**	**Test Scores**	**Letter Grade**		**Grade Table**				
4	Brown	Bernice	78	C						
5	Espinoza	Marlo	87	B						
6	Kim	Alicia	95	A						
7	Lee	Jimmy	82	B						
8	Savant	Susan	34	F						
9	Soth	Ashley	91	A						
10	Sulai	Raj	94	A						
11	Warren	Reed	67	D						

31. **Save** the changes and **close** the workbook.

REINFORCE YOUR SKILLS 14.3

Use the VLOOKUP Function and Error Checking

In this exercise, you will create a simple financial worksheet that uses tax rates from a table array to calculate the Net Profit. The tax rate calculations have been simplified to make the data easy to understand. You will use Error Checking to locate the source of a formula error.

Calculate the Five-Year Growth Using Percentages

1. **Open** the rs-Financial Projections workbook from the Lesson 14 folder.
   The owner of King's Bakery is projecting sales growth of 27 percent for each of the next five years. These calculations appear in rows 4–9.

Use Error Checking and Create a Formula

The gross profit is equal to the projected sales in row 4 minus the expenses in rows 5–9. You will calculate the gross profit with a formula that uses the SUM function to sum the expenses and then subtracts the result from the projected sales.

2. In **cell B10**, enter **=B4-(B5:B9)**.
   Cell B10 should display an error.
3. Choose **Formulas→Formula Auditing→Error Checking** from the Ribbon.
   Take a moment to read the information on the left side of the Error Checking dialog box, which cannot pinpoint the exact location of the error.
4. Click the **Show Calculation Steps** button in the dialog box.
   Cell B4 is evaluated as 400000, which is correct.

5. Click the **Evaluate** button in the Evaluate Formula dialog box.
   The next formula expression –(B5:B9) evaluates as a #VALUE! error. Evaluating the formula helped to locate the problem area in the formula. The function SUM is missing.
6. Click **Close** in the Evaluate Formula dialog box.
7. Click the **Edit in Formula Bar** button in the Error Checking dialog box.
8. Click in the **Formula Bar** between the minus (–) sign and the parenthesis, type **`SUM,`** and **tap** [Enter].
   The result equals $15,000. You may nest functions like SUM inside a formula.

Calculate the Total Taxes Using the VLOOKUP Function

9. Drop down the **Name** list to the left of the Formula Bar and choose **Tax_Table**.
   The tax table at the bottom of the worksheet is selected. This table array was assigned the defined name Tax_Table when the worksheet was first created.
10. In **cell B11**, enter **`=B10*VLOOKUP(B10,Tax_Table,2)`**.
    The result equals $1,500. In this example, the total taxes are calculated as the gross profit in cell B10 multiplied by the tax rate returned by the VLOOKUP function.

Calculate the Net Profit and Format All Cells

11. In **cell B12**, enter a formula to calculate the net profit as Gross Profit–Total Taxes.
    The result equals $13,500.
12. Use **AutoFill** to copy the formulas in the **range B10:B12** across the rows.
    Rows 10–12 should match the following illustration.

10	Gross Profit	$ 15,000	$ 61,850	$ 127,530	$ 218,041	$ 341,148
11	Total Taxes	$ 1,500	$ 15,463	$ 47,186	$ 85,036	$ 133,048
12	Net Profit	$ 13,500	$ 46,388	$ 80,344	$ 133,005	$ 208,100

13. **Save** the changes and **close** the workbook.

REINFORCE YOUR SKILLS 14.4

Use the COUNTIF and COUNTIFS Functions

In this exercise, you will use the COUNTIF function to count students who achieved a minimum test score on one test and COUNTIFS for multiple tests.

Create a COUNTIF Formula

1. **Open** the rs-Test 3 Grades workbook from the Lesson 14 folder.
   In the next steps, you will create a formula to count students who earned at least 70 points on Test 1.
2. Select **cell C13** and click the **Insert Function** button in the Formula Bar.
3. Choose the **Statistical** category and **double-click** the COUNTIF function in the list.
   The Function Arguments dialog box displays.
4. Select **cells C4:C11** in the worksheet for Range.

5. Type **>=70** in the Criteria box and click **OK**.
   The result is 6. Excel added quotation (") marks around the criteria in the formula =COUNTIF(C4:C11,">=70").

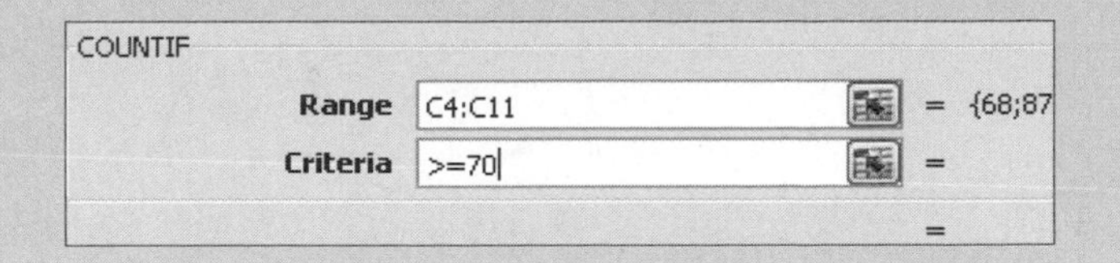

6. Copy the formula in **cell C13** to the **range D13:E13**.

Create a COUNTIFS Formula

In the next steps, you will create a formula to count students who earned at least 70 points on every test. Only records meeting all the criteria in the COUNTIFS formula are counted.

7. Select **cell E14** and click the **Insert Function** button in the Formula Bar.
8. Choose the **Statistical** category and **double-click** the COUNTIFS (not COUNTIF) function in the list.
   The Function Arguments dialog box displays.
9. Select the **range C4:C11** in the worksheet for Criteria Range1.
10. Type **>=70** in the **Criteria1** box.
    Excel will add quotation (") marks around the criteria when you click the next text box.
11. Click in the **Criteria Range2** box and select the **range D4:D11** in the worksheet.
12. Copy ">=70" from the **Criteria1** box and paste it in the **Criteria2** box.
13. Click in the **Criteria Range3** box and select the **range E4:E11** in the worksheet.
14. **Tap** Tab to display the **Criteria3** box.
    Only five text boxes display in the dialog box at one time.

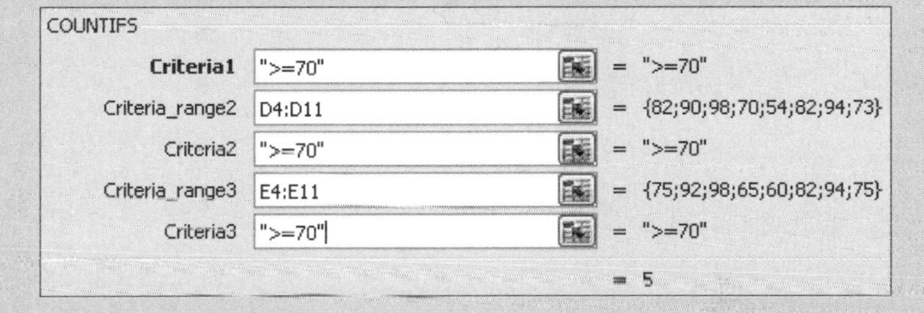

15. Paste ">=70" in the **Criteria3** box.
16. Click **OK**.
    The result is 5, indicating that five students earned a minimum score of 70 on each of the three tests. The COUNTIFS function may have up to 127 sets of criteria ranges and criteria.

    Your worksheet should look like the illustration to the right.
17. **Save** the changes and **close** the workbook.

	A	B	C	D	E
1	**Test 3 Grade Calculations**				
2					
3	**Last**	**First**	**Test 1**	**Test 2**	**Test 3**
4	Brown	Bernice	68	82	75
5	Espinoza	Marlo	87	90	92
6	Kim	Alicia	95	98	98
7	Lee	Jimmy	82	70	65
8	Savant	Susan	34	54	60
9	Soth	Ashley	91	82	82
10	Sulai	Raj	94	94	94
11	Warren	Reed	75	73	75
12					
13	**Count >= 70**		6	7	6
14	**All tests**				5

REINFORCE YOUR SKILLS 14.5

Use the Subtotal Function

In this exercise, you will filter a list to display students who have taken Level 1 Excel training tests. Then you will use the SUBTOTAL function to count just the filtered records. You also will create a SUBTOTAL formula to find the maximum value among the filtered test values.

Name and Filter the List

1. **Open** rs-Training Roster from the Lesson 14 folder.
2. Select **cell C3**, and choose **Data→Sort & Filter→Filter** from the Ribbon.
   Each column heading in row 3 displays an AutoFilter button.
3. In **cell C3**, choose the Level column heading **AutoFilter** button.
4. Point to **Number Filters** in the context menu, and choose **Equals**.
5. In the **Custom AutoFilter** dialog box, enter **1** and **tap** [Enter] to choose **OK**.
   There should be eight records showing.

Count Filtered Items

6. Select **cell C22**.
7. **Type** the formula **`=subtotal(2,c4:c21)`** and **tap** [Enter].
   The result should be 8. The argument 2 performs a count of only the displayed values in the filtered range C4:C21.

Find the Maximum Value

8. Copy the formula in **cell C22** to **cell D22**.
9. Edit the formula to change the argument from **2** to **4**.
   The result should be 100. In the formula =SUBTOTAL(4,D4:D21), the argument 4 performs a MAX function on only the displayed values in the filtered range D4:D21.
10. Use the **Format Painter** to copy the number formatting from **cell D19** to **cell D22**.
11. Choose **Data→Sort & Filter→Clear** from the Ribbon to remove the filter.
    The SUBTOTAL formulas in row 22 recalculate for all 18 records.
12. **Save** the changes, and leave the workbook **open**.
    You will continue to use this workbook in the next exercise.

REINFORCE YOUR SKILLS 14.6

Use the AND and OR Functions

In this exercise, you will use the AND function to list students who completed Level 1 and earned a score of 100 on the test. You will use the OR function to list students who earned either a score of 100 on the test or a letter grade of A for the class.

***Before You Begin:** You must have completed Reinforce Your Skills 14.5, and the rs-Training Roster workbook should be open.*

Use the AND Function

1. Type **100 and A** in **cell F3**, and type **100 or A** in **cell G3**.
2. Select **cell F4**, and choose **Formulas→Function Library→Logical** →**AND** from the Ribbon.
   The Function Arguments dialog box opens. You may use the Function Library as an alternative to using the Insert Function button on the Formula Bar.
3. Type **D4=100** in the **Logical1** box.
4. Type **E4="A"** in the **Logical2** box, and click **OK**.
   The formula =AND(D4=100,E4="A") displays in the Formula Bar. The result appears as FALSE because the Logical2 condition was not met.

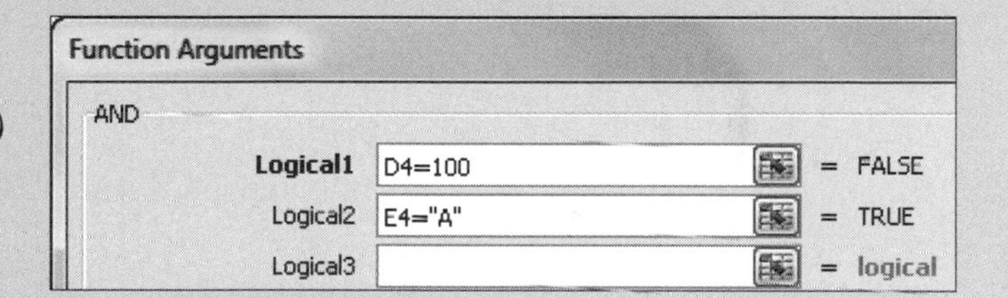

5. Use **AutoFill** to copy the formula in **cell F4** to the **range F5:F21**.
   The result is TRUE in cells F9 and F20. Two students met both conditions.

Use the OR Function

6. Select **cell G4**, and choose **Formulas→Function Library→Logical** →**OR** from the Ribbon.
   The Function Arguments dialog box opens.
7. If necessary, move the **Function Arguments** dialog box out of the way by dragging its title bar until you can see **columns D–G**.
8. For the **Logical1** entry, select **cell D4** in the worksheet and type **=100**.
9. For the **Logical2** entry, select **cell E4** in the worksheet and type **="A"** and then click OK.

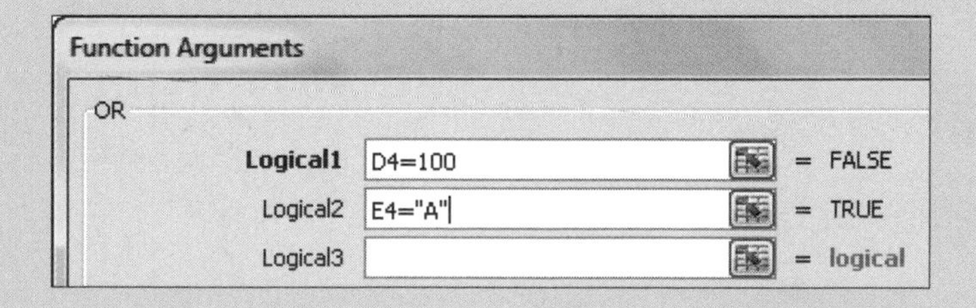

   The formula =OR(D4=100,E4="A") displays in the Formula Bar. The result appears as TRUE because either the Logical1 or Logical2 condition was met.

10. Use **AutoFill** to copy the formula in **cell G4** to the **range G5:G21**.

Add the IF Function

Now you will modify the formula by using the IF function to display Yes *if true or a blank if false.*

11. Select **cell G4**.
12. In the **Formula Bar**, click between the equals (=) sign and O.
13. Taking care to include the parenthesis, type **IF(** and then **tap** the [End] key on the keyboard to position the **insertion point** at the end of the formula.
14. Type **,"Yes","")** and click the **Enter** ✓ button on the Formula Bar to complete the formula.
    The formula is =IF(OR(D4=100,E4="A","Yes",""). The OR function serves as the argument to be evaluated as true or false by the IF function.
15. Use **AutoFill** to copy the formula in **cell G4** to the **range G5:G21**; center-align the range.
    Displaying Yes *or a blank makes it easier to read the results.*
16. **Save** the changes and **close** the workbook.

Apply Your Skills

APPLY YOUR SKILLS 14.1

Use Auditing Tools

In this exercise, you will respond to messages about possible formula errors.

1. **Open** the as-Vehicle Sales workbook in the Lesson 14 folder.
2. Display the **Robert Sales** worksheet.
   Cell E15 displays a triangle icon in the upper-left corner of the cell.
3. Trace precedents for the formula in **cell E15** and determine whether the formula includes the appropriate cell range. Leave the tracer arrow displayed.
4. Use the error checking menu on **cell E15** to review possible causes for the triangle icon alert. Determine whether the formula for new vehicle sales is correct or needs to be changed. Choose an appropriate command in the menu to remove the triangle icon from the cell.
5. Display the **Sales Summary** worksheet.
6. Use the **Error Checking** dialog box to find and repair formulas containing errors. Each linking formula should point to the grand total sales in a salesperson's worksheet.
   The formula results are shown in the following illustration.

	A	B	C
1	Ritzer's Auto Sales		
2	**Sales for January**		
3			
4	**Sales**		
5	New		
6	Used		
7	**Grand Total**		
8			
9			
10			
11			
12	**Salesperson**		**Total Sales**
13	Robert	Bendel	$251,190
14	David	Johnson	$122,620
15	Gwen	Wenski	$193,160

7. **Save** the changes.
   You will continue to use this workbook in the next exercise.

APPLY YOUR SKILLS 14.2

Create 3-D Cell References

In this exercise, you will use 3-D cell references in formulas.

***Before You Begin:** You must have completed Apply Your Skills 14.1, and the as-Vehicle Sales workbook should be open.*

1. Display the **Sales Summary** worksheet in the as-Vehicle Sales workbook.
2. In the appropriate cell, create a formula with a **3-D cell reference** that sums new vehicle sales for the three salespeople.
3. Create similar **formulas** for sales of used vehicles and the grand totals.
   The formula results are shown in the illustration to the right.
4. **Save** the changes and **close** the workbook.

	A	B
1	Ritzer's Auto Sales	
2	Sales for January	
3		
4	Sales	
5	New	$ 452,780
6	Used	$ 114,190
7	Grand Total	$ 566,970

APPLY YOUR SKILLS 14.3

Create a Table Array and VLOOKUP Function

In this exercise, you will use the VLOOKUP function to determine how many free rentals the customer receives.

1. **Open** the as-Frequent Renters workbook from the Lesson 14 folder.
2. Set up the **table array** under the worksheet data as shown here:

	A	B	C	D	E
1	Jenco Equipment Rentals - Frequent Renter Awards				
2					
3		Customer		Frequent Renter Points Earned	Number of Free Rentals
4	Hansen	Leslie	A	6	1
5	Liu	Shen		17	3
6	Ortiz	Maria	D	3	0
7	Park	Young	Min	22	4
8	Randall	Lynn	G	11	2
9	Salcedo	Nicolas		4	0
10	Tate	Deborah	M	14	2
11					
12				Free Rentals Table	
13				Frequent Renter Points	Free Rentals
14				0	0
15				5	1
16				10	2
17				15	3
18				20	4
19				25	5

3. Assign the defined name **`Free_Rentals_Table`** to the table array.

4. Use the VLOOKUP function in **column E** to determine the number of free rentals each customer should receive. The function should use the frequent renter points earned in column D as the lookup value and search the Free_Rentals_Table for the correct number of free rentals.
5. **Save** the changes and **close** the workbook.

APPLY YOUR SKILLS 14.4

Use the NOT Function

In this exercise, you will create a NOT function to indicate whether a person has or has not worked exactly 40 hours per week.

1. **Open** the as-Weekly Payroll workbook from the Lesson 14 folder.
2. In **cell I4**, create a NOT function that indicates whether Millie Aberdeen has worked 40 hours this week. The result TRUE or FALSE should display in the cell.

Reg Hours Worked	Overtime Hourly Rate	Overtime Hours Worked	Gross Pay	Did Not Work 40 hours
40	$18.00	4	$552.00	FALSE

3. Copy the formula in **cell I4** down **column I** for the other employees.
   A TRUE result indicates the employee did not work exactly 40 hours.
4. Apply conditional formatting to the **column I** formula cells to draw attention to the TRUE results.
5. **Save** the changes and **close** the workbook.

Critical Thinking & Work-Readiness Skills

In the course of working through the following Microsoft Office-based Critical Thinking exercises, you will also be utilizing various work-readiness skills, some of which are listed next to each exercise. Go to labyrinthelab.com/workreadiness *to learn more about the work-readiness skills.*

14.1 Use the Error Checking Feature

WORK-READINESS SKILLS APPLIED

- Serving customers/clients
- Showing responsibility
- Using computers to process information

Sandra Chavez-Hall, chief development officer for Raritan Clinic East Foundation, requests a daily operating report from her administrative assistant. The report is almost ready to give to Sandra. Your job is to finish it. Open ct-Raritan Clinic East Patient Roster (Lesson 14 folder). Run the error-checking function and fix the two formulas with errors. Make certain the formulas work correctly and that the worksheet contains no errors. Save your work as **`ct-Raritan Clinic East Patient Roster [Your Last Name]`**. Keep the file open.

14.2 Use the COUNTIF Function

WORK-READINESS SKILLS APPLIED

- Solving problems
- Using computers to process information
- Organizing and maintaining information

In order to cover appointments for two doctors attending a conference, the operations director needs to check on the number of patients scheduled for doctor appointments today. Open ct-Raritan Clinic East Patient Roster [Your Last Name], if necessary. Create a COUNTIF formula in cell F2 to show how many patients Dr. R. Lawrence has today. In cell F3, show how many patients Dr. J. Ottome has scheduled. Save your work and keep the file open.

14.3 Define a Table Array and Use the VLOOKUP Function

WORK-READINESS SKILLS APPLIED

- Serving customers/clients
- Using computers to process information
- Reasoning

The operations director is researching drug trials to help patients pay for their medications. In this case, she is examining the Pickard Trial to see how it may help with the specific patients' drug costs. If necessary, open ct-Raritan Clinic East Patient Roster [Your Last Name]. Define data provided in columns L and M as a table array for drug costs that this particular grant will reimburse. Name the table array **`Trial_Reimbursement`**. Use the VLOOKUP function to create formulas in the range H7:H16. The formulas should look up the drug cost in the table array and return the reimbursement percentage. Conditional formatting has been applied to the formula range. Save and close the file when you are finished.

Using Advanced Formatting and Analysis Tools

LESSON OUTLINE

LEARNING OBJECTIVES

After studying this lesson, you will be able to:

- Group worksheets for efficient data entry
- Consolidate data from multiple worksheets by position and category
- Set data validation rules to restrict data entry
- Remove duplicate records from data
- Create data tables to perform what-if analyses
- Develop trendlines and sparklines to analyze chart data

You can summarize data using such features as linking formulas and 3-D cell references in formulas. In this lesson, you will consolidate data from detail worksheets by position and category. Occasionally, you may need to set up multiple worksheets before data common to all of them are available. You will group worksheets to enter the data into multiple worksheets simultaneously. Many Excel workbooks are designed by experienced users but used by individuals with little Excel experience. Excel's Data Validation tool can assist users of all levels with data entry by forcing values to fall within a specified range. When data are combined or imported from different sources, duplicate records may exist. Excel's Remove Duplicates tool may be used to delete them. Data tables assist with what-if analyses by adjusting variables in a formula. Trendlines are another aid to analysis, helping you perceive and forecast trends in chart data. You also will create sparklines, or mini charts, to present changing data patterns in cells right next to the worksheet data.

Student Resources labyrinthelab.com/excel10

CASE STUDY

Consolidating and Validating Data

Sandra Chavez-Hall is the chief development officer at Raritan Clinic East. She will present quarterly fundraising results to the clinic's foundation board using charts and tables, but first she must gather the numbers for the contributions achieved. Sandra needs a workbook to store detailed information in separate sheets. She will use Excel's consolidation feature to summarize the data into a summary sheet without manually creating formulas. In addition, she will use data validation and other tools to format the workbook and create sparklines to show trends in data. Sandra will use a data table to forecast net income for an upcoming fundraising event.

	A	B	C	D	E	F
1	Raritan Clinic East	**Capital Campaign**				
2	Pediatric Diagnostic Specialists	**All Sources**				
3						
4	**Pledge Level**	**Q1**	**Q2**	**Q3**	**Q4**	**By Quarter**
5	Level 1	16,541,676	30,201,177	32,114,970	38,409,659	
6	Level 2	-	2,000,000	2,253,988	2,000,075	
7	Level 3	202,373	222,645	479,673	412,892	
8	Level 4	100,891	50,000	51,209	-	
9	Level 5	8,647	13,043	17,921	18,676	
10	Level 6	1,262	2,889	4,600	6,435	
11	**Total Contributions**	**16,854,849**	**32,489,754**	**34,922,361**	**40,847,737**	**125,114,701**

Sparkline

A consolidated worksheet summarizing quarterly totals from multiple source sheets

Variables for tickets sold

	A	B	C	D	E	F	G
1	**Net Income $ Goal**	**Net Income % Goal**					
2	$ 75,000	70%					
3					**Ticket Sales Above (Below) Goal**		
4			**Tickets Sold**				
5			600	650	700	750	800
6	**Ticket Price**	$ 100	(33,000)	(29,500)	(26,000)	(22,500)	(19,000)
7		$ 150	(12,000)	(6,750)	(1,500)	3,750	9,000
8		$ 200	9,000	16,000	23,000	30,000	37,000
9		$ 250	30,000	38,750	47,500	56,250	65,000
10		$ 300	51,000	61,500	72,000	82,500	93,000

Variables for ticket price

A data table showing the various results when two variables are adjusted in a formula; the data table formula is hidden in cell B5

15.1 Working with Grouped Worksheets

Video Lesson labyrinthelab.com/videos

You may temporarily group two or more worksheets to save time when entering data, creating formulas, and formatting worksheets. When worksheets are grouped, whatever you type is entered on all sheets simultaneously. The same is true of formatting. For example, changing the column width on one worksheet also affects the same column on the other grouped worksheets. You may copy data from an ungrouped worksheet and paste to all worksheets in a group.

Grouping Worksheets

By grouping worksheets, you work with them as a set. For example, imagine that you used a budget template to create a workbook with 12 monthly worksheets. Rather than typing or pasting the same row labels multiple times, you may group the sheets and type the labels just once. You may group contiguous or noncontiguous worksheets using the Shift and Ctrl keys, just as you do when selecting multiple cells. In this lesson, you will work with contiguous worksheets. When worksheets are grouped, their sheet tabs change color, and *[Group]* displays in the window's title bar.

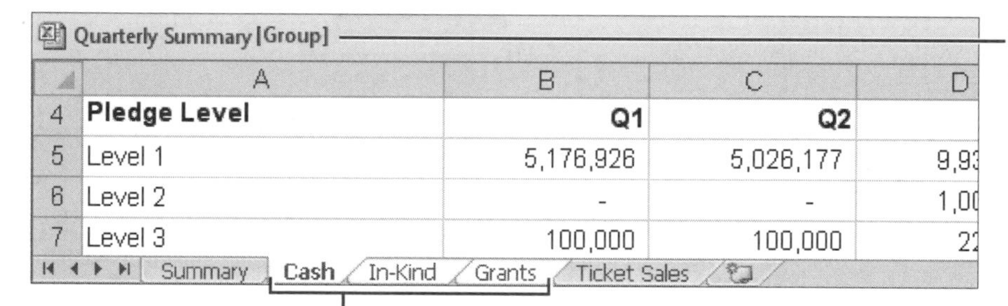

The title bar indicates that worksheets are grouped.

The sheet tabs turn white when worksheets are grouped.

Ungrouping Worksheets

Grouping and ungrouping actually are selecting and deselecting procedures. The Ungroup Sheets command in the sheet tab pop-up, or context, menu removes the grouping so that you may work in one worksheet at a time.

If all sheets in a workbook are grouped, you may simply click on any sheet tab, other than the first one, to ungroup them.

QUICK REFERENCE	GROUPING AND UNGROUPING WORKSHEETS
Task	**Procedure**
Group contiguous worksheets	■ Click the first sheet tab to be grouped. ■ Hold down [Shift] and click the last sheet tab to be grouped.
Group noncontiguous worksheets	■ Click the first sheet tab to be grouped. ■ Hold down [Ctrl] and click the individual sheet tabs to be grouped with the first.
Copy and paste cells to grouped worksheets	■ Select cells to be copied and use [Ctrl]+[C] to copy. ■ Select the destination cell in one of the grouped sheets. ■ Group the sheets to receive the copied cells. ■ Use [Ctrl]+[P] to paste.
Ungroup worksheets	■ Right-click a sheet tab and choose Ungroup Sheets from the context menu.

DEVELOP YOUR SKILLS 15.1.1

Group Worksheets

In this exercise, you will explore the structure of summary and detail worksheets. You will group four worksheets, enter new data, copy existing data, and apply formatting to all sheets simultaneously.

Explore the Workbook

1. **Start** Excel and **open** the Quarterly Summary workbook from the Lesson 15 folder in your file storage location.
2. Take a few moments to study the **Summary** and **three source** worksheets.
   The number cells are empty in the Summary sheet. Later in this lesson, these cells will receive data from the Cash, In-Kind, and Grants sheets through the Consolidation command. Some row and column headings are missing from the four worksheets. You will group the worksheets and type the labels once.

Group Worksheets

3. Follow these steps to group the four worksheets:

A Click the Summary sheet tab.
Summary
Cash
In-Kind
Grants
B Hold down Shift and click the Grants sheet tab. Release Shift.

The four sheets are now grouped. Notice [Group] in the title bar and that the grouped sheet tabs are white.

Enter Data in Grouped Worksheets

The ranges A14:A17 and B4:E4 are empty in all four worksheets. You will enter data once into these cells for all grouped worksheets.

4. In **cell A14**, type **`Web/Social Media Development`** and **tap** [Enter].
5. Continue entering the following labels in **cells A15:A17**: **`Print Materials, Events`**, and **`Salaries - Grant Proposals`**.
6. In **cell B4**, type **`Q1`** and **right-align** the label. Apply **bold**.
7. Use **AutoFill** to extend the series through **cell E4**.
   The range B4:E4 should display Q1, Q2, Q3, and Q4.
8. **Deselect** the highlighted cells.

Ungroup the Worksheets

9. **Right-click** the Summary sheet tab and choose **Ungroup Sheets** from the context menu.
10. Display each of the **source** worksheets.
    Notice that the labels you entered in the ranges A14:A17 and B4:E4 are now on all of the worksheets.

Copy and Paste Cells to Grouped Worksheets

Some row headings on the Summary worksheet should be included on the source worksheets.

11. Display the **Summary** worksheet.
12. Select the **range A5:A10**, and use [Ctrl]+[C] to copy.
13. Display the **Cash** worksheet and select **cell A5**, the destination cell.
14. **Hold down** [Shift] and click the **Grants** sheet tab to select all source sheets.
15. Use [Ctrl]+[V] to paste.
    The labels were pasted to cells A5:A10 in the three source worksheets.
16. Deselect the cells.

Format Grouped Worksheets

Now you will apply formatting to cells in a worksheet group.

17. Display the **Summary** worksheet.
18. **Tap** [Esc] to clear the marquee surrounding the **range A5:A10**.
19. **Group** the four worksheets again.

20. Follow these steps to select the desired cells to format:

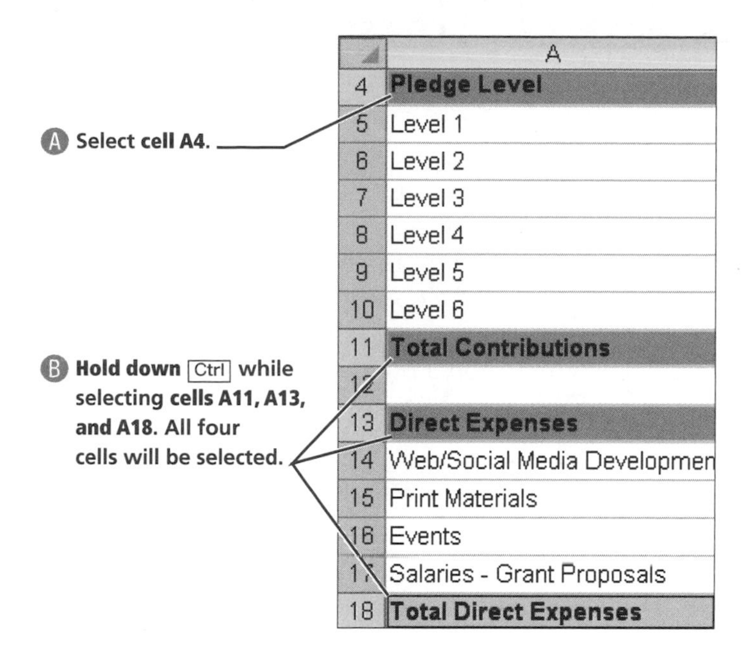

21. Choose **Home→Styles→Cell Styles→Themed Cell Styles→20% - Accent6**, and then apply **Bold** from the Ribbon.
    The selected cells display a light purple fill.
22. **Deselect** the cells.
23. Take a few moments to view the changes that were made to each worksheet.
    All the worksheets should have the same formatting as the Summary sheet.
24. Experiment with **grouping** and **ungrouping** contiguous and noncontiguous sheets.
    Remember, use the Shift key to group contiguous sheets and the Ctrl key to group noncontiguous sheets.
25. When finished, make certain to **ungroup** the worksheets.
26. **Save** the changes, and leave the workbook **open**.

15.2 Consolidating Worksheet Data

Video Lesson labyrinthelab.com/videos

Excel's Consolidate command combines values from source worksheets into a destination worksheet. You select an entire range, and all its value and formula cells (but not text cells) are consolidated simultaneously to the destination worksheet. Only one range may be consolidated from each source worksheet. The calculation results are values rather than formulas unless you select the Create Links to Source Data option. When the results are values, you must repeat the Consolidate command if values change later in the source worksheets. You may redisplay the Consolidate dialog box to add a reference range for any worksheet added to the workbook, and you may delete any reference range.

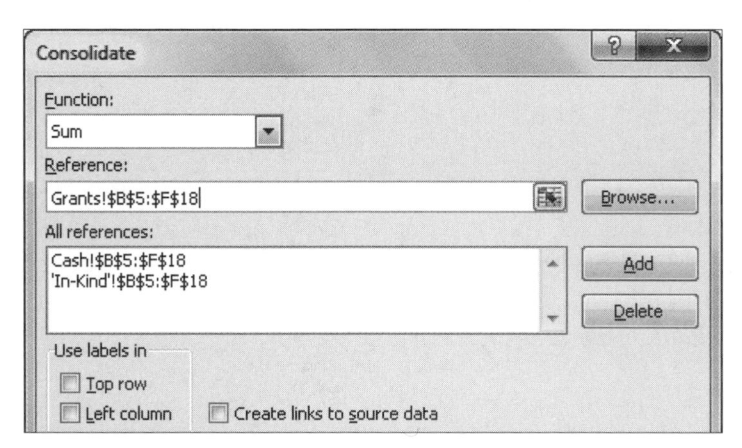

A consolidation reference being created to the Grants worksheet in the Consolidate dialog box

The Browse button in the Consolidate dialog box allows you to navigate to other workbooks and consolidate data from them.

Consolidation Functions

The SUM function is the most commonly used consolidation function. You also may use AVERAGE, MIN, MAX, and some other statistical functions when consolidating. You choose the desired function in the Consolidate dialog box when you set up the consolidation.

Types of Consolidation

You may consolidate data using either of the following methods:

- **By Position—**This method is useful when all worksheets have the same layout. To consolidate by position, specify the same range in all worksheets. Excel uses the function you choose to consolidate values in the same cell of each of the specified worksheets.
- **By Category—**This method is used when the supporting worksheets have different layouts but identical row or column labels that refer to the common data. A worksheet may contain labels for categories that other worksheets do not include. Excel uses the row and column headings to determine which rows or columns to consolidate with the other consolidation ranges you specify. The consolidation produces one row or column in the summary sheet for each unique row or column encountered in the supporting sheets. The consolidated data contains no blank rows or text formatting from the source worksheets, but you can format the summary sheet results after the consolidation.

Creating Links to Source Data

By default, consolidated data is not linked to the source cells. The Create Links to Source Data option does create linking formulas on the summary worksheet. For example, cell C5 contains the linking formula =Cash!$B$5 as shown in the following illustration. The consolidated data are formatted as an outline that may be expanded to view the source data or collapsed to view the totals. Any changes to source data on the original worksheets will update in the summary sheet.

Level 1 is expanded to display the data from three source worksheets, one sheet per row. The source workbook name for each sheet displays in column B. All three sheets are in the same Quarterly Summary workbook in this example.

Cell C5 in the Summary sheet contains a linking formula to refer to the cell B5 value in the Cash worksheet.

C5 =Cash!$B$5

	A	B	C	D	E
4	Pledge Level		Q1	Q2	
5		Quarterly Summary	5,176,926	5,026,177	9,9
6		Quarterly Summary	11,364,750	21,175,000	22,1
7		Quarterly Summary	-	-	
8	Level 1		16,541,676	30,201,177	32,1
12	Level 2		-	2,000,000	2,2
16	Level 3		202,373	222,645	4

The Level 1 total for Q1 is the sum of the three linked cells in the range C5:C7.

The labels for each quarter were entered manually after the consolidation. Only values are transferred from the source sheets.

Data consolidated by category and linked in an outline format to the source data

The column A text labels are included in the summary because the Left Column option was selected in the Consolidate dialog box to create a consolidation by category.

QUICK REFERENCE CONSOLIDATING DATA

Task	Procedure
Consolidate by position or category	■ Select a cell in the destination worksheet to be used as the starting point for the consolidation. *By category:* This range should include column and/or row labels. ■ Choose Data→Data Tools→Consolidate from the Ribbon. ■ Choose a consolidation function (usually SUM) in the Consolidate dialog box. ■ Click in the Reference box. ■ Click the sheet tab of the first source worksheet and select the data range. *By category:* The range must include either row or column labels. ■ Click the Add button to add the range to the All References list. ■ Click the next source sheet tab, and click Add to add the same range to the All References list. *By category:* Select a different range, if desired. ■ Continue adding the remaining source sheet ranges. *By category:* Place a checkmark in the Top Row box in the Use Labels In area if you included column labels or in the Left Column box if you included row labels. ■ Place a checkmark in the Create Links to Source Data box, if desired, and click OK. Using this option avoids having to update the consolidation manually after changes are made to the source data. ■ Format the consolidated data in the summary sheet as necessary.
Update the consolidation manually after changing values in source worksheets	■ Choose Data→Data Tools→Consolidate  from the Ribbon and click OK.

DEVELOP YOUR SKILLS 15.2.1

Consolidate Data

In this exercise, you will use the Consolidate command to consolidate the pledge level contributions and expenses related to fund raising. You will consolidate from the Cash, In-Kind, and Grants worksheets by position. This is possible because all worksheets have the same layout.

Consolidate by Position

1. Display the **Summary** worksheet in the Quarterly Summary workbook.
2. Select **cell B5** as the starting point for the consolidated data.
3. Choose **Data→Data Tools→Consolidate** from the Ribbon.
4. If necessary, move the **Consolidate** dialog box until **cell B5** in the Summary sheet and the sheet tabs at the bottom of the Excel window are visible.
5. Follow these steps to set consolidation options in the Consolidate dialog box:

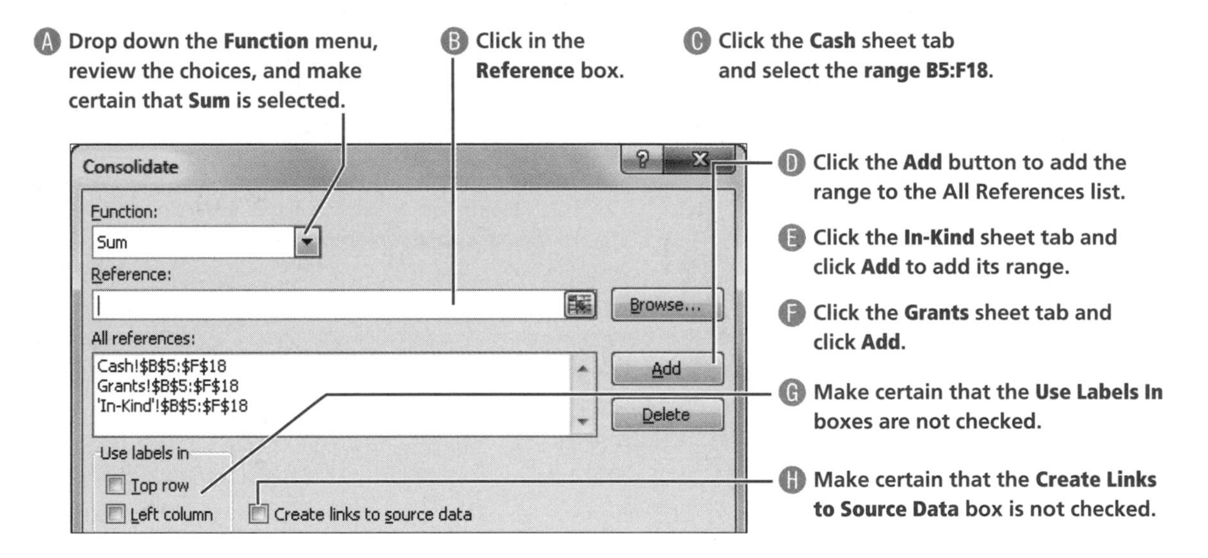
A Drop down the Function menu, review the choices, and make certain that Sum is selected.
B Click in the Reference box.
C Click the Cash sheet tab and select the range B5:F18.
Consolidate
Function:
Sum
Reference:
Browse...
All references:
Cash!$B$5:$F$18
Grants!$B$5:$F$18
'In-Kind'!$B$5:$F$18
Add
Delete
Use labels in
Top row
Left column
Create links to source data
D Click the Add button to add the range to the All References list.
E Click the In-Kind sheet tab and click Add to add its range.
F Click the Grants sheet tab and click Add.
G Make certain that the Use Labels In boxes are not checked.
H Make certain that the Create Links to Source Data box is not checked.

Review the references in the All References list. You build a consolidation range by adding references to this list.

6. Click **OK**.
   Excel consolidates the data into the Summary sheet. The Summary worksheet should display the consolidated numbers shown in the following illustration.

4	Pledge Level	Q1	Q2	Q3	Q4	
5	Level 1	16,541,676	30,201,177	32,114,970	38,409,659	
6	Level 2	-	2,000,000	2,253,988	2,000,075	
7	Level 3	202,373	222,645	479,673	412,892	
8	Level 4	100,891	50,000	51,209	-	
9	Level 5	8,647	13,043	17,921	18,676	
10	Level 6	1,262	2,889	4,600	6,435	
11	**Total Contributions**	16,854,849	32,489,754	34,922,361	40,847,737	125,114,701
12						
13	**Direct Expenses**					
14	Web/Social Media Developmen	3,500	3,500	3,500	37,000	
15	Print Materials	947	977	1,699	864	
16	Events	12,589	22,753	10,465	45,872	
17	Salaries - Grant Proposals	6,000	6,000	6,000	6,000	
18	**Total Direct Expenses**	23,036	33,230	21,664	89,736	167,666

Examine the Results

Notice that the number format in the range B5:F18 was transferred from the source worksheets sheets to the summary sheet. The bold text formatting, however, was not transferred.

7. Select any cell in the **range B5:F18** in the Summary worksheet.
   The Formula Bar displays a value rather than a formula. The Consolidate command sums the values in the specified ranges and enters the results as values in the Summary sheet. You would need to give the Consolidate command again if the numbers in the detail worksheets were updated. Assume that you did not switch on Create Links to Source Data in the Consolidate dialog box because you will not update the data.
8. **Save** the changes, and leave the workbook **open**.

15.3 Working with Data Validation

Video Lesson labyrinthelab.com/videos

Excel's data validation tool lets you restrict data entry in cells. The default validation setting for a cell is Any Value, meaning that until you specify a validation setting and criteria, any value may be entered in the cell.

Restricting Data Entry Using Criteria

You may restrict both the type and range of acceptable values. For example, you may want to restrict data entry to whole numbers between 0 and 100,000. You may also create an input message and error alert message to guide the user in entering acceptable data. An input message appears whenever the restricted cell is selected. An error message appears whenever data entry is attempted and the data is not of the correct type or within the accepted range.

Data validation operates only when the user attempts to type directly in a cell. No alert occurs when cell contents result from using the fill handle, Paste command, or an incorrect cell reference in a formula.

The following table describes the available validation criteria.

Type	Entries Must Be
Any Value	No restrictions; may display an input message without checking for valid entries
Custom	A formula, expression, or reference to a calculation in another cell
Dates	Dates
Decimal	Numbers or fractions
List	Only those in a specified list
Text Length	A specific number of characters
Time	Times
Whole Number	Integers without decimal places

If the values in the worksheet are formatted with decimal places, use Decimal rather than Whole Number.

Copying a Data Validation Rule

A data validation rule must be created while a single worksheet is selected and cannot be set up while worksheets are grouped. You may, however, copy a cell containing a validation rule. Then, you may use the Validation option of the Paste Special command on the Ribbon to apply a data validation rule from that cell to other cells on the same worksheet, another sheet, or grouped sheets. You may edit a validation rule. The Apply These Changes to All Other Cells with the Same Settings option in the Data Validation dialog box updates cells only in the active worksheet. You must use the Validation option of the Paste Special command to apply the revised rule to cells on other sheets.

DEVELOP YOUR SKILLS 15.3.1

Set Up Data Validation

In this exercise, you will set up data validation in a specified cell range and create an error alert message for incorrect entry attempts. You will use the Text Length option to restrict the Level 1–6 label entries. You also will create a data validation rule using a drop-down list to indicate that each fundraising goal was met or not met.

Set Data Validation for Numeric Entries

First, you will set up a data validation rule for the direct expense values. You usually would set up the rule before entering the data, but you will reenter some values to test the rule.

1. Display the **Cash** worksheet of the Quarterly Summary workbook.
2. Select the values in the **range B14:E17** as shown in the following illustration. (Make certain that the expense labels in column A and the total cells in row 18 are **not** selected.)

	A	B	C	D	E
14	Web/Social Media Development	1,500	1,500	1,500	35,000
15	Print Materials	500	500	500	563
16	Events	12,321	22,753	10,465	45,657
17	Salaries - Grant Proposals	-	-	-	-
18	**Total Direct Expenses**	**14,321**	**24,753**	**12,465**	**81,220**

3. Choose **Data→Data Tools→Data Validation** from the Ribbon.
4. Follow these steps to set the data entry restrictions:

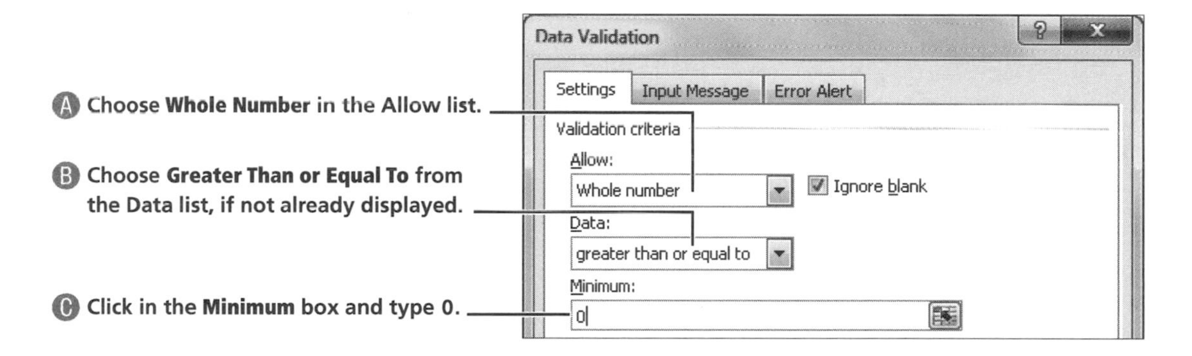

5. Display the **Input Message** tab in the dialog box.
   Notice that you may create an input message that appears whenever a restricted cell is selected. You will not use this option in this exercise. You will use an error alert message instead.
6. Display the **Error Alert** tab.

7. Follow these steps to set an error alert message:

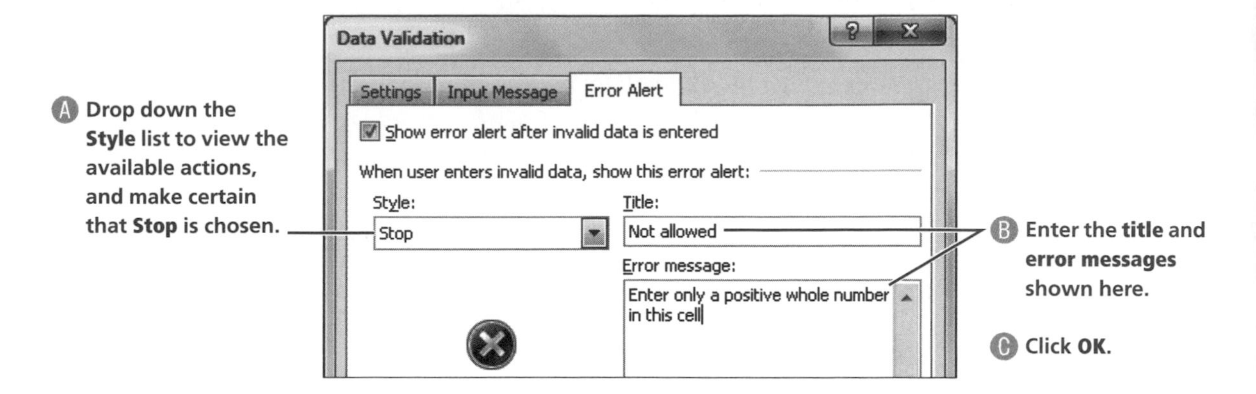
Data Validation
Settings
Input Message
Error Alert
Show error alert after invalid data is entered
When user enters invalid data, show this error alert:
Style:
Stop
Title:
Not allowed
Error message:
Enter only a positive whole number in this cell
A Drop down the Style list to view the available actions, and make certain that Stop is chosen.
B Enter the title and error messages shown here.
C Click OK.

Test the Data Validation

8. Select **cell B14** in the **Cash** sheet.
9. **Type** the negative number **-1000** and **tap** [Enter].
   The error alert message appears. The data validation restriction allows you to enter only a positive whole number in this cell.
10. Click the **Retry** button in the message box.
    Retry lets you edit an incorrect entry, while Cancel deletes the entry.
11. Type **1000.50** and **tap** [Enter].
    Once again, the entry is not accepted because it is not a whole number.
12. Click the **Retry** button and **enter** the original number **1500**.

Validate Label Entries Using Text Length

13. Select the **range A5:A10**.
    Notice that all text entries are seven characters in length in the selected range. You will create a data validation rule based on the text length.
14. Choose **Data→Data Tools→Data Validation** from the Ribbon.
15. Follow these steps to set up the data entry restriction:

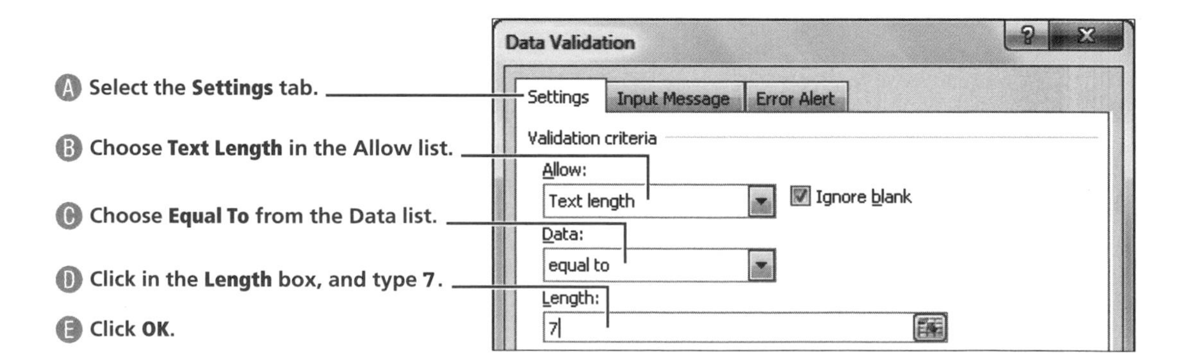
A Select the Settings tab.
B Choose Text Length in the Allow list.
C Choose Equal To from the Data list.
D Click in the Length box, and type 7.
E Click OK.
Data Validation
Settings
Input Message
Error Alert
Validation criteria
Allow:
Text length
Ignore blank
Data:
equal to
Length:
7

You did not set an input message, and the default error alert message will apply for this rule.

16. Select **cell A5**.

17. Type **Level 22** and **tap** [Enter].
    The default error message displays.

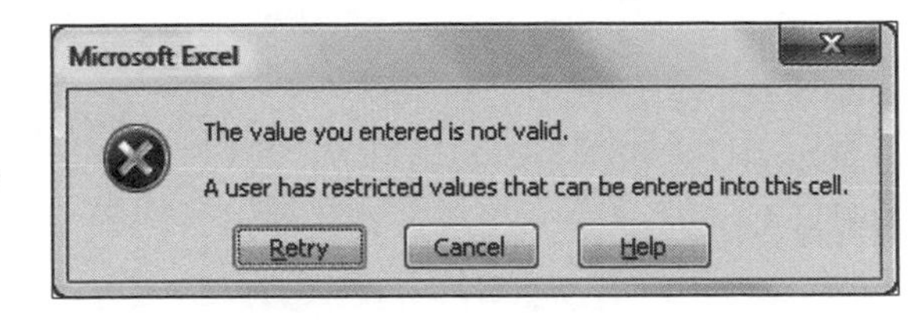

18. Click the **Cancel** button in the error message dialog box to leave the original entry unchanged.

Copy and Paste a Data Validation Rule

You cannot set up a data validation rule while sheets are grouped, but you may paste a validation format to a range in a group.

19. **Right-click** cell B14, and choose **Copy** from the context menu.
    This cell is formatted with the data validation rule for direct expense values you set up. In the next few steps, you will apply only the validation formatting to the direct expenses range of the In-Kind and Grants worksheets.
20. Select the **In-Kind** sheet tab, **hold down** [Shift], and select the **Grants** sheet tab.
    The two grouped sheet tabs have a white background.

21. Select the **range B14:E17**.
22. Choose **Home→Clipboard→Paste menu ▾→Paste Special** from the Ribbon.
    If an error message appears because you chose the Paste command rather than the Paste menu, click Cancel and repeat this step.
23. Choose **Validation** in the Paste Special dialog box, and click **OK**.

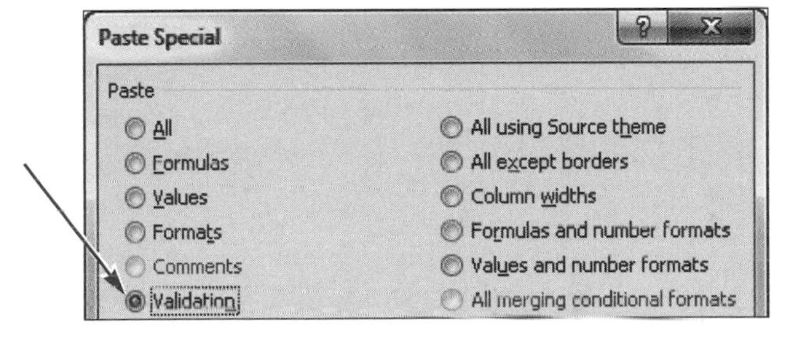

24. Select **cell B14** to deselect the range in both grouped sheets.
25. **Right-click** the Grants sheet tab, and choose **Ungroup Sheets** from the context menu.
    Now only the Grants worksheet is active.
26. Type **web** in cell B14 of the **Grants** worksheet, and **tap** [Enter].
    The Not Allowed error message displays because you applied the data validation rule.
27. Click **Cancel** in the error message dialog box to restore the original value.
28. **Save** the changes, and leave the workbook **open**.

Creating Drop-Down Lists for Data Entry

Video Lesson labyrinthelab.com/videos

The data validation List option allows you to restrict data entry for a cell to a choice contained in a drop-down list. For example, the acceptable entries for a product's status could be *In Stock* and *Reorder*. An error message displays if the user attempts to type an entry.

Specifying List Items

You may type the list items separated by commas (,) in the Data Validation dialog box. As a recommended alternative, you may enter the list choices in cells down a column of a worksheet and give the range where the entries are stored. Revising the list choices often is easier with the in-worksheet method. Including a blank cell at the end of the list range allows the user to reset the cell contents to a blank when appropriate. You may wish to lock the cell range containing the list entries and turn on worksheet protection (see the Excel Help topic about locking cells and protecting a worksheet, if necessary).

Specifying Other Options

The In-Cell Dropdown option must be checked for the drop-down list to be displayed in the specified cells. The Ignore Blanks option must be unchecked if you wish to prevent users from typing entries in cells formatted with a list.

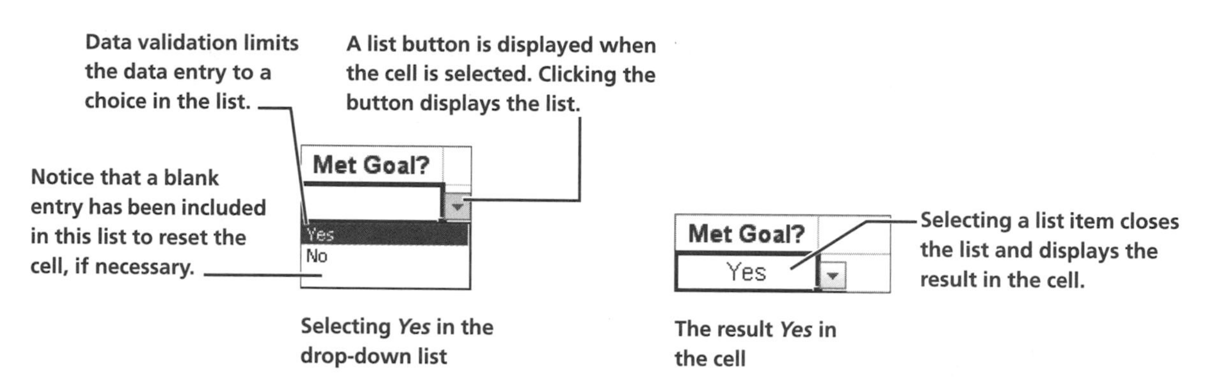
Data validation limits the data entry to a choice in the list.
A list button is displayed when the cell is selected. Clicking the button displays the list.
Notice that a blank entry has been included in this list to reset the cell, if necessary.
Met Goal?
Yes
No
Met Goal?
Yes
Selecting a list item closes the list and displays the result in the cell.

Selecting *Yes* in the drop-down list

The result *Yes* in the cell

QUICK REFERENCE — VALIDATING DATA ENTRIES

Task	Procedure
Set validation criteria and messages except for a list	■ Select the cells to be validated. ■ Choose Data→Data Tools→Data Validation from the Ribbon. ■ Choose the desired category from the Allow list. (Choose Custom if you wish to enter a formula.) ■ Choose the criteria for data to be entered in the cells. ■ If desired, set an input message and/or error alert message using the tabs in the Data Validation dialog box.

QUICK REFERENCE	VALIDATING DATA ENTRIES (continued)
Task	**Procedure**
Set validation criteria and messages for a list	■ Type the list items in a named worksheet range. The range may include a blank entry, if desired. ■ Select the cells to be validated. ■ Choose Data→Data Tools→Data Validation from the Ribbon. ■ Choose List from the Allow list. ■ Remove the checkmark next to Ignore Blank, and place a checkmark next to In-Cell Dropdown. ■ Click in the Source box, and select the named range containing the list items in the worksheet. ■ If desired, set an input message and/or error alert message using the tabs in the Data Validation dialog box.
Copy a validation rule to other cells	■ Right-click the cell containing the validation rule, and choose Copy from the context menu. ■ Select the cell range that will receive the validation formatting. ■ Choose Home→Clipboard→Paste menu ▼→Paste Special from the Ribbon. ■ Choose the Validation option in the Paste Special dialog box. Paste
Locate cells formatted with data validation rules in the active worksheet	■ Choose Home→Editing→Find & Select →Validation from the Ribbon. The data validation cells will be selected.

DEVELOP YOUR SKILLS 15.3.2

Use a Drop-Down List

In this exercise, you will set data validation to restrict data entry to items in a drop-down list.

Create and Name the List

1. Display the **Summary** worksheet of the Quarterly Summary workbook.
2. Type **Yes** in **cell G1**.
3. Type **No** in **cell G2**.
4. Select the **range G1:G3**.
   This range will contain the entries in the drop-down list. Notice that you included a blank cell so users may reset a cell to a blank when necessary.
5. Click in the **Name** box to the left of the Formula Bar.
6. Type **List** and **tap** Enter to assign the name to the range.

List
A

Set Data Validation

7. In **cell G4**, type **Met Goal?** Center align the entry, and choose **bold**, if necessary.
8. Select the **range G5:G10**; **center-align** the cells.
   The range should still be selected.
9. Choose **Data→Data Tools→Data Validation** from the Ribbon.

10. Follow these steps to set up the data entry restriction:

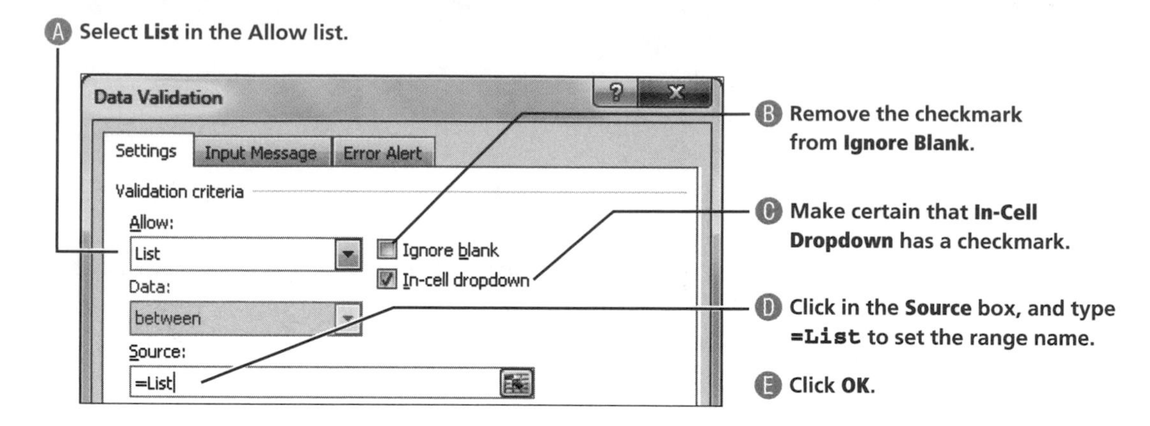
A Select List in the Allow list.
Data Validation
Settings
Input Message
Error Alert
Validation criteria
Allow:
List
Ignore blank
In-cell dropdown
Data:
between
Source:
=List
B Remove the checkmark from Ignore Blank.
C Make certain that In-Cell Dropdown has a checkmark.
D Click in the Source box, and type =List to set the range name.
E Click OK.

You did not enter an input message, and the default error alert message will be used.

Use the List to Enter Data

11. Select **cell G5**.
12. Follow these steps to enter data from the drop-down list:

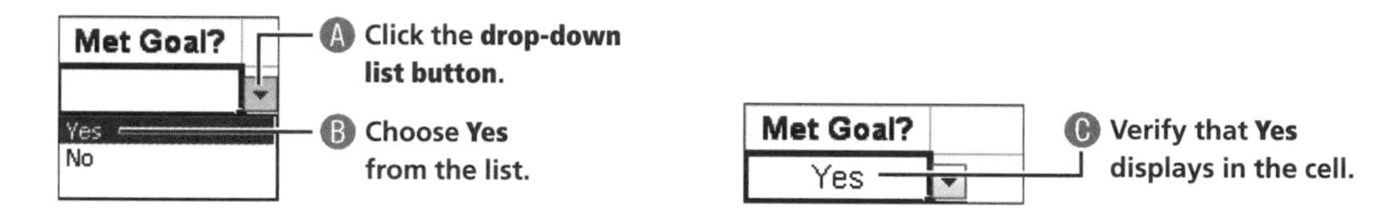
Met Goal?
Yes
No
A Click the drop-down list button.
B Choose Yes from the list.
Met Goal?
Yes
C Verify that Yes displays in the cell.

13. Select **cell G6**, and choose **No** from the in-cell drop-down list.
14. Select **cell G7**, and choose **No**.
    Assume that now you wish to reset this entry to a blank until you obtain more information.
15. Click the **drop-down list button** on **cell G7**, and choose the **blank item** below No.
    Cell G7 is now blank. Providing a blank choice in the list allows the user to reset the cell entry.
16. Select **cell G8**, type **Maybe**, and **tap** [Enter].
    An error message appears because you unchecked the Ignore Blanks option in the Data Validation dialog box. With the option off, the user is not allowed to type an entry into the cell unless it matches an entry contained in the drop-down list.
17. Read the error message, and click **Cancel**.
18. **Save** the changes, and leave the workbook **open**.

15.4 Circling Invalid Data

Video Lesson labyrinthelab.com/videos

At times, data may already be entered in worksheet cells before data validation rules are created. Some cells then may contain invalid data, so you should use the Circle Invalid Data command to find them. The command does just what the name implies: it places circles around any data that does not conform to the validation rules set for the cells. Once the data is circled, you may ignore or correct an entry. The red circles are easy to spot and do not print.

Circles around invalid data are temporary. Even if you don't clear the circles before you close the file, they will be gone when you reopen the file. You may, however, choose the Circle Invalid Data command again.

QUICK REFERENCE — CIRCLING INVALID DATA

Task	Procedure
Circle invalid data entered prior to creation of validation rules	■ Choose Data→Data Tools→Data Validation menu ▼→ Circle Invalid Data from the Ribbon. ■ Edit or ignore circled cells, as desired.
Remove validation circles	■ Perform any one of the following: ◆ Enter valid data in the cells. ◆ Choose Data→Data Tools→Data Validation menu ▼→ Clear Validation Circles from the Ribbon. ◆ Close the workbook.

DEVELOP YOUR SKILLS 15.4.1

Circle Invalid Data

In this exercise, you will reset data validation for a range of cells and then circle invalid data. You will edit values flagged as invalid. Finally, you will consolidate data again to update the totals on the Summary sheet.

Change Data Validation for a Range

In the first steps, you will revise a data validation rule only for the expense values in the Cash worksheet.

1. Display the **Cash** worksheet of the Quarterly Summary workbook.
2. Taking care not to select the totals in row 18, select the expense values in the **range B14:E17**.
3. Choose **Data→Data Tools→Data Validation** from the Ribbon.
4. Display the **Settings** tab in the Data Validation dialog box, if necessary.
   Recall that you set validation options to a whole positive number earlier in this lesson.

5. Follow these steps to restrict expense values to a maximum of $32,000:

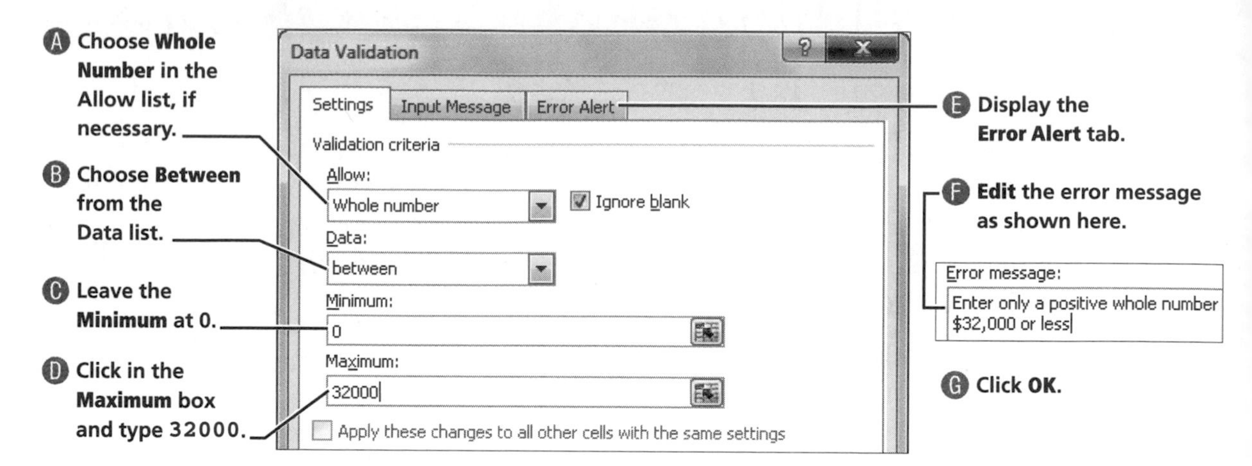

Test Data Validation

6. Enter **41500** in **cell B15**.
7. Read the error message, click **Retry,** and enter **1200**.

Circle Invalid Data

8. Choose **Data→Data Tools→Data Validation menu ▾→Circle Invalid Data** from the Ribbon.
Red circles appear around the cells that do not meet the validation set for those cells.

13	Direct Expenses				
14	Web/Social Media Development	1,500	1,500	1,500	35,000
15	Print Materials	1,200	500	500	563
16	Events	12,321	22,753	10,465	45,657
17	Salaries - Grant Proposals	-	-	-	-

9. Select **cell E14** and enter **1500**.
Notice that the red circle disappeared after you completed a valid entry.

Clear Validation Circles

10. Leave the value in **cell E16** as is.
At times you may want to keep previous values in the worksheet even if they do not meet the validation rules.
11. Choose **Data→Data Tools→Data Validation menu ▾→Clear Validation Circles**  from the Ribbon.
The remaining validation circle disappears.

Consolidate Data

You edited some values on the Cash worksheet in this exercise. Recall that a consolidated worksheet is not updated automatically unless the links option is switched on. In the next few steps, you will consolidate data again manually on the Summary worksheet.

12. Display the **Summary** worksheet.
    Notice that the direct expense total in cell F18 is 167,666 from the previous consolidation.
13. Select **cell B5**.
    Cell B5 is the starting cell in the consolidation cell range B5:F18.
14. Choose **Data→Data Tools→Consolidate** from the Ribbon.
    The Consolidate dialog box appears with the ranges still set for the Cash, Grants, and In-Kind worksheets.
15. Click **OK**.
    The sums are recalculated, and cell F18 should display 134,866.
16. **Save** the changes, and **close** the workbook.

15.5 Removing Duplicate Records

Video Lesson labyrinthelab.com/videos

When you combine or import records into a worksheet, duplicate records may then exist in multiple rows of the worksheet. Excel provides several methods to identify and remove duplicates that contain the same cell entries as those in another row. The records are not considered duplicates if the data are formatted differently.

Filtering for unique records does not delete any duplicate records, but the Remove Duplicates command does delete them.

Filtering for Unique Records

You may perform an advanced filter to temporarily hide duplicate records. You may filter a list or table in place, as shown in the following illustration. You also may choose to copy unique records to another area of the same worksheet or a different worksheet.

Duplicate records in rows 5 and 7 are hidden temporarily.

	A	B	C
3	Pledge Level	Team Leader	Sponsor Category
4	Level 5	Abbott	Organization Contrib
6	Level 4	Faber	Corporate Sponsors
8	Level 1	Lemus	Federal Government
9	Level 3	Faber	Corporate Sponsors
10	Level 6	Nguyen	Individual Contributio

The result of an advanced filter for unique records

Removing Duplicates

The Remove Duplicates command on the Ribbon deletes duplicate records from a list. You specify the columns in which Excel is to look for an exact match. Choosing all columns will ensure that only the records that match in every cell will be deleted. You may undo the action if the result is not what you expect.

QUICK REFERENCE **FILTERING AND REMOVING DUPLICATE RECORDS**

Task	Procedure
Filter to hide duplicate records in a list or table	■ Select any cell in the list or table. ■ Choose Data→Sort & Filter→Advanced from the Ribbon. ■ Verify that the default list range is correct in the Advanced Filter dialog box. ■ Choose to filter the list in place or copy to another location. ■ Place a checkmark next to Unique Records Only.
Remove duplicate records from a list or table	■ Select any cell in the list or table. ■ Choose Data→Data Tools→Remove Duplicates from the Ribbon. ■ Verify that a checkmark is next to My Data Has Headers if column headings are included as the first row of data. ■ Select the desired columns that contain duplicate data. (Select all columns to require an exact match of all data in rows.)

DEVELOP YOUR SKILLS 15.5.1

Filter Unique Records and Remove Duplicates

In this exercise, you will perform an advanced filter to hide duplicate records. You also will remove duplicates permanently.

Perform an Advanced Filter

1. **Open** the Combined Contributions workbook from the Lesson 15 folder.
   Duplicate records exist in rows 4–5 and 6–7.
2. Select **cell D4.**
3. Choose **Data→Sort & Filter→Advanced** from the Ribbon.
4. Follow these steps to filter the list for unique records:

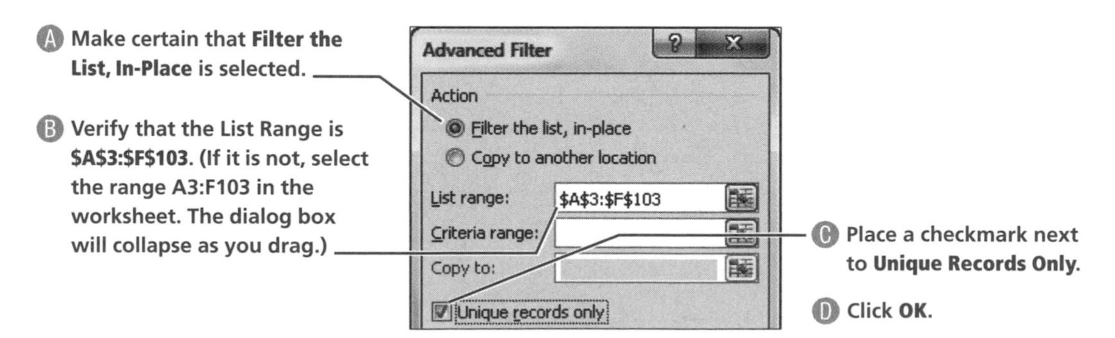

Ⓐ Make certain that **Filter the List, In-Place** is selected.
Ⓑ Verify that the List Range is **$A$3:$F$103.** (If it is not, select the range A3:F103 in the worksheet. The dialog box will collapse as you drag.)
Advanced Filter
Action
Filter the list, in-place
Copy to another location
List range:
$A$3:$F$103
Criteria range:
Copy to:
Unique records only
Ⓒ Place a checkmark next to **Unique Records Only.**
Ⓓ Click **OK.**

The duplicate rows 5 and 7 are hidden, and the Status Bar at the lower-left corner of the window indicates that 98 unique records were found.

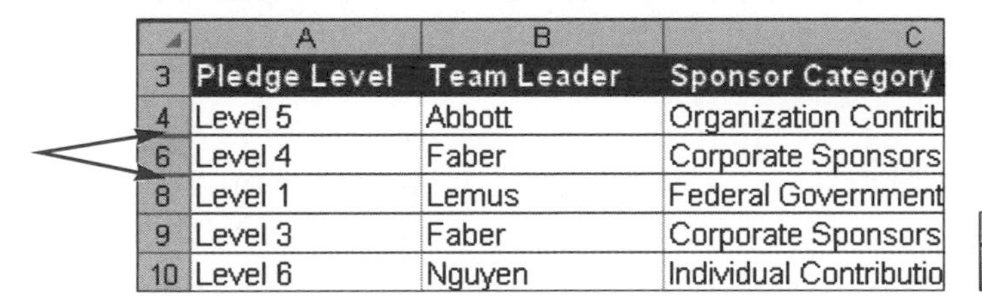

	A	B	C
3	Pledge Level	Team Leader	Sponsor Category
4	Level 5	Abbott	Organization Contrib
6	Level 4	Faber	Corporate Sponsors
8	Level 1	Lemus	Federal Government
9	Level 3	Faber	Corporate Sponsors
10	Level 6	Nguyen	Individual Contributio

5. Choose **Data→Sort & Filter→Clear** from the Ribbon.
   The duplicate records reappear in the list. Filtering did not delete the records.

Remove Duplicates

6. Make certain that **cell D4** or another cell in the list is selected.
7. Choose **Data→Data Tools→Remove Duplicates** from the Ribbon.

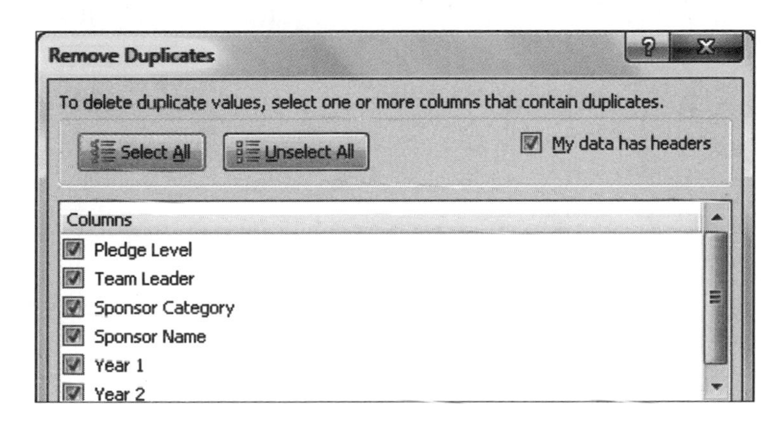

Notice that all columns are selected with a checkmark in the Remove Duplicates dialog box.

8. Make certain **My Data Has Headers** has a checkmark in the upper-right corner of the dialog box, and click **OK**.
   Excel looks for an exact match in all columns of records to find duplicate rows.
9. Read the message indicating that two records were removed, and click **OK**.
   The Remove Duplicates command deleted the records without asking for confirmation. You could undo the command if the results were incorrect.
10. **Save** and **close** the workbook.

15.6 Using Data Tables

Video Lesson labyrinthelab.com/videos

Data tables are different from the tables that allow you to sort, filter, and create totals for data. Data tables preview the effect that changing some values would have on a formula's result. A data table is structured around a specific formula to perform a what-if analysis. Various values from a list are substituted for either one or two cell references in the formula. The Data Table command calculates the formula result for each value listed.

One-Variable Data Tables

One-variable data tables compute results for various values substituted for a cell reference in a formula. For example, the data table may display the result for a FV (Future Value) formula with the monthly payment as a variable in increments of $20. This example is shown in the following illustration, where the empty Payment cell (B5) is known as the input cell. Each value from Payment column C of the data table is substituted in the input cell, and its corresponding Future Value result displays in column D.

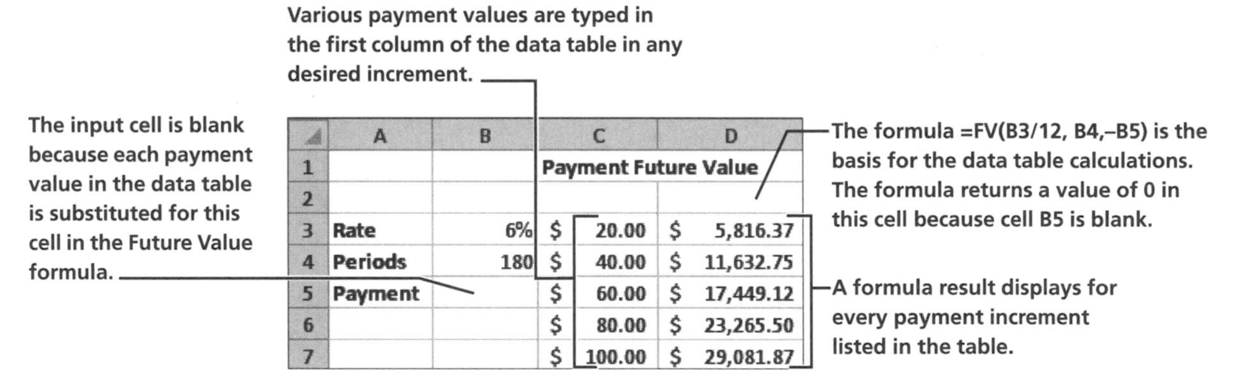

	A	B	C	D
1			Payment	Future Value
2				
3	Rate	6%	$ 20.00	$ 5,816.37
4	Periods	180	$ 40.00	$ 11,632.75
5	Payment		$ 60.00	$ 17,449.12
6			$ 80.00	$ 23,265.50
7			$ 100.00	$ 29,081.87

Various payment values are typed in the first column of the data table in any desired increment.
The input cell is blank because each payment value in the data table is substituted for this cell in the Future Value formula.
The formula =FV(B3/12, B4,–B5) is the basis for the data table calculations. The formula returns a value of 0 in this cell because cell B5 is blank.
A formula result displays for every payment increment listed in the table.

A one-variable data table for a Future Value formula

Two-Variable Data Tables

You will work with two-variable data tables in this lesson. While a one-variable data table has one input cell, this type has two input cells. Values are substituted for two cell references in the formula. The following illustration shows the layout of a two-variable data table using the same Future Value formula as in the previous example. Take a few moments to review this illustration carefully.

The formula =FV(B3/12, B4,–B5) is the basis for the data table calculations. The formula returns a value of 0 in this cell because cells B3 and B5 are blank.

Various payment values are typed into the first column of the data table, and rates are entered into the first row.

The input cells are blank because each rate and payment value in the data table are substituted for these cells in the Future Value formula.

	A	B	C	D	E	F	G
1			Payment Future Value				
2			$ -	4%	5%	6%	7%
3	Rate		$ 20.00	$ 4,921.81	$ 5,345.78	$ 5,816.37	$ 6,339.25
4	Periods	180	$ 40.00	$ 9,843.62	$ 10,691.56	$ 11,632.75	$ 12,678.49
5	Payment		$ 60.00	$ 14,765.43	$ 16,037.34	$ 17,449.12	$ 19,017.74
6			$ 80.00	$ 19,687.24	$ 21,383.12	$ 23,265.50	$ 25,356.98
7			$ 100.00	$ 24,609.05	$ 26,728.89	$ 29,081.87	$ 31,696.23

A two-variable data table for a Future Value formula

A formula result displays for every combination of rate and payment listed in the table.

QUICK REFERENCE CREATING DATA TABLES

Task	Procedure
Create a one-variable data table	■ Enter a formula in the worksheet. The formula must include a reference to one input cell outside the data table. ■ Enter input variable values down the column (under the formula cell) to substitute for one cell address in the formula. ■ Select the data table, including the formula cell, all input variable values, and the cells that will hold the calculated results. ■ Choose Data→Data Tools→What-If Analysis →Data Table from the Ribbon. ■ In the Data Table dialog box, specify the column input cell that is outside the data table and used in the formula.
Create a two-variable data table	■ Enter a formula as the upper-left cell in the data table. The formula must include references to two input cells outside the data table. ■ Enter input variable values across the first row (to the right of the formula cell) to substitute for one cell address in the formula. ■ Enter input variable values down the first column (under the formula cell) to substitute for one cell address in the formula. ■ Select the data table, including the formula cell, all input variable values, and the cells that will hold the calculated results. ■ Choose Data→Data Tools→What-If Analysis →Data Table from the Ribbon. In the Data Table dialog box, specify the row input cell and column input cell that are outside the data table and used in the formula.

DEVELOP YOUR SKILLS 15.6.1

Create a Two-Variable Data Table

In this exercise, you will create a data table with two variables. The data table formula will calculate the amount above or below the net income goal for a fundraising event for each combination of ticket price and tickets sold.

Set Up the Data Table

1. **Open** a new, blank workbook.
2. Enter the following data into **Sheet1**, formatting the numbers and text as shown.

	A	B	C	D	E	F	G
1	**Net Income $ Goal**	**Net Income % Goal**					
2	$ 75,000	70%					
3			**Ticket Sales Above (Below) Goal**				
4			**Tickets Sold**				
5			600	650	700	750	800
6	**Ticket Price**	$ 100					
7		$ 150					
8		$ 200					
9		$ 250					
10		$ 300					

A two-variable data table is always set up this way. One set of variables is placed immediately to the right of the formula (the tickets sold from 600 to 800 in this exercise). The other set of variables is placed immediately below the formula (the dollar amounts). The Tickets Sold and Ticket Price labels may be placed anywhere as long as they do not interfere with the table.

3. Select **cell B5**.
   You will create a formula with references to two input cells. Any two blank cells may be used as the input cells as long as they are outside the data table range. You will use cell B3 as the tickets sold (row) variable and cell B4 as the ticket price (column) variable.
4. **Enter** the formula **=(B2*B3*B4)-A2** in **cell B5**.
   The result equals –75000, the entire net income goal, because cells B3 and B4 used in the formula are blank. This formula first calculates the net income as 70 percent of tickets sold at the specified price. From the result, the $75,000 net income goal is subtracted to calculate the dollar amount of ticket sales that is above or below the goal. A positive number is acceptable.
5. Select **cell B5**, and change the text color to **white** to **hide** the formula result.
   The result of the formula cell is not a relevant value for your ticket sales analysis.

Complete the Data Table

The final steps in creating the data table are selecting the table range and issuing the Data Table command.

6. Select the **range B5:G10** as shown.

	A	B	C	D	E	F	G
4			Tickets Sold				
5			600	650	700	750	800
6	Ticket Price	$ 100					
7		$ 150					
8		$ 200					
9		$ 250					
10		$ 300					

When selecting the range for a data table, you must include the formula, variables, and cells that will hold the calculated results in the selection. Notice that the text labels and input cells are not included.

7. Choose **Data→Data Tools→What-If Analysis** →**Data Table** from the Ribbon.
8. Follow these steps to choose the input cells:

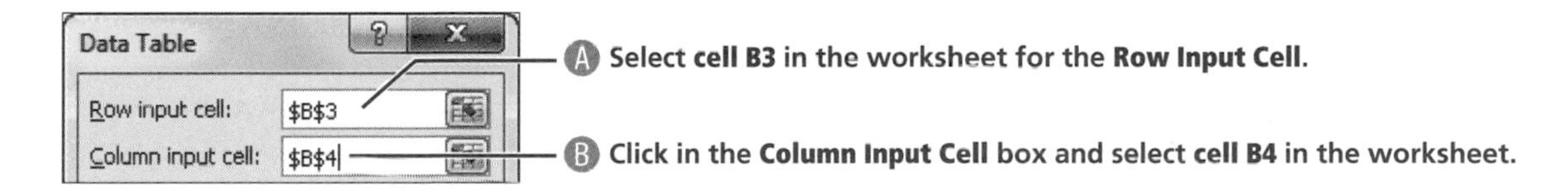

Data Table
Row input cell: $B$3
Column input cell: $B$4
A Select cell B3 in the worksheet for the Row Input Cell.
B Click in the Column Input Cell box and select cell B4 in the worksheet.

The Row Input Cell is the cell in which you want the row variables (tickets sold) to be substituted. Likewise, the Column Input Cell substitutes the column variables (ticket prices). If you look at the formula in cell B5, you will see that these substitutions make sense.

9. Click **OK** in the Data Table dialog box.
The data table is completed as shown in the following illustration.

	A	B	C	D	E	F	G
3			Ticket Sales Above (Below) Goal				
4			Tickets Sold				
5			600	650	700	750	800
6	Ticket Price	$ 100	(33,000)	(29,500)	(26,000)	(22,500)	(19,000)
7		$ 150	(12,000)	(6,750)	(1,500)	3,750	9,000
8		$ 200	9,000	16,000	23,000	30,000	37,000
9		$ 250	30,000	38,750	47,500	56,250	65,000
10		$ 300	51,000	61,500	72,000	82,500	93,000

10. Select the **range C6:G10**, and choose **Comma Style with no decimals** from the Ribbon.
Notice the positive numbers in the data table. Any positive number indicates that net income would be above the goal. At a ticket price of $150, more than 700 tickets must be sold to achieve the desired net income amount. Any ticket price of $200 or more would achieve the goal, but a higher price might result in fewer tickets sold.
11. **Save** the changes as **`Tickets Data Table`** in the Lesson 15 folder in your file storage location.

12. Feel free to experiment with your data table. For example, try changing the ticket prices in **column B** to increments of $25 rather than $50. How would the results change if the net income percentage in cell B2 were 65%?
    The data table will be recalculated each time you change a variable.
13. When you are finished, **close** the workbook **without** saving again.

15.7 Creating Trendlines

Video Lesson labyrinthelab.com/videos

Trendlines are used on charts for data analysis and prediction. A trendline visually displays the trend (increasing or decreasing) of one data series in a chart. There are several types of trendlines available, each suited to the display of particular types of data. For example, a linear trendline works well with data that follow a fairly straight path. A moving average trendline smoothes out fluctuations in data by averaging two or more adjacent data points for each trendline data point.

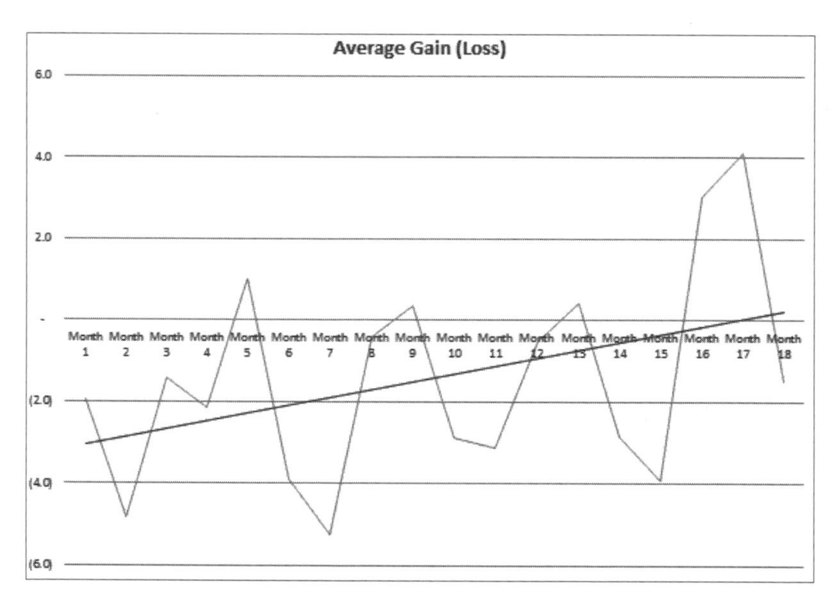

This linear trendline depicts the upward trend for average weight of patients enrolled in a clinical study over 18 months.

You cannot add a trendline to certain types of charts, such as 3-D, pie, and area charts.

DEVELOP YOUR SKILLS 15.7.1

Add a Trendline

In this exercise, you will add a trendline to an existing chart. You will format the trendline to show trends based on various time periods.

Insert a Trendline

1. **Open** the Contributions Trend workbook from the Lesson 15 folder.
   The Summary worksheet and trend chart summarize net sales for four quarters of a year.
2. Display the **Trend Chart** worksheet.
3. **Select** the chart.
4. Choose **Chart Tools Layout→Analysis→Trendline** →**Linear Trendline** from the Ribbon.
   The new trendline appears. This best-fit line indicates that net sales are increasing at an excellent rate.

Edit the Trendline

5. Taking care to position the tip of the pointer arrow against the trendline as shown, select the **trendline**. (If the trendline does not display handles at its endpoints, reposition the tip of the mouse pointer at the trendline and select again.)

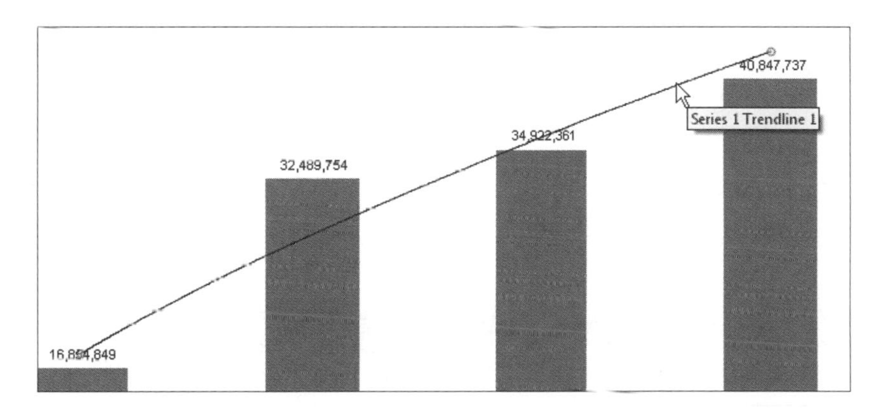

6. Choose **Layout→Analysis→Trendline→Linear Forecast Trendline**.
   The trendline lengthens to forecast net sales in the next two quarters.
7. Select the trendline, and choose **Layout→Analysis→Trendline** →**More Trendline Options** from the Ribbon.
8. In the **Forecast** area in the lower part of the Format Trendline dialog box, change **Forward** from 2.0 periods to **1**.
9. Take a few moments to view the other options in the dialog box.
10. Click **Close**.
    The trendline now forecasts only one quarter in the future, a more conservative analysis.

11. With the trendline still selected, choose **Layout→Analysis→Trendline→Two Period Moving Average** from the Ribbon.

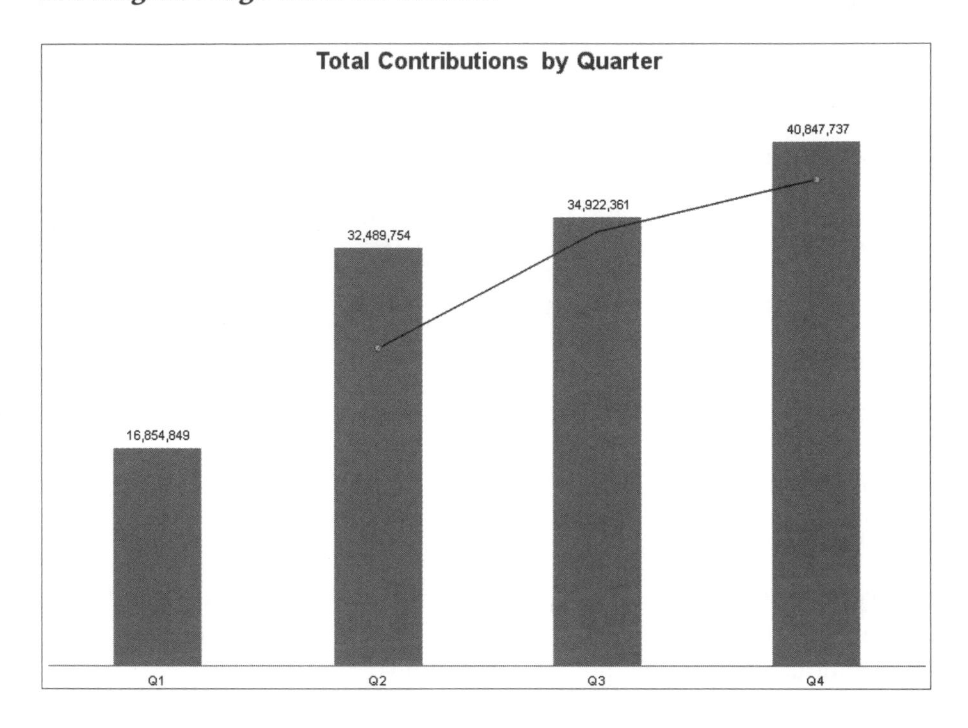

The trendline shortens to begin at the second quarter and displays an angle to reflect the fewer number of data points being averaged for each point on the trendline. This type of trendline follows data fluctuations. To use trendline options effectively, an understanding of statistics in math is helpful.

12. **Save** the changes, and leave the workbook **open**.

15.8 Creating Sparklines in Cells

Video Lesson labyrinthelab.com/videos

Sparklines appear as miniature charts in worksheet cells. New in Excel 2010, sparklines allow you to show the data graphically without all the steps required in creating a normal chart. You also may select a cell range and create sparklines for every row or column at once. Changes to data are reflected immediately in sparklines right next to the data. Each sparkline charts the data in one row or column.

	A	B	C	D	E	F
4	**Pledge Level**	**Q1**	**Q2**	**Q3**	**Q4**	**By Quarter**
5	Level 1	16,541,676	30,201,177	32,114,970	38,409,659	
6	Level 2	-	2,000,000	2,253,988	2,000,075	
7	Level 3	202,373	222,645	479,673	412,892	
8	Level 4	100,891	50,000	51,209	-	
9	Level 5	8,647	13,043	17,921	18,676	
10	Level 6	1,262	2,889	4,600	6,435	
11	**Total Contributions**	**16,854,849**	**32,489,754**	**34,922,361**	**40,847,737**	**125,114,701**

Sparklines in column F with dot markers to show upward and downward trends for each pledge level of contributions during the year

Formatting Sparklines

You may format sparklines as lines, columns, or win-loss columns. The win-loss format shows the increase or decrease as compared to a previous period. You may format sparklines with styles and choose to display data points in various ways. For example, the Markers option displays a dot for each value along a sparkline formatted as a line. The same formatting must be applied to sparklines created all at once, while unique formatting may be applied to each sparkline created one at a time.

QUICK REFERENCE **CREATING TRENDLINES AND SPARKLINES**

Task	Procedure
Add a trendline to a chart	■ Display the chart to which you wish to add a trendline. ■ Choose Chart Tools Layout→Analysis→Trendline from the Ribbon. ■ Choose a trendline type. ■ Select a data series in the Add a Trendline Based on Series dialog box, if more than one exists in the chart.
Change the trendline type	■ Select the trendline. ■ Choose Chart Tools Layout→Analysis→Trendline from the Ribbon. ■ Choose a trendline type.
Format the trendline	■ Select the trendline. ■ Choose the desired options on the Format ribbon.
Add objects specific to the chart type and trendline type	■ Select the trendline. ■ Display the Chart Tools Layout ribbon and choose options from those displayed in the Analysis group.
Create a sparkline	■ Select the cell to contain the sparkline, or select a cell range to place a sparkline in each row or column. ■ Choose the Insert ribbon, and choose the desired sparkline type from the Sparklines group on the Ribbon. ■ In the Create Sparklines dialog box, select the data range containing the source values. ■ Verify the location range of cells to contain the sparkline(s), and click OK.
Format a sparkline	■ Select the desired cell(s) containing a sparkline. ■ Choose the desired options on the Sparkline Tools Design ribbon.

DEVELOP YOUR SKILLS 15.8.1

Create Sparklines

In this exercise, you will create sparklines in a fundraising summary worksheet to show upward and downward trends in the contributions raised each quarter.

Create Sparklines as Line Charts

1. Display the **Summary** sheet in the Contributions Trend workbook.
2. Select the **range F5:F10**.
   These cells will contain the sparklines for each contribution level.
3. Choose **Insert→Sparklines→Line** from the Ribbon.
4. Follow these steps to complete the Create Sparklines dialog box:

Ⓐ Move the dialog box, if necessary, to view **column B** in the worksheet.

Ⓑ For the Data Range, select the **range B5:E10** in the worksheet. (The dialog box will collapse as you drag.)

Ⓒ Make certain that the Location Range is **$F$5:$F$10**.

Ⓓ Click **OK**.

Create Sparklines
Choose the data that you want
Data Range: B5:E10
Choose where you want the sparklines to be placed
Location Range: $F$5:$F$10

   A sparkline appears in each cell of the range.

5. Choose **Sparkline Tools Design→Show→Markers** from the Ribbon to place a checkmark next to Markers.

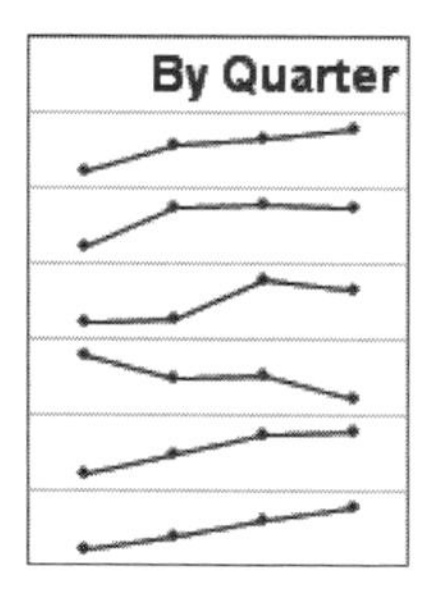

   The sparklines display a dot marker for each quarter, thus making the upward and downward trends easier to understand.

6. Read the other options in the Design ribbon, and then **deselect** the range.
7. **Save** the changes.

Create Sparklines as Column Charts

8. Select **cell F14**, and choose **Insert→Sparklines→Column** from the Ribbon.
9. In the **Create Sparklines** dialog box, set the Data Range to **B14:E14**, verify that the Location Range is **$F$14**, and click **OK**.
   This time you created a single sparkline.

10. Repeat **steps 8–9** to create a column sparkline in **cell F15**. Then, repeat twice more for **cells F16 and F17**.

	B	C	D	E	F
13	Q1	Q2	Q3	Q4	By Quarter
14	3,500	3,500	3,500	37,000	
15	947	977	1,699	864	
16	12,589	22,753	10,465	45,872	
17	6,000	6,000	6,000	6,000	

Notice the values in the range B14:E14. The sparkline chart in cell F14 represents these values in relation to each other. The fourth column in the sparkline is larger to represent the value 37,000 as compared to the value 3,500 in the other three cells. The columns in cell F17 are an equal size because the values in the range B17:E17 are equal. The sparklines do not compare values from one row to values in another row.

Format Sparklines

11. Select **cell F15**, and follow these steps to change the sparkline style:

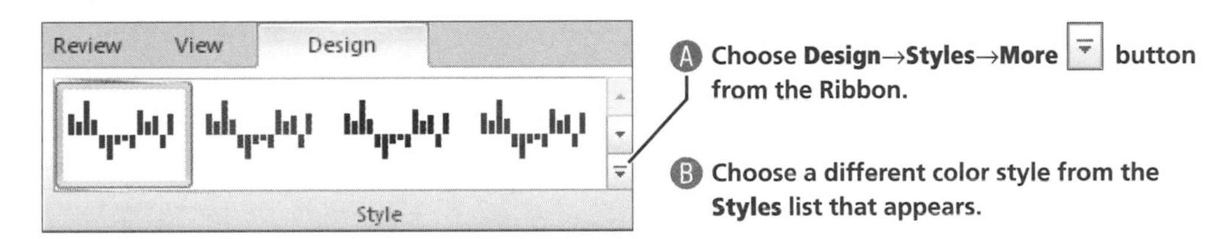

Review
View
Design
Style
A Choose Design→Styles→More button from the Ribbon.
B Choose a different color style from the Styles list that appears.

Notice that you could format a single sparkline because you created each sparkline separately in the range F14:F17.

12. Repeat the above step **twice** to apply different sparkline styles to **cells F16 and F17**.
13. Select **cell F5**.
    The range F5:F10 is surrounded by an outline to indicate that the six sparklines are selected. You previously created these sparklines all at once.
14. Choose **Design→Style→More** button, and choose a different style from the Ribbon.
15. Feel free to experiment with any other options in the Show group of the Design ribbon to format the sparklines.
16. **Save** the changes, and **close** the workbook.

15.9 Concepts Review

Concepts Review labyrinthelab.com/excel10

To check your knowledge of the key concepts introduced in this lesson, complete the Concepts Review quiz by going to the URL listed above. If your classroom is using Labyrinth eLab, you may complete the Concepts Review quiz from within your eLab course.

Reinforce Your Skills

REINFORCE YOUR SKILLS 15.1

Group Worksheets and Consolidate Data by Category

In this exercise, you will complete a workbook that tracks compensation paid to independent contractors. The employer issues 1099 statements (similar to W-2 forms) to independent contractors at the end of the year for their income tax returns. The workbook contains a Year-to-Date worksheet as well as worksheets for each month. You will group the worksheets and enter the headings for all the sheets. In addition, you will use the Consolidate by Category option to consolidate the monthly data in the Year-to-Date worksheet.

Browse the Workbook

1. **Open** the rs-Consolidated Compensation workbook from the Lesson 15 folder.
   Notice that the Year-to-Date worksheet has column headings in row 3 but no data. The Consolidation command will insert the data.
2. Display the **January** worksheet.
   Six 1099 recipients are listed with their respective number of hours and compensation. This recipient list is different for each month because these temporary contractors come and go on a regular basis.
3. Select **cell C4**.
   Notice that the compensation is calculated as the hours multiplied by $21.35. The Consolidate command will combine the hours and compensation from the monthly worksheets. You can consolidate cells with both values and formulas, as in this exercise.
4. Display the **February** worksheet.
   Seven recipients are listed for February. Several of these recipients differ from those in the January worksheet.
5. Display the **March** worksheet and notice that, again, the recipient list has changed.
   In a later step, you will use the Consolidate command for the Year-to-Date worksheet. You cannot consolidate by position, as you did in the Quarterly Summary workbook previously in this lesson, because the monthly sheets have different layouts. The list of independent contractors varies.

Group Multiple Worksheets

Next you will group the worksheets to prepare for data entry and formatting.

6. Display the **Year-to-Date** worksheet.
7. **Hold down** [Shift] and click the **March** sheet tab.
   Notice that the sheets are now grouped so that whatever you do on one worksheet occurs simultaneously on all worksheets in the group.

Enter and Format Labels Across Worksheets

8. Select **cell A1** in the Year-to-Date worksheet and enter **Compensation**.
9. Merge and center the label in **cell A1** across **cells A1:C1**.
10. With cells A1:C1 still selected, choose **Home→Styles→Cell Styles→Themed Cell Styles→Accent1** (white text with dark blue fill) from the Ribbon.

11. Select **cells A3:C3** and choose **Home→Styles→Cell Styles→Themed Cell Styles→20% - Accent1** (black text with light blue fill) from the Ribbon.
12. **Deselect** the highlighted cells.
13. **Right-click** the Year-to-Date sheet tab and choose **Ungroup Sheets** from the context menu.
14. Edit **cell A1** in the Year-to-Date worksheet to **`1099 Recipient Compensation`**.
15. Display each of the **monthly** worksheets.
    Notice that the formatting you applied while the worksheets were grouped appears on every worksheet. You edited the title in cell A1 while the worksheets were ungrouped, so only the Year-to-Date worksheet reflects that change.

Select Data to Consolidate

16. Display the **Year-to-Date** worksheet and select **cell A4** as the starting point for the consolidated data.
17. Choose **Data→Data Tools→Consolidate** from the Ribbon.
    In the next few steps, you will specify the range references you wish to consolidate. You will do this by selecting the ranges in the various sheets and adding them to the All References list.
18. Follow these steps to set consolidation options in the Consolidate dialog box:

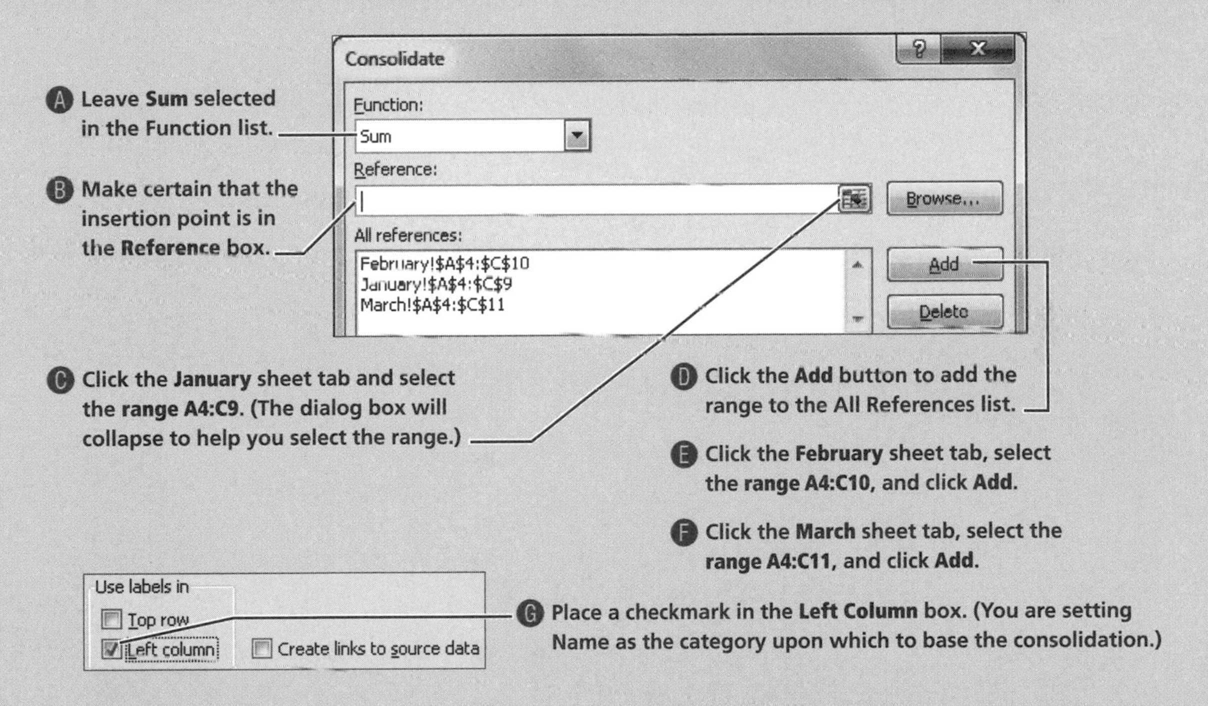

Consolidate
Function:
Sum
Reference:
Browse...
All references:
February!$A$4:$C$10
January!$A$4:$C$9
March!$A$4:$C$11
Add
Delete
A Leave Sum selected in the Function list.
B Make certain that the insertion point is in the Reference box.
C Click the January sheet tab and select the range A4:C9. (The dialog box will collapse to help you select the range.)
D Click the Add button to add the range to the All References list.
E Click the February sheet tab, select the range A4:C10, and click Add.
F Click the March sheet tab, select the range A4:C11, and click Add.
Use labels in
Top row
Left column
Create links to source data
G Place a checkmark in the Left Column box. (You are setting Name as the category upon which to base the consolidation.)

Review the references in the All References list. You build a consolidation by adding references to this list. Notice that the row labels in column A are included in the references. The Consolidate command will use the labels in the left column (column A) to determine which rows to consolidate from the monthly sheets. Excel will create one consolidated row in the Year-to-Date worksheet for each name. For example, the name Dennis Johnson appears in two worksheets. Excel will create one Dennis Johnson row in the Year-to-Date sheet summing his numbers.

19. Click **OK** in the Consolidate dialog box.
The Year-to-Date worksheet displays the consolidated numbers shown in the following illustration.

	A	B	C
1	1099 Recepient Compensation		
2			
3	Name	Hours	Compensation
4	Johnson, Dennis E.	27	576.45
5	Lake, Cheryl Y.	77	1,643.95
6	Parson, Robin J.	67	1,430.45
7	Williams, Scott G.	35	747.25
8	Richardson, Eddie	46	982.10
9	Jones, William T.	51	1,088.85
10	Thomas, Wanda M.	65	1,387.75
11	Wilson, Leslie A. Jr.	38	811.30
12	Simpson, Lakisha D.	12	256.20
13	Ellis, Ellen E.	10	213.50
14	Williams, Stewart M.	8	170.80

Notice that each name appears just once in the consolidated list. Feel free to browse through the monthly sheets. You will notice that the consolidated numbers are sums of the numbers for the individual months.

20. **Deselect** the highlighted range.

Add Another Worksheet

You can easily consolidate the data again by adding a consolidation range for any monthly worksheet added later. In the next few steps, you will add an April worksheet and reconsolidate the data.

21. Copy the **March** worksheet and name the new sheet `April`.
22. In the **April** worksheet, select **rows 6 and 7** and use the **Delete** command to remove them.
Scott Williams and Eddie Richardson did not receive compensation in April.
23. Add the recipients and hours shown to **rows 10 and 11**.
Excel will automatically calculate the compensation in cells C10 and C11 when you Tab *through the cells during data entry.*

10	Sanchez, Pedro	23	491.05
11	Yee, Doness U.	21	448.35

Consolidate Again

24. Display the **Year-to-Date** worksheet.
25. Select all consolidated data in the **range A4:C14** and **tap** the Delete key.
It is best to delete the existing data before reconsolidating because the new consolidation will overwrite the existing data. If the new consolidation has fewer rows than the original consolidation, there will be leftover (and incorrect) rows at the bottom of the consolidated data.
26. Select **cell A4** and choose **Data→Data Tools→Consolidate** from the Ribbon.
Notice that the consolidation ranges you chose are still in the All References list. Now you need only add the April range.
27. Make certain that the insertion point is in the **Reference** box.
28. Click the **April** sheet tab and select the **range A4:C11** in the worksheet.

29. Click the **Add** button in the dialog box.

30. Click **OK** to complete the consolidation.
The updated consolidation includes 13 unique names in rows 4–16.

31. **Deselect** the highlighted range.

32. **Save** the changes, and **close** the workbook.

REINFORCE YOUR SKILLS 15.2

Construct a Loan Payment Data Table

In this exercise, you will create a two-variable data table. The data table will calculate monthly payments on a car loan using various interest rates and payment periods.

Set Up the Data Table

1. **Start** a new workbook and **enter** the data shown. Make certain that the numbers in **column B** are formatted with percent symbols.

	A	B	C	D	E	F	G
1	Car Loan Analysis						
2							
3	Opening Balance		$ 22,000				
4							
5			Months				
6			36	42	48	54	60
7	Rate	2%					
8		3%					
9		4%					
10		5%					
11		6%					
12		7%					
13		8%					
14		9%					

2. Select **cell B6**, the upper-left corner cell of the data table.
In the next step, you will enter a formula that uses the PMT function. The PMT function calculates payments using a monthly interest rate, number of payments, and opening balance as arguments.

3. **Enter** the formula **= -PMT(B5/12,A6,C3)** and **complete** the entry.
The result displays as #NUM! because cells B5 and A6 (the input cells for the data table) are empty. You will respond to this message later. The formula is interpreted as follows.

The B5/12 reference is the interest rate argument. The B5 reference is divided by 12 because the payments will be made monthly, and the rates in column B are annual rates. The interest rates in column B will be substituted into input cell B5 when the Data Table command is issued.

The A6 reference is the second input cell. The months in row 6 will be substituted into this cell when the Data Table command is issued.

Cell C3 contains the loan amount. The PMT function always returns a negative number, so you added a minus (–) sign to reverse the formula result to a positive number.

Complete the Data Table

4. Select the **range B6:G14** and choose **Data→Data Tools→What-If Analysis** →**Data Table** from the Ribbon.
5. Enter **A6** as the **row input** cell and **B5** as the **column input** cell.
6. Click **OK** and the table is calculated.
7. Taking care not to select the months in row 6 or rates in column B, select the **range C7:G14**.
8. Format the selected cells as **Comma Style with two decimal places**.

Adjust the Loan Amount

Now imagine that you want to see the same analysis for a different loan amount. This is easily accomplished by changing the loan amount in cell C3.

9. Select **cell C3** and change 22000 to **25000**.
10. **Complete** the entry, and the data table will recalculate.
    Assume that your budget allows a maximum payment of $550. Read across each row of the data table to determine the loan length. For example, at the 2 percent rate, the loan term must be 48 months.

	A	B	C	D	E	F	G
3	Opening Balance		$ 25,000				
4							
5			Months				
6		#NUM!	36	42	48	54	60
7	Rate	2%	716.06	616.81	542.38	484.49	438.19
8		3%	727.03	627.78	553.36	495.49	449.22
9		4%	738.10	638.87	564.48	506.65	460.41
10		5%	749.27	650.08	575.73	517.96	471.78
11		6%	760.55	661.41	587.13	529.42	483.32
12		7%	771.93	672.86	598.66	541.04	495.03
13		8%	783.41	684.42	610.32	552.81	506.91
14		9%	794.99	696.11	622.13	564.73	518.96

Respond to an Alert

If the Enable Background Error Checking option is switched on in Excel Options, the PMT formula cell displays a small triangle icon in the upper left of the cell to alert you to the #NUM! error. For the purpose of the data table, this is not actually an error.

11. Select **cell B6**, click the **alert** button displayed to the left of the cell, and choose **Ignore Error** from the context menu.

    If you determine that #NUM! would confuse other workbook users, you may format the cell with a white font to "hide" the message, or you could hide the cell and turn on worksheet protection.
12. **Save** as **rs-Loan Data Table** in the Lesson 15 folder; then **close** the workbook.

REINFORCE YOUR SKILLS 15.3

Work with Trendlines and Sparklines

In this exercise, you will add a trendline to the data on an existing chart. You will create sparklines to chart the net sales performance for each quarter during a four-year period.

Create and Format a Trendline

1. **Open** the rs-Trendline workbook from the Lesson 15 folder and take a moment to review the data.
   The Net Sales worksheet depicts the quarterly net sales over the course of four years.
2. Display the **Trend Chart** worksheet.
   This chart displays the four years of data. Notice that the data pattern fluctuates up and down. A linear trendline would not provide much help in analyzing the trends.
3. Select the chart and choose **Chart Tools Layout→Analysis→Trendline→More Trendline Options** from the Ribbon.
4. Move the **Format Trendline** dialog box to one side of the workbook window as you work so that you can view the trendline.
5. Under **Trend/Regression Type** in the Format Trendline dialog box, choose **Polynomial**.
   This trendline type is useful for tracking fluctuations in data. Inspecting the columns in the chart indicates several significant changes over the four-year period.
6. Use the spinner button to set the **Order** option to **4** as shown.
   Each click displays an additional rise or dip in the trendline.

One way to compare the accuracy of a trendline is to display its R-squared value. The closer a trendline's R-squared value is to 1, the better it fits the data.

7. Place a checkmark in the **Display R-squared Value on Chart** option near the bottom of the dialog box.
   The R-squared value displays near the end of the trendline as R^2=0.5312.

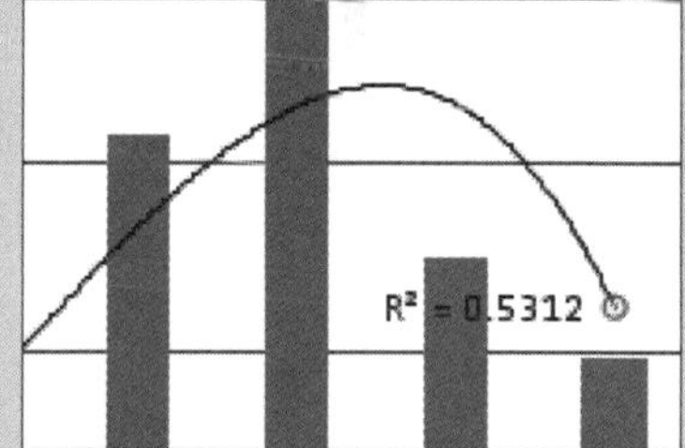

8. Change the **Order** option to **6** next to Polynomial and click **Close**.
   The trendline displays R^2 = 0.6286. Since its value is closer to 1, this trendline represents a more accurate forecast. An ideal trendline would have an R^2 value very close to 1.
9. **Save** the changes.

Create Sparklines

10. Display the **Sales Change** worksheet.
    On this sheet, the data are rearranged by each quarter of the fiscal year. You will create sparklines to quickly chart the changes from year to year and identify the lowest year in each row.
11. Select the **range F5:F8**.
12. Choose **Insert→Sparklines→Line** from the Ribbon.
13. On the Sparkline Tools Design ribbon, navigate to the **Show** group and place a checkmark next to both **Markers** and **Low Point**.
    The markers indicate each fiscal year on a sparkline. Notice that the low point has a slightly different color than the other markers. Next, you will choose a color with more contrast so the low point stands out.
14. Choose **Design→Style→Marker Color→Low Point**, and choose a contrasting theme color.
    Now the sparklines present the lower sales performance in fiscal years 1 and 3 more clearly.

	A	B	C	D	E	F
1	Net Sales					
2	Fiscal Years 1–4					
3						
4	**Quarter**	**FY 1**	**FY 2**	**FY 3**	**FY 4**	**Change**
5	**Q1**	**$1,375,950**	**$3,072,567**	**$ 1,376,950**	**$3,072,567**	
6	**Q2**	**$2,975,324**	**$3,254,087**	**$ 1,484,565**	**$4,235,210**	
7	**Q3**	**$4,195,000**	**$2,752,200**	**$ 1,257,535**	**$2,752,200**	
8	**Q4**	**$2,000,058**	**$2,484,384**	**$ 2,005,486**	**$2,484,384**	

15. **Save** the changes, and **close** the workbook.

Apply Your Skills

APPLY YOUR SKILLS 15.1

Consolidate Data by Category

In this exercise, you will consolidate the shares bought and sold each month into a summary investment portfolio worksheet.

1. **Open** as-Consolidated Portfolio from the Lesson 15 folder in your file storage location.
   The workbook contains a Beginning Balance worksheet showing the number of shares owned at the beginning of the year. The January and February worksheets include the shares purchased, reinvested, and sold.
2. Copy a worksheet to create the **March** worksheet and **Portfolio Activity** worksheet shown in the illustrations below. (Copying will ensure that the column widths and cell formats are the same as in the other worksheets.) Make certain to enter the data in the correct cells as shown because you will consolidate the data by position later in this exercise.

	A	B	C	D	E
1	March				
2					
3	**Investment Name**	**Shares Purchased**	**Shares Reinvested**	**Shares Sold**	**Net Shares**
4	Prigem			12.39	(12.39)
5	American Fund	40.52	1.23		41.75
6	Guardian Balanced Fund	12.31	4.70		17.01

	A	B	C	D	E
1	Portfolio Activity				
2					
3	**Investment Name**	**Shares Purchased**	**Shares Reinvested**	**Shares Sold**	**Net Shares**

3. **Rename** the sheet tabs using the entries from **cell A1**.
4. Use the **Consolidate** command to combine the Beginning Balance and three monthly worksheets into the **Portfolio Activity** worksheet.
   The names of eight investments and their consolidated numbers should result.
5. **Sort** the investments into alphabetical order on the **Portfolio Activity** worksheet.
6. **Save** the changes, and **close** the workbook.

APPLY YOUR SKILLS 15.2

Construct a Mortgage Payment Data Table

In this exercise, you will create a data table to calculate monthly payments for a home mortgage using various interest rates and periods.

1. **Start** a new workbook.
2. Begin creating the **data table** by typing labels in cells as needed.
3. **Enter** the loan amount **`$200,000`** in **cell C3**.
4. **Enter** interest rates from **`6%`**, **`6.5%`**, and up through **`8.5%`** in **column B**.
5. **Enter** the number of *months* for loan periods of 15, 20, 25, and 30 years in **row 6**.
6. Use the **PMT** function to create a formula in the appropriate cell. You used the PMT function in Reinforce Your Skills 15.2.
7. Issue the **Data Table** command.
8. **Format** the values in the data table as **Comma Style with two decimal places**.
9. Optional: Apply a **conditional format** that changes the font and fill color when a data table value is less than 1,550.01.
10. Clear any **alert** or **error message** that appears in a cell.
11. **Save** with the name **`as-Mortgage Data Table`** in the Lesson 15 folder; then **close** the workbook.

APPLY YOUR SKILLS 15.3

Present Data with Sparklines

In this exercise, you will add a trendline to a column chart.

1. **Open** the as-Projected Revenue workbook.
2. Create sparklines in **column G** to present the projected yearly changes in revenue, gross profit, and net profit.
3. **Format** the sparklines appropriately.
4. **Save** the changes, and **close** the workbook.

Critical Thinking & Work-Readiness Skills

In the course of working through the following Microsoft Office-based Critical Thinking exercises, you will also be utilizing various work-readiness skills, some of which are listed next to each exercise. Go to labyrinthelab.com/workreadiness *to learn more about the work-readiness skills.*

15.1 Group Sheets and Summarize Data

Sandra Chavez-Hall, chief development officer for Raritan Clinic East Foundation, has asked you to summarize direct expenses for Quarter 1. Open ct-Expense Summary (Lesson 15 folder). Group the January, February, and March sheets, and apply Comma Style to the numbers in column B. Then, copy cell B4 from the January worksheet to the Summary, February, and March worksheets by grouping sheets as necessary. Consolidate the January, February, and March expenses into column B of the Summary sheet. Save as **`ct-Expense Summary [Your Last Name]`**, and then close the file.

WORK-READINESS SKILLS APPLIED

- Solving problems
- Thinking creatively
- Arithmetic/ mathematics

15.2 Create a Two-Variable Data Table

Sandra is ready to study the mortgage payments for Phase 2. She requests a two-variable data table. Your job is to set it up for her. Open a new workbook. Create a two-variable data table for a mortgage of $1,500,000. Enter a set of variables to the right of the data table formula as the months for 10, 15, 20, and 25 years. Create the set of variables below the formula as interest rates of 7.5%, 7.75%, 8%, 8.25%, 8.5%, 8.75%, and 9%. Save your work as **`ct-Phase 2 [Your Last Name]`** in your Lesson 15 folder, and then close the file.

WORK-READINESS SKILLS APPLIED

- Solving problems
- Using computers to process information
- Arithmetic/ mathematics

15.3 Display Trends in Cells

The operations director at Raritan Clinic East needs to evaluate the cost of three drugs used at the clinic. She has data showing the cost of each drug over a period of five years. Open ct-Drug Cost (Lesson 15 folder). Use sparklines to show the cost trend for each of the three drugs. Apply appropriate formatting to the sparklines. Then, type a brief label in one cell to describe the purpose of the sparklines. Save and close the file when you are finished.

WORK-READINESS SKILLS APPLIED

- Seeing things in the mind's eye
- Interpreting and communicating information
- Using computers to process information

Collaborating in Excel

LESSON OUTLINE

LEARNING OBJECTIVES

After studying this lesson, you will be able to:

- Create folders to organize project documents
- Manage and print comments in workbooks
- Track and consolidate changes made by multiple authors to a single workbook copy
- Prepare and share workbooks for collaboration
- Merge multiple versions of a shared workbook

Collaborating on projects is a typical business activity. The Internet simplifies exchanging documents and other types of information to coordinate geographically diverse activities. However, the lack of face-to-face contact also places a premium on sharing information efficiently. In this lesson, you will learn how to participate in workbook collaboration. You will set up folders for project files, place comments into an Excel workbook, and prepare the workbook to be distributed to other people. The ability to create shared workbooks is one of Excel's most powerful collaboration features. You can set up a workbook that several other users can access simultaneously on a network server, or intranet. Excel's change history tracking feature can help you avoid and resolve potential conflicts when data is edited by multiple users. You will learn how to merge all of the users' changes automatically into one workbook.

Student Resources labyrinthelab.com/excel10

CASE STUDY

Collaborating on Grant Reports

Grace Vargas is the grant and contract coordinator for Raritan Clinic East. She administers grant funds awarded to the medical center to support various research studies and uses Excel for several of the project activities. Grace administers a Connections medical research grant project that involves Raritan's cardiology and orthopedics departments. She must assemble financial data from both departments each quarter and submit it to the granting agency to show how the funds were spent. Grace and her colleagues use email and an intranet to transmit information back and forth in the form of messages and Excel workbooks.

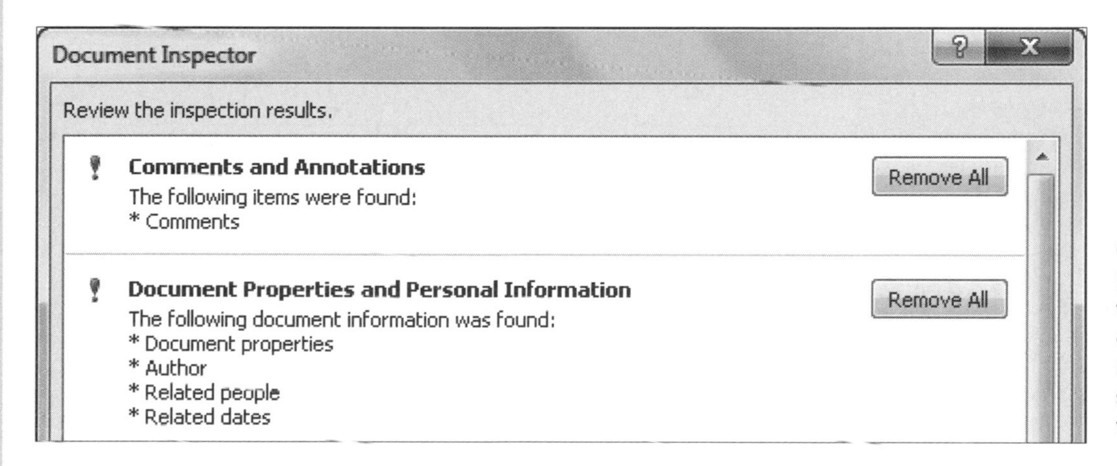

Grace uses the Document Inspector tool to remove items containing personal information prior to sharing the workbook with coworkers.

Grace and her colleagues use comments to ask questions and make suggestions. Comments can also help everyone involved in the project understand special formulas and values contained in worksheet cells.

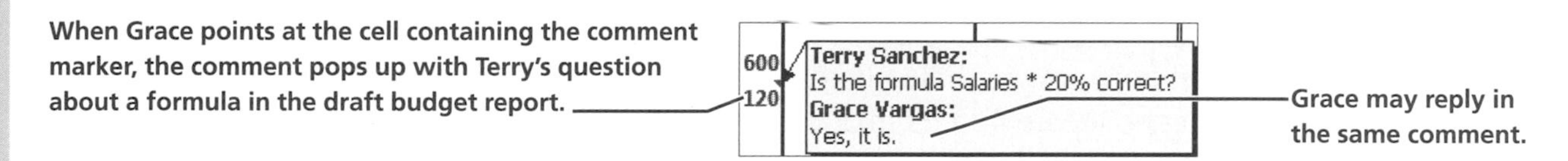

When Grace points at the cell containing the comment marker, the comment pops up with Terry's question about a formula in the draft budget report.

Grace may reply in the same comment.

Grace may also share a workbook with others working on the project. As they return revisions to the workbook, Grace uses Excel's Compare and Merge Workbooks command. Excel automatically enters all revisions from the other workbooks and marks them to be accepted or rejected. This allows Grace to review everyone's revisions in a single workbook.

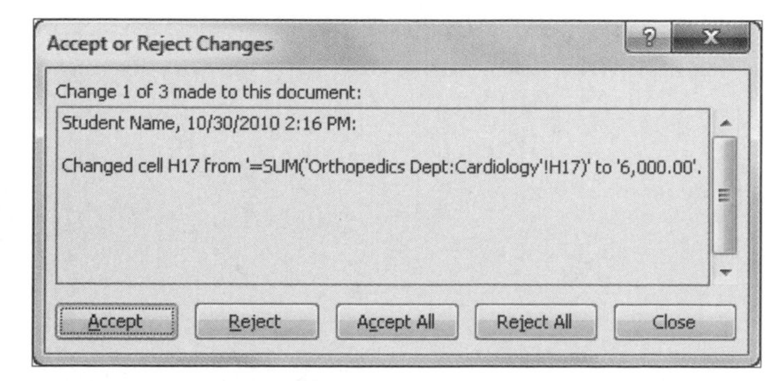

Grace may accept or reject each change that other collaborators made to the workbook.

16.1 Creating Folders in Excel

Video Lesson labyrinthelab.com/videos

When you work on a project, you usually will create one or more folders on your computer to store the documents and other types of files with which you will work. This topic will give you practice in creating folders and teach you techniques to access the new folders quickly.

Working with Project Folders

Depending on the size of the project and the number of files you must organize, you may need to create more than one folder. You may create a main folder for the project as well as subfolders inside of it for major types of documents or major sections of the project. The following diagram displays an example of project folders.

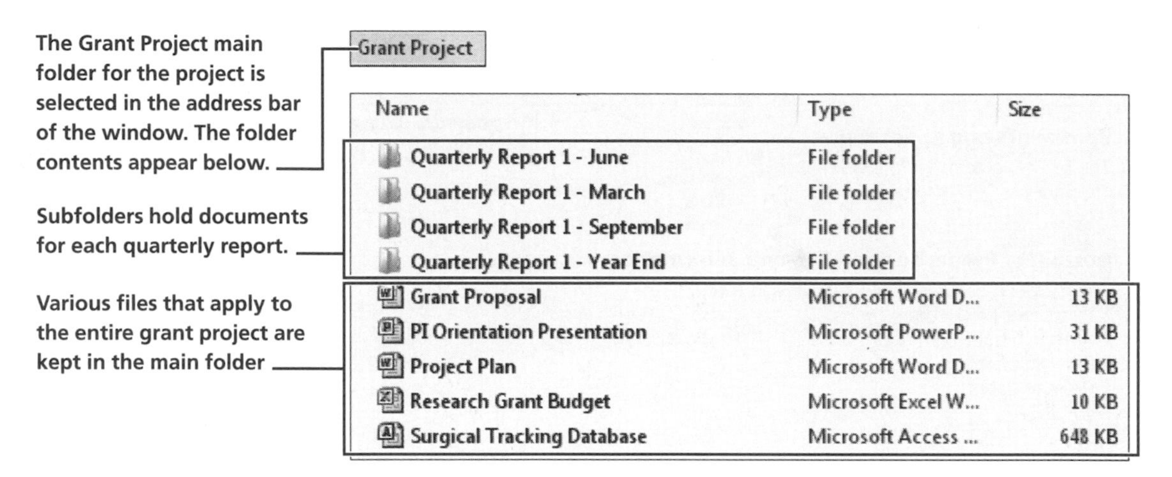

Creating Folders

You don't need to leave Excel to create a new folder. Simply choose the Open or Save As command, and then click the New Folder button (or Create New Folder button, depending on your Windows version) on the dialog box toolbar. You may create a single folder or several. If desired, you may also create folders inside other folders.

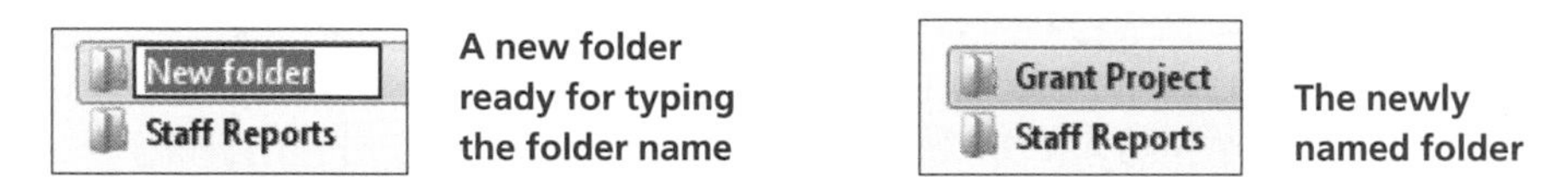

Renaming Folders

You may rename folders from within Excel by right-clicking the folder and choosing Rename from the context menu. Or you may click once on the folder, pause one second, and click again to select the folder name for renaming.

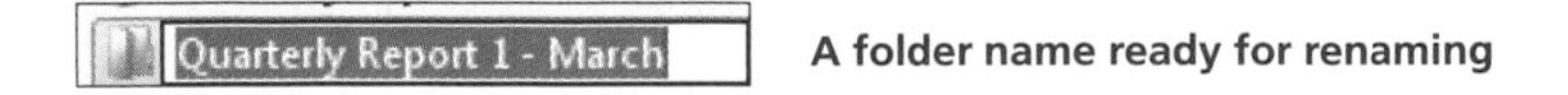

DEVELOP YOUR SKILLS 16.1.1

Create and Rename a Project Folder

In this exercise, you will create a folder from within the Excel program.

1. Start **Excel** and choose **File→Open** .
2. Follow these steps to begin creating the new folder:

The dialog box may appear slightly different depending on your Windows version.

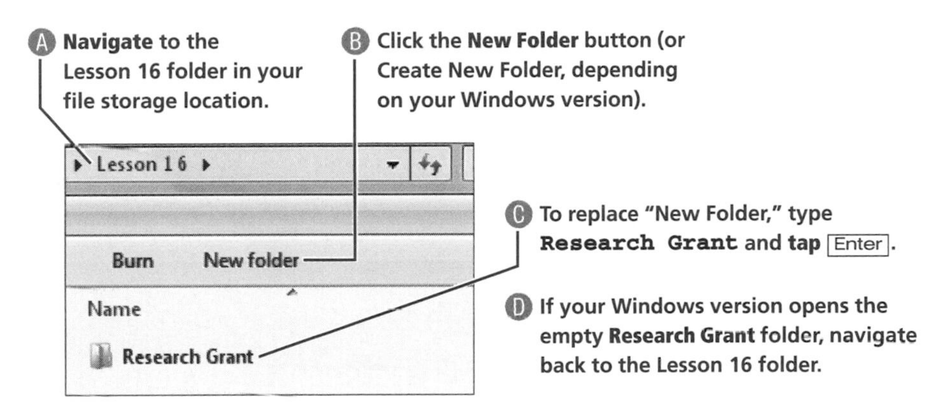

A Navigate to the Lesson 16 folder in your file storage location.
B Click the New Folder button (or Create New Folder, depending on your Windows version).
Lesson 16
Burn
New folder
Name
Research Grant
C To replace "New Folder," type Research Grant and tap Enter.
D If your Windows version opens the empty Research Grant folder, navigate back to the Lesson 16 folder.

The new folder appears at the top of the file list. It is now ready to store files.

3. **Right-click** the Research Grant folder and choose **Rename** from the bottom of the context menu.
   The folder name is selected for renaming.
4. Type **`Grant Project`** and **tap** Enter.
5. Click the **Cancel** button in the Open dialog box.
   This cancels the Open command, not the creation of the new folder.
6. Leave the Excel window **open**.

Organizing Workbooks in Folders

Video Lesson labyrinthelab.com/videos

Many computer users store their files in the Documents or My Documents folder found on most Windows systems. Sometimes you will store files in a separate folder such as the one you just created. This allows you to place your project on a portable drive to use at another computer. Excel's Open and Save As dialog boxes allow you to move or copy files to different folders and to delete files from within Excel.

QUICK REFERENCE	ORGANIZING WORKBOOKS IN FOLDERS
Task	**Procedure**
Create a new folder	■ Choose File→Open. ■ Navigate to the folder that will contain the new folder. ■ Click the New Folder button in the dialog box toolbar. ■ Type the folder name and tap [Enter].
Rename a folder	■ Choose File→Open. ■ Navigate to the folder containing the folder to be renamed. ■ Right-click the desired folder, type the new name, and tap [Enter].
Copy or move files	■ Choose File→Open. ■ Navigate to the folder containing the files to be copied or moved. ■ Select the desired file. Use [Ctrl] or [Shift] to select multiple files. ■ Use [Ctrl]+[C] to copy or [Ctrl]+[X] to cut the files. ■ Navigate to the destination folder. ■ Use [Ctrl]+[V] to paste the files.

DEVELOP YOUR SKILLS 16.1.2

Move and Copy Files to a Folder

In this exercise, you will move and copy some files into the folder you created in the previous exercise and then open a workbook from that folder.

Move a File to a Folder

1. Choose **File→Open**, and navigate to the Lesson 16 folder in your file storage location.
2. **Single-click** the Shared Budget file to select it.
3. Use [Ctrl]+[X] from the keyboard to cut the file.
   The file's icon is dimmed to indicate the cut.
4. **Double-click** the Grant Project folder to open it.
5. Use [Ctrl]+[V] from the keyboard to paste the file.

The file display may appear slightly different depending on your Windows version and the type of view selected.

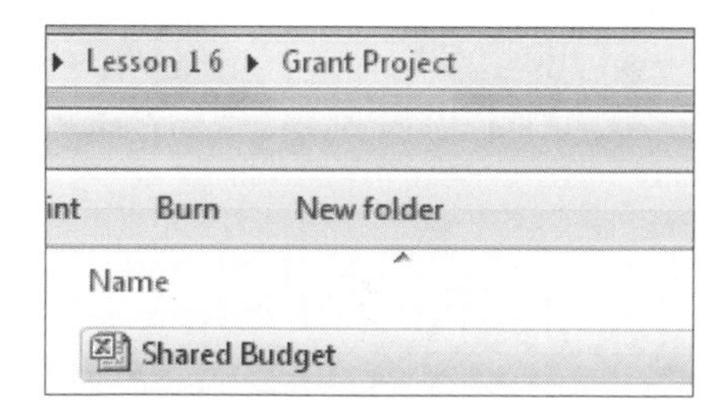

The Shared Budget file appears in the Grant Project folder.

6. Navigate back to the Lesson 16 folder in the **Open** dialog box.
   The Shared Budget file is no longer in the Lesson 16 folder because you moved the file rather than copying it.

Copy Three Files to a Folder

In the next few steps, you will place a copy of three files in the Grant Project folder. The original files will remain in the Lesson 16 folder.

7. Follow these steps to copy the files:

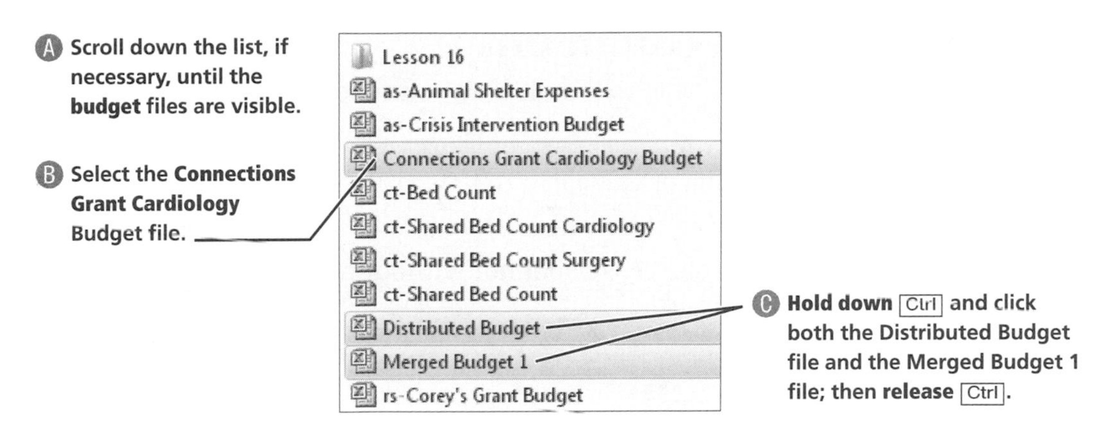

A Scroll down the list, if necessary, until the budget files are visible.
B Select the Connections Grant Cardiology Budget file.
C Hold down Ctrl and click both the Distributed Budget file and the Merged Budget 1 file; then release Ctrl.
Lesson 16
as-Animal Shelter Expenses
as-Crisis Intervention Budget
Connections Grant Cardiology Budget
ct-Bed Count
ct-Shared Bed Count Cardiology
ct-Shared Bed Count Surgery
ct-Shared Bed Count
Distributed Budget
Merged Budget 1
rs-Corey's Grant Budget

   The Ctrl *key allows you to select multiple adjacent or nonadjacent files.*

8. Use Ctrl + C from the keyboard to **copy** the files to the Clipboard.
   The files' appearance does not change, but the files have been copied.

9. **Scroll up**, if necessary, until the Grant Project folder is visible at the top of the file list, and then **double-click** the folder to open it.

10. Use Ctrl + V from the keyboard to **paste** the files.
    The files are copied into the Grant Project folder.

11. Navigate back to the Lesson 16 folder.

12. **Select** the original three files you selected in **step 7, tap** Delete, and choose **Yes** to confirm the deletion.
    You will use the file copies in the Grant Project folder during this lesson.

Open a File in the Folder

13. Open the **Grant Project** folder.
    Navigating to a folder and opening files from it is easy as long as you keep track of the locations of your folders.

14. Open the **Connections Grant Cardiology Budget** workbook file, and leave the file **open** for the next exercise.

16.2 Inserting and Viewing Comments

Video Lesson labyrinthelab.com/videos

Excel's Comment feature is a great tool for online collaboration. A comment is a text note that you can embed inside a workbook cell without cluttering the normal view of the workbook. You may display all comments on a worksheet and even print them.

When to Use a Comment

Comments are an excellent way to handle many situations. You may want to insert a comment:

- To document the formula or value in a cell.
- To record a question about the worksheet data to be followed up later.
- To ask a question of an online collaborator without placing it into the normally printed page of the workbook.

Viewing Comments

When someone inserts a comment, Excel places a small red triangle at the top-right corner of the cell. When you point at the cell containing the red triangle, Excel displays the name of the author and the text of the comment. You also may display or hide one or all comments using commands in the Comments group on the Review Ribbon. The following illustration shows a cell and its associated comment.

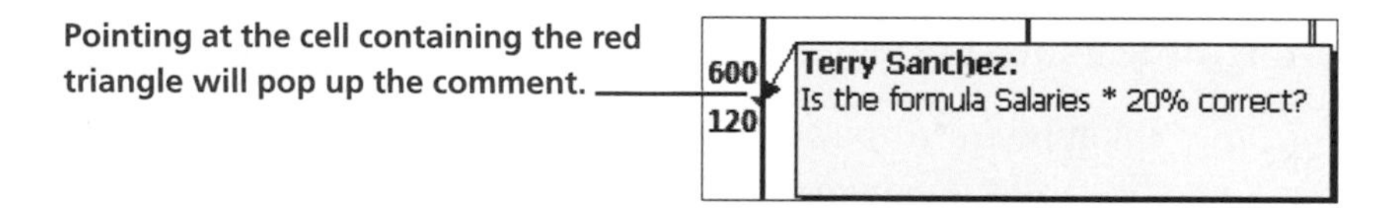
Pointing at the cell containing the red triangle will pop up the comment.
600
120
Terry Sanchez:
Is the formula Salaries * 20% correct?

Navigating Through Comments

You may jump from one comment to the next with the Next and Previous commands in the Ribbon. Using these commands is especially useful in large worksheets. When you reach the last comment in the workbook, the Next command starts over with the first comment in the workbook. The following figure displays the Comments group commands on the Ribbon.

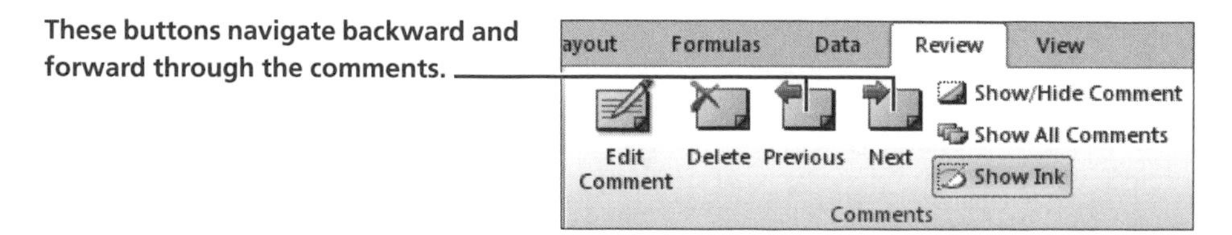
These buttons navigate backward and forward through the comments.
ayout
Formulas
Data
Review
View
Edit Comment
Delete
Previous
Next
Show/Hide Comment
Show All Comments
Show Ink
Comments

DEVELOP YOUR SKILLS 16.2.1

Review Comments

In this exercise, you will review comments inserted into the workbook by Terry Sanchez.

1. Follow these steps to display some comments on the Cardiology worksheet of the Connection Grant Cardiology Budget workbook:

	A	B	C	D	E	F	G	H
9	EXPENSES							
10	PROJECT STAFF							
11	Salaries		1,462	600	1,224	600	1,224	600
12	Benefits		284	120	194	120	194	120
13								
14	OPERATING COSTS							
15	Curriculum development		1,010		1,010		1,010	
16	Staff development						216	
17	Supplies				400			8,000

Ⓐ Point at this cell containing a **comment triangle** and read Terry Sanchez's comment.

Ⓑ Point at each of these cells and read the comments.

2. Choose **Review→Comments→Show All Comments** from the Ribbon.
   All comments on the worksheet are displayed when you choose this command.
3. Choose **Review→Comments→Show All Comments** from the Ribbon again to toggle off the display of the comments.
4. Choose **Review→Comments→Next** from the Ribbon
5. Repeat the **Next** command to view the second comment.
6. Choose **Review→Comments→Previous** from the Ribbon.
   The Next and Previous commands are useful for navigating through comments one by one.
7. Issue the **Next** command three times until prompted that you are at the end of the workbook.
8. Click **OK** in the Microsoft Excel dialog box to start over at the first comment.
9. Select any cell to hide the comment, and leave the workbook **open**.

Setting the Username

Video Lesson labyrinthelab.com/videos

Before you insert comments, you should set the username to identify that the comment came from you. You make this setting in the Excel Options window in the General category. Once you set the username, Excel will keep this setting until the username is changed to something else.

You may not have permission rights to change the username on a classroom computer. The computer number may display as the username on a network of computers, or all computers may have the same username.

Inserting and Deleting Comments

FROM THE KEYBOARD
[Shift]+[F2] to insert comment

You may insert a comment into any cell with the New Comment command on the Ribbon or by right-clicking a cell and choosing Insert Comment from the context menu. A comment is specific to a cell; you cannot assign a comment to a range of cells. You cannot insert more than one comment box in a cell, but you may add to an existing comment. After you give the command, a comment box appears in which you may type the text of the comment. Clicking outside the comment box hides it when Show All Comments is turned off. The Delete command on the Review ribbon will remove the selected comment from its cell.

Adding to Comments

You may add to comments made by other authors by clicking in the comment box and typing. If the comment is not displayed, you may select the cell and choose Edit Comment from the Ribbon or context menu. Typing your name in bold is recommended to identify your portion of the comment.

The New Comment command on the Ribbon changes to Edit Comment when a comment box is selected.

Example of an Edited Comment

As you read comments inserted by your co-worker in another department, you notice one that asks a question. Rather than insert a new comment, you decide to add your answer by editing the existing comment. You also may apply a different text color to this edit so that the other readers can readily distinguish your addition from the original comment.

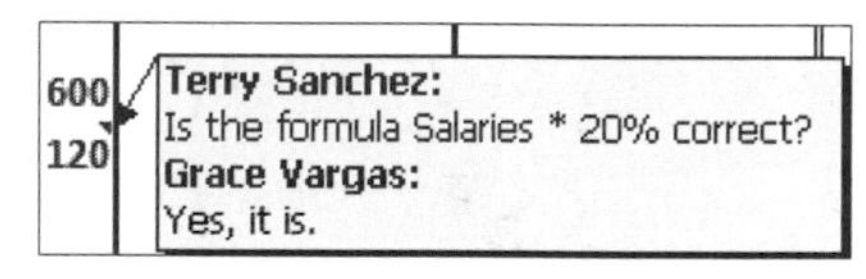

Formatting Comment Text

You may change most text attributes for your comment using commands on the Home Ribbon, but the Font Color command is not available on the Ribbon. Instead, you should use the Format Comment command in the context menu to display a dialog box, where you may change the font color.

Positioning and Sizing a Comment

A comment box may be moved by dragging its border or using the cursor keys to nudge the box. You may resize a comment box by dragging any of the eight resizing handles that appear around its edge. A comment box does not expand automatically to display all the text of a lengthy comment. You may use cursor keys to scroll through text in a comment, but resizing the comment box will ensure that everyone can read the entire comment.

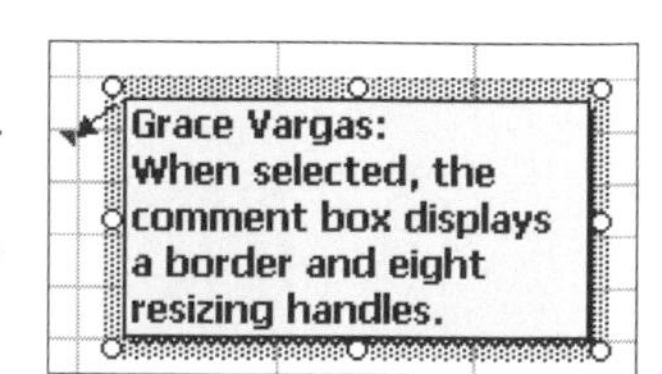

Is the formula Salaries * 20% correct?
Grace Vargas:
When selected, the
comment box displays
a border and eight
resizing handles.

QUICK REFERENCE — WORKING WITH COMMENTS

Task	Procedure
Associate your name with new comments	■ Choose File→Options →General category. ■ Under Personalize Your Copy of Microsoft Office, enter your name in the User Name box.
Insert a comment in a worksheet cell	■ Select the desired cell. ■ Choose Review→Comments→New Comment from the Ribbon (or right-click on the desired cell and choose Insert Comment from the context menu). ■ Type the desired text in the comment box. ■ Click outside the comment box to complete the comment.
Make a comment pop up and then hide it	■ Point at the cell containing the comment triangle for about one second to make the comment box pop up. ■ Point at any other cell to hide the comment.
Show or hide a comment	■ Select the cell containing the comment triangle. ■ Choose Review→Comments→Show/Hide Comment from the Ribbon (or right-click the cell and choose Show/Hide Comments from the context menu).
Show or hide all comments in a workbook	■ Choose Review→Comments→Show All Comments from the Ribbon.
Navigate through comments	■ Choose Review→Comments→Next from the Ribbon to find the next comment. ■ Choose Review→Comments→Previous from the Ribbon to go back one comment.
Add to a comment	■ Select the cell containing the comment. ■ Choose Review→Comments→Edit Comment from the Ribbon (or right-click on the cell with the comment and choose Edit Comment from the context menu) if the comment box is not visible. ■ Edit the comment text normally. You may change the text color of your addition if you like. ■ Click outside the comment box to complete the comment.
Format comment text	■ Select the desired comment cell. ■ Choose Review→Comments→Edit Comment or Edit Comment from the Ribbon, as needed (or right-click the cell and choose the command from the context menu). ■ Select existing text or position the insertion point for new next. ■ Choose Home→Cells→Format →Format Comment from the Ribbon (or right-click inside the comment box and choose Format Comment from the context menu). ■ Change the font, size, and color, as desired.
Move and resize a comment	■ Display the comment. ■ Drag its border to move the comment box. ■ Drag one of the eight resizing handles to resize.
Delete a comment	■ Select the desired comment cell. ■ Choose Review→Comments→Delete Comment from the Ribbon (or right-click on the cell and choose Delete Comment from the context menu).

DEVELOP YOUR SKILLS 16.2.2

Insert and Add to Comments

In this exercise, you will insert a new comment into a cell and edit an existing comment with an answer to a question. Then you will move comments so that the underlying cells are visible.

Before You Begin: *Verify with your instructor, staff, or class notes whether you have permission to change the username on your computer. Verify the procedure for restoring the original username if you do have permission.*

Set the Username

1. Choose **File→Options** . Display the **General** category, if not already displayed.
2. Under Personalize Your Copy of Microsoft Office, notice the current **User Name**.

Click Cancel and skip to step 5 if you do not have permission to change the username on your computer.

3. As directed by your instructor, write the current username *exactly as shown* so that you may restore that name at the end of this exercise, or write the restoration procedure in the space provided:

   ____

4. Change the existing username in the User Name box to **your first name and last name**, and click **OK** to save the change.

Insert a Comment

5. Verify that the Connections Grant Cardiology Budget workbook in the Grants Project folder is **open**.
6. **Right-click** cell G20 and choose **Insert Comment** from the context menu.
   A comment box appears. Notice that the username is exactly as entered in the User Name box.
7. Type the following comment in the comment box:
   `Participation in the League for Innovation conference`.
8. **Tap** [Enter], and then select **cell G20** to close the Edit Comment box and hide your comment.
9. Point at **cell G20** to pop up your comment.

Add to a Comment

10. **Right-click** cell D12 and choose **Edit Comment** from the context menu.
    The comment box appears and displays Terry Sanchez's question followed by the insertion point (text cursor).
11. Use [Ctrl]+[B] to turn on bold, **type** your name followed by a colon (:), **tap** [Enter], and use [Ctrl]+[B] to turn off bold.

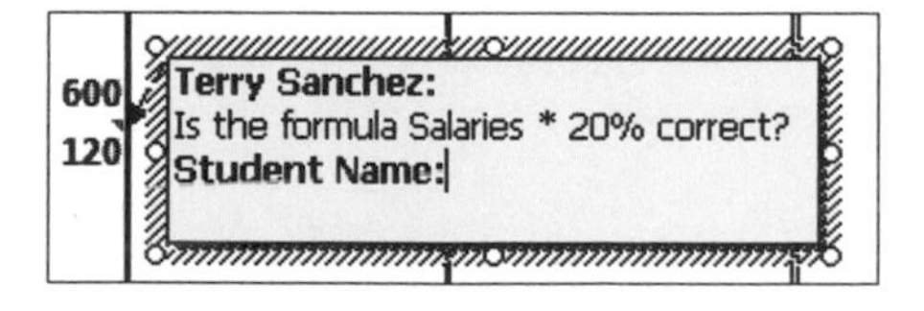

12. **Drag down** the center-bottom handle of the comment box to enlarge the box, if necessary.
13. **Right-click** anywhere in the comment text and choose **Format Comment** from the context menu.
14. In the Format Comment dialog box, drop down the **Color** list, choose a new text color, such as Blue, and then click **OK**.
15. **Type** the following: **`Yes, it is`**.
16. Select **cell D12** to close the comment box.
17. **Right-click** cell D12 and choose **Show/Hide Comments** from the context menu.
    Only your comment text changes color to help other readers notice that the comment has been edited. Terry Sanchez's comment is not affected. You could also drag to select your name and change its color using the Format Comment command.

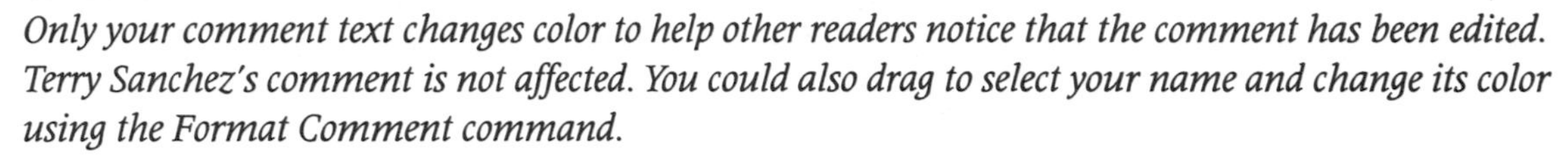

Move a Comment

18. Choose **Review→Comments→Show All Comments** from the Ribbon to display all comments.
    Notice that some comments cover worksheet data or overlap another comment. You will move a comment off the data portion of the workbook.
19. Click in the **cell D12** comment box to select it.
20. Follow these steps to change the location of a comment on the worksheet:

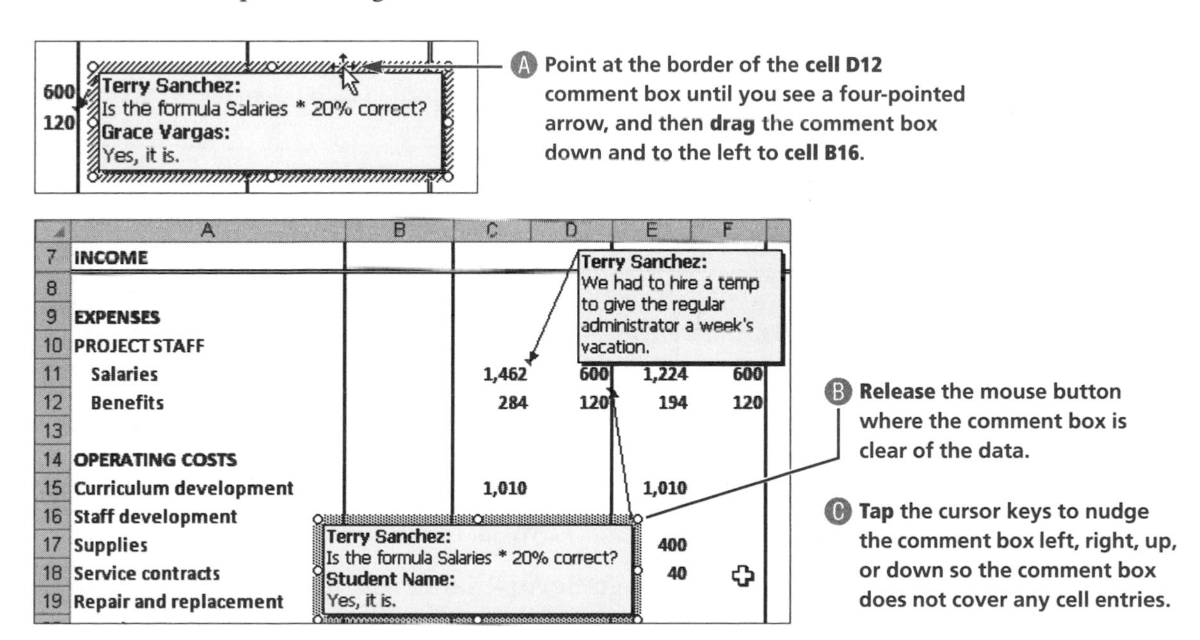

A line still connects the comment to its cell. You may move a comment box to any location on the worksheet so it is out of the way of important data. This may be necessary before you print the comments on the worksheet, as you will learn to do in the next topic.

Delete a Comment and Save the Workbook

21. **Right-click** cell H17 and choose **Delete Comment** from the context menu.
    The triangle icon disappears from the cell to indicate that it no longer contains a comment.
22. **Save** the changes, and leave the workbook **open** for the next exercise.

Printing Comments

Video Lesson labyrinthelab.com/videos

Excel's default setting is to suppress the printing of comments. To print the comments in a workbook, you choose a comments printing mode in the Page Setup dialog box. You may print each currently displayed comment where it appears on the worksheet or print all comments (whether displayed or not) on a separate sheet.

QUICK REFERENCE **PRINTING COMMENTS**

Task	Procedure
Print the comments in a workbook	■ If you are going to print comments as they appear on the worksheets, display all comments that you want printed. ■ Choose Page Layout→Page Setup dialog box launcher from the Ribbon. Page Setup ■ Display the Sheet tab in the Page Setup dialog box. ■ Under Print, choose a print mode from the Comments list.
Switch off printing comments	■ Choose Page Layout→Page Setup dialog box launcher from the Ribbon. ■ Under Print, choose (None) from the Comments list.

DEVELOP YOUR SKILLS 16.2.3

Print Comments

In this exercise, you will make settings to control the printing of comments. Then you will print the worksheet with comments printed on a separate sheet. Finally, you will switch off the printing of comments and restore the original username if you changed it to your name.

1. Choose **Review→Comments→Show All Comments** from the Ribbon to display all comments, if not already displayed.
   Notice that all of the comments on the worksheet are displayed. One of the page setup options prints comments as they are currently displayed on the worksheet.
2. Choose **Page Layout→Page Setup dialog box launcher** from the Ribbon.
3. Display the **Sheet** tab in the Page Setup dialog box.
4. Under Print, drop down the Comments list and choose **As Displayed on Sheet**.

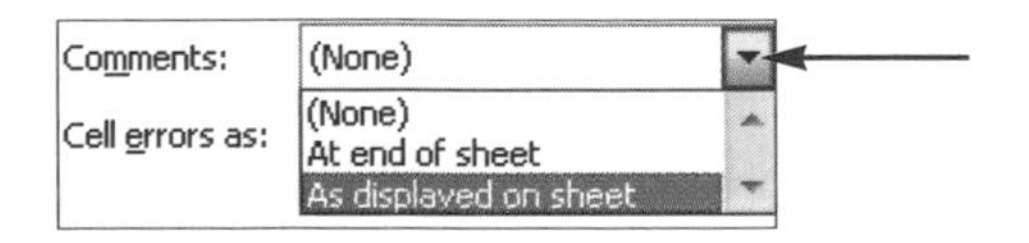

5. Click the **Print Preview** button near the bottom of the Sheet tab in the dialog box.
   Excel displays the Print tab of Backstage view. The comments will print exactly as shown. You moved a comment in Develop Your Skills 16.2.2 to avoid covering important worksheet data.
6. Click the **Page Setup** link at the bottom-left corner of Backstage view.

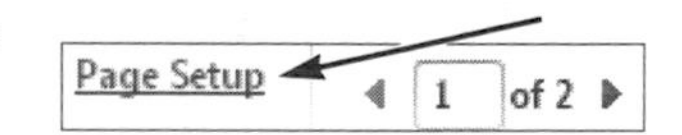

7. Display the **Sheet** tab in the Page Setup dialog box.
8. Choose **At End of Sheet** from the Comments list, and click **OK**.
   The Print tab of Backstage view displays the worksheet in the preview.
9. Click the **Next Page** button at the bottom of Backstage view to display page 2.
   A second sheet has been added to the printout. This prints the comments along with their cell references. Since the comments print on a separate sheet, they will not cover any of the data as they could with the As Displayed on Sheet option.
10. Click the **Print** button at the upper-left corner of Backstage view to print the worksheet with a separate comments page.
11. Retrieve the printout from the printer.

Switch Off Printing Comments

12. Choose **Page Layout→Page Setup dialog box launcher** from the Ribbon.
13. Display the **Sheet** tab in the Page Setup dialog box.
14. Choose **(None)** from the Comments list and click **OK**.
    Now the printing of comments is suppressed until you switch on this option again.
15. **Save** the changes, and **close** the workbook. Leave Excel **open**.

Skip steps 16–17 if you did not change the username in Develop Your Skills 16.2.2. If you did change the username, refer to the procedure that you wrote in step 3 of that exercise to restore the original username, which may vary from the following steps.

Restore the Username

16. Choose **File→Options**. Display the **General** category, if not already displayed.
17. Under **Personalize Your Copy of Microsoft Office**, carefully **type** the original username that you wrote down during Develop Your Skills 16.2.2 in the User Name box and click **OK**.

16.3 Preparing Workbooks for Distribution

Video Lesson labyrinthelab.com/videos

Assume that you created a workbook and checked its contents for accuracy. You wouldn't want your colleagues or clients to make changes or view confidential information unless authorized. You can perform a few more steps to enhance data security before sharing the workbook with other people.

Inspecting Workbooks for Personal Information and Hidden Data

The Document Inspector tool can search for certain items in a workbook that you may not wish other people to see. The following table gives examples of data that you may include in a search and items that will *not* be found.

Examples of items that may be included in a search	Examples of items NOT included in a search
■ Hidden worksheets, rows, and columns	■ Hidden cells
■ Comments in cells	■ Comments resulting from edits by multiple authors
■ Document properties, such as the author's name	■ Data entered in out-of-the-way areas of a worksheet
■ Headers and footers	■ White text on a white background
■ Comments next to named ranges in the Name Manager	■ A shape covering worksheet data
■ Objects formatted as hidden or invisible	■ Invisible objects pasted from Web pages
	■ Hyperlinks and other workbook metadata that give the path to the source data's storage location

When the Document Inspector displays the search result, you may choose to remove items from the workbook from within the search result. The removal may be permanent, and you cannot choose specific instances within a category. For example, you may choose to remove all document property types listed in the search result but not just some of them. You may, however, choose not to remove all in Document Inspector and instead delete any single item manually in the workbook as you would normally.

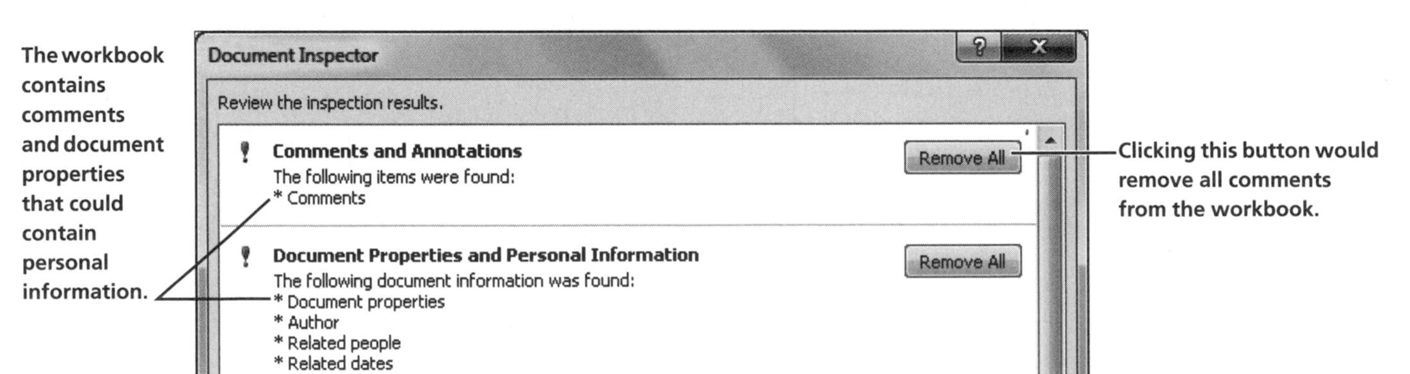
The workbook contains comments and document properties that could contain personal information.
Document Inspector
Review the inspection results.
Comments and Annotations
The following items were found:
* Comments
Remove All
Document Properties and Personal Information
The following document information was found:
* Document properties
* Author
* Related people
* Related dates
Remove All
Clicking this button would remove all comments from the workbook.

The Document Inspector report

Some removed content cannot be restored. If you are uncertain, close Document Inspector, locate and remove items manually, and inspect again.

Marking a Workbook as Final

The Mark as Final command in the Info tab of Backstage view saves the workbook and sets the file as read-only. A co-worker can view the workbook but cannot enter, change, or format data. This feature is not foolproof, though. Anyone who opens the workbook can turn off the "final" status.

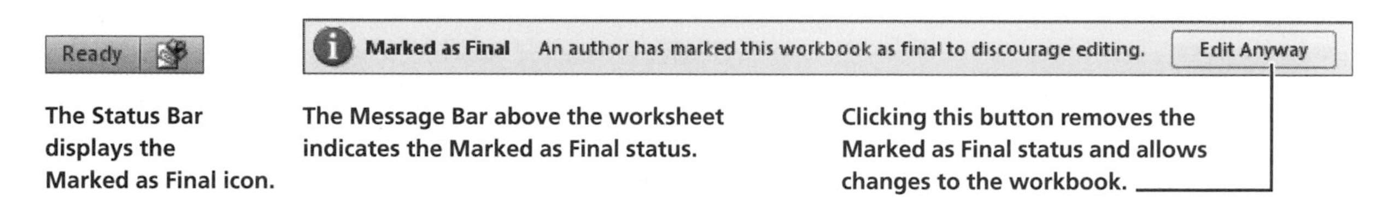

The Status Bar displays the Marked as Final icon.

The Message Bar above the worksheet indicates the Marked as Final status.

Clicking this button removes the Marked as Final status and allows changes to the workbook.

Granting a User Permission to View or Edit a Workbook

In addition to locking cells on a worksheet and protecting the workbook, you may control who may open a workbook and whether they may edit, print, or copy data from it. You also may set a permission expiration date. Your network administrator may set up rights management on your intranet server. As an alternative, you may sign up for a Windows Live account and use the free Windows Rights Management Services Client software to embed your chosen permissions and restrictions in the workbook file. When users try to open the file, they receive a message to connect to the licensing server. If the user's credentials are verified as valid, the server downloads a license to use the file and the workbook opens. Otherwise, a message indicates that the user does not have permission rights for the file.

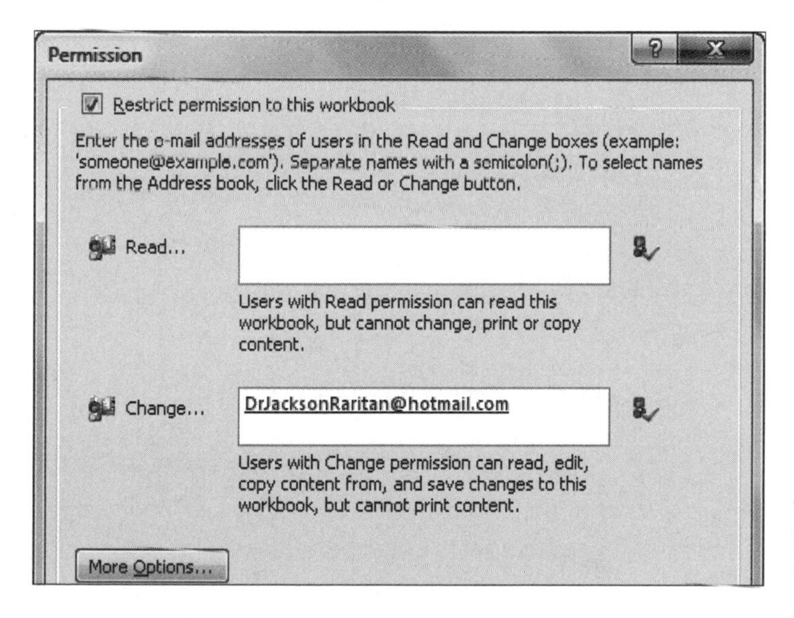

This Permission dialog box indicates that one user may open and change the workbook.

Ready

The Status Bar displays an icon to indicate that a permission policy is applied to the workbook.

QUICK REFERENCE	INSPECTING, MARKING AS FINAL, AND RESTRICTING ACCESS TO WORKBOOKS
Task	**Procedure**
Inspect a workbook for hidden data and personal information	■ Save a copy of the original workbook in case you need to recover hidden data or document attributes. ■ Choose File→Info, and choose Check for Issues menu ▼→Inspect Document in the Info tab of Backstage view. ■ Check or uncheck the desired options for inspection. ■ Click Inspect. ■ In the Document Inspector dialog box, click Remove All next to any item to remove all instances of that item, or click Close and remove items manually from the workbook.
Mark a workbook as final	■ Choose File→Info, and choose Protect Workbook menu ▼→Mark as Final in the Info tab of Backstage view. ■ Click OK to confirm, and click OK in the message box. The Permissions indicator will be highlighted in Backstage view.
Remove final status from a workbook	■ Follow one of these steps: ◆ Click the Edit Anyway button in the Message Bar above the worksheet. *or* ◆ Choose File→Info, and choose Protect Workbook menu ▼→Mark as Final in the Info tab of Backstage view to toggle off the option.
Allow access to a workbook only to certain people	■ Save the workbook. ■ Choose File→Info, and choose Protect Workbook menu ▼→Restrict Permission by People→Restricted Access in the Info tab of Backstage view. ■ Follow the prompts to sign up for the Information Rights Management Services, if necessary. ■ Follow the prompts to use an existing Windows Live ID or create an account ID, and then log in with your email address and password. ■ In the Select User dialog box, choose the desired user account for granting permission, and click OK. ■ In the Permissions dialog box, place a checkmark next to Restrict Permission to This Workbook, and enter the users' email addresses in the Read box and Change box, as desired. ■ To set an expiration date, click the More Options button, and enter an expiration date.
Remove restrictions for accessing a workbook	■ Choose File→Info, and choose Protect Workbook menu ▼→Restrict Permission by People→Unrestricted Access in the Info tab of Backstage view. ■ Click Yes to confirm that anyone can open and edit the workbook.
Access a restricted workbook after permission is granted	■ Make certain your Internet or network connection is active. ■ Choose File→Open, navigate to the storage location containing the desired file, and double-click the file. A blank workbook appears. ■ Click OK when prompted to connect to the licensing server. After your credentials are verified, the workbook appears.

DEVELOP YOUR SKILLS 16.3.1

Inspect and Mark a Workbook as Final

In this exercise, you will use Document Inspector to search for data items you may not wish other people to see when you share the workbook. You also will mark the workbook as final to help prevent unintended changes.

Use Document Inspector

1. **Open** the Distributed Budget workbook from the Grant Project folder in the Lesson 16 folder.
2. Choose **File→Save As**, change the filename to **`Distributed Budget Final`**, make certain that the **Grant Projects** folder is active, and click **Save**.
   The file copy is saved in the Grant Project folder within the Lesson 16 folder. Inspecting a copy of the original workbook is recommended to preserve original data that may be lost during inspection.
3. Choose **File→Info,** and choose **Check for Issues menu ▾→Inspect Document** in the Info tab of Backstage view.

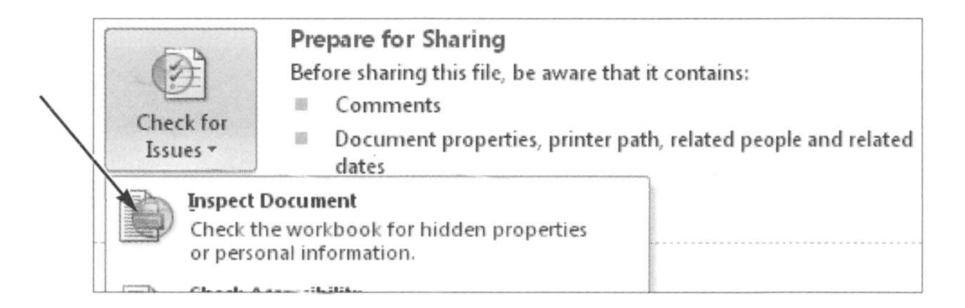

   The Document Inspector dialog box displays seven selected categories. You could deselect any categories, if desired.
4. Read the inspection categories, and then click **Inspect** at the bottom of the dialog box.
   The inspection report appears.

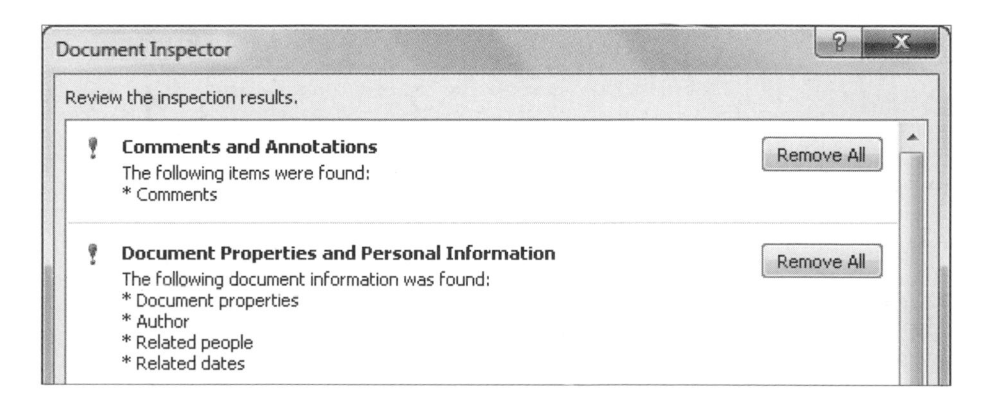

   Two categories of data that may contain personal information were found in the workbook. Each category is indicated by a red exclamation (!) mark. Under the Comments and Annotations category, notice that Comments were found. Also, several types of document properties were found.

5. Click **Remove All** at the right of Comments and Annotations.
   The Comments and Annotations category now indicates that all comment items were successfully removed.
6. Click **Remove All** at the right of Document Properties and Personal Information.
   All seven categories now display a blue checkmark.
7. Close the **Document Inspector** dialog box.
   Notice that only the size, last modified date, and created date properties remain at the right of the Info tab in Backstage view. The author name was removed.

Properties ▾	
Size	20.0KB
Title	Add a title
Tags	Add a tag
Categories	Add a category
Related Dates	
Last Modified	Today, 7:19 PM
Created	2/18/1998 4:29 PM
Last Printed	6/26/2010 4:52 PM
Related People	
Author	Add an author
Last Modified By	Student Name

8. **Tap** [Esc] to exit Backstage view, and notice that all comments were removed.
   You cannot undo to restore the comments. The Remove All button should be used with care.

Mark the Workbook as Final

9. Choose **File→Info**, and choose **Protect Workbook menu ▾→Mark as Final** in the Info tab of Backstage view.

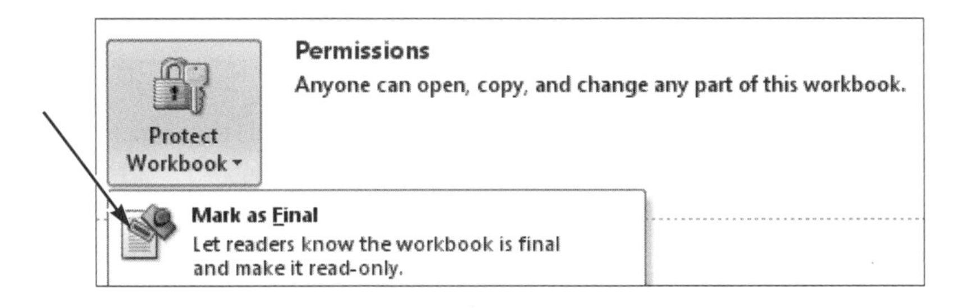

10. Read the Microsoft Excel message, and click **OK**.
11. Read another message, if one appears, and click **OK**.

The Permissions heading changes color and indicates the workbook status.

12. **Tap** [Esc] to exit Backstage view, and read the Message Bar about the workbook.
13. Select any cell in the worksheet, and attempt to enter data.
    You cannot type into a cell. Notice that formatting comments on the Ribbon are dimmed.
14. Click the **Edit Anyway** button in the Message Bar.
    The Marked as Final status is removed, and the document may be edited and formatted as usual.
15. **Save** the changes, and **close** the workbook.

16.4 Sharing Workbooks Without a Network

In a workgroup environment, several team members may need to access the same workbook simultaneously. For example, they may be independently checking data, entering data into areas of a project workbook assigned to them, or updating rapidly changing data. You may set up a shared workbook for other users to edit. If your organization does not have a computer network available, you may distribute the shared workbook using either of the following methods:

1. Sending one copy to the first team member to make changes and then routing the same file to the next user
2. Giving each user his/her own copy in which to make changes

You will set the workbook as shared, track changes made by the various users, and review the changes. The Excel commands that you use will vary depending on the method.

16.5 Tracking Changes to Workbooks

Video Lesson labyrinthelab.com/videos

When several people make changes to the same workbook, one person usually is assigned to review and approve each change. Excel can maintain a change history that tracks each change to the workbook. The change history displays the username of the person who made each change along with the original and new contents of each cell. The change history lets you review each change and accept or reject it. A changed cell may be identified by its border and a triangle in the upper-left corner. Each user's changes are marked in a different color.

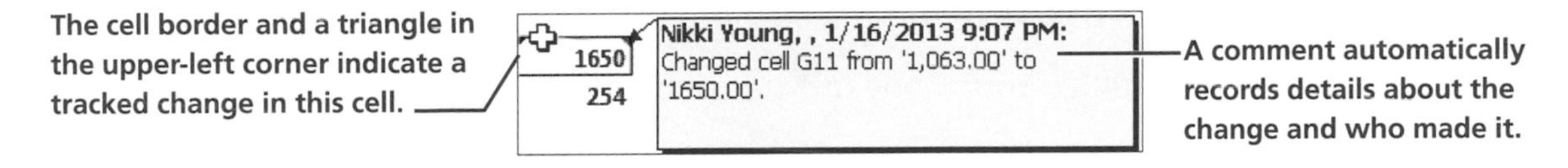
The cell border and a triangle in the upper-left corner indicate a tracked change in this cell.
1650
254
Nikki Young, , 1/16/2013 9:07 PM:
Changed cell G11 from '1,063.00' to '1650.00'.
A comment automatically records details about the change and who made it.

Example of Tracked Changes at Work

You turn on the Track Changes feature and then give the workbook file to your assistant. You ask him to contact two grant and contract specialists and then input any expenditures not yet included in the workbook. You turn on the Track Changes feature so you can quickly see and review all changes your assistant makes. You may also turn on the Track Changes feature for one workbook copy before passing it from one person to another for changes and then back to the project manager to approve the changes. Switching on Track Changes also sets that workbook to be shared. In this case, you need not also use the Share Workbook command described later in this lesson.

QUICK REFERENCE	TRACKING CHANGES TO A WORKBOOK
Task	**Procedure**
Switch on tracking changes for a workbook	■ Choose Review→Changes→Track Changes →Highlight Changes from the Ribbon. ■ Make certain that the box next to Track Changes While Editing has a checkmark. This option also sets the workbook to be shared. ■ Under When, Who, and Where in the Highlight Changes dialog box, choose the options for the changes that should be highlighted. ■ Set whether you wish the changed cells to be highlighted on the screen and click OK. ■ Choose Yes when prompted to save the workbook. You must save the workbook to activate tracking changes.
Switch off tracking changes	■ Choose Review→Changes→Track Changes →Highlight Changes from the Ribbon. ■ Remove the checkmark from the box next to Track Changes While Editing. Note that the change history will be erased.

DEVELOP YOUR SKILLS 16.5.1

Track Changes to a Workbook

In this exercise, you will switch on the Track Changes feature and then edit several workbook cells. As you work, your edits will be recorded for later review.

1. **Open** the Shared Budget workbook from the Grant Project folder, which is within the Lesson 16 folder in your file storage location.

Check the Username

Because Track Changes records the name of each user who edits the workbook, you will check the username and change it to your own name, if necessary.

2. Choose **File→Options** . Display the **General** category, if not already displayed.
3. Under Personalize Your Copy of Microsoft Office, notice the name in the **User Name** box.

Click Cancel and skip to step 5 if you do not have permission rights to change the username on your computer.

4. Change the existing name in the **User Name** box to your first name and last name, and click **OK**.

Switch On Track Changes

5. Choose **Review→Changes→Track Changes** →**Highlight Changes** from the Ribbon.
6. Follow these steps to set up tracking changes:

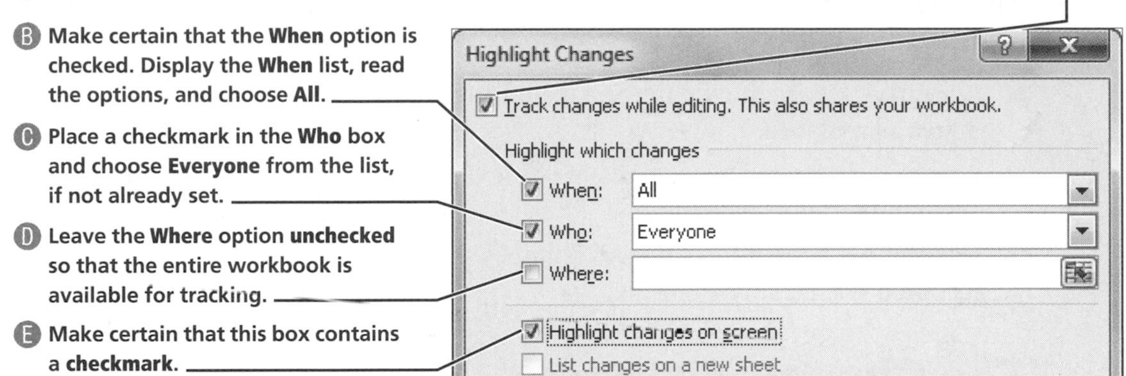
A Make certain that this box contains a checkmark to turn on tracking changes and share the workbook.
B Make certain that the When option is checked. Display the When list, read the options, and choose All.
C Place a checkmark in the Who box and choose Everyone from the list, if not already set.
D Leave the Where option unchecked so that the entire workbook is available for tracking.
E Make certain that this box contains a checkmark.
Highlight Changes
Track changes while editing. This also shares your workbook.
Highlight which changes
When:
All
Who:
Everyone
Where:
Highlight changes on screen
List changes on a new sheet

7. Click **OK** to close the dialog box, and then click **OK** when prompted to save the workbook.
   You must save the file to activate the tracking changes feature. Now Excel is set up to record every change made to the workbook. Notice that [Shared] *appears after the filename in the title bar at the top of the window, as shown in the following illustration. You will learn more about sharing workbooks later in this lesson.*

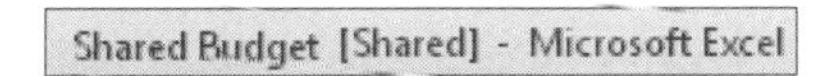
Shared Budget [Shared] - Microsoft Excel

Edit the Workbook

8. Display the **Orthopedics Dept** worksheet.
9. Select **cell E21**, which currently has a value of 2,308, and enter **1725**.
   Notice the border around the cell and the small triangle in the upper-left corner. This mark tells you that the cell has been edited since Track Changes was activated.
10. **Right-click** cell E21 and choose **Insert Comment** from the context menu. Type the comment **Network server was repaired.**
11. Click **outside** the comment box.
12. Point at **cell E21** but do not click. In the pop-up box that appears, read the change history and your comment for cell E21.
13. If the comment box remains visible when you point to a different cell, choose **Review→Comments→Show All Comments** from the Ribbon to turn off the display of comments.
14. Select **cell G16** and **enter** a value of **725**.
15. Select **cell G11** and change the value to **5844**.
16. **Save** the changes.
    You are finished editing the workbook. Now read on to see how the workbook author reviews the edits.

Reviewing Tracked Changes

Video Lesson labyrinthelab.com/videos

You may review changes to a workbook that has the Track Changes feature switched on. When you review changes, Excel can jump from one change to the next, giving you the opportunity to accept or reject each change. After you have reviewed a change, Excel keeps a record of the change until you deactivate the Track Changes feature. The following list describes your review options.

- **Accept—**An accepted change is kept in the cell. The change history records the old value that was replaced.
- **Reject—**A rejected change restores the old value in the cell. The change history records the new value that was rejected.
- **Accept All or Reject All—**All changes that have not yet been reviewed may be rejected or accepted with a single command.

The Change History

After you have reviewed changes to a worksheet, the change history retains a copy of the reviewed cells, including their old and new values and any rejected values. Thus, even after you accept a change, you may refer to the change history and manually reinstate an old or rejected value. You may view the change history by displaying a separate History worksheet. This worksheet is deleted automatically when you save the workbook, but you may give the command again.

When you switch off track changes, the change history is erased.

QUICK REFERENCE **REVIEWING TRACKED CHANGES**

Task	Procedure
Review and approve changes to a workbook	■ Choose Review→Changes→Track Changes →Accept/Reject Changes from the Ribbon. ■ Choose OK when prompted to save the workbook. ■ Choose the categories of changes you wish to review in the Select Changes to Accept or Reject dialog box and click OK. ■ Use the buttons in the Accept or Reject Changes dialog box to navigate through the changes and accept or reject them as desired.
View the change history for a workbook	■ Choose Review→Changes→Track Changes →Accept/Reject Changes from the Ribbon. ■ Place a checkmark in the box next to List Changes on a New Sheet and click OK. The new History worksheet will remain visible until you give the Save command.

DEVELOP YOUR SKILLS 16.5.2

Review the Changes

In this exercise, you will take on the role of Grace Vargas reviewing the changes.

Before You Begin: You may not have permission rights to change the username on your computer. If directed by your instructor, close the Shared Budget workbook and open it on a different computer. That way, you may still use a different username while reviewing the changes.

Set the Username

1. Choose **File→Options** . Display the **General** category, if not already displayed.
2. Under Personalize Your Copy of Microsoft Office, notice the current **User Name**.

Click Cancel and skip to step 4 if you do not have permission rights to change the username on your computer.

3. Enter **Grace Vargas** in the User Name box, and click **OK** to save the change.
   Notice that the borders around the changed cells have changed color. This alerts you that the cells were changed by someone other than Grace Vargas, the current user.

Accept or Reject Changes

4. Choose **Review→Changes→Track Changes** →**Accept/Reject Changes** from the Ribbon.
   A dialog box appears in which you can select the changes to accept or reject.
5. Follow these steps to examine your choices:

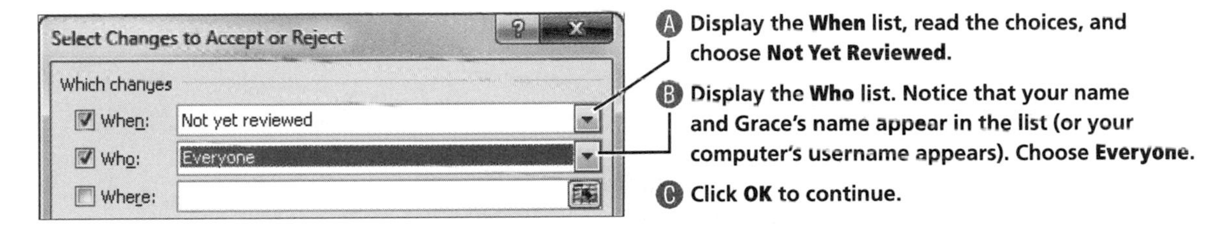

Select Changes to Accept or Reject
Which changes
When:
Not yet reviewed
Who:
Everyone
Where:
A Display the When list, read the choices, and choose Not Yet Reviewed.
B Display the Who list. Notice that your name and Grace's name appear in the list (or your computer's username appears). Choose Everyone.
C Click OK to continue.

The Accept or Reject Changes dialog box appears so that you may navigate from one changed cell to the next, as shown in the following illustration.

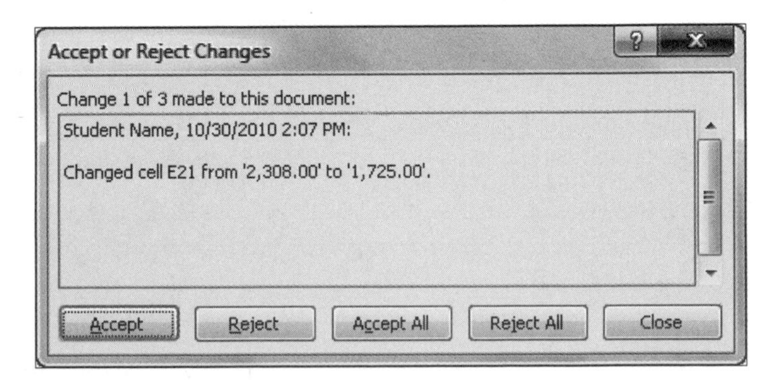

6. If necessary, drag the title bar to move the **Accept or Reject Changes** dialog box so that **cell E21** is visible.
   Notice that the first cell that you changed already has a marquee around it.
7. Point at **cell E21**, but do not click.
   Notice that you cannot view the comment. Before reviewing a changed worksheet, you may want to display or review any comments first.
8. Click the **Accept** button to accept this change to the workbook.
   Notice that cell E21 no longer has a change box around it. The change has been reviewed. The marquee moves on to the next changed cell, G16. You recognize this figure as advance payment for travel by a medical staff member to a training seminar. You decide to reject this change because you know that this expense should not be recorded until next quarter, when the training actually takes place.
9. Click the **Reject** button.
   Cell G16 reverts to its old value, which is blank.
10. Click the **Accept** button for **cell G11**.
    Notice that the change boxes have returned to cells E21 and G11, where you accepted the change. These cells will remain marked until you switch off Track Changes.
11. Scroll down so that **row 16** is at the top of the window.
    This allows enough space to view the comment in cell E21, which you will do next.
12. Point at **cell E21**.
    Notice that the entry from the change history appears for this cell as in the previous exercise. It tells you the name of the person who changed the cell, the old and new values, and the name of the person who entered the comment.
13. Scroll up until **row 1** is visible.
14. **Save** the workbook.
    The change history is not complete unless you save the workbook. Next you will create a change history worksheet.

View the Change History

15. Choose **Review→Changes→Track Changes** **→Highlight Changes** from the Ribbon.
16. Place a checkmark in the box next to **List Changes on a New Sheet** near the bottom of the dialog box and click **OK**.

	A	B	C	D	E	F	G	H	I	J	K
1	Action Number	Date	Time	Who	Change	Sheet	Range	New Value	Old Value	Action Type	Losing Action
2	1	5/21/2010	10:22 PM	Student Name	Cell Change	Orthopedics Dept	E21	1725	2308		
3	2	5/21/2010	10:22 PM	Student Name	Cell Change	Orthopedics Dept	G16	725	<blank>		
4	3	5/21/2010	10:22 PM	Student Name	Cell Change	Orthopedics Dept	G11	5844	1063		
5	4	5/21/2010	10:35 PM	Grace Vargas	Cell Change	Orthopedics Dept	G16	<blank>		Result of rejected action	2
6											
7	The history ends with the changes saved on 5/21/2010 at 10:35 PM.										

The History worksheet appears. (Your Date, Time, and Who entries will vary from the illustration.) The change history maintains a complete record of every change to the workbook. Notice that the last action line even describes how cell G16 reverted to blank as a result of a rejected change.

17. **Save** the workbook.
    The temporary History worksheet disappears after you save the workbook, and the first worksheet in the workbook is displayed.

Switch Off Track Changes

Now that you have reviewed the changes, you no longer need to track them.

18. Choose **Review→Changes→Track Changes** →**Highlight Changes** from the Ribbon.
19. Remove the checkmark from the **Track Changes While Editing** box and click **OK**.
20. Click **Yes** when asked to confirm removal of the change history and workbook sharing.
    Wait briefly as Excel deletes the hidden change history data from the workbook.
21. Display the **Orthopedics Dept** worksheet.
    Notice that the changed cells contain the accepted values but no longer display borders.
22. **Close** the workbook, and leave Excel **open**.

Restore the Username

Skip steps 23 and 24 if you did not change the username. If you did change the username, refer to the procedure you wrote in step 3 in Develop Your Skills 16.2.2 to restore the original username, which may vary from the following steps.

23. Choose **File→Options**. Display the **General** category, if not already displayed.
24. Under **Personalize our Copy of Microsoft Office**, carefully **type** the original username you wrote down during Develop Your Skills 16.2.2 in the User Name box and click **OK**.

16.6 Merging Multiple Workbooks

Video Lesson labyrinthelab.com/videos

You may choose to share a workbook by distributing a copy to each user rather than placing it on a network server. The Compare and Merge Workbooks command gives you the capability to merge the multiple copies of the workbook containing all user changes into a single workbook. This saves you the tedium of opening each workbook individually and then selecting, copying, and pasting the necessary cells into the primary workbook. The files to be merged must all be copies of the *original* workbook, and the copies must have unique filenames. For example, users may add their initials to the filename, such as mw-Budget and tg-Budget.

You may only merge the edited copies of the workbook when it has been set up as a shared workbook with Track Changes. The Compare and Merge Workbooks command is dimmed for normal (unshared) Excel workbooks.

Example of a Merge

You create a shared workbook. You send the workbook to several people by email as an attachment and request that the recipients fill in data on specific sections. After the workbook copies are returned, you use the Compare and Merge Workbooks command to merge them into your original shared workbook. You will not have to look for, copy, and paste the data. Then, you use the Accept/Reject Changes command to resolve any changes that multiple users made to the same cell.

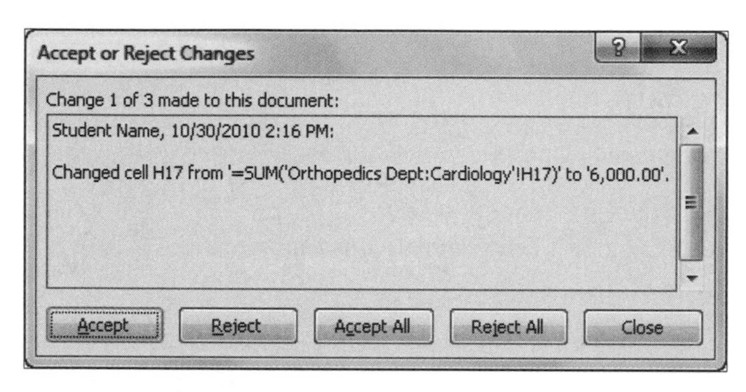

The Compare and Merge Workbooks command displays all changes made to a cell.

The Compare and Merge Workbooks command does not appear on the Ribbon. You must add it to the Quick Access toolbar or a main tab on the Ribbon.

What Happens When Workbooks Are Merged

Excel performs several operations when you merge workbooks. The details are described in the following table.

Change	Description
Data is merged into the currently active workbook	Whichever copy of the shared workbook you have open when you give the Compare and Merge Workbooks command is the one that receives the merged data. The copies of the workbook you are merging from do not receive merged data.
Merged data replaces original data	Data merged from other workbook(s) will replace any data already existing in the same cells of the workbook into which you are merging.
A change history is recorded	Excel records all changes that occur during the merge, including where the data came from and who made the change. You may review the changes and accept any one change to a cell.

Merged Cells Compared to Merged Workbooks

Do not confuse the Compare and Merge Workbooks command with merged cells. Merged cells allow you to combine a range of cells and center a label across the cells. You cannot merge cells in a shared workbook. You must either merge cells before sharing the workbook or turn off sharing.

QUICK REFERENCE	MERGING MULTIPLE VERSIONS OF A SHARED WORKBOOK
Task	**Procedure**
Add the Compare and Merge Workbooks command to the Quick Access toolbar	■ Choose File→Options→, and choose the Quick Access Toolbar category in the Excel Options dialog box. ■ Choose Commands Not in the Ribbon from the Choose Commands From list. ■ Scroll down the list, select Compare and Merge Workbooks, and click the Add button.
Merge multiple copies of a shared workbook	■ Set up the workbook to be shared. Distribute copies of the original shared workbook to others who will contribute data. The files must have unique filenames. ■ After the workbook copies are edited and returned, open the one file into which all others will be merged. ■ Make certain that all other workbooks to be merged are closed. ■ Choose Compare and Merge Workbooks from the Quick Access toolbar. ■ In the dialog box, select the workbook to be merged or use Ctrl or Shift to select multiple files.
Review merged changes to a workbook	■ Choose Review→Changes→Track Changes →Accept/Reject Changes from the Ribbon. ■ Choose the types of changes you wish to review and click OK. ■ Use the buttons in the dialog box to navigate through the changes and accept or reject changes as desired.

Protecting Elements in a Shared Workbook

You may protect worksheet elements before setting the workbook to be shared. For example, you may lock or unlock cells and then turn on worksheet protection. The Protect and Share Workbook command sets the workbook to be shared and provides two additional protection levels. The share and track changes features are dimmed in dialog boxes to prevent users from switching them off in an individual copy of a shared workbook. You may also set a password to ensure that only designated users may alter this protection. This password is distinct from any passwords set to protect cells or worksheets.

When you use the Protect and Share Workbook command, the shared workbook is automatically created and the Track Changes feature is activated. Thus, you do not have to execute the Share Workbook command separately.

QUICK REFERENCE	SETTING PASSWORD PROTECTION FOR WORKBOOK SHARING
Task	**Procedure**
Share a workbook and protect the change history from being disabled	■ Choose Review→Changes→Protect and Share Workbook from the Ribbon. ■ In the Protect Shared Workbook dialog box, place a checkmark in the box next to Sharing with Track Changes. ■ Enter a password, if desired, and reenter the password when prompted to confirm. Users must enter the password to alter protection. ■ If desired, choose Review→Changes→Share Workbook from the Ribbon and set options in the Advanced tab of the Share Workbook dialog box.
Switch off workbook sharing and password protection for the change history	■ Choose Review→Changes→Unprotect Shared Workbook from the Ribbon. ■ Enter the password. ■ Click Yes to confirm removing the workbook from shared use.

DEVELOP YOUR SKILLS 16.6.1

Merge Two Workbooks

In this exercise, you will merge changes from a copy of a shared workbook into the original shared workbook.

Before You Begin: The Compare and Merge Workbooks command should be available on the Quick Access toolbar, or you must have permission rights to add the command.

Set the Username

Skip to step 3 if you do not have permission rights to change the username on your computer.

1. Choose **File→Options**. Display the **General** category, if not already displayed.
2. Under **Personalize Your Copy of Microsoft Office**, enter your **first and last name** in the User Name box and click **OK**.

Create a Shared Workbook with Track Changes Protection

In this section of the exercise, you will create a protected shared workbook. You will then create a second copy of the workbook with a different name.

3. **Open** the Merged Budget 1 workbook.
4. Choose **Review→Changes→Protect and Share Workbook** from the Ribbon.
5. Place a checkmark in the box next to **Sharing with Track Changes** and click **OK**.
   You just turned on workbook sharing and track changes, and you protected both features. Excel warns you that the workbook will now be saved.
6. Click **OK** to confirm saving the shared workbook.

7. Choose **Review→Changes→Share Workbook** from the Ribbon.
   Notice that the Allow Changes by More than One User option is dimmed. Users cannot switch off workbook sharing, nor can they switch off change tracking in the Highlight Changes dialog box.
8. Click **Cancel** to exit the dialog box without making any changes.

Copy the Shared Workbook

You will save a second copy with a different name. You can do this to create as many copies of the shared workbook as you need. Excel will still recognize these variously named workbooks as being shared with the original workbook.

9. Choose **File→Save As**. Change the number from 1 to **2** in the filename and click **Save**.
   The new filename is Merged Budget 2. Notice that the title bar displays [Shared] *after the filename.*

Enter Data in the Workbook Copy

10. Display the **Cardiology** worksheet.
    When you merge data into a workbook, the new data in a cell being merged always replaces any data already in the cell. You will place a new value in one of the cells and see how Excel helps you catch any potential problems during the merge.
11. Select **cell H17** and enter **6000** as the new value.
12. Enter **600** in **cell H11**.
13. Enter **120** in **cell H12**.
14. **Close** the workbook and choose to **save** when you are asked to save the changes.
    You cannot merge from an open workbook.

Merge the Workbooks

Now that the Cardiology worksheet is edited, you will merge the changes into the original workbook.

15. Verify that the **Compare and Merge Workbooks** command is installed on the Quick Access toolbar. If it is not, follow these steps to install the command:

(A) Choose **File→Options**→Quick Access Toolbar category.

(B) Choose **Commands Not in the Ribbon** from the **Choose Commands From** list.

(C) Scroll down the command list and select **Compare and Merge Workbooks**.

Choose commands from:
Commands Not in the Ribbon
Compare and Merge Workbooks...
Constrain Numeric

(D) Click the **Add** button in the center of the dialog box.

(E) Click **OK**.

16. **Open** the Merged Budget 1 workbook.
17. Display the **Cardiology** worksheet.
    Notice that no data values are entered into cells H11 and H12 of this worksheet.

18. Choose **Compare and Merge Workbooks** from the Quick Access toolbar.
    A dialog box opens from which you can select one or more files to merge. To select more than one file from the list, you would hold down the Ctrl *key as you make your selections. In this exercise, you will merge just one file.*

19. **Double-click** the Merged Budget 2 workbook to merge it into your open workbook.
    Excel saves the workbook as it processes the merge. All data for the Cardiology worksheet have been merged into place. Notice that the newly merged number 6000 in cell H17 that you entered into the Merged Budget 2 workbook has replaced the old figure of 8000. *However, you still have the opportunity to review the changes and reject incorrect merge results.*

Visually Review the Changes

You will use two methods to survey the results. First, you will perform a visual review of highlighted changes. Then you will use the Accept/Reject Changes command to review them.

20. Choose **Review→Changes→Track Changes** →**Highlight Changes** from the Ribbon.

21. Follow these steps to display the change history worksheet:

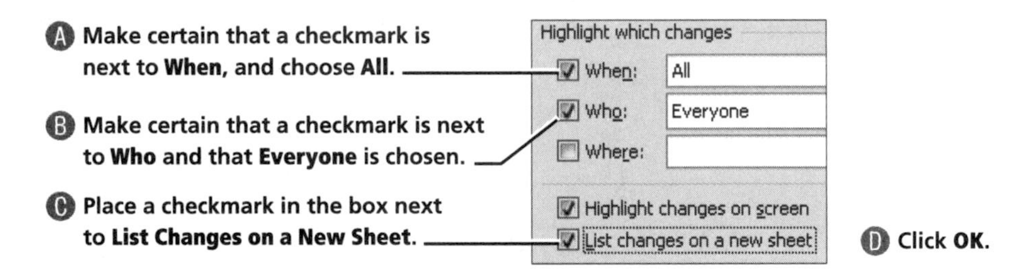

A Make certain that a checkmark is next to **When**, and choose **All**.
B Make certain that a checkmark is next to **Who** and that **Everyone** is chosen.
C Place a checkmark in the box next to **List Changes on a New Sheet**.
D Click **OK**.
Highlight which changes
When:
All
Who:
Everyone
Where:
Highlight changes on screen
List changes on a new sheet

22. Examine **columns H and I** of the History worksheet. These columns display a new and an old value for **cell H17**.

23. Display the **Cardiology** worksheet.
    Notice the change box around the changed cell, another visual indication that a change you might not want has taken place. You could manually change this cell if necessary. However, you will use the Accept/Reject Changes command instead.

Accept and Reject Changes

24. Choose **Review→Changes→Track Changes** →**Accept/Reject Changes** from the Ribbon.

25. Make certain that the dialog box is set as shown at right, and click **OK**.
    The first change is displayed. In fact, it's the only one we need to worry about.

Select Changes to Accept or Reject
Which changes
When: Not yet reviewed
Who: Everyone
Where:

26. Click **Reject** to replace 6000 with the old value.
    Now you see the next change on the Cardiology worksheet. You know that this and the next change values are good. Rather than click Accept for changes one by one, you can simply accept them all.

27. Click **Accept All** to accept all remaining changes.
    That saved some time! Now you will turn off sharing on this workbook.

Disable Sharing for the Workbook

28. Choose **Review→Changes→Unprotect Shared Workbook** from the Ribbon.
Although protection has been removed, the workbook is still shared. You must use the Share Workbook command to switch off sharing.
29. Choose **Review→Changes→Share Workbook** from the Ribbon.
30. On the **Editing** tab, uncheck the box next to **Allow Changes by More than One User at the Same Time**, and click **OK**.
31. Click **Yes** to confirm removing the workbook from shared use.
Now that the workbook is no longer shared, you cannot perform any additional merge commands. You would need to share the workbook again and then create additional copies to merge with this workbook. Notice that the change boxes are no longer visible because the change history has also been deactivated.
32. **Save** the changes, and **close** the workbook.

Restore the Username

Skip steps 33 and 34 if you did not change the username. If you did change the username, refer to the procedure that you wrote in step 3 in Develop Your Skills 16.2.2 to restore the original username, which may vary from the following steps.

33. Choose **File→Options** and display the **General** category, if not already displayed.
34. Under **Personalize Your Copy of Microsoft Office**, carefully **type** the original username that you wrote down during Develop Your Skills 16.2.2 in the User Name box and click **OK**.

Remove a Button from the Quick Access Toolbar

Your instructor may request that you skip the next step.

35. **Right-click** the Compare and Merge Workbooks button on the Quick Access toolbar, and choose **Remove from Quick Access Toolbar** in the context menu.

16.7 Concepts Review

Concepts Review labyrinthelab.com/excel10

To check your knowledge of the key concepts introduced in this lesson, complete the Concepts Review quiz by going to the URL listed above. If your classroom is using Labyrinth eLab, you may complete the Concepts Review quiz from within your eLab course.

Reinforce Your Skills

REINFORCE YOUR SKILLS 16.1

Create a New Folder

In this exercise, you will create a new folder for a project from within Excel's Save As dialog box.

1. **Open** the rs-Expense Report workbook from the Lesson 16 folder in your file storage location.
2. Choose **File→Save As** from the Ribbon.
3. Follow these steps to create a new folder:
   Your dialog box may appear slightly different from what is shown here, depending on your version of Windows.

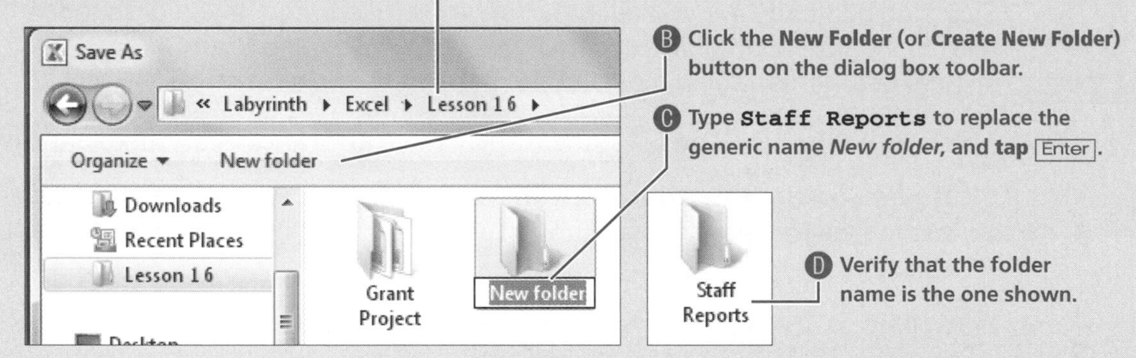

A Navigate to the Lesson 16 folder in your storage location, if not already displayed.
Save As
« Labyrinth ▸ Excel ▸ Lesson 16 ▸
Organize ▾
New folder
Downloads
Recent Places
Lesson 16
Grant Project
New folder
Staff Reports
B Click the New Folder (or Create New Folder) button on the dialog box toolbar.
C Type Staff Reports to replace the generic name New folder, and tap Enter.
D Verify that the folder name is the one shown.

NOTE

Skip to **step 5** if your Windows version opened the empty Staff Reports folder.

4. **Double-click** the Staff Reports folder in the Save As dialog box to open the folder.
   Notice the new folder name in the Save In box. Excel immediately opened the new folder after you named it.
5. **Save** the workbook in the folder you just created, and leave the workbook **open**.
   Now you have two copies of this workbook file in your file storage location: one where you opened the file originally and one in the new folder. You will use the copy in the Staff Reports folder in the next exercise.

REINFORCE YOUR SKILLS 16.2

Work with Comments

In this exercise, you will add comments to a workbook. You will also edit, move, delete, and print comments.

Before You Begin: You must have completed Reinforce Your Skills 16.1, and the rs-Expense Report workbook should be open. The Microsoft Office username should be set to your name if you have permission to do so (see steps 1–4 in Develop Your Skills 16.2.2).

Insert Comments

1. Select **cell B11** and then choose **Review→Comments→New Comment** from the Ribbon. **Enter** the following comment: **`Presentation binders and blank media`**
2. **Right-click** cell B12 and choose **Insert Comment** from the context menu. Enter the following comment: **`Photocopying, including 10 color pages`**
3. **Enter** the following comment in **cell I19**: **`Travel to/from airport at 50 cents per mile`**
4. **Enter** the following comment in **cell E22**: **`Find receipt`**
5. **Save** the changes.

Display and Hide the Comments

6. Choose **Review→Comments→Show All Comments** from the Ribbon.
   Notice that the comments for cells B11 and B12 overlap. You need to move them to new positions.
7. Follow these steps to move a comment:

(A) Click in the comment box for **cell B11**.

(B) Point at the **comment box border** until the pointer displays four arrows, and then **drag** the comment up so that it no longer overlaps the other comment.

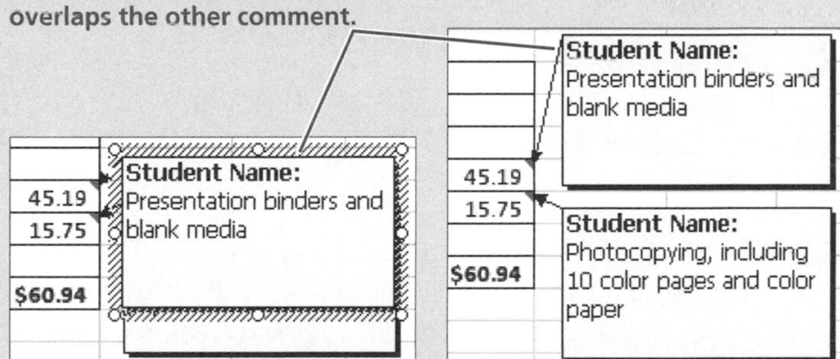

8. Move the comment for **cell B12** down.
9. Move the comment for **cell I19** up so it is above row 18 and no longer overlaps the data in **cells J19 and K19**.

Delete and Edit Comments

10. **Right-click** cell E22 and choose **Delete Comment** from the context menu.
11. Click in the comment box for **cell B12**, type **`and color paper`** at the end of the comment, and click **outside** the comment box.

Print the Comments

12. Choose **Page Layout→Page Setup dialog box launcher** from the Ribbon.

13. Display the **Sheet** tab in the Page Setup dialog box.
14. Under Print, drop down the **Comments** list and choose **As Displayed on Sheet**. Click **OK**.
15. Click **Print Preview** to make certain that the worksheet and comments will print on one page.
16. **Print** the workbook and retrieve your printout from the printer.
17. **Save** the changes and **close** the workbook.

REINFORCE YOUR SKILLS 16.3

Share a Workbook and Review Changes

In this exercise, you will set up a workbook to be routed to Corey Owens, a co-worker. First, you will inspect the document for potential security issues; then you will protect and share the workbook. Next, you will review the changes in a workbook that Corey returns to you. Finally, you will create the History worksheet to display the change history.

Before you Begin: The Microsoft Office username should be set to your name if you have permission to do so (see steps 1–4 in Develop Your Skills 16.2.2).

Use Document Inspector

1. **Open** the rs-Workforce Grant Budget workbook from the Lesson 16 folder.
2. Choose **File→Info**, and choose **Check for Issues menu ▾→Inspect Document** in the Info tab of Backstage view.
3. Choose to **save** the workbook if asked to save.
   The Document Inspector dialog box displays. A workbook must retain certain document properties to be shared, so you will not inspect for properties and personal information.
4. Remove the checkmark from **Document Properties and Personal Information**, and then click **Inspect**.
   After a few moments, the Document Inspector report displays. The report should not indicate any potential problems.
5. **Close** the Document Inspector and **exit** Backstage view.

Turn On Workbook Sharing and Track Changes

6. Choose **Review→Changes→Protect and Share Workbook** from the Ribbon.
7. Switch on **Sharing with Track Changes** but do **not** set a password.

8. Click **OK**, and then click **OK** again to confirm saving the workbook.
   The word [Shared] *appears after the filename in the title bar. Any changes that users make will be highlighted in the workbook.*
9. **Close** the workbook.
   Now the workbook is ready to distribute so that coworkers can input their data.

Review Changes in a Workbook

Assume that your coworker Corey Owens edited and returned the shared workbook to you.

10. **Open** the rs-Corey's Grant Budget workbook from the Lesson 16 folder.
11. Choose **Review→Changes→Track Changes→Highlight Changes** from the Ribbon.
    Notice that the Track Changes While Editing option is checked. Track Changes was switched on automatically when the command was given to share the workbook.
12. In the **Highlight Changes** dialog box, choose options to highlight all changes from everyone and click **OK**.

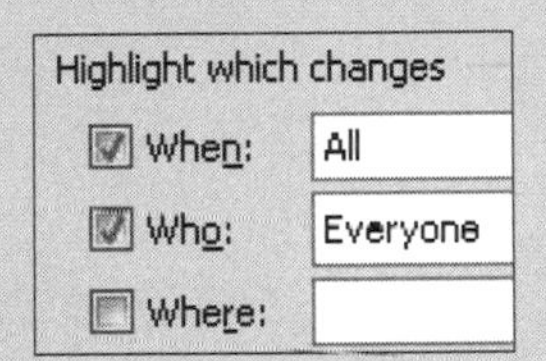

13. Choose **Review→Changes→Track Changes** →**Accept/Reject Changes** from the Ribbon.
14. Set options as shown in the following illustration.

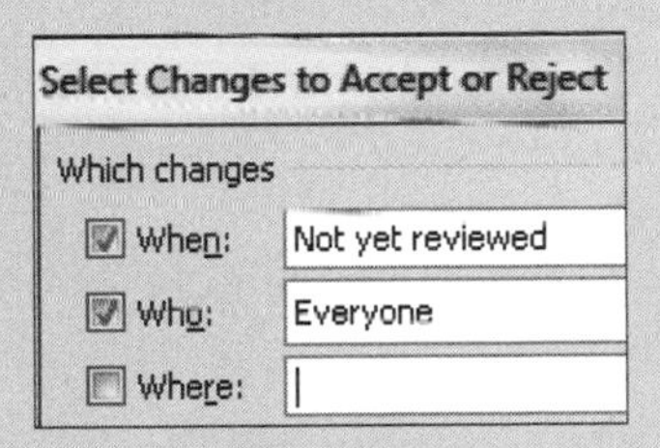

15. Click **OK** in the Select Changes to Accept or Reject dialog box.
16. Click **Accept** to accept the first edit in **cell C15**.
17. Read the details of the next change and notice that Corey entered a formula.
    Users may enter values, text, or formulas in cells.

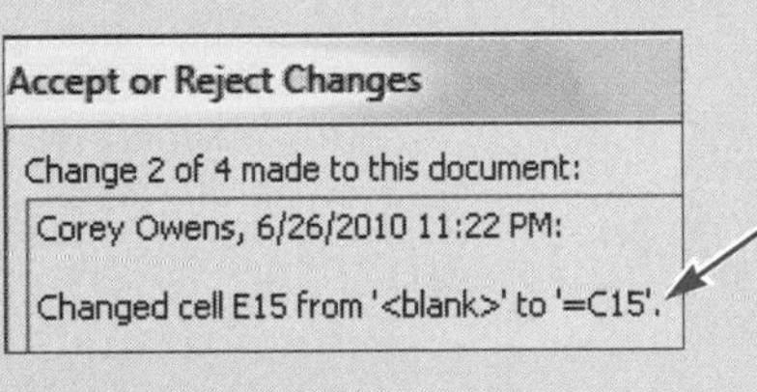

18. Accept this edit in **cell E15** and the next change for **cell G15**.

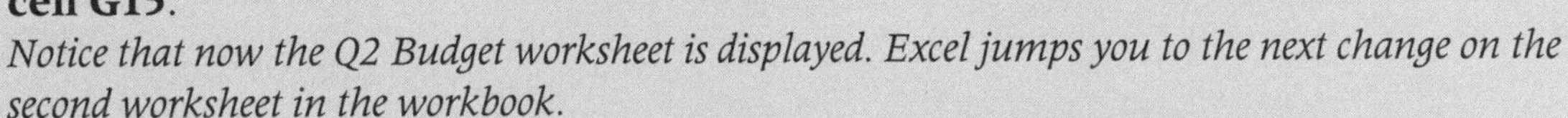

    Notice that now the Q2 Budget worksheet is displayed. Excel jumps you to the next change on the second worksheet in the workbook.
19. Click **Reject** to restore **cell E21** in the Q2 Budget worksheet to blank.
    After you have reviewed all of the changes, the dialog box disappears. Notice that the change boxes are still displayed, however. They remain until you switch off Track Changes.
20. **Save** the workbook.

Display and Print the Change History

Excel can display the change history of the workbook. This can be useful for reviewing edits.

21. Choose **Review→Changes→Track Changes** →**Highlight Changes** from the Ribbon.

22. Place a **checkmark** in the box next to **List Changes on a New Sheet** and click **OK**.
A History worksheet appears, listing all Corey's changes to the workbook that you accepted. Notice that the change to cell E21 of the Q2 Budget worksheet does not appear because you rejected it. Therefore, the original value was restored. Your Who, Date, and Time entries will vary from the following illustration.

	A	B	C	D	E	F	G	H	I	J	K
1	Action Number	Date	Time	Who	Change	Sheet	Range	New Value	Old Value	Action Type	Losing Action
2	1	6/26/2010	11:22 PM	Corey Owens	Cell Change	Q1 Budget	C15	2,000.00	<blank>		
3	2	6/26/2010	11:22 PM	Corey Owens	Cell Change	Q1 Budget	E15	"=C15	<blank>		
4	3	6/26/2010	11:22 PM	Corey Owens		Q1 Budget	G15	"=C16	<blank>		
5	4	6/26/2010	11:22 PM	Corey Owens	Cell Change	Q2 Budget	E21	500	<blank>		
6	5	6/26/2010	11:23 PM	Student Name	Cell Change	Q2 Budget	E21	<blank>		Result of rejected action	4
7											
8	The history ends with the changes saved on 6/26/2010 at 11:23 PM.										

23. **Print** the History worksheet and retrieve your printout from the printer.

24. **Close** the workbook.

REINFORCE YOUR SKILLS 16.4

Merge Workbooks

In this exercise, you will merge data from three copies of a shared workbook. Each copy was created from the original shared workbook and then changed by various coworkers.

Before You Begin: The Compare and Merge Workbooks command should be available on the Quick Access toolbar, or you must have permission rights to add the command. The Microsoft Office username should be set to your name if you have permission to do so (see steps 1–4 in Develop Your Skills 16.2.2).

Merge Data into the Shared Workbook

1. Verify that the **Compare and Merge Workbooks** command is installed on the Quick Access toolbar. If it is not, follow these steps to install the command:

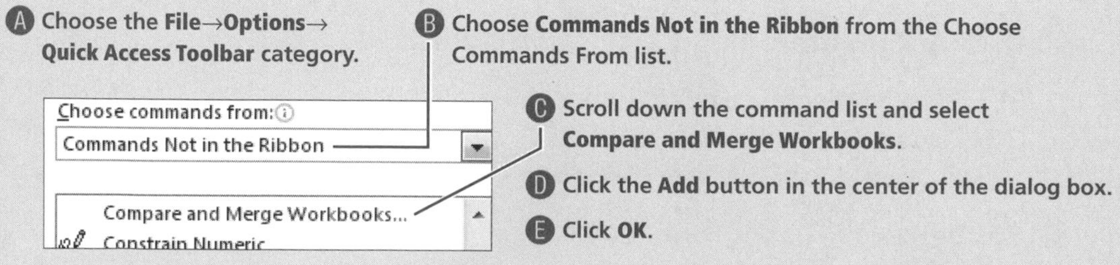

Ⓐ Choose the **File→Options→ Quick Access Toolbar** category.

Ⓑ Choose **Commands Not in the Ribbon** from the Choose Commands From list.

Choose commands from:
Commands Not in the Ribbon
Compare and Merge Workbooks...
Constrain Numeric

Ⓒ Scroll down the command list and select **Compare and Merge Workbooks.**

Ⓓ Click the **Add** button in the center of the dialog box.

Ⓔ Click **OK.**

2. **Open** the rs-Merged Budget 1 workbook from the Lesson 16 folder.
Look at the title bar at the top of the Excel window. Notice that this is a shared workbook.

3. Choose **Compare and Merge Workbooks** from the Quick Access toolbar, and click **OK** if a message appears that the workbook needs to be saved before continuing.
The Select Files to Merge into Current Workbook dialog box appears. Remember that you may merge only copies of workbooks made from the original shared workbook. The files on your file storage location have already been created and edited from the rs-Merged Budget 1 file you are sharing.

   Next you will choose the three edited copies of the workbook that were returned by your coworkers.

4. Navigate to the Lesson 16 folder and **click** rs-Merged Budget 2.
5. **Hold down** Shift and select rs-Merged Budget 4.

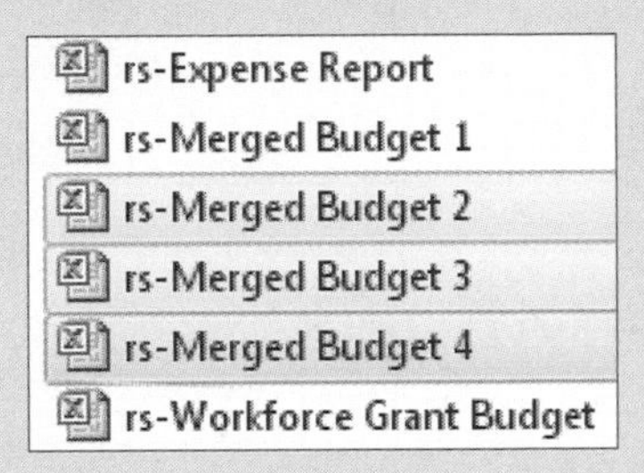

   Three files should appear selected for merging, including rs-Merged Budget 3. Using Shift includes all files between the first and last in the selection. During the next step, watch the Status Bar at the bottom of the Excel window to monitor the progress of the command. You also will see the values update in the Curriculum Development and Faculty/Staff Professional Development rows.

6. Click **OK** to start the merge.
After a few moments, all data is merged into the Q1 Budget worksheet and Q2 Budget worksheet. Excel automatically saved the rs-Merged Budget 1 file after the merge.

Accept and Reject Changes

7. Choose **Review→Changes→Track Changes** →**Accept/Reject Changes** from the Ribbon.
8. Make certain that the **Accept or Reject Changes** dialog box is set as shown at right, and click **OK**.
The dialog box displays a conflict for cell C15.

   Select Changes to Accept or Reject
   Which changes
   When: Not yet reviewed
   Who: Everyone
   Where:

9. **Resolve** the conflict by choosing Oscar Valencia's change of 1,000 and then click **Accept**.
Another conflict for cell E21 of the Q2 Budget worksheet is displayed. Lawrence Harris changed your original value of 1,000 to 5,000. You know that is not correct.
10. Click **Reject** to restore the **cell E21** value to 1,000. (Do not click Accept.)
11. Click **Accept All** to accept the remaining changes.
12. **Save** the workbook.

Display the Change History

13. Choose **Review→Changes→Track Changes** →**Highlight Changes** from the Ribbon.

14. Choose **All** from the **When** list. Make certain that **Who** has a **checkmark** and **Everyone** is chosen.

15. Place a **checkmark** in the box next to **List Changes on a New Sheet**, and click **OK**.
A History worksheet appears, listing all changes to the workbook that you accepted. Compare Action Numbers 2 and 10. You rejected Lawrence Harris's change to cell E21 of the Q2 Budget worksheet. Both changes to cell C15 are listed; the second change "won" because you accepted Oscar Valencia's number. The last change listed for a cell is the one that appears in the merged worksheet. Your Who, Date, and Time entries will vary from the illustration below.

	A	B	C	D	E	F	G	H	I	J	K
1	Action Number	Date	Time	Who	Change	Sheet	Range	New Value	Old Value	Action Type	Losing Action
2	1	6/27/2010	5:39 PM	Lawrence Harri	Cell Change	Q1 Budget	C15	4,500	<blank>		
3	2	6/27/2010	5:39 PM	Lawrence Harri	Cell Change	Q2 Budget	E21	5,000.00	1,000.00		
4	3	6/27/2010	5:41 PM	Iridza Paloma	Cell Change	Q1 Budget	C16	500	<blank>		
5	4	6/27/2010	5:41 PM	Iridza Paloma	Cell Change	Q1 Budget	E16	=C16	<blank>		
6	5	6/27/2010	5:41 PM	Iridza Paloma	Cell Change	Q1 Budget	G16	=C16	<blank>		
7	6	6/27/2010	5:41 PM	Iridza Paloma	Cell Change	Q2 Budget	G20	500	<blank>		
8	7	6/27/2010	5:43 PM	Oscar Valencia	Cell Change	Q1 Budget	C15	1,000.00	<blank>		
9	8	6/27/2010	5:43 PM	Oscar Valencia	Cell Change	Q1 Budget	E15	1,500.00	<blank>		
10	9	6/27/2010	5:43 PM	Oscar Valencia	Cell Change	Q1 Budget	G15	2,000.00	<blank>		
11	10	6/27/2010	5:43 PM	Student Name	Cell Change	Q2 Budget	E21	1000		Result of rejected action	2
12											
13	The history ends with the changes saved on 6/27/2010 at 5:56 PM.										

16. **Print** the History worksheet and retrieve your printout from the printer.
Normally you would remove workbook sharing after approving changes. In this exercise, however, you will leave the change history available to re-create the History worksheet, if necessary.

17. **Save** and **close** the workbook.

Apply Your Skills

APPLY YOUR SKILLS 16.1

Add Comments to a Workbook

In this exercise, you will insert a new comment and edit an existing comment on a worksheet.

***Before You Begin:** The Microsoft Office username should be set to your name if you have permission to do so (see steps 1–4 in Develop Your Skills 16.2.2).*

1. **Open** the as-Crisis Intervention Budget workbook from the Lesson 16 folder in your file storage location.
2. **Add** the following comment in **cell C6**: **`Added an evening volunteer coordinator to the hotline staff.`**
3. Edit the comment in **cell D7** by adding the following text below the existing comment text: **`Repairs were completed by November 18 within the originally estimated cost.`**
4. **Display** all comments.
5. **Move** comments below the data area so that all data is visible while the comments are displayed.
6. **Resize** comments as necessary to display all text in a comment.
7. Make certain that the worksheet and comments fit on **one page**.
8. **Print** the workbook with comments on the same sheet (not on a separate sheet).
9. **Save** and **close** the workbook.

APPLY YOUR SKILLS 16.2

Track Changes to a Workbook

In this exercise, you will set the workbook to track changes and make several edits in a worksheet. You will then review the edits and turn off the Track Changes feature.

1. **Open** the as-Animal Shelter Expenses workbook from the Lesson 16 folder.
   This workbook does not have data in it yet. You will enter data during the various Assessment exercises.
2. Set the workbook to **highlight and track changes** and use the appropriate options.
3. In **cell B5** of the Expense Report worksheet, create a linking formula to **cell E9** on the Cats worksheet.
4. In **cell B6**, create a linking formula to **cell E9** on the Dogs worksheet.
5. Create a formula in **cell B7** that sums the **range B5:B6**.
6. **Save** the workbook.
7. **Display** and **print** the change history for the workbook.

	A	B
4	Animal	Total Costs
5	Cats	$ -
6	Dogs	$ -
7	Total Costs	$ -

8. Give the command to **accept or reject changes** and **approve all** changes you made to the workbook.
9. **Turn off** Track Changes and click **Yes** when alerted that the change history and workbook sharing will be removed.
10. **Save** the workbook and leave it **open** for the next exercise.

APPLY YOUR SKILLS 16.3

Share a Workbook

In this exercise, you will share a workbook file and then create two copies of it to merge in the next exercise.

***Before You Begin:** You must have completed Apply Your Skills 16.2, and the as-Animal Shelter Expenses workbook should be open.*

1. **Share** the workbook.
2. Create **two copies** of the shared workbook, one named **`as-Animal Shelter Cats`** and the other named **`as-Animal Shelter Dogs`**.
   Remember that each must be a copy of the original workbook. You cannot copy the Cats workbook to create the Dogs workbook.
3. **Close** any workbook still open.

APPLY YOUR SKILLS 16.4

Merge Workbooks

In this exercise, you will edit the two copies of the shared workbook you created in Apply Your Skills 16.3. Then you will merge the contents of the edited workbooks into the as-Animal Shelter Expenses workbook.

***Before You Begin:** You must have completed Apply Your Skills 16.2 and Apply Your Skills 16.3, and the as-Animal Shelter Expenses workbook should be open. The Compare and Merge Workbooks command should be available on the Quick Access toolbar.*

Edit and Merge Workbook Copies

1. **Open** the as-Animal Shelter Cats workbook from the Lesson 16 folder.
2. **Type** new data into the Cats worksheet to match the data items shaded in gray in the following illustration.

Animal	Age	Health	Date Arrived	Shelter Cost
Cat	Adult	Healthy	1-May	$ 82.50
Cat	Adult	Healthy	9-May	$ 60.50
Cat	Kitten	Healthy	10-May	$ 57.75
Cat	Adult	Healthy	30-May	$ 2.75

3. **Save** and **close** the as-Animal Shelter Cats workbook.
4. **Open** the as-Animal Shelter Dogs workbook.

5. **Type** new data into the Dogs worksheet to match the data items shaded in gray in the following illustration.

Animal	Age	Health	Date Arrived	Shelter Cost
Dog	Adult	Healthy	2-May	$ 79.75
Dog	Adult	Healthy	8-May	$ 63.25
Dog	Pup	Sick	15-May	$ 44.00
Dog	Adult	Healthy	20-May	$ 30.25

6. **Save** and **close** the as-Animal Shelter Dogs workbook.
7. **Open** the as-Animal Shelter Expenses workbook.
8. **Merge** the contents of the as-Animal Shelter Cats and as-Animal Shelter Dogs workbooks into the as-Animal Shelter Expenses workbook.
Your data should appear in the Cats and Dogs worksheets. The Expense Report worksheet should display totals as shown on the right.

	A	B
4	Animal	Total Costs
5	Cats	$ 203.50
6	Dogs	$ 217.25
7	Total Costs	$ 420.75

Mark the Document as Final

9. Remove **workbook sharing** and mark the document as **final**.
10. **Close** the as-Animal Shelter Expenses workbook.

Restore the Username

Skip steps 11–12 if you did not change the username. If you did change the username, refer to the procedure that you wrote in step 3 in Develop Your Skills 16.2.2 to restore the original username, which may vary from the following steps.

11. Choose **File→Options** and display the **General** category, if not already displayed.
12. Under **Personalize Your Copy of Microsoft Office**, carefully type the original username that you wrote down during Develop Your Skills 16.2.2 in the User Name box and click **OK**.

Critical Thinking & Work-Readiness Skills

In the course of working through the following Microsoft Office-based Critical Thinking exercises, you will also be utilizing various work-readiness skills, some of which are listed next to each exercise. Go to labyrinthelab.com/workreadiness *to learn more about the work-readiness skills.*

16.1 Share a Workbook

WORK-READINESS SKILLS APPLIED

- Serving clients/customers
- Organizing and maintaining information
- Selecting technology

Dr. Edward Jackson, chief operating officer for Raritan Clinic East, is studying the efficiency of patient bed availability. Your job is to set up a shared workbook for him. Open ct-Bed Count (Lesson 16 folder). Protect the workbook for sharing with track changes, and save with the name **ct-Bed Count [Your Last Name]** in the Lesson 16 folder. Create a file copy for both Cardiology and Surgery. Close the files when you are finished.

16.2 Merge Edited Copies of a Shared Workbook

WORK-READINESS SKILLS APPLIED

- Serving clients/customers
- Organizing and maintaining information
- Selecting technology

Dr. Jackson wants to look at the bed space occupied on May 18 and has asked for your help. Open ct-Shared Bed Count(Lesson 16 folder), and merge it with the data from ct-Shared Bed Count Cardiology and ct-Shared Bed Count Surgery (also in the Lesson 16 folder). Highlight all changes, and accept the changes to cells C6 and C7 on the Surgery sheet. Save your work and keep the file open.

16.3 Work with Comments

WORK-READINESS SKILLS APPLIED

- Serving clients/customers
- Acquiring and evaluating information
- Reading

Deion Jennett is Dr. Jackson's administrative assistant. He wants to do a final review of the comments before turning the report over to Dr. Jackson to make sure they are all appropriate to room/bed space, and asks for your help. Open ct-Shared Bed Count, if necessary. Delete any comments that are not related to the room space, and adjust comments so that they do not overlap worksheet data. Create and print the change history. Then, save the workbook. Close the file when you are finished.

Sharing Workbooks on Networks and the Internet

LESSON OUTLINE

LEARNING OBJECTIVES

After studying this lesson, you will be able to:

- Share workbooks for simultaneous collaboration on an intranet
- Share workbooks via the web in Windows Live SkyDrive
- Edit workbooks online using Excel Web App 2010

An organization's employees and clients may work from different locations and in different time zones. They often need the capability to access documents 24/7 from a central storage location. Desktop and mobile devices allow people to view and collaborate on documents from almost anywhere. In this lesson, you will learn how to set up a workbook that several other users can access simultaneously on a network server, or intranet. Cloud computing is a technology that allows users to share and edit files using software stored centrally on the Internet. You will learn how to store workbooks online in Windows Live SkyDrive and edit a workbook with the Excel 2010 Web App from any computer with Internet access.

Student Resources labyrinthelab.com/excel10

CASE STUDY

Sharing Workbooks in a Central Storage Location

Grace Vargas is the grant and contract coordinator for Raritan Clinic East. She needs to upload various documents on her medical center's network server so other employees can view them. In addition, she will ask employees in various departments to update the expense numbers in a budget workbook stored on the server. First, Grace will set up the workbook in Excel for sharing on the intranet. Then, Raritan's network administrator will create a network folder where Grace will upload her workbook file. Grace realizes that some employees who are traveling will need to access documents from a wireless device, such as a mobile phone, that may not have Excel installed or the capability to connect to Raritan's intranet. She decides to store certain documents on Windows Live SkyDrive. Other collaborators only need a web browser on their devices to access the documents. Or, they can download a workbook to a computer that has Excel installed, edit, and then upload the file back to SkyDrive.

	A	B	C	D	E	F	G	H	I	J	K
1	Action Number	Date	Time	Who	Change	Sheet	Range	New Value	Old Value	Action Type	Losing Action
2	1	5/21/2010	11:16 PM	Student Name	Cell Change	Orthopedics Dept	C15	3,250.00	1,134.00		
3	2	5/21/2010	11:16 PM	Student Name	Cell Change	Orthopedics Dept	G16	350	<blank>		
4	3	5/21/2010	11:38 PM	Grace Vargas	Cell Change	Orthopedics Dept	H18	700	<blank>		
5	4	5/21/2010	11:38 PM	Grace Vargas	Cell Change	Orthopedics Dept	G15	1,450.00	<blank>		
6											
7	The history ends with the changes saved on 5/21/2010 at 11:38 PM.										

Grace uses the workbook's change history to track all updates that users make to the shared workbook stored on the network server.

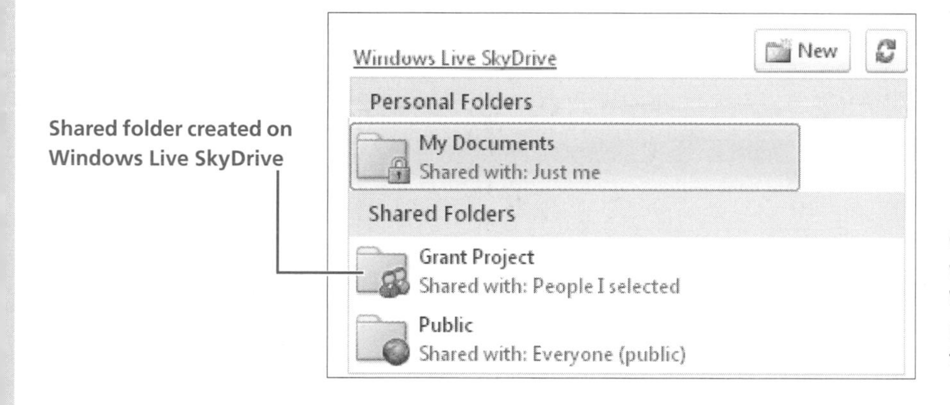

Grace may use Excel to upload a workbook to a shared folder on Windows Live SkyDrive and give permission to other people to edit the workbook or only to view it.

17.1 Sharing Workbooks on a Network

Video Lesson labyrinthelab.com/videos

Excel's Share Workbook command lets you set up a workbook for sharing and choose options for recording a history of changes to the workbook. Then you can review the change history for any conflicts between entries to the same cells and see how they were resolved. When the shared workbook is stored on a network drive on your organization's intranet and you have the file open, you may have Excel give you automatic updates of all user changes. When sharing files, you should give users clear instructions about the data that they should and should not change.

Characteristics of Shared Workbooks

When you set up a workbook for sharing on a network, several features work together to coordinate the use of the workbook.

- **Shared Access—**Multiple users can access the same file at once and see which other users currently have the file open.
- **User Settings—**Users may save their own printing and filtering settings as a custom view with the file.
- **Change History—**The change history is activated automatically whenever you create a shared workbook. This feature must be active as long as the workbook is shared.
- **Resolving Conflicts—**When changes are saved to a shared workbook, Excel displays a dialog box to help you review and resolve any conflicts between what you and another user have entered.

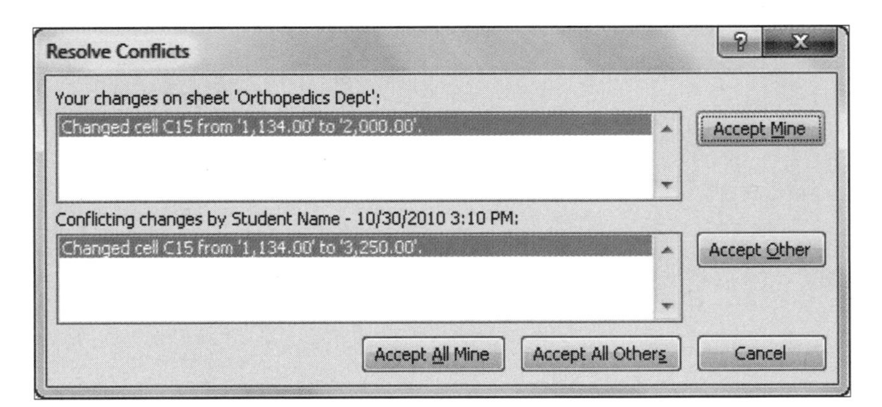

The Resolve Conflicts dialog box appears after two users change the same cell and save a shared workbook.

Simultaneous Access to Shared Workbooks

When you share a workbook on a network drive, several users can open and change the workbook simultaneously. Changes saved by multiple users are recorded in the change history for later review. When two users change the same cell and the second user gives the Save command, Excel analyzes the change history and alerts the second user to review both changes and choose one. Excel cannot keep both changes in one cell.

If more than one person tries to open a standard (unshared) Excel workbook, the second person to open the workbook will receive a warning message and must open a read-only copy in order to view the file.

Disabled Features in Shared Workbooks

Several Excel features are disabled when a workbook is shared, whether on a network drive or distributed to individual users. For example, you cannot delete a worksheet or add tables and charts in a shared workbook. Nor can you change passwords to protect worksheets—although password protection applied before the workbook is shared remains in effect. For a complete list of disabled features, see the Use a Shared Workbook to Collaborate topic in Excel Help.

QUICK REFERENCE **SHARING A WORKBOOK**

Task	Procedure
Set up a workbook to be shared	■ Choose Review→Changes→Share Workbook from the Ribbon. ■ In the Editing tab of the Share Workbook dialog box, place a checkmark in the box next to Allow Changes by More Than One User at the Same Time. ■ Display the Advanced tab in the dialog box, choose any desired options, and click OK. ■ Click OK to confirm saving the workbook. ■ Copy the workbook to a network drive or other location where the entire workgroup has access to it, or make multiple copies of the original file and distribute a copy to each user.

DEVELOP YOUR SKILLS 17.1.1

Set Up and Edit a Shared Workbook

In this exercise, you will set up the Shared Budget workbook to be shared. Then you will open the workbook in two different Excel windows simultaneously to simulate multiple users working in a shared workbook on a network drive.

Before You Begin: *Verify with your instructor, staff, or class notes whether you have permission to change the username on your computer. Verify the procedure for restoring the original username if you do have permission.*

Set the Username

1. Choose **File→Options**. Display the **General** category, if not already displayed.
2. Under Personalize Your Copy of Microsoft Office, notice the current **User Name.**

Click Cancel and skip to step 5 if you do not have permission to change the username on your computer.

3. As directed by your instructor, write the current username *exactly as shown* so you may restore that name at the end of this exercise. Or, write the restoration procedure in the space provided:

    ____

4. Change the existing username in the User Name box to **Grace Vargas**, and click **OK** to save the change.

Set Up the Shared Workbook

5. **Open** the Shared Budget workbook from the Lesson 17 folder in your file storage location.
6. Choose **Review→Changes→Share Workbook** from the Ribbon.
7. On the **Editing** tab, place a checkmark in the box next to **Allow Changes by More than One User at the Same Time**.
8. Display the **Advanced** tab and read the various options.
9. Make certain that the **Ask Me Which Changes Win** option is chosen near the bottom of the dialog box, as shown at right.
   This option ensures that you can review and accept or reject any conflicting changes to cells whenever you save the workbook.

   Conflicting changes between users
   Ask me which changes win
   The changes being saved win

10. Click **OK**, and then click **OK** again to confirm saving the workbook.
    Notice that [Shared] *appears on the title bar next to the filename. This tells you that sharing has been enabled for this workbook.*

    Shared Budget [Shared] - Microsoft Excel

11. Choose **Review→Changes→Track Changes** **→Highlight Changes** from the Ribbon.
    Notice that the Track Changes While Editing option is checked. Track Changes was switched on automatically when you gave the command to share the workbook.
12. Make certain that **When** is set to **Since I Last Saved**.
13. Place a checkmark in the box next to **Who** and make certain that **Everyone** is chosen in the Who list.
    This sets the change history to display change boxes around the changes that everyone makes in the workbook. Remember that Grace Vargas (or your computer's username) is the username set in the Excel Options dialog box, so Excel considers her to have created this shared workbook.
14. Click **OK** in the dialog box. Click **OK** again in the dialog box with the message No Changes Were Found with the Specified Properties.
    Initially, Excel finds that no changes have yet been made after the workbook was saved.

Edit the Shared Workbook

Now you will play the role of Grace editing some data in the workbook.

15. Display the **Orthopedics Dept** worksheet.
16. Select **cell C15** and enter **2000** as the new value for the cell.
17. Select **cell H18**, a blank cell, and enter **700**.
18. Select **cell G15**, a blank cell, and enter **1450**.
19. Do **not** save yet.
    You set the When option to track changes from the last save. Saving now would not track the changes you just made.

Start a Second Copy of Excel

Now you will work as if you are accessing the workbook simultaneously with Grace.

This new window will be referred to as the second Excel window for the remainder of this exercise and the following exercise.

20. Display the **Start** menu in Windows and navigate to Excel to open a **second** Excel program window.

Change the Username

Skip to step 23 if you do not have permission rights to change the username on your computer.

21. Choose **File→Options**. Display the **General** category, if not already displayed.
22. Under **Personalize Your Copy of Microsoft Office**, enter your first name and last name in the User Name box and click **OK** to save the change.
    Now when you open the workbook, Excel will recognize you as a different user making changes to the workbook.

Open a Second Copy of the Workbook

23. **Open** the Shared Budget workbook from the Lesson 17 folder in your file storage location.
    Notice that [Shared] *appears just to the right of the filename on the title bar. You now have this file open in two Excel program windows at once. This is possible only with a shared workbook, not a standard Excel workbook.*
24. Choose **Review→Changes→Share Workbook** from the Ribbon, and notice that two users are listed under Who Has This Workbook Open Now (if you were allowed to change the username).
25. Click **Cancel** to exit the dialog box without making any changes.
26. Display the **Orthopedics Dept** worksheet, select **cell C15**, and enter **3250** as the new value for the cell.
    This new value will conflict with the 2000 *entry Grace made in step 16. However, as you will see later, Excel will help you catch conflicts like this. Notice also that, unlike the first copy, this second copy of the shared workbook does not display change boxes. The changes are being saved to the change history, though, and will be displayed later in the exercise when you review the changes.*
27. Select **cell G16** and enter **350**.
    This value does not conflict with any value entered by Grace.
28. **Save** the changes and leave the **second** Excel window open.
    Excel saves the changes to this second copy of the shared workbook in the change history. Later, Excel will use the change history to enter the data into Grace's copy of the workbook in the first Excel window and to resolve the conflict in cell C15.

Switch to the First Workbook and Resolve Conflicts

29. Follow these steps to switch to Grace Vargas' copy of the workbook:
Your buttons may look different. If they appear side by side, click the Microsoft Excel button to the left.

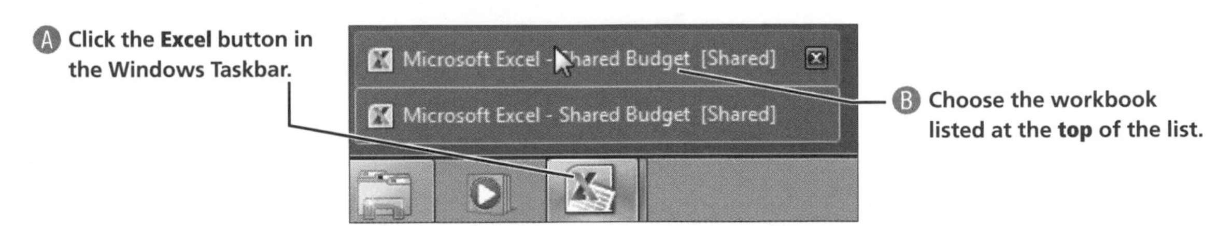

A Click the **Excel** button in the Windows Taskbar.
Microsoft Excel - Shared Budget [Shared]
Microsoft Excel - Shared Budget [Shared]
B Choose the workbook listed at the **top** of the list.

The first Excel window becomes the active window, and you are back to viewing Grace's work in this copy of the shared workbook. Notice that the changes you made in the second Excel window are not yet visible. They are in the change history. The changes won't be visible until Grace gives the Save command on her copy of the shared workbook.

30. **Save** the workbook in the first Excel window.
A Resolve Conflicts dialog box appears. This alerts Grace that her change conflicts with a change you made and saved in the second Excel window a few moments ago. Notice that Excel displays the name, time, and other details of the conflicting change. Based on her knowledge of the project, Grace recognizes that the higher figure is correct.

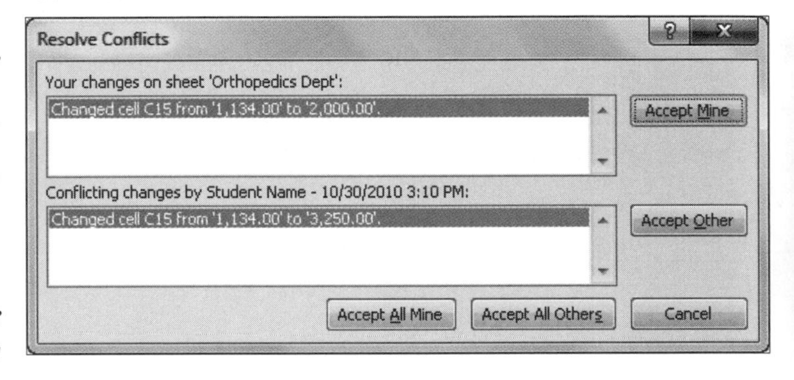

31. Click the **Accept Other** button on the right side of the dialog box.
32. Click **OK** to acknowledge the message that the workbook has been updated with the various changes.
Notice that the 350 in cell G16 of the second Excel window was entered automatically because it did not conflict with any other edits to the workbook.

Review Changes to the Shared Workbook

Now you will look over the change boxes on the worksheet and review the change history worksheet.

33. Choose **Review→Changes→Track Changes** **→Highlight Changes** from the Ribbon.
34. Follow these steps to review the change history:

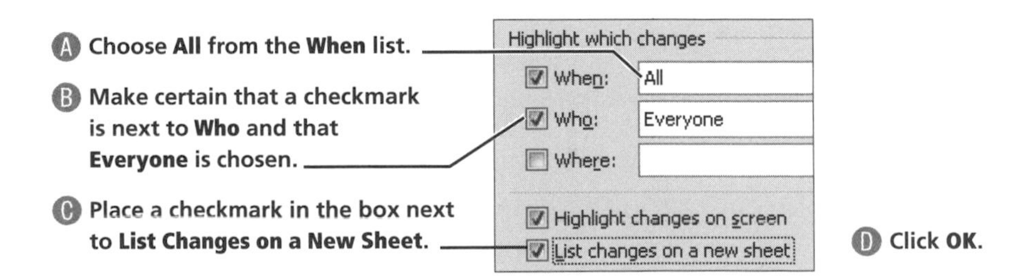

The History worksheet appears. Your Date, Time, and Who columns will differ from the illustration.

	A	B	C	D	E	F	G	H	I	J	K
1	Action Number	Date	Time	Who	Change	Sheet	Range	New Value	Old Value	Action Type	Losing Action
2	1	5/21/2010	11:16 PM	Student Name	Cell Change	Orthopedics Dept	C15	3,250.00	1,134.00		
3	2	5/21/2010	11:16 PM	Student Name	Cell Change	Orthopedics Dept	G16	350	<blank>		
4	3	5/21/2010	11:38 PM	Grace Vargas	Cell Change	Orthopedics Dept	H18	700	<blank>		
5	4	5/21/2010	11:38 PM	Grace Vargas	Cell Change	Orthopedics Dept	G15	1,450.00	<blank>		
6											
7	The history ends with the changes saved on 5/21/2010 at 11:38 PM.										

As you may expect, all changes are recorded here. Notice, however, that the 2000 entry made in cell C15 of the first Excel window is not recorded. That was the cell with the conflicting changes. Since you dismissed the 2000 value and kept the 3250 value, the change history does not record the conflict, just the resolution.

35. Display the **Orthopedics Dept** worksheet.
    Notice that change boxes have appeared around all four of the cells that were changed earlier in this exercise.
36. **Save** the workbook in the **first** Excel window.
    Notice that the History worksheet disappears after the save. However, you may still see the change boxes.
37. Leave both Excel windows **open** for the next exercise.

Switching Off Sharing

Video Lesson labyrinthelab.com/videos

You may want to switch off sharing only temporarily or after a project is completed. When you switch off sharing, the change history is erased and any unsaved changes by other users are lost. You should not turn off sharing to a workbook unless you are satisfied that everyone's data have been saved and that any conflicts have been resolved satisfactorily. Once you disable the sharing feature for a workbook, there is no turning back.

Before you turn off sharing, make certain that all other network users have saved their changes and closed the workbook. Otherwise, their changes will be lost.

QUICK REFERENCE **DISABLING WORKBOOK SHARING**

Task	Procedure
Disable workbook sharing	■ Print or copy the History worksheet to another workbook, if desired. ■ Make certain that all other users have saved their work. Otherwise, any unsaved changes are lost. ■ Choose Review→Changes→Share Workbook from the Ribbon. ■ In the Editing tab of the Share Workbook dialog box, remove the checkmark in the box next to Allow Changes by More than One User at the Same Time. ■ Click Yes when you are warned that the change history will be erased and that other users will not be able to save their work.

DEVELOP YOUR SKILLS 17.1.2

Stop Sharing the Workbook

In this exercise, you will disable sharing for the workbook. This command will also erase the change history and deactivate the Track Changes feature.

1. Verify that the active window is the **first** Excel window with Grace's work and the change boxes displayed. (If the change boxes do not display, choose **Review→Changes→Track Changes**, and click **OK**.)
2. Choose **Review→Changes→Share Workbook** from the Ribbon, and select the **Editing** tab in the Share Workbook dialog box, if necessary.
   Notice that the Who Has This Workbook Open Now list on the dialog box displays both Excel users. You should see your own name (or computer username) on the second line along with the time you opened the workbook in the second window. Although you could use the Remove User button near the bottom of the dialog box to close the other window, it is much more polite to contact the user and provide an opportunity to save the workbook. Otherwise, the unsaved changes will be lost.
3. Click **Cancel** to close the dialog box.

Turn Off Workbook Sharing

4. Make the **second** Excel window active by clicking the Excel button on the Windows Taskbar and selecting the bottom file in the list (or clicking the button to the right if the buttons are side by side on the Taskbar). Then **close** that Excel window without saving any changes.
5. Choose **Review→Changes→Share Workbook** from the Ribbon.
   The Who Has This Workbook Open Now list now shows just one open copy of the shared workbook. Now it is safe for Grace to turn off sharing for this workbook.
6. Uncheck the **Allow Changes by More than One User at the Same Time** option and click **OK**.
7. Click **Yes** to confirm removing the workbook from shared use.
   Now this workbook may be opened by only one user at a time.
8. **Close** the workbook and click **Yes** if prompted to save the changes.

Restore the Username

Skip steps 9 and 10 if you did not change the username. If you did change the username, refer to the procedure you wrote in step 3 in Develop Your Skills 17.1.1 to restore the original username, which may vary from the following steps.

9. Choose **File→Options.** Display the **General** category, if not already displayed.
10. Under **Personalize Your Copy of Microsoft Office,** carefully **type** the original username you wrote down during Develop Your Skills 17.1.1 in the User Name box and click **OK**.
11. **Exit** Excel.

17.2 Collaborating with Windows Live SkyDrive and Office Web Apps 2010

Video Lesson labyrinthelab.com/videos

You may not always be at your computer or have access to your hard drive when you need to edit a file. For example, you may need to edit an important work document from home, but have no access to your work computer. With Windows Live™ SkyDrive, you can store your files online so they are available from any computer with an Internet connection. With Office Web Apps 2010, you or your colleagues can edit those files residing on SkyDrive even if the actual Microsoft Office programs are not installed on the computer being used.

Creating a Windows Live ID Account

SkyDrive and Office Web Apps 2010 require you to have a Windows Live ID to sign in before the service can be used. A Windows Live ID is simply a free account with a Microsoft service such as Hotmail (email), Messenger (instant messaging), or Xbox LIVE (online gaming).

Adjust the steps in the following Quick Reference table if the Windows Live website has been updated.

QUICK REFERENCE — CREATING AND USING A WINDOWS LIVE ID

Task	Procedure
Create a free Windows Live ID	■ Verify that your Internet connection is active. From Excel: ■ Choose File→Save & Send→Save to Web. ■ In the Save to Windows Live area of Backstage view, click Sign Up for Windows Live. ■ Fill in the form to create your Windows Live ID. From a web browser: ■ Start Internet Explorer or another web browser, type **www.live.com** in the Address box at the top of the window, and tap [Enter]. ■ Click the Sign Up button on the Windows Live web page. ■ Fill in the form to create your Windows Live ID.
Sign in to Windows Live with an existing ID	From Excel: ■ Choose File→Save & Send→Save to Web. ■ In the Save to Windows Live area of Backstage view, click Sign In. ■ Enter your Windows Live ID email address and password, if not already displayed, and click OK. From a web browser: ■ Start Internet Explorer or another web browser, type **www.live.com** in the Address box at the top of the window, and tap [Enter]. ■ Click the Sign In button on the Windows Live web page. ■ Enter your Windows Live ID email address and password, if not already displayed, and click Sign In.

DEVELOP YOUR SKILLS 17.2.1

Create a Windows Live ID Account

WebSim labyrinthelab.com/excel10

In this exercise, you will sign up for a Windows Live ID by creating a new Hotmail email address. Then you will log off Windows Live.

1. **Type** the URL for the student web page (listed above) in the address bar of your web browser and **tap** [Enter].
2. From the left navigation bar, click **Lessons 12–18** and then **Lesson 17**; then click the **Develop Your Skills 17.2.1: Create a Windows Live ID Account** link.
   The WebSim loads. The browser is open to the Windows Live homepage. Websites are updated frequently, and the actual web pages may vary from those shown in the WebSim.
3. Work your way through the **on-screen exercise instructions**.
4. Click the **Back to Course** link at the top-right corner of your screen.

Storing Files on SkyDrive

Video Lesson labyrinthelab.com/videos

SkyDrive is a free service provided by Microsoft that allows you to store your files online. This online storage provides several benefits.

- You can access your files from any computer with an Internet connection.
- You don't need to worry about losing the files from your hard drive crashing or USB drive breaking because your files are stored on the SkyDrive servers. You should, however, make backup copies of important files.

Adjust the steps in the following Quick Reference table if the Windows Live website has been updated.

QUICK REFERENCE **SAVING AND ACCESSING FILES ON SKYDRIVE**

Task	Procedure
Navigate to SkyDrive in Windows Live	■ Choose Windows Live→SkyDrive from the menu bar at the top of the Windows Live web page.
Navigate to SkyDrive in Excel	■ Choose File→Save & Send→Save to Web. ■ Click Windows Live SkyDrive in the Save to Windows Live SkyDrive area of Backstage view, if necessary. ■ Log into Windows Live, if necessary.

QUICK REFERENCE	SAVING AND ACCESSING FILES ON SKYDRIVE (continued)
Task	**Procedure**
Upload a workbook in SkyDrive	■ Start your web browser, log into Windows Live, and navigate to SkyDrive. ■ Open the folder into which you wish to add the file. ■ Click the Add Files link. ■ Click a Browse button or choose Select Documents from Your Computer, depending on the command available. Navigate to the folder containing the desired file, and double-click the filename.
Save a workbook in Excel to a SkyDrive folder	■ Open the workbook that you wish to save to SkyDrive. ■ Choose File→Save & Send→Save to Web. ■ In the Save to Windows Live SkyDrive area of Backstage view, select the SkyDrive folder into which you wish to save the file. ■ Click Save As under the folders list. ■ In the Save As dialog box, verify the folder name, name the file, and click Save.
Access a file stored on SkyDrive	■ Start your web browser and navigate to www.live.com. ■ Sign in with your Windows Live ID and choose SkyDrive. ■ Select the folder containing the file that you wish to access. ■ Select the desired file to view it. Alternatively, point to the file you want to access and click an action, such as Edit in Browser, Share, or More.

DEVELOP YOUR SKILLS 17.2.2

Add a File on Windows Live SkyDrive

WebSim labyrinthelab.com/excel10

In this exercise, you will sign into Windows Live SkyDrive and upload a workbook file to an existing shared folder.

1. If necessary, **type** the URL listed above into the address bar of your web browser and **tap** [Enter].
2. From the left navigation bar, click **Lessons 12–18** and then **Lesson 17**; then click the **Develop Your Skills 17.2.2: Add a File on Windows Live SkyDrive** link.
   The WebSim loads. The browser is open to the Windows Live homepage. Websites are updated frequently, and the actual web pages may vary from those shown in the WebSim.
3. Work your way through the **on-screen exercise instructions**.
4. Click the **Back to Course** link at the top-right corner of your screen.

Saving a File to SkyDrive in Excel

Video Lesson labyrinthelab.com/videos

As you learned in the previous exercise, you may upload Excel workbooks after logging in to Windows Live in your web browser. As an alternative, you may log in to Windows Live and save a workbook to SkyDrive from within Excel.

DEVELOP YOUR SKILLS 17.2.3

Save a File in Excel to Windows Live SkyDrive

WebSim labyrinthelab.com/excel10

In this exercise, you will save a file to Windows Live SkyDrive from within Excel. You will save the workbook file using Backstage view.

1. If necessary, **type** the URL listed above into the address bar of your web browser and **tap** [Enter].
2. From the left navigation bar, click **Lessons 12–18** and then **Lesson 17**; then click the **Develop Your Skills 17.2.3: Save a File in Excel to Windows Live SkyDrive** link.
   The WebSim loads. The Shared Budget workbook is open in Excel.
3. Work your way through the **on-screen exercise instructions**.
4. Click the **Back to Course** link at the top-right corner of your screen.

Editing Files with Office Web Apps 2010

Video Lesson labyrinthelab.com/videos

Files that have been saved to SkyDrive can be edited online using Office Web Apps 2010. These applications can be considered as free online versions of Microsoft Office programs, but with limited functionality. Initially, Microsoft planned to support editing only in Word, Excel, PowerPoint, and OneNote documents with Office Web Apps 2010. The apps may feature different capabilities at a later time. The benefits and limitations of Office Web Apps 2010 are summarized in the following table.

Benefits of Office Web Apps 2010	Limitations of Office Web Apps 2010
■ Files can be edited from any computer with an Internet connection ■ No need for Microsoft Office to be installed ■ Document content and formatting are maintained between the Web App and the full Office application	■ Requires a Windows Live ID ■ Fewer features and capabilities than the full Microsoft Office applications

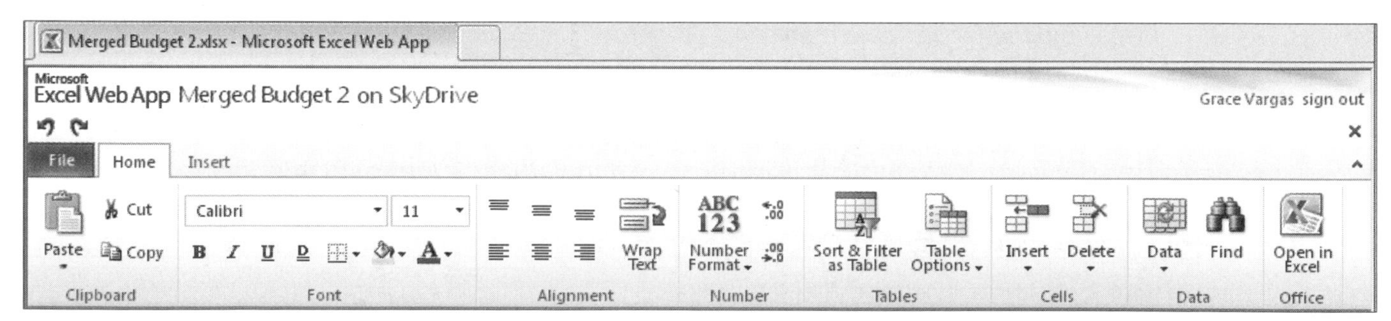

The Excel Web App features a similar Ribbon as in the full version of Excel, but lacks much of the functionality.

Adjust the steps in the following Quick Reference table if the Office Web Apps have been updated.

QUICK REFERENCE	EDITING A SKYDRIVE WORKBOOK IN EXCEL WEB APP 2010 OR EXCEL
Task	**Procedure**
Edit a workbook on SkyDrive using the Excel Web App	■ In SkyDrive, open the folder containing the file to be edited. ■ Click the desired file to view the workbook. ■ Choose Edit in Browser from the menu bar above the worksheet to open the workbook in the Excel Web App. ■ Respond to accept the service agreement if a message appears. ■ Edit the workbook. The Ribbon does not contain all of the commands that are in the full Excel version. ■ When you are finished editing, click either Close [X] or Sign Out at the upper-right above the Ribbon. The file is saved automatically.
Edit a workbook on SkyDrive using the full Excel version	■ In SkyDrive, open the folder containing the file to be edited. ■ Click the desired file to view the workbook. ■ Choose Open in Excel from the menu bar above the worksheet to open the workbook in Excel on your computer. ■ Click OK to respond to the message about opening web files. ■ Edit the workbook, click Save, and close Excel. ■ In the SkyDrive window, your changes may not appear automatically. Close and reopen the workbook on SkyDrive to verify that the changes were saved.

DEVELOP YOUR SKILLS 17.2.4

Edit a Workbook Using the Excel Web App

WebSim labyrinthelab.com/excel10

In this exercise, you will access a workbook on Windows Live SkyDrive. Assume that you are using a computer with Internet access but without Excel installed. You will edit the workbook using the Excel Web App.

1. If necessary, **type** the URL listed above into the address bar of your web browser and **tap** [Enter].
2. From the left navigation bar, click **Lessons 12–18** and then **Lesson 17**; then click the **Develop Your Skills 17.2.4: Edit a Workbook Using the Excel Web App** link.
   The WebSim loads. Assume that you have signed in to Windows Live SkyDrive. Internet Explorer displays the Grant Project folder in your SkyDrive storage location.
3. Work your way through the **on-screen exercise instructions**.
4. Click the **Back to Course** link at the top-right corner of your screen.

Sharing Files with SkyDrive

Video Lesson labyrinthelab.com/videos

In addition to editing files stored on SkyDrive with Office Web Apps 2010, you can share files and allow others to edit or comment on them. Alternatively, you can share files and allow others to only view or comment on them.

Creating and Sharing SkyDrive Folders

When you share a file on SkyDrive, you actually share the SkyDrive folder containing the file. Therefore, all files stored in the SkyDrive folder are shared. You can easily create additional SkyDrive folders to more easily manage permissions. For example, you can create one folder that stores files you allow others to edit and create another folder that stores files you allow the same people to only view. Files you store in the Public folder are available to anyone with a Windows Live ID who knows their location.

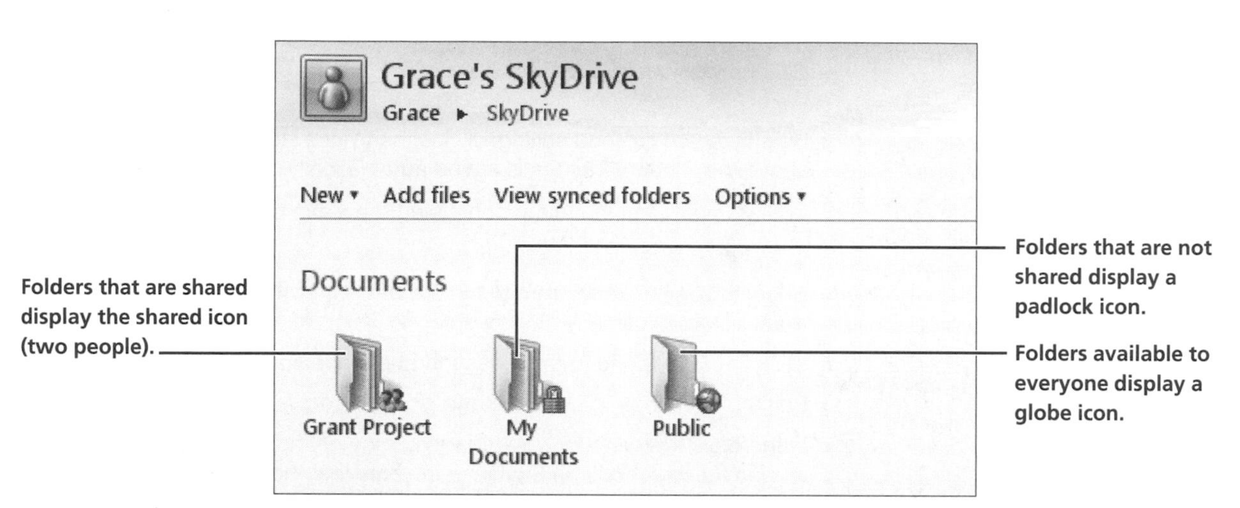
Grace's SkyDrive
Grace ▸ SkyDrive
New ▾ Add files View synced folders Options ▾
Documents
Grant Project
My Documents
Public
Folders that are shared display the shared icon (two people).
Folders that are not shared display a padlock icon.
Folders available to everyone display a globe icon.

QUICK REFERENCE	WORKING WITH SKYDRIVE FOLDERS
Task	**Procedure**
Create a folder in SkyDrive	■ Navigate to SkyDrive. ■ Choose New ▾ menu→Folder from the web page menu bar above the SkyDrive folder icons. ■ Type a folder name in the Name box. ■ Leave the Share With setting as Just Me, or click Change to set up sharing with other people. ■ Click Next to begin adding files to the folder. (Click Cancel if you do not wish to add files at this time.)
Share a SkyDrive folder	■ In SkyDrive, select the folder to open it. ■ Choose Share ▾ menu→Edit Permissions from the web page menu bar. ■ Enter the email address of the person with whom you would like to share the folder and tap Enter. Repeat this step to add additional people, if desired. ■ Choose the desired permission level from the list next to each person's email address. ■ Click Save. ■ Type a message to include in the invitation email, and click Send. (Click Skip This if you do not wish to send an invitation.)
Access a shared folder	■ Click the link to the shared folder in the invitation email you received from the file's owner. ■ Click the View Folder button in the email. ■ Point to the file you wish to view or edit and choose an action.

DEVELOP YOUR SKILLS 17.2.5

Create a SkyDrive Folder

WebSim labyrinthelab.com/excel10

In this exercise, you will create a SkyDrive folder to store shared documents.

1. If necessary, **type** the URL listed above into the address bar of your web browser and **tap** Enter.
2. From the left navigation bar, click **Lessons 12–18** and then **Lesson 17**; then click the **Develop Your Skills 17.2.5: Create a SkyDrive Folder** link.
   The WebSim loads and the SkyDrive start page appears. You are already logged in as GraceVargasRaritan@hotmail.com.
3. Work your way through the **on-screen exercise instructions**.
4. Click the **Back to Course** link at the top-right corner of your screen.

Moving Files

Video Lesson labyrinthelab.com/videos

Because permissions are set on folders and not individual files, you may find it necessary to move files from one SkyDrive folder to another.

DEVELOP YOUR SKILLS 17.2.6

Move Files

WebSim labyrinthelab.com/excel10

In this exercise, you will move a file from one SkyDrive folder to another.

1. If necessary, **type** the URL listed above into the address bar of your web browser and **tap** Enter.
2. From the left navigation bar, click **Lessons 12–18** and then **Lesson 17**; then click the **Develop Your Skills 17.2.6: Move Files** link.
   The WebSim loads and the SkyDrive start page appears. You are already logged in as GraceVargasRaritan@hotmail.com.
3. Work your way through the **on-screen exercise instructions**.
4. Click the **Back to Course** link at the top-right corner of your screen.

Setting the Folder Permission Level

Video Lesson labyrinthelab.com/videos

Once a folder is created, you can set its permission level, allowing others to view or edit the files inside. SkyDrive lets you set global permissions and share a folder with the general public, or you can specify individuals by their email addresses. Any files stored in the folder will inherit the folder's permissions. While granting permission, you may send an email to invite the specified people to access the shared folder.

DEVELOP YOUR SKILLS 17.2.7

Share a Folder Using Permissions

WebSim labyrinthelab.com/excel10

In this exercise, you will share a SkyDrive folder and all the files within.

1. If necessary, **type** the URL listed above into the address bar of your web browser and **tap** [Enter].
2. From the left navigation bar, click **Lessons 12–18** and then **Lesson 17**; then click the **Develop Your Skills 17.2.7: Share a Folder Using Permissions** link.
   The WebSim loads and the SkyDrive page appears. The contents of the For Revision folder are displayed. You are already logged in as GraceVargasRaritan@hotmail.com.
3. Work your way through the **on-screen exercise instructions**.
4. Click the **Back to Course** link at the top-right corner of your screen.

Accessing Shared Files

Video Lesson labyrinthelab.com/videos

Once a file has been shared with you, accessing it is simple. You click the View Folder button in the invitation email, log in with your Windows Live ID if prompted, and edit the file just as if it were one of your own files on SkyDrive. Make certain you keep the invitation email because using the View Folder button is the easiest way to access the files.

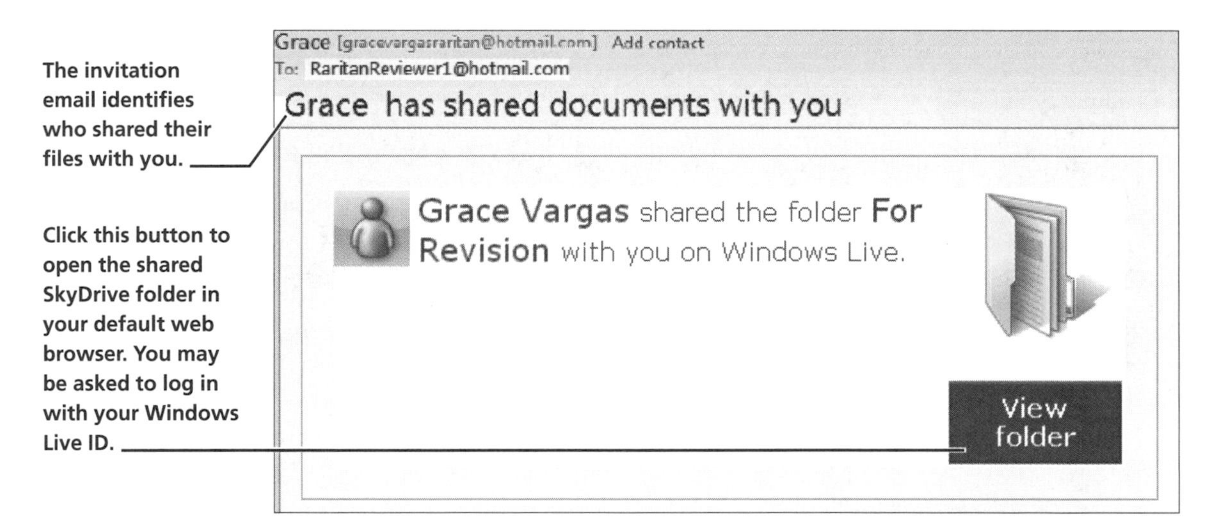
The invitation email identifies who shared their files with you.
Click this button to open the shared SkyDrive folder in your default web browser. You may be asked to log in with your Windows Live ID.
Grace [gracevargasraritan@hotmail.com] Add contact
To: RaritanReviewer1@hotmail.com
Grace has shared documents with you
Grace Vargas shared the folder For Revision with you on Windows Live.
View folder

17.3 Concepts Review

Concepts Review labyrinthelab.com/excel10

To check your knowledge of the key concepts introduced in this lesson, complete the Concepts Review quiz by going to the URL listed above. If your classroom is using Labyrinth eLab, you may complete the Concepts Review quiz from within your eLab course.

Reinforce Your Skills

REINFORCE YOUR SKILLS 17.1

Set Up a Workbook for a Network Share

In this exercise, you will create a shared workbook for access by other users on a network.

1. **Open** the rs-Network Share Budget workbook from the Lesson 17 folder.
2. Choose **Review→Changes→Share Workbook** from the Ribbon.
3. Place a **checkmark** in the box next to **Allow Changes by More than One User at the Same Time**.
4. Display the **Advanced** tab and follow these steps to set options in the dialog box.

Track changes
Keep change history for: 7 days
Don't keep change history
Update changes
When file is saved
Automatically every: 15 minutes
Save my changes and see others' changes
Just see other users' changes
Conflicting changes between users
Ask me which changes win
The changes being saved win

A Set **7 days** in the Keep Change History For box.

B Make certain that the other settings match the illustration.

Saving the change history for seven days rather than 30 days reduces the potential size of the file. The longer changes are kept and the more changes that are tracked, the larger the workbook file will become.

5. Click **OK**, and then click **OK** again to approve saving the workbook.
   Notice the word [Shared] *to the right of the filename in the title bar.*
6. Choose **Review→Changes→Track Changes** **→Highlight Changes** from the Ribbon.
   Notice that the Track Changes feature has been switched on. This was done automatically when you set the workbook for sharing. Notice also that the When setting is Since I Last Saved. This causes the highlight around changes to disappear each time you save the workbook. However, all changes will still be listed in the Change History.
7. Click **Cancel** in the dialog box.
8. Have your instructor or a teaching assistant initial that you have successfully shared the workbook. __________
9. **Close** the workbook.
   The workbook is now ready to be placed on a network drive for multiple users to open and work on the file simultaneously.

REINFORCE YOUR SKILLS 17.2

Create a Windows Live ID

In this exercise, you will create a Windows Live ID to use in later exercises as you work in Windows Live SkyDrive.

Before You Begin: *It is recommended that you use the Internet Explorer browser for the textbook exercises. You may use the Firefox or Safari browsers if Internet Explorer is not available.*

Websites are updated frequently, and the actual web pages may vary from those shown in the exercises of this book. Adjust the step instructions if the Windows Live website has been updated.

Create a Windows Live ID Account

1. **Start** your web browser.
2. Type **`www.live.com`** in the address bar of the web browser, and **tap** [Enter].
   The Windows Live homepage includes a link to sign up for a Hotmail email account and a link to sign into Windows Live.
3. Click the **Sign Up** button at the bottom-left of the web page.
4. Complete the form to create your Windows Live ID. Do **not** click the I Accept button at the bottom of the page yet.
5. Write down your Windows Live ID and password for future reference:
   - Windows Live ID:______________________________@hotmail.com
   - Password:______________________________

   It is recommended that you use this account only for the exercises in this book. Your account information is not secure, as anyone can look over your shoulder and learn your account password.
6. Click **I Accept** at the bottom of the page to complete the registration.
   Your Windows Live account is created, and your Hotmail page appears. You could access Windows Live SkyDrive from this window. However, you will sign out now.

Sign Out from Windows Live

7. Click Sign Out at the upper-right corner of the browser window.
   You are signed out of Hotmail and redirected to another Microsoft web page.

8. Leave your web browser **open** and continue with the next exercise.

REINFORCE YOUR SKILLS 17.3

Create a Folder and Share a Workbook in Windows Live SkyDrive

In this exercise, you will sign in to Windows Live. You will access SkyDrive, create a new shared folder, and upload an Excel workbook to the folder. Then you will sign out of Windows Live.

***Before You Begin:** You must have completed Reinforce Your Skills 17.2, and your web browser should be open.*

Sign In to Windows Live

1. Type **`www.live.com`** in the address bar of the web browser, and **tap** [Enter].
   The Windows Live sign-in page displays.
2. Type the **Windows Live ID** (such as yourname22@hotmail.com) that you created in step 5 of Reinforce Your Skills 17.2, and **tap** [Tab].
3. Type your **password**, and **tap** [Enter] to sign in.
   Your Windows Live homepage displays.

Navigate to SkyDrive

4. Point at **Windows Live** in the upper-left corner of your homepage window and choose **SkyDrive** from the menu.
   Your SkyDrive web page displays. You can choose SkyDrive on the navigation menu as shown below to move back to this view whenever you wish to view your folder list, create a folder, or open a different folder.

Create a Folder in SkyDrive

5. Notice that the My Documents folder was created automatically. Its icon has a padlock to indicate that the folder is not shared with anyone but you.
6. Choose **New ▾ menu→Folder** from the menu bar above the My Documents folder.
   The Create a Folder page displays.

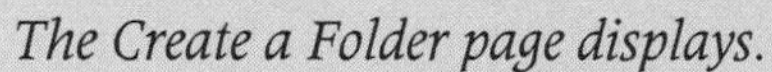

7. Type **`Budget Drafts`** as the folder name.

Share the Folder

In the next few steps, you will change the folder permissions to share the folder with another co-worker.

8. Click **Change** to the right of Share With: Just Me. (If you accidentally continued to the next screen, click Just Me instead. Then, click Edit Permissions in the Permissions for Budget Drafts screen.)

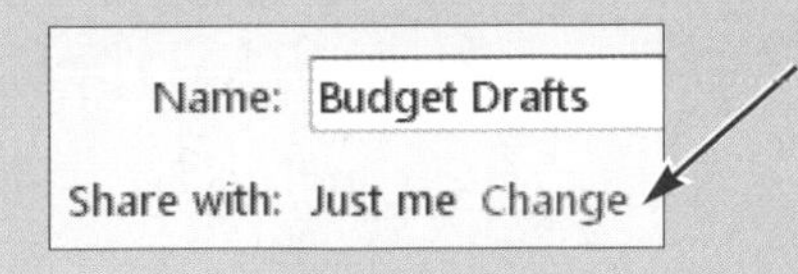

9. Under Add Specific People, type **`nikkiyoung@raritan.com`** in the Enter a Name or an E-Mail Address box, and **tap** [Enter].
   The email address displays with a checkmark and Nikki Young's current permission rights near the bottom of the window. Nikki's email account does not actually exist, so you will not use it to access any files.
10. Click the permission rights menu ▾ arrow, and choose **Can Add, Edit Details, and Delete Files**, if not already selected.

nikkiyoung@raritan.com | Can add, edit details, and delete files ▾

11. Click **Next** to display the Budget Drafts folder page.

Add a Workbook File to the Folder

Some of the next steps contain an alternate instruction for you to follow if the Silverlight add-in program is installed on your computer.

12. Choose **Add Files** from the Budget Drafts folder menu bar.
13. Click the **Browse** button for the first Add Document text box. (If the Add Document text boxes do not display, choose **Select Documents from Your Computer** instead.)
14. Navigate to the Lesson 17 folder in your file storage location and **double-click** the rs-Orthopedics Dept Budget workbook.
15. Click the **Upload** button. (If the file uploaded automatically, click the **Continue** button at the bottom of the window instead.)
    The file uploads, and the icon for the rs-Orthopedics Dept Budget file displays in the folder.
16. Click **Sign Out** in the upper-right corner of the window to exit Windows Live.
17. **Close** your web browser window.

REINFORCE YOUR SKILLS 17.4

Edit a Workbook with Excel Web App

In this exercise, you will save a workbook from within Excel to a folder in your Windows Live SkyDrive storage location. Then, you will edit the workbook in Excel Web App as if you are working from a computer that does not have Excel installed.

***Before You Begin:** You must have completed Reinforce Your Skills 17.2.*

Create a New Workbook in Excel

1. **Start** a new, blank workbook in Excel.
2. **Enter** data of your choice in a few cells.
3. **Format** the data appropriately, such as applying colors, changing alignment, or adjusting column widths.

Save the Workbook to Windows Live SkyDrive

4. Choose **File→Save & Send→Save to Web.**
   The Save to Windows Live SkyDrive pane displays in Backstage view.
5. Click the **Sign In** button in the Windows Live SkyDrive pane.
6. In the dialog box that appears, enter the **email address** and **password** you created in Reinforce Your Skills 17.2, and **tap** [Enter].
   You are now logged in to Windows Live, and your folder list appears as shown. The Budget Drafts folder displays only if you completed Reinforce Your Skills 17.3.

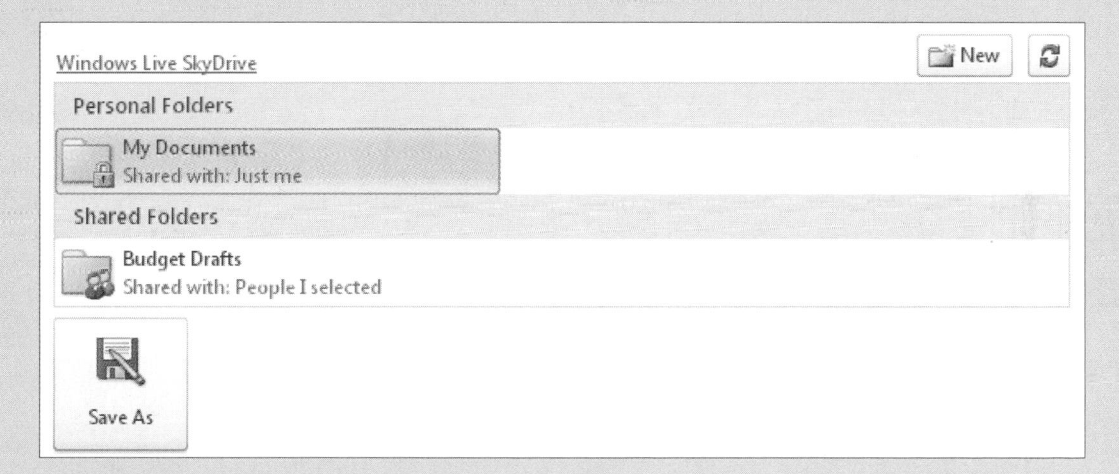

7. Choose the **My Documents** folder under Personal Folders, if not already selected.
   The folder name is highlighted. Under My Documents, notice that Shared With: Just Me indicates you have not shared the folder. Other people cannot access documents you place in this folder. You could change the folder permission properties, if you wished.
8. Click the **Save As** button.
   After a few moments, the Save As dialog box appears. The address bar displays an alphanumeric entry for your SkyDrive main folder and ^.Documents (or a similar name) to indicate that My Documents is the currently active folder.

9. Enter the filename **rs-SkyDrive Workbook** and click **Save**.
   Your workbook has been saved to SkyDrive, and the workbook redisplays in Excel. You could continue editing and then save again to SkyDrive, if you wished.
10. **Exit** Excel.

Edit the Workbook in Excel Web App

Now assume that you are using a computer in an Internet café. You wish to edit your workbook, but this computer does not have Excel installed.

11. **Start** your web browser and navigate to **www.live.com**.
12. **Sign in** with your Windows Live ID and password. (See step 5 of Reinforce Your Skills 17.2, if necessary.)
13. Choose the **My Documents** folder, if it is not open already.
    The My Documents folder page appears and contains the rs-SkyDrive Workbook folder you just saved.
14. **Click** the rs-SkyDrive Workbook file.
    The workbook displays below a menu of available actions.
15. Try to change the contents of any cell.
    The cell contents are not changed. Currently, you only may view the workbook. To edit the workbook, you must choose either the Open in Excel or Edit in Browser command.
16. Click **Edit in Browser** in the menu.

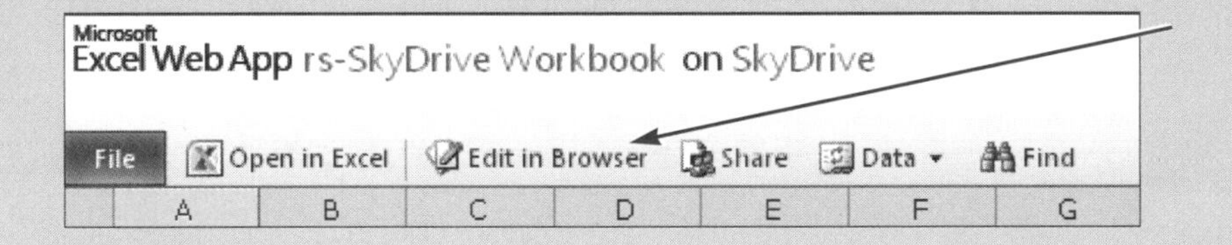

    You are now viewing your workbook in Excel Web App. Notice that fewer tabs and commands are available on the Ribbon than in the full version of Excel. The Web App, however, allows you to edit the workbook when Excel isn't installed on the computer you are using.

17. Take a moment to browse through the **File**, **Home**, and **Insert** tabs of the Ribbon to become familiar with the commands available, and then return to the Home tab.
18. Experiment by editing a cell's entry, applying various formatting to cells, and cutting and pasting data to a different row or column.
    Notice that the context, or popup, menu is not available when you right-click a cell or cell range.

Sign Out from Windows Live

19. Click **Sign Out** at the upper-right corner when you finish editing the workbook.
    Signing out or clicking the Back button in the browser window automatically saves your changes and closes the workbook.
20. **Close** your web browser.

Apply Your Skills

APPLY YOUR SKILLS 17.1

Create and Share a Folder on SkyDrive

In this exercise, you will sign in to your Windows Live account. Then you will navigate to SkyDrive and create a new folder.

1. **Start** your web browser and navigate to **www.live.com**.
2. **Sign in** using the Windows Live ID and password you created in step 5 of Reinforce Your Skills 17.2. (Follow steps 3–6 of that exercise if you did not create a Windows Live account.)
3. Navigate to your **SkyDrive** storage location in Windows Live.
4. Create a new folder named **Raritan Shared Documents** in SkyDrive. Choose options to **share** the folder with nikkiyoung@raritan.com. Allow Nikki to **view** documents in the folder but not to edit or delete them. If you are asked to send a notification to Nikki, click **Skip This**. Do not send a notification to her fictitious email address.
5. Leave your browser window **open** and continue with the next exercise.

APPLY YOUR SKILLS 17.2

Add a File to the SkyDrive Folder

In this exercise, you will upload a workbook to your Raritan Shared Documents folder on Windows Live SkyDrive.

***Before You Begin:** You must have completed Apply Your Skills 17.1. Your web browser should be open, and you should be signed in to your Windows Live account.*

1. Navigate to the **Raritan Shared Documents** folder in Windows Live SkyDrive, if necessary. You created this folder in Apply Your Skills 17.1.
2. Add the as-Cardiology Dept Budget workbook from the Lesson 17 folder in your file storage location to the **Raritan Shared Documents** folder in SkyDrive.
3. Click **Sign Out** in the top-right area of the web page.
4. Leave your browser window **open** and continue with the next exercise.

APPLY YOUR SKILLS 17.3

Edit a Workbook Using Excel Web App

In this exercise, you will upload a workbook to your Raritan Shared Documents folder on Windows Live SkyDrive.

Before You Begin: *You must have completed Apply Your Skills 17.1 and 17.2. Your web browser should be open, and you should be signed in to your Windows Live account.*

1. Navigate to the **Raritan Shared Documents** folder in Windows Live SkyDrive, if necessary. You created this folder in Apply Your Skills 17.1.
2. Choose the as-Cardiology Dept Budget workbook. You added this file in Apply Your Skills 17.2.
3. Choose to edit the workbook using **Excel Web App**.
4. Select **cell E11,** and change the May grant salaries to **1597**.
   The total grant amount in cell I11 should be 4,283.
5. Click the **Back** button in your web browser.
6. **Open** the as-Cardiology Dept Budget workbook, and verify that the change was saved.
7. Have your instructor or a teaching assistant initial that you successfully saved the revised as-Cardiology Dept Budget workbook in the Raritan Shared Documents folder on SkyDrive: ____________
8. **Sign out** from Windows Live, and **close** your browser window.

Critical Thinking & Work-Readiness Skills

In the course of working through the following Microsoft Office-based Critical Thinking exercises, you will also be utilizing various work-readiness skills, some of which are listed next to each exercise. Go to labyrinthelab.com/workreadiness *to learn more about the work-readiness skills.*

17.1 Set Up a Workbook for a Network Share

Elias Carpenter is a nurse supervisor at Raritan Clinic East. He coordinates a free testing program to screen patients for diabetes. He uses Excel to keep a record of the screening costs. These costs include medical and office supplies as well as physician, medical professional, and administrative time. Your job is to set up his workbook to be shared on Raritan Clinic's intranet, or network. Open ct-Diabetes Screening Clinic (Lesson 17 folder). Save with the name **ct-Diabetes Screening Clinic [Your Last Name]** in the Lesson 17 folder. Take a few moments to review the worksheets. Two sheets contain PivotTables that organize the personnel costs by patient age group and test result. Then, set up the workbook to be shared on the network so that multiple users can enter data simultaneously. Display each tab in the Ribbon and determine which commands are unavailable until sharing is switched off. Close the workbook when finished.

WORK-READINESS SKILLS APPLIED

- Understanding systems
- Participating as a member of a team
- Reasoning

17.2 Create a SkyDrive Folder and Add a File

Elias will be away from Raritan Clinic while attending a conference and cannot access the Raritan Clinic intranet then. In this scenario, he wishes to use Windows Live SkyDrive to continue working on his unshared workbook. Log in to Windows Live using the ID and password you created in Reinforce Your Skills 17.1. Navigate to SkyDrive and create a folder named **Diabetes Screening**. Upload the *original* ct-Diabetes Screening Clinic workbook (Lesson 17 folder) to the newly created folder. Leave SkyDrive open for the next exercise.

WORK-READINESS SKILLS APPLIED

- Selecting technology
- Applying technology to a task
- Organizing and Maintaining information

17.3 Edit a Workbook Stored on SkyDrive

Elias is attending the conference and needs to change some personnel costs in his workbook. He is using a computer that has the full version of Excel 2010 installed. Log in to Windows Live, if necessary. Open the ct-Diabetes Screening Clinic workbook from the Diabetes Screening folder on SkyDrive. You may choose to edit the workbook either in Excel or Excel Web App. In the Costs worksheet, sort the records by screening result. Change the personnel cost to **$30** for all patients whose test result indicated Type 1 or Type 2 diabetes. Do *not* change the cost for patients whose test result was normal or borderline. Use the Data tab of the Ribbon (Excel) or the HomeData menu ▾ (Excel Web App) to refresh all connections so that the costs update in the PivotTable worksheets. Save the workbook, and close it in SkyDrive. Reopen the workbook in SkyDrive to verify the changes were saved. Sign out from Windows Live when you are finished.

WORK-READINESS SKILLS APPLIED

- Applying technology to a task
- Organizing and Maintaining information
- Making decisions

Integrating Excel with Other Programs

LESSON OUTLINE

LEARNING OBJECTIVES

After studying this lesson, you will be able to:

- Save workbooks for use with prior Excel versions
- Convert workbooks to text, PDF, and XPS file formats
- Share Excel data with Word, PowerPoint, and Access
- Import text and data from external sources into Excel workbooks
- Save workbook elements as a web page

Information is shared electronically in many ways. In this lesson, you will learn how to make Excel 2010 workbooks compatible with prior Excel versions so that all project collaborators may share data. You will learn how to convert workbooks to other file formats, including PDF and XPS for document sharing. A program other than Excel may be the basis for a project. For example, you often will create reports using Word and make presentations using PowerPoint. Through the power of application integration, you may link or embed Excel data, tables, and charts in those documents. You also will bring data into Excel from external sources such as a plain-text file or Word document. Documents often are shared electronically as web pages. You will learn how to save an entire workbook as a web page, as well as save a single worksheet and selected elements from a sheet.

Student Resources labyrinthelab.com/excel10

CASE STUDY

Producing an Annual Report

Deion Jenett is administrative assistant to Dr. Edward Jackson, the chief operating officer at Raritan Clinic East. Deion is halfway through a project to produce Raritan's annual report. He coordinates the efforts of the production team to get various parts of the publication ready for printing and publishing to the clinic's website. Deion assembles information about the production tasks and the schedule into an Excel workbook and then publishes the workbook in a universal file format so everyone can review it. As part of his normal job duties, Deion also merges Excel workbook data into forms or letters addressed to multiple recipients.

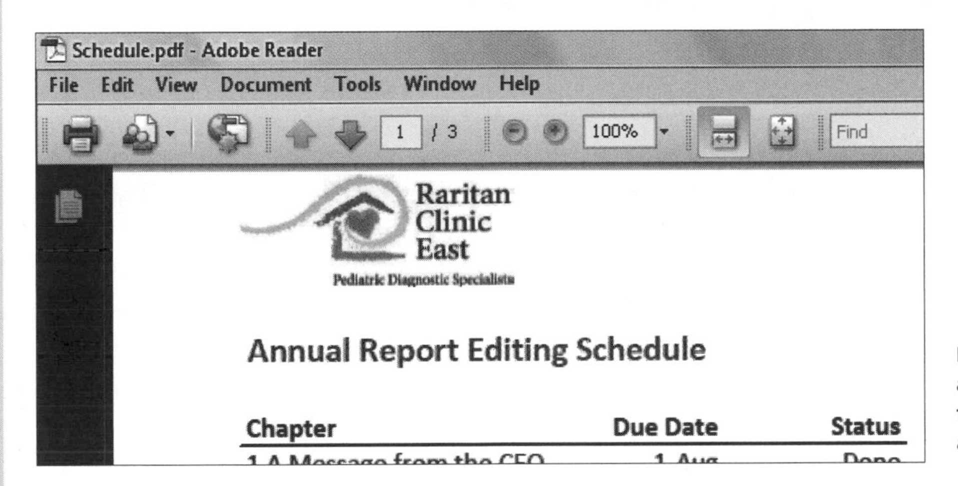

Deion saves an Excel workbook as a PDF file, a universal file format that may be viewed by anyone in a PDF reader.

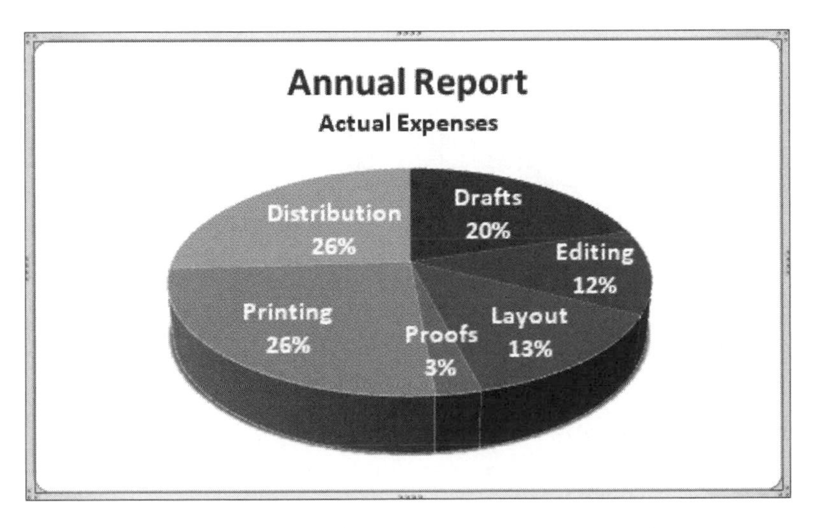

The Copy and Paste commands are used to import a linked Excel chart into a PowerPoint slide.

Employee Name:	«First» «Last»
Employee ID:	«Exployee ID»
Job Title:	«Position»

Employee Name:	Nadia Andrews
Employee ID:	NA34
Job Title:	Nurse Aide

Data from an Excel workbook is inserted into merge fields, and then Word's Mail Merge feature is used to assemble personalized forms.

18.1 Maintaining Compatibility with Previous Versions of Excel

Video Lesson labyrinthelab.com/videos

You can open and work with Excel workbooks saved in Excel 2010 or earlier versions such as Excel 97, 2000, 2003, and 2007. At times, you will need to share your workbooks and templates with others who have one of the earlier Excel versions or may not have Excel installed. You must ensure that files are saved in a format that those users can open.

About File Formats

A file format is a structure for storing data in a computer file. An application program uses specific file formats to save anything that you create in that program. The format that an application program normally uses to save files is called its *native* file format. For example, Word saves files using the format Word Document (.docx), and a web page editor may use the HTML file format.

Identifying a File's Format

When you give Excel's Save As command, you may choose from a number of file formats in the Save As Type list in the Save As dialog box. The default is Excel Workbook. While browsing filenames in Excel or Windows Explorer, you may identify files that are compatible with Excel by viewing the icons next to the filenames. You may also read the extension at the end of the filename, if extensions are displayed. For example, the extension .xls indicates a spreadsheet workbook saved for use with a previous Excel version.

Can't view any filename extensions? See the Working with File Formats Quick Reference table on page 700 for the procedure to switch on their display.

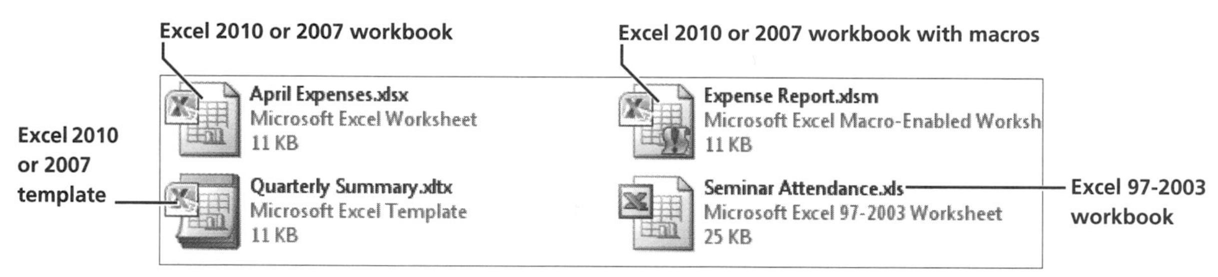

The file's icon and extension in the filename identify the file type

The following table shows the file formats that you may use to save workbooks for various Excel versions along with their file extensions.

All Excel filename extensions begin with the letters *xl* and contain additional letters that have special meanings. In Excel 2010, the third letter is *s* for spreadsheet (workbook), *t* for template, or *a for add-in. The fourth letter x indicates that the file is* without macros, and *m* indicates that it does have macros.

File Type	Excel Version	Description	File Extension
Excel Workbook	2010 or 2007	Workbooks without macros	.xlsx
Excel Macro-Enabled Workbook	2010 or 2007	Workbooks with macros	.xlsm
Excel Template	2010 or 2007	Template workbooks without macros	.xltx
Excel Macro-Enabled Template	2010 or 2007	Template workbooks with macros	.xltm
Excel 97-2003 Workbook	97–2003	Workbooks with or without macros	.xls
Excel 97-2003 Template	97–2003	Template workbooks with or without macros	.xlt
Excel Binary Workbook	97–2007	Non-XML workbooks	.xlsb
Microsoft Excel 5.0/95 Workbook	95	Early-version workbooks	.xls

Excel 2010 Open XML File Formats

As you can see from the preceding table, Excel 2010 has more file formats than most previous versions to help identify files containing macros and reduce the file size, which is beneficial when you share files. The file structure, called Open XML, is based on the Extensible Markup Language (XML) used by software developers. XML is is one standard for the exchange of structured data on the Internet.

Earlier Excel File Formats

Versions prior to Excel 2010 and 2007 use different file formats than XML. For this reason, some Excel 2010 and 2007 features are not viewable in the earlier versions. Files saved in these formats display the words *[Compatibility Mode]* in the Excel title bar as shown in the following illustration.

Schedule [Compatibility Mode] - Microsoft Excel

You have the following two options to enable users of earlier versions to open and work with your Excel 2010 file.

- **Save in a Non-XML File Format—**You may save your workbook in a file format that removes the incompatible features.
- **Use the Compatibility Pack—**Users may download and install a file converter that hides the incompatible features.

QUICK REFERENCE	WORKING WITH FILE FORMATS
Task	**Procedure**
Save a workbook in an Excel 97-2003 file format	■ Choose File→Save As →Excel 97-2003 Workbook. (Two files will now exist if you previously saved the file in Excel Workbook format.) ■ Correct any issues reported by the Compatibility Checker.
Display filename extensions	■ Open Windows Explorer. ■ Choose (Win 7/Vista) Organize→Folder and Search Options or (Win XP) Tools→Folder Options. ■ Display the View tab, and under Advanced Settings remove the checkmark next to Hide Extensions for Known File Types.
Identify the format of files	■ Choose File→Open or open Windows Explorer. ■ Navigate to the folder containing the file(s) in your file storage location. ■ Display the Files of Type list and choose All Files if working in Excel's Open dialog box. ■ Click the Views menu button on the dialog box or Explorer toolbar and choose Details. ■ Look at the icon next to the filename, read the filename extension (if displayed), and read the file type.

DEVELOP YOUR SKILLS 18.1.1

Save a Workbook for an Earlier Excel Version

In this exercise, you will save an Excel 2010 workbook in a file format compatible with an earlier version of Excel. You will view file details to identify file formats.

Save the Workbook

1. **Start** Excel and **open** the Schedule workbook from the Lesson 18 folder in your file storage location.
2. **Maximize** the window.
   This workbook contains three worksheets. Notice that the words [Compatibility Mode] *do not appear after the filename in the title bar. This workbook was saved in Excel 2010, and all its features are visible.*
3. Choose **File→Save As** .
   The Save As dialog box opens.
4. Follow these steps to save the workbook in Excel 97–2003 file format:
   Filenames in your dialog box will display extensions if the Windows Explorer option is set to do so. Filename extensions are not displayed in the illustrations of this exercise except those Excel displays. No other filenames now appear in the dialog box because you are currently filtering for only this Excel 97–2003 type. Other files do exist in the folder, but they are not in this file format.

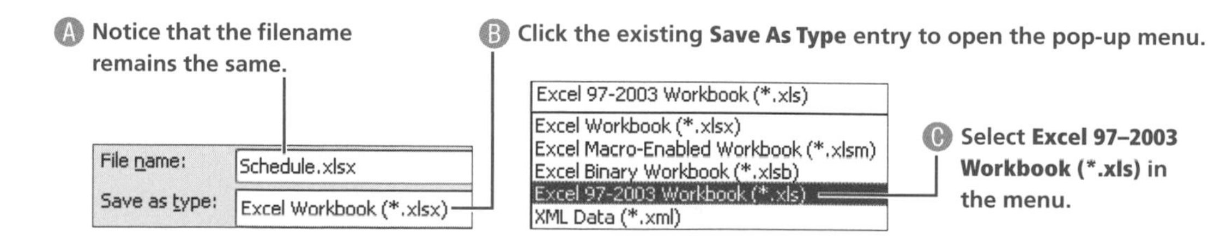

5. Click **Save**.
   No alerts appeared because Excel found no compatibility issues in this workbook. This file could be opened and edited in Excel versions 97 through 2003.

Identify the Format of Files

Next you will display the filenames in the Lesson 18 folder and review their file formats.

6. Choose **File→Open**, and navigate to the Lesson 18 folder, if not already displayed.
7. Follow these steps to display details about the files in the folder:
   Your dialog box displays more files than shown here. The dialog box may vary slightly from the illustration depending on your Windows version.

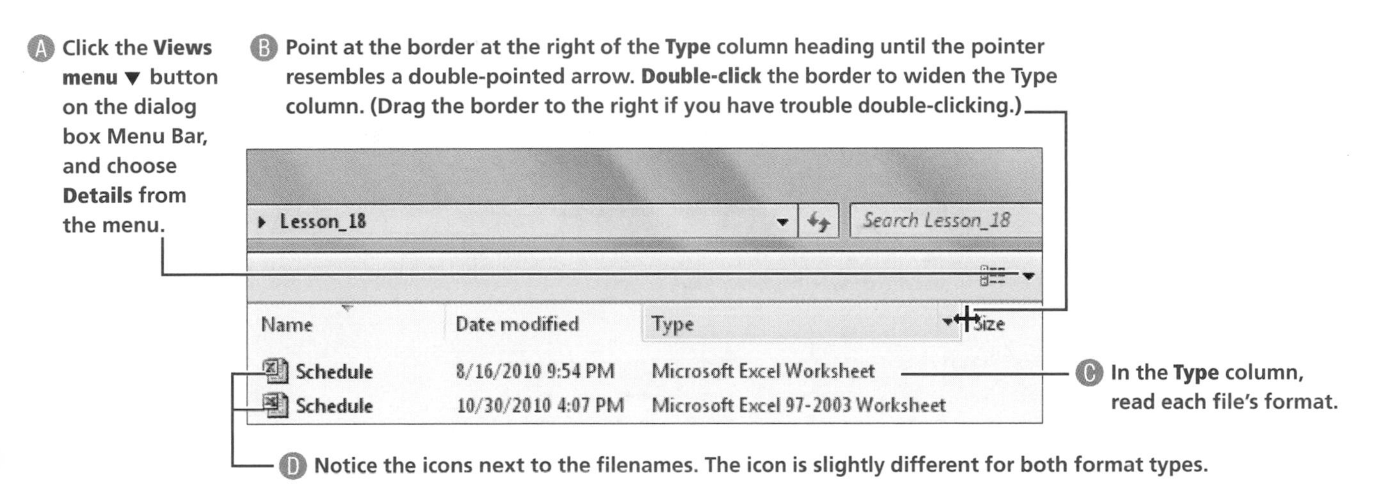

A Click the Views menu ▼ button on the dialog box Menu Bar, and choose Details from the menu.
B Point at the border at the right of the Type column heading until the pointer resembles a double-pointed arrow. Double-click the border to widen the Type column. (Drag the border to the right if you have trouble double-clicking.)
Lesson_18
Search Lesson_18
Name
Date modified
Type
Size
Schedule
8/16/2010 9:54 PM
Microsoft Excel Worksheet
Schedule
10/30/2010 4:07 PM
Microsoft Excel 97-2003 Worksheet
C In the Type column, read each file's format.
D Notice the icons next to the filenames. The icon is slightly different for both format types.

   Also, each filename displays a filename extension, such as .xlsx, if the display option is switched on in Windows.

8. Click **Cancel** to exit the Open dialog box.
9. **Close** the workbook, and leave Excel **open**.

Checking for Excel Version Compatibility

Video Lesson labyrinthelab.com/videos

Check for Issues

The Compatibility Checker scans your workbook and identifies any features that would not be included if you were to save the workbook in a non-XML (nonnative) file format. The report summarizes various incompatibilities as significant or minor, and it provides a Find button to help you locate each occurrence in the workbook. You may decide to proceed if the compatibility check reports only a minor loss of fidelity, such as table formatting. Significant issues usually must be resolved. The dialog box contains an option that, when switched on, will check for compatibility every time the workbook is saved.

The Compatibility Checker automatically scans any file that you save in a non-XML format even if you did not run the Checker before giving the Save As command.

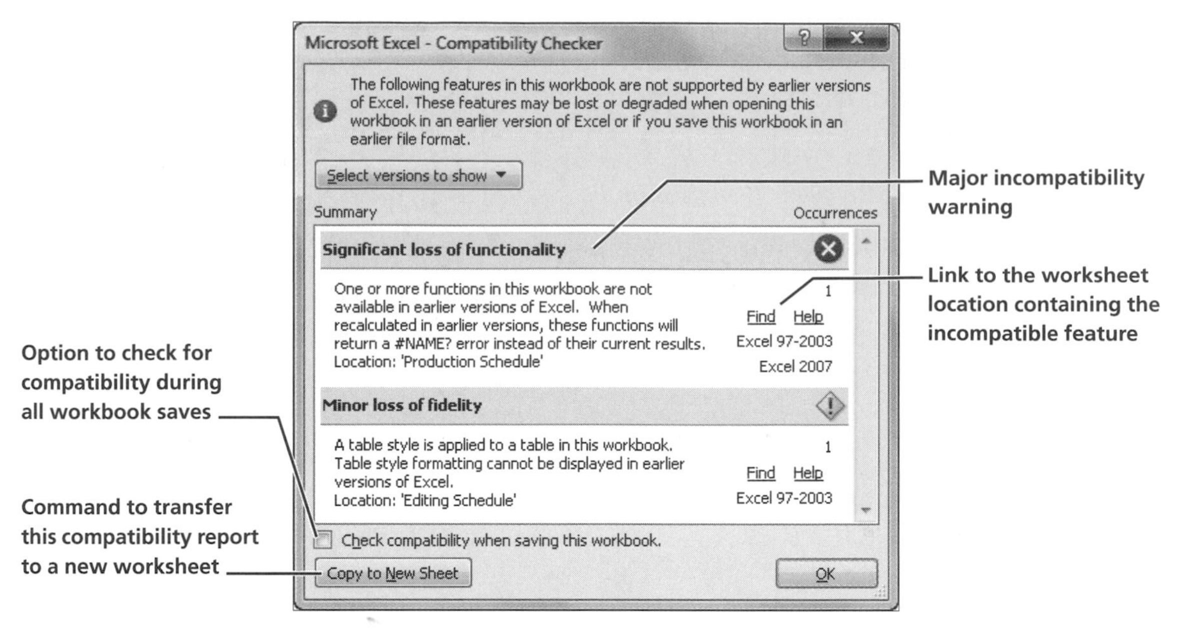

A report displayed by the Compatibility Checker before or while a file is saved

DEVELOP YOUR SKILLS 18.1.2

Check Excel Version Compatibility

In this exercise, you will run the Compatibility Checker to check for compatibility issues before attempting to save a file in the Excel 97-2003 file format.

1. **Open** the Compatibility Check workbook from the Lesson 18 folder.
   Notice that the Editing Schedule worksheet contains a table style, which is not supported in older Excel versions.

Run the Compatibility Checker

If you accidentally close the Compatibility Checker window in the following steps, just give the command again.

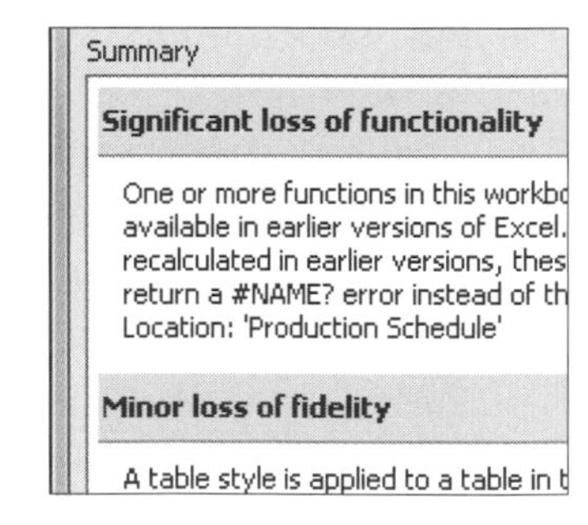

2. Choose **File→Info**. In the Info tab of Backstage view, choose **Check for Issues menu ▾**, and choose **Check Compatibility**.
   After a few moments, the Microsoft Excel – Compatibility Checker window appears with its report of two issues found in the workbook.
3. **Scroll** through the window and read both messages.
4. Click the **Help** link under Minor Loss of Fidelity.
   The Excel Help window appears so you may search for information to help resolve table compatibility issues.
5. **Close** the Help window.

6. In the Compatibility Checker window, **scroll up** and click the **Find** link under Significant Loss of Functionality.
   The pointer jumps to cell D13 on the Production Schedule worksheet. This cell contains a formula using the WORKDAY.INTL function. This function is new in Excel 2010 and is not backward compatible. You would edit the workbook to correct this significant compatibility issue before saving. However, you are not required to make any corrections in this exercise.
7. Notice that the Compatibility Checker window is closed because you used the Find link.
   You may run the Compatibility Checker again as needed, and any resolved issues will no longer display.

Use Save As

Next, you will give the Save As command with the intent to save the file for an earlier Excel version. Remember that two compatibility issues still exist in the workbook.

8. Choose **File→Save As** .
9. In the Save As dialog box, drop down the **Save As Type** list, and choose **Excel 97-2003 Workbook**.

File name:	Compatibility Check.xls
Save as type:	Excel 97-2003 Workbook (*.xls)

10. Click **Save**.
    The Compatibility Checker window appears. Excel automatically runs the checker whenever you attempt to save a workbook in a non-XML file format. Notice the buttons at the bottom of the dialog box. The Continue button would save the file with the issues unresolved. That might be appropriate for minor compatibility issues but is not the action that you want to take now.
11. Click **Copy to New Sheet**.
    The compatibility issues report, including cell locations, is transferred to a separate worksheet for documentation and printing. You could use this information to continue resolving any compatibility issues until the workbook would be ready for saving.
12. **Close** the workbook without saving again.

Using the Compatibility Pack

Video Lesson labyrinthelab.com/videos

A free compatibility download from Microsoft allows users of previous Excel 2000, XP (2002), and 2003 versions to open and work with Excel 2010 files. Users are prompted to download and install the Microsoft Office Compatibility Pack the first time they attempt to open an Excel 2010 file. Thereafter, any opened Excel 2010 files will be converted automatically. Any formatting or other features specific to Excel 2010 do not display when the file is opened in the previous version but are preserved when the file is reopened in Excel 2010. Having that capability may be worth asking other users to take the time to install the Compatibility Pack.

If asking others to install the Compatibility Pack could cause a problem—perhaps inconveniencing your best customers—you may opt to save files in the Excel 97-2003 file format as previously described in this lesson. Just remember that some Excel 2010 features may be removed permanently from those files.

Converters

A converter is a small program that allows an application program such as Excel to open files that are not in the program's native file format. For example, you may need to import data from a Word document into a worksheet. Excel features a variety of converters that are installed automatically. You also may download and install additional converters that may become available as new file formats are introduced. For example, when a new version of an application program is released, it often introduces a new native file format.

Example of Using a Converter

You send a workbook saved in an Excel 2010 file format to another user who uses Excel 2003. The other user installs the Compatibility Pack, which includes converter programs. When she opens your Excel 2010 file, it is converted to a format that is compatible with her Excel version. Any incompatible features will be hidden.

QUICK REFERENCE	CHECKING WORKBOOK COMPATIBILITY WITH EARLIER EXCEL VERSIONS
Task	**Procedure**
Check a workbook for features incompatible with earlier Excel versions	■ With the workbook open, choose File→Info. In the Info tab of Backstage view, choose Check for Issues menu ▾, and choose Check Compatibility. ■ Click the Find link in the Compatibility Checker dialog box to locate the first incompatible cell, if any issues are reported. ■ Edit the worksheet to correct a major incompatibility. ■ Run Compatibility Checker again to verify that the previous issue is no longer reported. Find and, if necessary, correct any additional major issues. Correct minor issues as necessary.
Install the Microsoft Office Compatibility Pack	■ Start Internet Explorer, navigate to the Microsoft Office 2010 Downloads web page, enter *Compatibility Pack* in the Search box, and initiate the search. ■ Follow instructions to download and install the Microsoft Office Compatibility Pack for Word, Excel, and PowerPoint 2007 file formats. This Compatibility Pack also is used for Excel 2010.

18.2 Converting Workbooks to Other File Formats

Video Lesson labyrinthelab.com/videos

At times, you may need to save worksheet data to use in a program other than Excel or upload a worksheet onto a web page. You may choose from several file formats in the Save As dialog box, such as XML Data or Web Page. This topic explains two common methods of sharing data between incompatible programs or with users who do not have the original program.

Text File Formats

Text file formats are commonly used to export data to or from another program that is incompatible with Excel. All worksheet formatting, such as fonts, colors, and graphics, is removed. Two types of text files are used most often in conjunction with Excel: comma delimited and tab delimited.

Comma Delimited

A comma delimited text file uses a comma to separate two columns of data. The following illustration shows an example of Excel data converted in a comma delimited file. When saving a workbook in this file format, you would choose CSV (Comma Delimited) from the Save As Type list. The filename extension .csv is added to the filename.

```
First,Last,Phone,City
Deion,Jenett,619-555-7823,San Diego
Jacqueline,Chan,303-555-8989,Denver
Jason,Stevens,540-555-2220,Bristol
```

Excel column data converted to the comma delimited format

Tab Delimited

A tab delimited file uses a tab character to separate two columns of data. In the following example of a tab delimited file, each small arrow represents a non-printing tab code. When saving a workbook in this file format, you would choose Text (Tab Delimited) from the Save As Type list. The filename extension .txt is added to the filename.

```
First →       Last →      Phone →         City
Deion →       Jenett →    619-555-7823 →  San Diego
Jacqueline →  Chan →      303-555-8989 →  Denver
Jason →       Stevens →   540-555-2220 →  Bristol
```

Excel column data converted to the tab delimited format

Limitations of File Formats

Some file formats will not save all information in the workbook file. For example, a tab delimited file won't save data on multiple worksheets or any cell formatting. Excel will warn you about features, formatting, or data you might lose in the new file format. When you save a workbook to a non-Excel file format, a second file is created. The original workbook file is not changed.

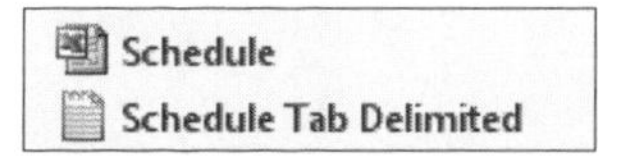

Icons and filenames for an original Excel workbook and a version saved in tab delimited format

Example of a File Format Limitation

You decide to convert a workbook to tab delimited format. Excel warns you that only the currently selected worksheet can be saved to the new file. So, you perform a save command for each worksheet in the workbook. Now each worksheet is contained in a separate file. You also notice that comments on the worksheets are not saved in the tab delimited format.

QUICK REFERENCE **CONVERTING WORKSHEET DATA TO A TEXT FORMAT**

Task	Procedure
Save workbook data in comma delimited or tab delimited format	▪ Choose File→Save As. ▪ In the Save As dialog box, choose CSV (Comma Delimited) or Text (Tab Delimited) from the Save As Type list. ▪ Enter the name in the File Name box and click Save.

DEVELOP YOUR SKILLS 18.2.1

Convert Excel Data to Text

In this exercise, you will use the Save As command to save a copy of a worksheet in a different file format. You will then use the Notepad application to view the workbook in its new file format.

Convert a Worksheet to Text

1. **Open** the original Schedule workbook that is in the Excel Workbook file format. Its icon is shown to the right. Display the **Details** view to determine the correct file in the Save As dialog box, if necessary.

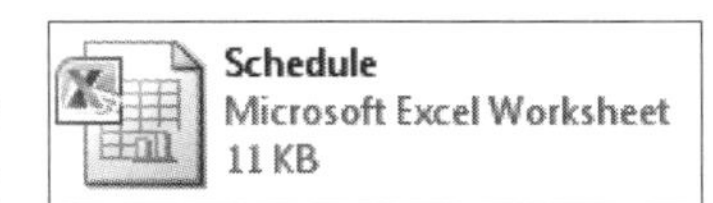
Schedule
Microsoft Excel Worksheet
11 KB

2. Display the **Editing Schedule** worksheet, if not already displayed.
3. Choose **File→Save As**.
4. Follow these steps to save the workbook in the tab delimited file format:

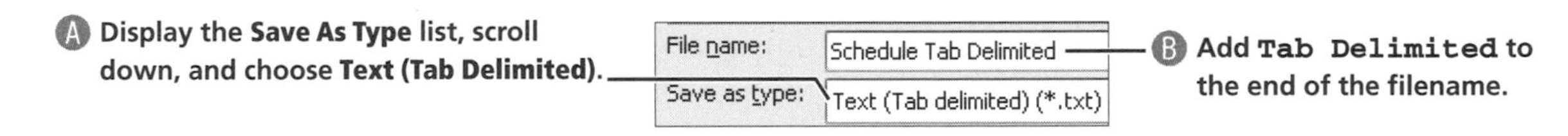
A Display the Save As Type list, scroll down, and choose Text (Tab Delimited).
File name:
Schedule Tab Delimited
Save as type:
Text (Tab delimited) (*.txt)
B Add Tab Delimited to the end of the filename.

5. Click the **Save** button and read the warning box.
Excel warns you that the selected file type cannot save a file containing multiple worksheets. It will save only the active worksheet.
6. Click **OK** to acknowledge the warning, and then review the next warning box that appears.
Excel now warns you that the tab delimited file format may not be compatible with features in your workbook file. Features other than the text in cells, such as cell formatting, will be removed in the resulting file.

7. Choose **Yes** to continue the conversion to the tab delimited format.
Excel completes the conversion. Notice that the worksheet tab has been renamed to the new filename. Although the name of the new file appears in the Excel title bar, you are not really viewing the converted file. You must open the newly converted file to see the changes.

8. Use [Ctrl]+[W] to close the workbook. Choose **not** to save when you are asked if you wish to save the workbook.

View the Converted Data

9. Choose **File→Open** and navigate to the Lesson 18 folder, if necessary.
Notice that the newly converted file is not listed. That's because Excel is displaying only workbook files. A tab delimited file is saved in text format. In the next step, you will tell Excel to display all text format files.

10. Choose **Text Files** from the Files of Type list, as shown below. Your dialog box may differ depending on your Windows version.

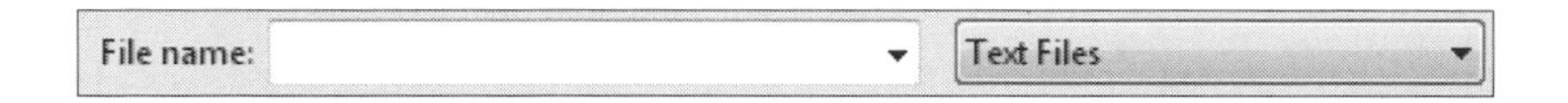

Three files with this file format display. You used the Open dialog box only to navigate to and view filenames. In the next step, you will open the file using a different program. The Notepad applet is a simple text editor that comes with Windows. It allows you to view exactly what the data in your converted file looks like.

11. Follow these steps to open the text file in Notepad:

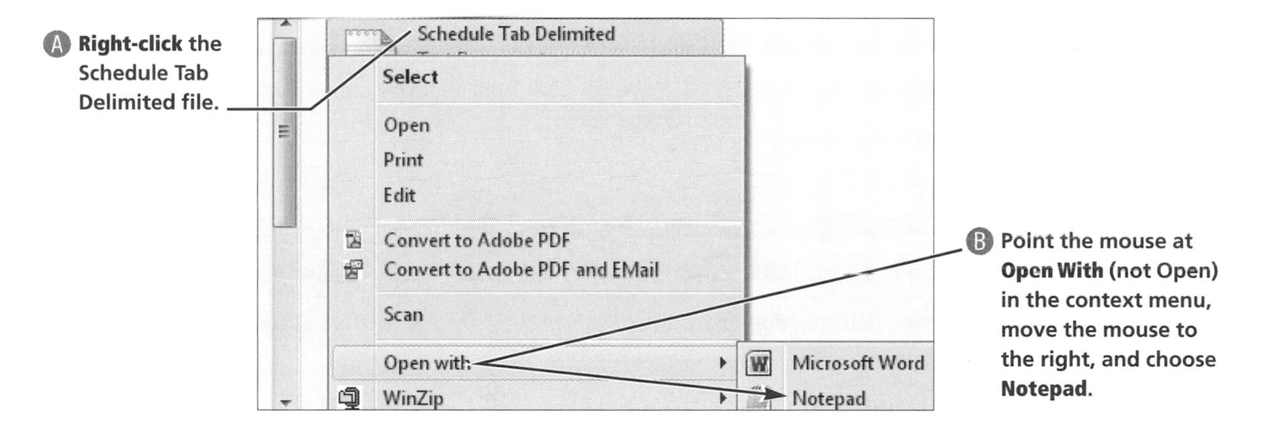

The file opens in Notepad, the Windows text editor program. Notice that the file contains only plain text separated by tabs. The original worksheet's cell formatting and the logo graphic were removed. This file format, however, may be the only means of bringing the data into certain programs that are not compatible with Excel.

12. **Close** the Notepad window. Choose **not** to save if you are asked to save changes to the file.

13. **Cancel** Excel's Open dialog box.

PDF and XPS File Formats

Video Lesson labyrinthelab.com/videos

The PDF (Portable Document Format) and XPS (XML Paper Specification) file formats may be applied to Excel workbooks and many other types of documents. These file formats allow colleagues to view and print a workbook with all formatting intact even if they don't have any Excel version, and it also prevents them from making any changes or accessing any hidden information. For example, a user who installs the free Adobe Acrobat Reader may view a PDF document. You may use either the Save As command in the File tab or the Create PDF/XPS command in the Save & Send tab of Backstage view to publish the document. You may publish a selected range, a worksheet, or the entire workbook.

Personal information from the document's properties, such as your Microsoft Office user name, are saved with the PDF or XPS document unless you choose Options and uncheck Document Properties.

QUICK REFERENCE **PUBLISHING A WORKBOOK IN PDF OR XPS FORMAT**

Task	Procedure
Publish a PDF or XPS document	■ To save part of a workbook, display the desired worksheet. Select a range, if desired. ■ Choose File→Save As, or choose File→Save & Send→Create PDF/XPS Document→Create PDF/XPS from Backstage view. ■ Enter the workbook name in the File Name box. ■ Choose PDF (or choose XPS Document) from the Save As Type list. ■ Choose an Optimize For option, and then choose other options as desired. ■ Click Save (or click Publish if you chose the Create PDF/XPS command in Backstage view).

DEVELOP YOUR SKILLS 18.2.2

Publish Excel Data as a PDF Document

In this exercise, you will convert a workbook to the PDF file format, and then you will view the file in a PDF reader program.

Before You Begin: Your computer must have a PDF reader such as Adobe Acrobat Reader installed.

1. **Open** the original Schedule workbook. Its icon is shown to the right. If necessary, change Files of Type to Excel Files to see the filename.

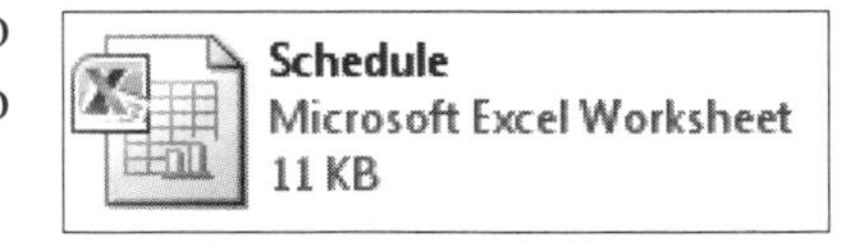

2. Choose **File→Save As**, and choose **PDF** in the Save As Type list.
   The PDF publishing options appear along the bottom of the Save As dialog box. The filename Schedule should already be entered, and the file type is PDF. Notice that the Open File After Publishing option is switched on if your computer has a PDF reader installed.

3. Click the **Options** button near the lower-left corner of the dialog box.
4. Under **Publish What** in the Options dialog box, choose **Entire Workbook**.
   Notice that you may publish a selected range, the active worksheet, the entire workbook, or a table (available when a table range is selected). The Ignore Print Areas option is used to disregard any print area set in Excel.

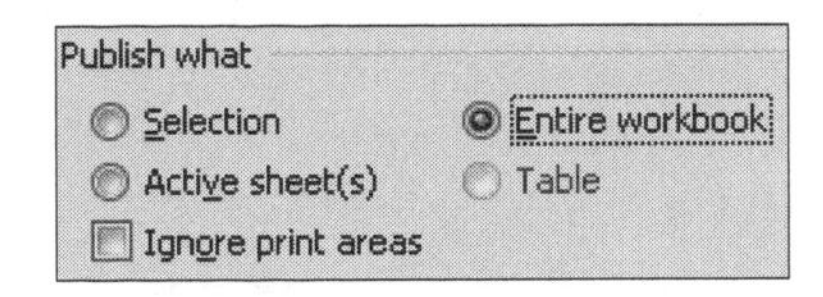

5. Click **OK**.
6. Click the **Save** button in the Save As dialog box.
   After a few moments, the published workbook displays in an Adobe Acrobat (or other PDF reader) window. This occurs because the Open File After Publishing option was switched on. Depending on the PDF reader you use, the filename Schedule.pdf usually appears in the window's title bar.
7. **Maximize** the PDF reader window.
8. Use the following tools to browse through the document (your reader window may differ from the one shown):

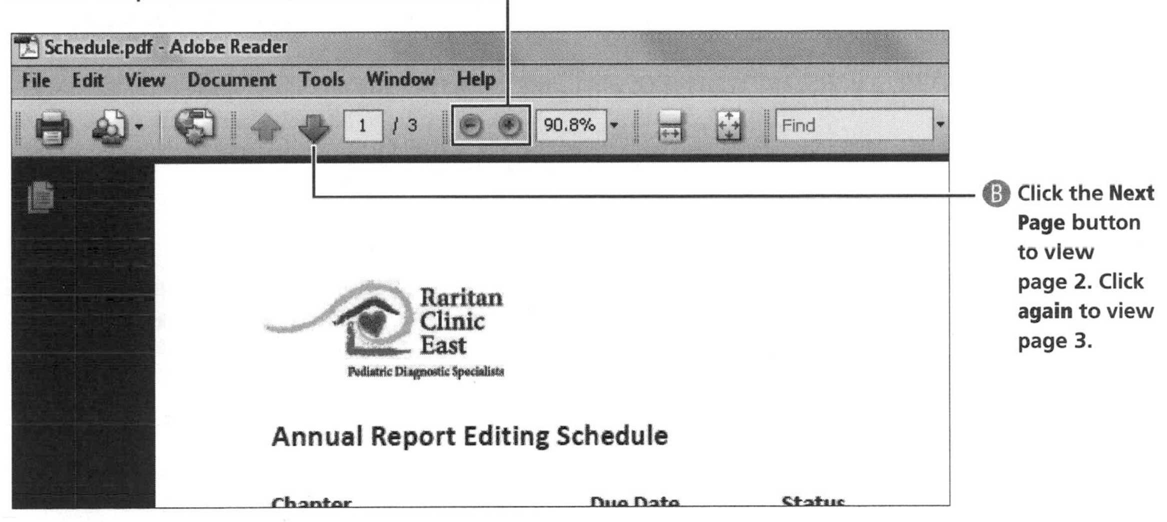

The toolbar buttons allow you to print or select and copy text and objects, but you cannot alter anything in this document.

9. **Close** the reader window.
10. **Close** the Schedule workbook, and leave Excel **open**. Choose **not** to save if you are asked to save.

18.3 Using Excel Tables with Word Mail Merge

Video Lesson labyrinthelab.com/videos

You may wish to send multiple customers a letter or an envelope containing marketing materials. Word's mail merge feature helps you prepare a standard message (called the main document) and personalize each copy with the customer's name, address, most recent order date, and other data unique to that customer. You may use a list or table from an Excel worksheet as a data source for these and other documents in Word. In this lesson, you will work with tables. A table should be set up with each field (column) containing one type of data, such as the order date. You insert various field names in the main document to personalize the message. When the mail merge is completed, data from each record (row) of the data source replace the field names, and you have a personalized document copy for each record.

For a successful mail merge, break up data into its smallest segments. For example, each of the following segments in an address list should be in a separate column: title, first name, middle initial, last name, street, city, state, and ZIP code.

QUICK REFERENCE USING EXCEL TABLES WITH WORD MAIL MERGE

Task	Procedure
Create the table and name the worksheet in Excel	■ Create the table in an Excel workbook. For best results, enter the table column headings in row 1 of the worksheet. ■ Double-click the sheet tab, type the sheet name, and tap [Enter]. ■ Save the workbook.
Start the mail merge in Word	Do one of the following: ■ Open the desired main document. ■ Start a new, blank document in Word. ■ Choose Mailings→Start Mail Merge→Start Mail Merge and choose the document type from the Ribbon.
Choose an Excel worksheet as the data source	■ Choose Mailings→Start Mail Merge→Select Recipients →Use an Existing List from the Ribbon. ■ In the Select Data Source dialog box, select the Excel file containing the table and click Open. ■ In the Select Table dialog box, choose the desired worksheet, place a checkmark in the box next to First Row of Data Contains Column Headers, and click OK.
Select records	■ Choose Mailings→Start Mail Merge→Edit Recipient List from the Ribbon. ■ Use options to sort, filter, find, and deselect records, as desired.

QUICK REFERENCE	USING EXCEL TABLES WITH WORD MAIL MERGE (continued)
Task	**Procedure**
Complete the main document	■ Type text and use Mailings→Write & Insert Fields→Insert Merge Field from the Ribbon.
Preview the merged copies	■ Choose Mailings→Preview Results→Preview Results from the Ribbon. ■ Use navigation buttons in the Preview Results group on the Ribbon to view the document for any one record.
Print or email the completed document copies	■ Choose Mailings→Finish→Finish & Merge →Print Documents (or Send E-mail Messages) from the Ribbon.

After starting the mail merge, you use commands in sequence on the Mailings Ribbon from left to right. The next command usually is dimmed until you complete the preceding step.

DEVELOP YOUR SKILLS 18.3.1

Mail Merge Excel Table Data in Word

In this exercise, you will merge a form document with employee data from an Excel table to fill in the form with each employee's name, identification number, and so on.

View the Table Data

1. **Open** the Employee List workbook from the Lesson 18 folder in your file storage location. If necessary, change Files of Type to **All Excel Files** to see the filename in the Open dialog box.
2. Display the **Orthopedics** worksheet.
   Notice that the table's column headings are in row 1 of the worksheet. This helps you work with the data more easily during the merge. Each column (field) contains a specific category of data, such as last name. Each row (record) contains the data for one employee.
3. **Close** the workbook.

Start the Merge

4. Start **Word** and **open** Seminar Form from the Lesson 18 folder.
   This is the main document that you will merge with employee data from the Excel table. You may also start with a new, blank document and enter the necessary information for the main document.

   Next you will use commands on the Mailings Ribbon. After using a Ribbon command, you will use the command to its right until you complete the merge.
5. Choose **Mailings→Start Mail Merge→Start Mail Merge** from the Ribbon.
   Notice that the formatting choices on the menu include letters, envelopes, labels, an address directory, and a normal document. You would select one of these to start the main document if one were not already created.
6. **Press** [Esc] to cancel the menu.

Connect to the Data Source

7. Choose **Mailings→Start Mail Merge→Select Recipients** →**Use Existing List** from the Ribbon.
8. In the **Select Data Source** dialog box, navigate to the Lesson 18 folder in your file storage location, choose the Employee List workbook, and click **Open**.
9. Follow these steps to select the Orthopedics worksheet:

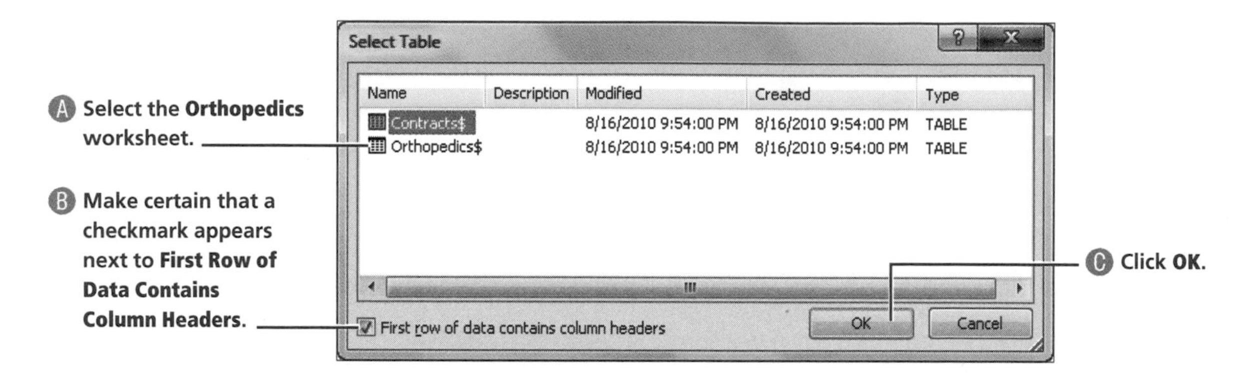

10. Choose **Mailings→Start Mail Merge→Edit Recipient List** from the Ribbon.
11. In the **Mail Merge Recipients** dialog box, click in the checkbox next to employees Gonzalez, Howard, and Lawrence to deselect the department's physicians and department chief.

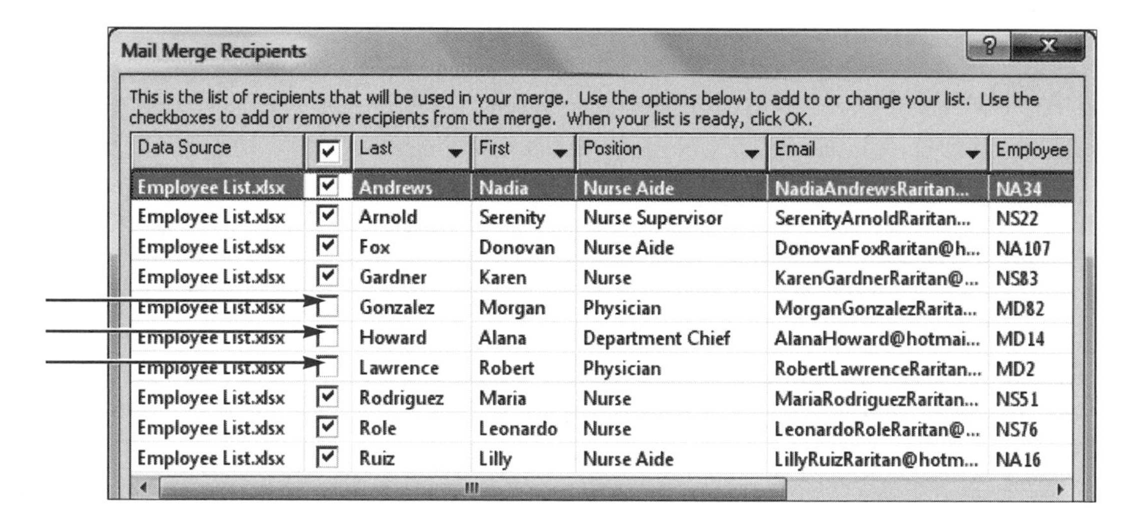

Notice the commands to sort, filter, and find records in the lower half of the dialog box. You may also perform these tasks by clicking the triangle next to a column heading, which displays a menu. You may edit the worksheet and refresh the list from within this dialog box.

12. Click **OK** in the Mail Merge Recipients dialog box.

Insert Merge Fields

You will insert field names in the form. Word will substitute one employee's data in those locations on each copy of the form.

13. **Click** in the blank to the right of Employee Name in the form.

14. Choose **Mailings→Write & Insert Fields→Insert Merge Field** menu ▾→**First** from the Ribbon, and then **tap** Spacebar.
15. Choose **Mailings→Write & Insert Fields→Insert Merge Field** menu ▾→**Last** from the Ribbon.
16. Use the preceding step to add the **Employee ID** and **Position** fields as shown in the following illustration.

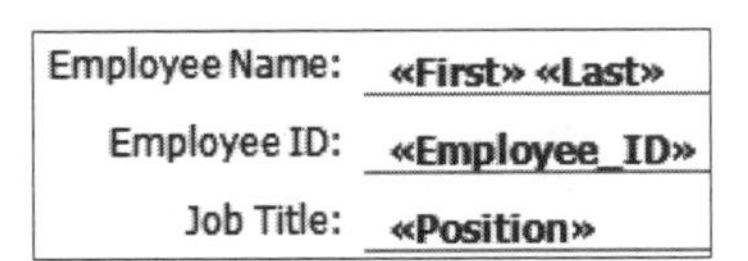

You may insert field names within a paragraph or in a mailing address to create a business letter, envelope, or labels. You type punctuation and spaces between words as necessary.

17. **Click** in the blank to the right of Dept. Head and type **Alana Howard, MD**.

Dept. Head: Alana Howard, MD

You typed directly in the form because all employees have the same department head. All text typed in the main document appears in every individualized copy.

18. **Click** in the blank to the right of Department and type **Orthopedics**.
19. Choose **Mailings→Write & Insert Fields→Highlight Merge Fields** from the Ribbon.
The field names are identified with a gray background to show you the location of inserted fields in the entire document.
20. Choose **Mailings→Write & Insert Fields→Highlight Merge Fields** from the Ribbon again to toggle off the highlighting.
If displayed, the highlighting would appear in printed copies, which is not desirable.

Preview the Form Copies

21. Choose **Mailings→Preview Results→Preview Results** from the Ribbon.
The view switches to the form for the first employee in the table. (If the tenth record displays, click the First Record button in the Preview Results group on the Ribbon.)
22. Choose **Mailings→Preview Results→Next Record** in the Ribbon. Click the button again to view the next few records.
Records 5–7 for Gonzalez, Howard, and Lawrence do not display because you unchecked them in step 11 of this exercise.

Print a Copy

23. Choose **Mailings→Finish→Finish and Merge** →**Print Documents** from the Ribbon.
24. In the Merge to Printer dialog box, choose **Current Record** and click **OK**.
25. Click **OK** in the Print dialog box to print one copy of the form.
26. Retrieve the printout from the printer.
27. **Save** the changes, and exit **Word**.

18.4 Sharing Excel Data with Access

Video Lesson labyrinthelab.com/videos

Access, a software application in Microsoft Office, stores data in tables that look similar to Excel worksheets. While you usually may format data and create calculations more easily in Excel, the database capabilities of Access allow you to filter large amounts of data using queries and to combine data from multiple sources to create various reports. When you import an Excel worksheet into a new Access table, you have the option to link the data. Then, any updates made to the original worksheet data in Excel are shown when you reopen the database and the related Access table. Without linking, the data is not updated in Access. Linked data cannot be edited in Access.

If the original linked Excel workbook is moved or deleted, its link is broken and the data is not available in Access. The Linked Table Manager command in Access allows you to give the new location if the file was moved. Make frequent backups of linked workbooks in case a file is deleted inadvertently.

QUICK REFERENCE — IMPORTING EXCEL DATA INTO ACCESS

Task	Procedure
Import worksheet data as a new Access table or into an existing table	■ Open the Access database. ■ Choose External Data→Import→Excel from the Ribbon. ■ In the Get External Data – Excel Spreadsheet dialog box, click Browse and choose the desired workbook. ■ Choose an import option and click OK. ■ In the Import Spreadsheet Wizard dialog box, place a checkmark in the box next to First Row Contains Column Headings. ■ Continue choosing options and clicking Next in the wizard. ■ Enter the name for the new or existing Access table and click Finish. ■ Respond to any message box that appears. ■ Display All Tables in the Navigation Pane, and double-click the table to open it.

DEVELOP YOUR SKILLS 18.4.1

Import Worksheet Data into Access

In this exercise, you will import employee data from an Excel worksheet as a new table in the database. Then you will import the same worksheet but set a link to observe the difference.

1. Start **Access**.
   The New tab of Backstage view, where you may start a new database, appears. You wish to open an existing database.
2. Click **Open** on the File tab, navigate to the Lesson 18 folder, and **open** the Raritan Employees database.
3. If a security warning appears above the database, click **Enable Content**.
   The title bar displays the name of the database and (Access 2007) to indicate the version in which it originally was created. The design of this database is not yet complete. The Navigation Pane on the left contains the names of various tables, queries, forms, and reports that make up the database.

Import a Worksheet as a New Table

4. Choose **External Data→Import & Link→Excel** from the Ribbon.
5. In the Get External Data – Excel Spreadsheet dialog box, click **Browse** and choose the **Nurse Aides** workbook from the Lesson 18 folder.
   Read the three options for importing worksheet data in the dialog box.
6. Make certain that the **Import the Source Data into a New Table in the Current Database** option is selected, and then click **OK**.
   The Import Spreadsheet Wizard dialog box appears and displays a preview of the Nurse Aides worksheet. (If the workbook contained multiple worksheets, you would be prompted to select one.) Notice that the column headings display as the first data row as shown to the right. They should be above row 1, and you will correct this in the next step.

1	Nurse Aide ID	Last Name	First Name
2	NA1	Hardy	Brenda B.

7. Place a checkmark in the box next to **First Row Contains Column Headings**.
   The column headings display above the first row of data. Remember to choose this option, or the worksheet data will not import correctly.
8. Click **Next** and review the options.
   The wizard displays options to format the worksheet columns as fields in the database. You will not change any options.
9. Click **Next**, review the options, and click **Next** again.
10. In the **Import to Table** box, change the existing name to **`Employees`**.
    You are naming the new Access table. You need not use the worksheet name.
11. Click **Finish**, and click **Close** in the next window. (Do not select the Save Import Steps option.)
    The new Employees table name displays under the Tables group in the Navigation Pane on the left.

Tables
Employees
General Employees

12. **Double-click** Employees to open the table.
    Notice that Access added ID as the first field in the table and automatically numbered the records. Depending on the database design, you may want to delete this field in the Import Spreadsheet Wizard dialog box while importing the data.

Import as a Linked Worksheet

Now you will import the same data by linking to the original worksheet to observe the difference.

13. Choose **External Data→Import→Excel** from the Ribbon.
14. In the Get External Data – Excel Spreadsheet dialog box, click **Browse** and choose the **Nurse Aides** workbook.
15. Choose **Link to the Data Source by Creating a Linked Table** and click **OK**.
16. Place a checkmark in the box next to **First Row Contains Column Headings**.
17. Click **Next**.
    This time no field options appear because you are linking to the worksheet.

Conflicting changes between users

Ask me which changes win

The changes being saved win

18. Leave the Linked Table Name as **Nurse Aides**, and then click **Finish**. Click **OK** when alerted that the link has been completed.
    Notice that the icon next to All Staff in the Navigation Pane indicates a linked Excel worksheet.
19. **Double-click** Nurse Aides in the Navigation Pane to open the table.
20. **Click** in any cell and try to type a different entry.
    You cannot edit the data from within Access. You may only edit the original worksheet in Excel.
21. **Exit** Access. Click **Yes** if prompted to save the table design.

18.5 Inserting Excel Charts in PowerPoint

Video Lesson labyrinthelab.com/videos

Using the Paste command is usually the best method for inserting an existing Excel chart in PowerPoint. If no chart yet exists, you may create one entirely in PowerPoint using the same commands and options as in Excel, as long as Excel is installed on the same computer.

PivotCharts are converted to normal charts when pasted in a presentation. You may adjust formatting but cannot adjust fields and calculations.

Linking Compared to Embedding

You may choose to paste a chart by converting the chart to a picture, embedding, or linking. The embedding and linking options are more useful because you can edit the chart data. Embedding places a standalone copy of the chart in the destination document. Sharing the PowerPoint presentation is simplified because the original workbook need not be distributed with the presentation. Any changes to the workbook, however, are not updated in the document holding the embedded copy. Linking a chart means that if the worksheet data is updated and saved, the chart automatically updates in the PowerPoint presentation. When you choose to paste, the embedding and linking options also allow you convert the chart to the theme of the destination document or retain the original colors and fonts.

Embedding a chart in another document gives users access to the entire workbook upon which the chart is based. If that is not desirable, you should copy a worksheet and its chart to a separate workbook.

The Paste menu with options to embed, link, or convert the chart to a picture

Take care not to delete the original linked worksheet data or the workbook file because the link would be broken. Distributing the presentation via email would also break the link to the original workbook storage location.

QUICK REFERENCE	LINKING AND EMBEDDING EXCEL CHARTS IN A POWERPOINT SLIDE
Task	**Procedure**
Link or embed an Excel chart on a slide	■ Create and save the worksheet and chart in Excel. ■ Right-click in a blank area of the chart and choose Copy from the context menu. ■ Close the workbook. ■ Open the desired presentation in PowerPoint and create a slide using a layout containing a content placeholder. ■ Right-click the content placeholder and choose the desired option under Paste from the context menu.
Update a linked chart in PowerPoint	■ Right-click on the chart and choose Edit Data from the context menu. ■ Edit the worksheet upon which the chart is based. ■ Close the workbook and choose to save when asked if you want to save.
Edit an embedded chart on a slide	■ Right-click on the chart and choose Edit Data from the context menu. ■ In the displayed Excel worksheet, edit the desired data. ■ Close the workbook; you are not asked to save it.

DEVELOP YOUR SKILLS 18.5.1

Link a Chart in PowerPoint

In this exercise, you will copy a chart from an Excel workbook and paste the chart onto a PowerPoint slide. Then you will change a value on the linked worksheet from within PowerPoint to update the chart.

1. **Open** the AR Project Expenses workbook.
2. **Right-click** in a blank area of the chart and choose **Copy** from the context menu.

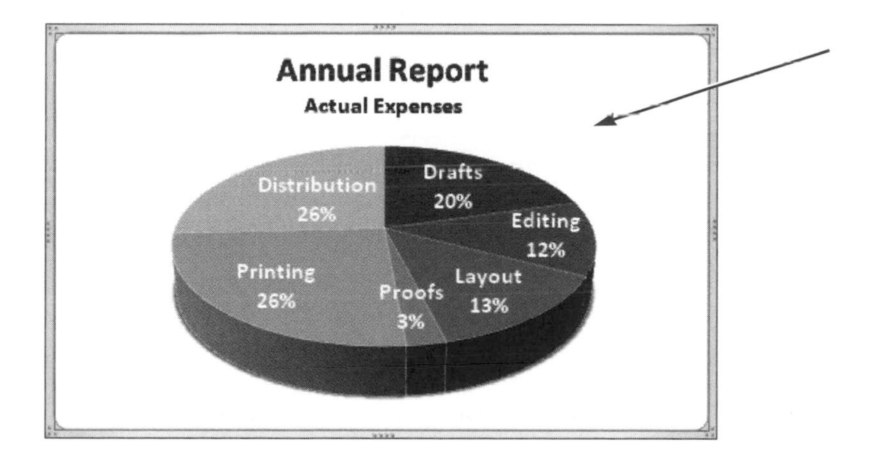

3. Leave the workbook **open**.
   The chart is copied to the Clipboard.
4. Start **PowerPoint** and open the Project Budget presentation from the Lesson 18 folder.
5. Select **slide 2 in** the Slides tab at the left of the window.
   This slide has the Title and Content layout.

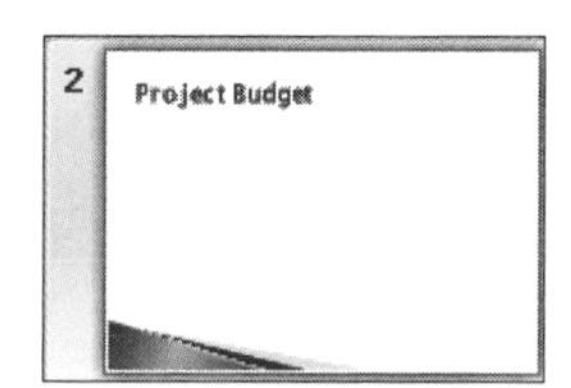

6. Follow these steps to paste the chart on slide 2:

Ⓐ In the Slide Pane, **right-click** in a blank area within the content placeholder to display the context menu.

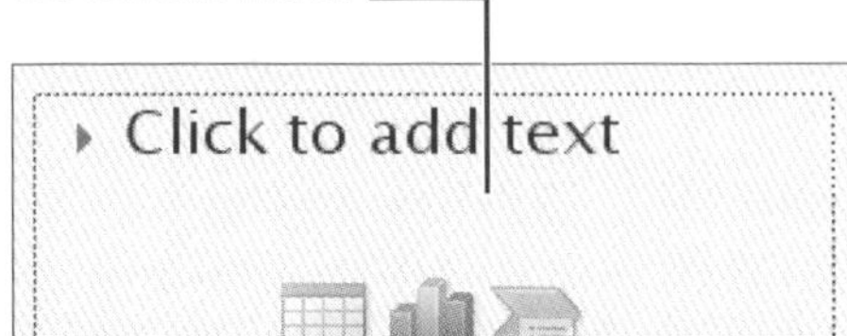

Ⓑ In the context menu, point to each button under Paste Options to read its ScreenTip. Choose **Use Destination Theme & Link Data.**

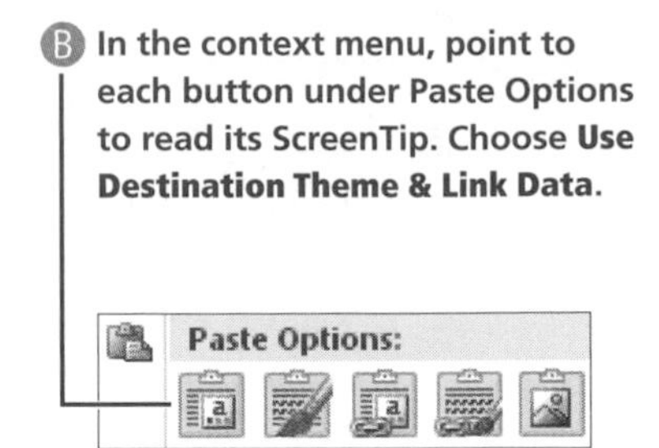

Because you selected the placeholder prior to pasting, the chart fills the placeholder and you need not resize or center the chart on the slide. The chart's colors change to match the theme of the presentation.

7. **Close** Excel and leave PowerPoint **open**.

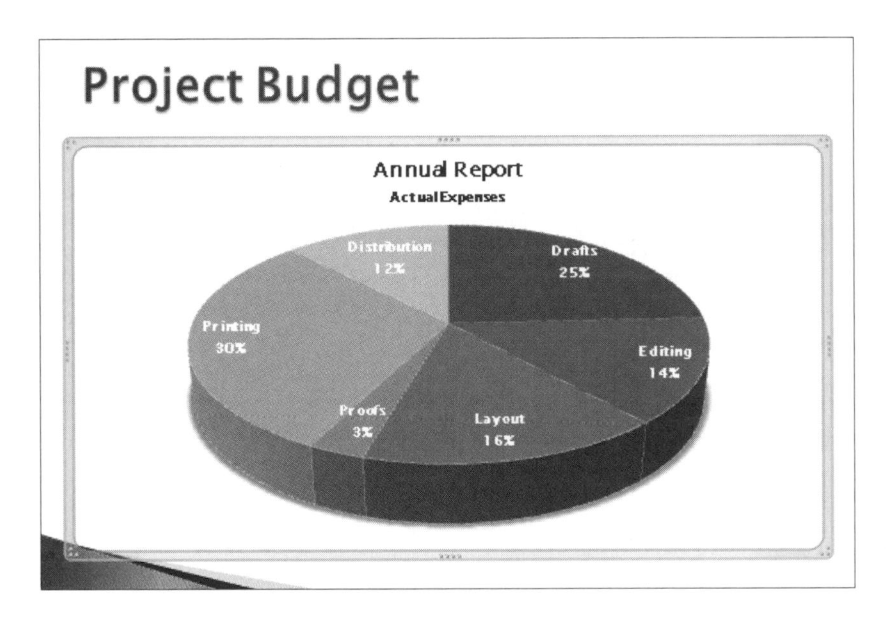

Update the Linked Chart

Next you will change a worksheet value and the chart from within PowerPoint.

8. **Right-click** anywhere on the chart and choose **Edit Data** from the context menu.
   Excel opens and displays the original worksheet.
9. In **cell D14**, notice that Distribution is 12 percent of the total expenses. Scroll to the **right**, if necessary, to see that 12 percent is also shown in the Distribution pie slice.
10. Change **cell C14** to **1000**.
    The percentage changes to 26 percent.
11. **Close** the workbook and choose to **save** when asked if you want to save.
    Saving the changes will update the linked chart in PowerPoint. Notice that Distribution is now 26 percent in the PowerPoint chart.
12. **Close** PowerPoint and choose to **save** when asked if you want to save.

18.6 Importing External Data

Video Lesson labyrinthelab.com/videos

You can bring data from other application programs into Excel. This is called *importing*. For example, if a coworker types some information in Word, you may import this data directly into an Excel worksheet. Excel can import a variety of data into your workbooks. You may import data from as many sources as needed to complete a document. Converters are installed in Excel to import data from many popular applications.

If Excel can't import a specific type of data, check in the source application to see if you can save the data in another file format that is compatible with Excel. Some loss of formatting may occur.

The three methods that you may use to import data into an Excel worksheet are the following:

- **Copy and Paste—**You may use standard copy and paste commands to bring text, images, and charts into a worksheet.
- **Drag and Drop—**You may select data in another application program, use the mouse to drag the selection into an Excel worksheet, and release the mouse button.
- **Import a File—**The Get External Data command on the Data ribbon is used to import an entire text file, Access table, web page table, or data from other sources such as a network server.

Using Copy and Paste

You may copy and paste data between another application and an Excel workbook. For example, you may copy and paste a table or text from a Word document into an Excel worksheet. You simply select the data in the other document window, cut or copy the selection, and paste it into the desired cell in the Excel window. You may also use the Paste Special command to paste data, such as images, into Excel in a specific format.

Importing Data with Drag and Drop

You may drag and drop data between another application window and an Excel workbook. For example, you may drag and drop a table or text from a Word document into an Excel worksheet. You select the data to be imported and then drag and drop it onto the desired worksheet. When you use this technique, the data is cut from the source file. However, if you then close the source file without saving, the original data will be retained.

QUICK REFERENCE	IMPORTING DATA BETWEEN DOCUMENTS
Task	**Procedure**
Import text data with Copy and Paste	■ Open the application window. ■ Select the text in the source document and choose Home→Clipboard→Copy (or use [Ctrl]+[C]). ■ Select the desired cell of the worksheet and choose Home→Clipboard→Paste (or use [Ctrl]+[V]). ■ Format the pasted text as desired.
Import text data with Drag and Drop	■ Display the Excel worksheet window and an application window containing the text data side by side. ■ Drag to select the text data in the other program. Point to the selection, drag toward the Excel window, point to a cell in the worksheet, and release the mouse button.

DEVELOP YOUR SKILLS 18.6.1

Import Data between Documents

In this exercise, you will insert a logo at the top of a worksheet and then use the Copy and Paste commands to add the logo to other worksheets. You will drag and drop text from a Word document into the workbook. Finally, you will copy a table and text from Word and paste it in the workbook.

Insert and Duplicate the Logo

1. **Open** the AR Production Schedule workbook and **maximize** the window.
2. Select **cell A1** on the Editing Schedule worksheet, if not already selected, and then choose **Insert→Illustrations→Picture** from the Ribbon.
3. Navigate to the Lesson 18 folder in your file storage location, if not already displayed. *Excel displays only one picture file in the Insert Picture dialog box. Notice that Files of Type near the bottom of the dialog box is set to All Pictures.*
4. **Double-click** Raritan Clinic Logo to insert the image in **cell A1**.
5. With the image still selected, choose **Format→Size→Shape Height,** type **.64**, and **tap** [Enter].

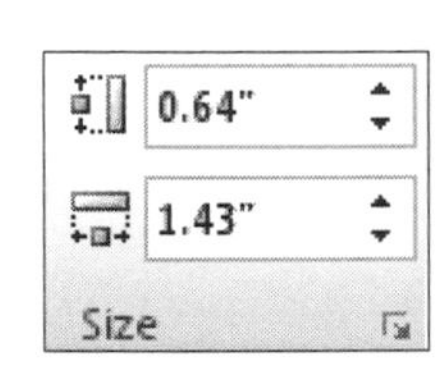

6. **Right-click** the image and choose **Copy** from the context menu.
7. Display the **Layout Schedule** worksheet.
8. **Right-click** cell A1 and choose **Paste** from the context menu. *The Clipboard retains the most recently copied or cut items. Thus, you can paste the logo multiple times after you give the Copy command.*
9. Display the **Production Schedule** worksheet and paste the logo into **cell A1**.

Drag and Drop Text

Another staff member used Word to compose her status list. You will use drag and drop to copy a heading from her Word document into Excel.

10. Display the **Layout Schedule** worksheet.
11. Start **Word** and **open** the AR Layout Schedule document.
12. **Right-click** in a blank area of the Windows taskbar at the bottom of the screen and choose **Show Windows Side by Side** (or **Tile Windows Vertically,** depending on your Windows version) from the context menu.
    The Excel and Word windows display side by side. This will make it easy for you to drag and drop from one window to the other. If any other window also displays, minimize it and repeat the Show Windows Side by Side (or Tile Windows Vertically) command.
13. Click the **AR Layout Schedule** button in the Windows taskbar to activate the Word document.
14. Follow these steps to drag and drop text into the worksheet:

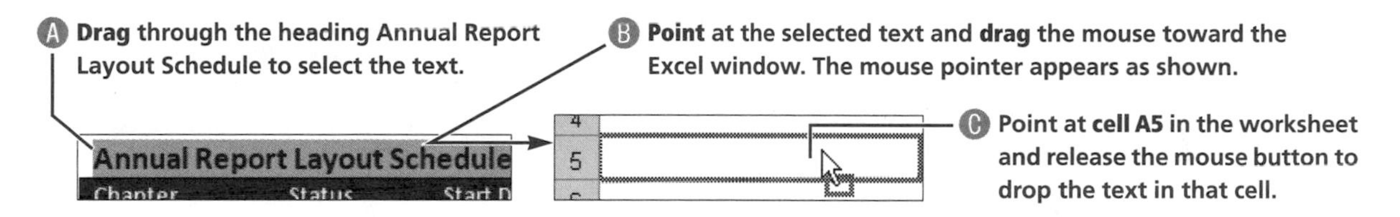

A Drag through the heading Annual Report Layout Schedule to select the text.
B Point at the selected text and drag the mouse toward the Excel window. The mouse pointer appears as shown.
C Point at cell A5 in the worksheet and release the mouse button to drop the text in that cell.
Annual Report Layout Schedule
5

    Notice that the heading text disappeared from the Word document. A drag and drop cuts the selection from the source document. Leave the Word document open.

15. In the Excel window, **click** the first navigation button on the workbook tabs toolbar at the lower left of the window to display and select the Editing Schedule tab, as shown to the right.
16. Use the **Format Painter** on the Ribbon to copy the formatting from **cell A5** in the Editing Schedule worksheet to **cell A5** that you just added in the Layout Schedule worksheet.

Copy and Paste a Word Table and Text

Now you will transfer the remainder of the Word document. You could use drag and drop, but you may find copying and pasting to be easier for a longer selection.

17. **Maximize** the Word window.
18. Follow these steps to copy the Word table and legend text:

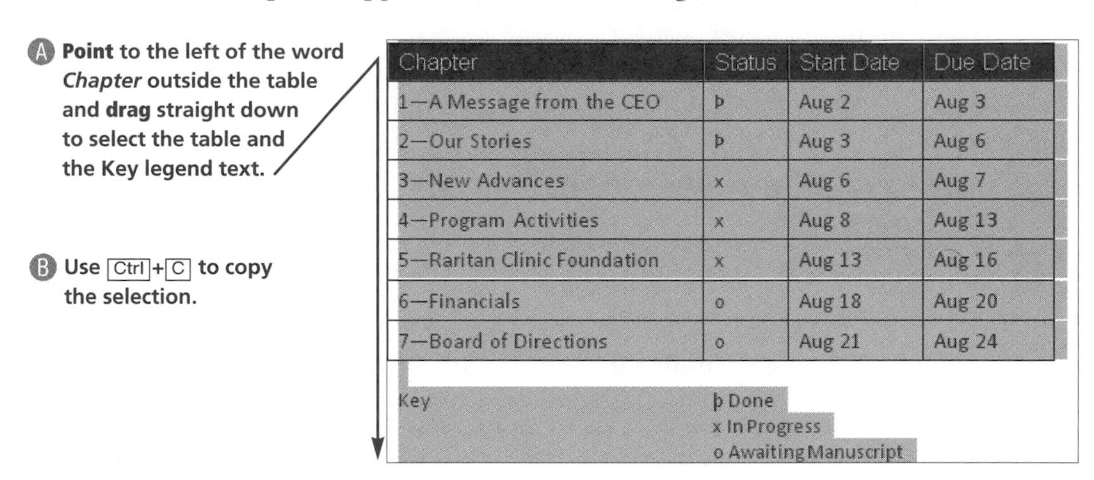

A Point to the left of the word Chapter outside the table and drag straight down to select the table and the Key legend text.
B Use Ctrl+C to copy the selection.

Chapter	Status	Start Date	Due Date
1—A Message from the CEO	þ	Aug 2	Aug 3
2—Our Stories	þ	Aug 3	Aug 6
3—New Advances	x	Aug 6	Aug 7
4—Program Activities	x	Aug 8	Aug 13
5—Raritan Clinic Foundation	x	Aug 13	Aug 16
6—Financials	o	Aug 18	Aug 20
7—Board of Directions	o	Aug 21	Aug 24

Key þ Done
x In Progress
o Awaiting Manuscript

19. Switch to the **Excel** window in the Windows taskbar.
20. **Maximize** the Excel window.
21. Select **cell A7** in the Layout Schedule worksheet, and then use Ctrl+V to paste.
Thanks to Excel's Word converter, the formatting carried over into the Excel worksheet. The table cells from Word display in separate cells of the worksheet. The tab codes in the Key legend text caused that text to be placed into two columns. Notice that Excel reformatted the dates in Custom format, such as 2-Aug.
22. Format the **range A7 through D18** in Calibri font and a font size of 11.
You may format imported text just like any other text in the worksheet.
23. **Deselect** the range.
24. Widen **column A** to display all the text in the **range A8:A14**, if necessary.
25. **Right-align** the Start Date and Due Date labels over their numbers.
Your worksheet should look similar to the illustration at right.

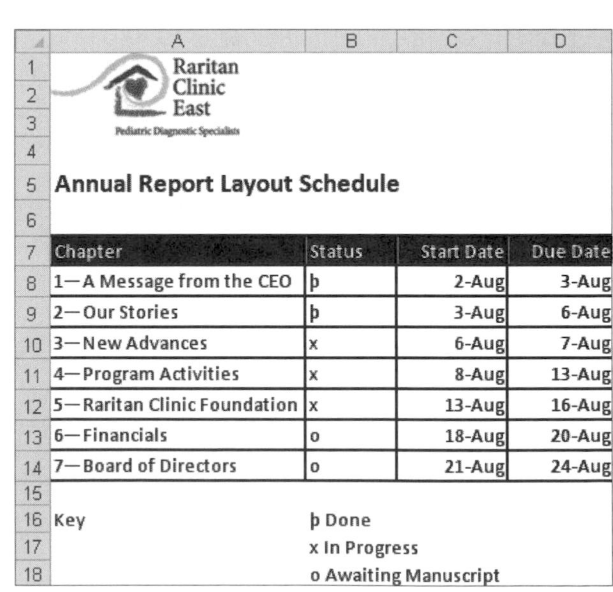

Raritan Clinic East
Pediatric Diagnostic Specialists

	A	B	C	D
1				
2				
3				
4				
5	Annual Report Layout Schedule			
6				
7	Chapter	Status	Start Date	Due Date
8	1—A Message from the CEO	þ	2-Aug	3-Aug
9	2—Our Stories	þ	3-Aug	6-Aug
10	3—New Advances	x	6-Aug	7-Aug
11	4—Program Activities	x	8-Aug	13-Aug
12	5—Raritan Clinic Foundation	x	13-Aug	16-Aug
13	6—Financials	o	18-Aug	20-Aug
14	7—Board of Directors	o	21-Aug	24-Aug
15				
16	Key	þ Done		
17		x In Progress		
18		o Awaiting Manuscript		

26. **Close** Word and choose **not** to save when asked if you want to save.
This prevents the loss of the text that you dragged and dropped. If you were to reopen this document, all of the content would reappear.
27. **Save** the changes in Excel, and leave the workbook **open**.

Importing a Text File

Video Lesson labyrinthelab.com/videos

The From Text command imports an entire text file into an Excel worksheet as data. The source file format may be either tab delimited (.txt) or comma delimited (.csv). When another program is not compatible with Excel, you may need to save its data as text in one of those two formats. When you import a text file, Excel examines the file to determine whether the formatting in the file will help lay out the data neatly into rows and columns. For example, if the text file is comma delimited, Excel will place each data item following a comma in a separate column. The From Text command can also help you deal with certain formatting problems that you may encounter with tab delimited or comma delimited text files.

QUICK REFERENCE	IMPORTING A TEXT FILE INTO EXCEL
Task	**Procedure**
Import a tab delimited or comma delimited text file into an Excel worksheet	■ Display the worksheet in which you wish to import the text file data. ■ Choose Data→Get External Data→From Text from the Ribbon. ■ Navigate to the folder containing the text data file, select the file, and click Import. ■ Follow the instructions in the Text Import Wizard, and then click Finish. ■ In the Import Data dialog box, choose the cell where you wish to begin the data import (or choose New Worksheet). ■ Click Properties and change any desired options to refresh or format data.

DEVELOP YOUR SKILLS 18.6.2

Import Data from a Text File

In this exercise, you will import a tab delimited text file into a worksheet.

Before You Begin: You must have completed Develop Your Skills 18.2.1 to create the Schedule Tab Delimited file, and the AR Production Schedule workbook should be open. If you reopened the file and a Data Connections Have Been Disabled warning appears, click the Enable Content button.

Import a Text File

1. Display the **Editing Schedule** worksheet of the AR Production Schedule workbook.
2. If a warning appears above the worksheet (or in a dialog box), read the warning and click **Enable Content** (or **OK**) to confirm that you trust the website source.
3. Choose **Data→Get External Data→From Text** from the Ribbon.
4. Navigate to the Lesson 18 folder, if necessary.
   Notice that Files of Type is set to Text Files near the bottom of the dialog box. The Schedule Tab Delimited filename is displayed, but not the Word file that you used previously because its file format is Word Document (.docx).
5. Select the Schedule Tab Delimited text file and click **Import**.
   The Text Import Wizard dialog box appears. This wizard will guide you through the steps of importing the text file data. In the upper half of the dialog box, notice that Delimited is selected. The wizard always analyzes text files to determine whether they are a specific type of file that can aid the import process.

6. In the preview of the text file in the lower portion of the dialog box, scroll until **row 7** is visible.
   You want to leave out the blank rows and headings in rows 1 through 6, so you will start the import process with row 7.

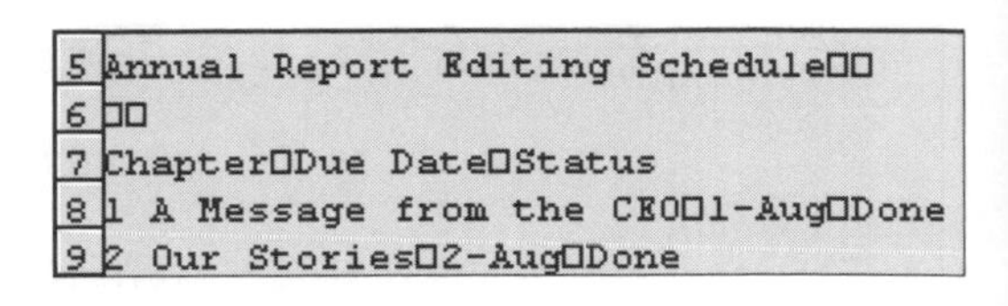

7. In the **Start Import at Row** box, enter **7** as shown to the right.

8. Click the **Next** button.
   Step 2 of the wizard displays the next set of options. Since the file to be imported is recognized as tab delimited, Tab has already been chosen for you under Delimiters.
9. Scroll in the **Data Preview** section to see that text displays correctly in columns.
   The text converter places the text following a tab code into the next column.
10. Click **Next** to continue with step 3 of the wizard.
    This step lets you select one or more columns and change their format to text or adjust the date format. You may even exclude selected columns from being imported.
11. Read the description of **General** format in the upper-right area of the dialog box.
    The three columns are formatted in General format. You need not make any changes to the options.
12. Click **Finish** to display the Import Data dialog box.
    The wizard asks you where you want to put the data. You can specify the top-left cell of the range to receive the data.

Specify the Location for the Imported Text

13. Select **cell A7** in the Editing Schedule worksheet, and click **OK**.
    The text data appear on the worksheet. Notice that the dates are converted to day/month format.

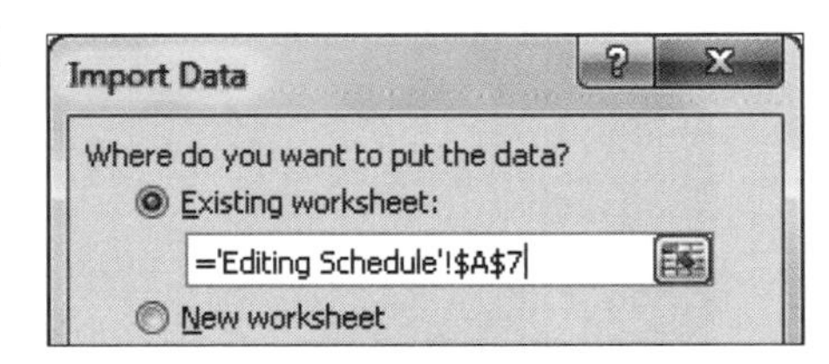

Format the Text

14. Select the **range A7:C7** and add bold and a bottom border.
    Your worksheet should look similar to the following illustration.

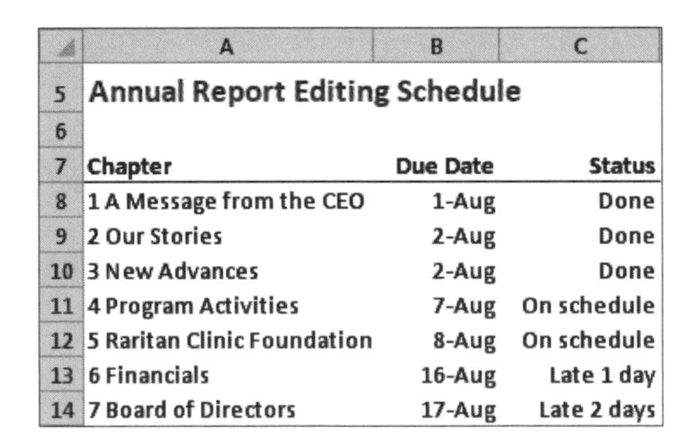

	A	B	C
5	Annual Report Editing Schedule		
6			
7	Chapter	Due Date	Status
8	1 A Message from the CEO	1-Aug	Done
9	2 Our Stories	2-Aug	Done
10	3 New Advances	2-Aug	Done
11	4 Program Activities	7-Aug	On schedule
12	5 Raritan Clinic Foundation	8-Aug	On schedule
13	6 Financials	16-Aug	Late 1 day
14	7 Board of Directors	17-Aug	Late 2 days

15. Add any other formatting that you think will make the text easier to read.
16. **Save** the changes, and leave the workbook **open**.

Converting Text to Columns

Video Lesson labyrinthelab.com/videos

The Text to Columns command allows you to split cell entries on a worksheet into multiple columns. For example, cells containing a full employee name may be split into two columns for first name and last name. Cells containing the city and state may be split into two columns. The Convert Text to Columns wizard operates in a similar way to the Text Import Wizard you use to import a text file. You may split text by specifying a delimiter, such as a comma (,) or a space. You also may specify a column width. In the following illustration to the left, column A contains the chapter number and chapter name separated by a space. In the illustration below and to the right, the text has been split into columns A and B.

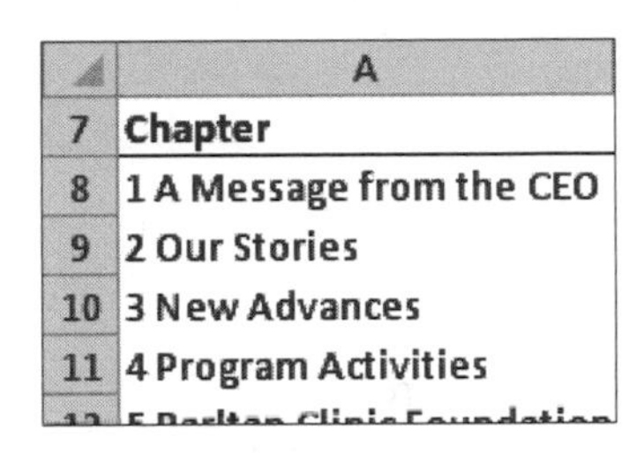

Text in a single column...

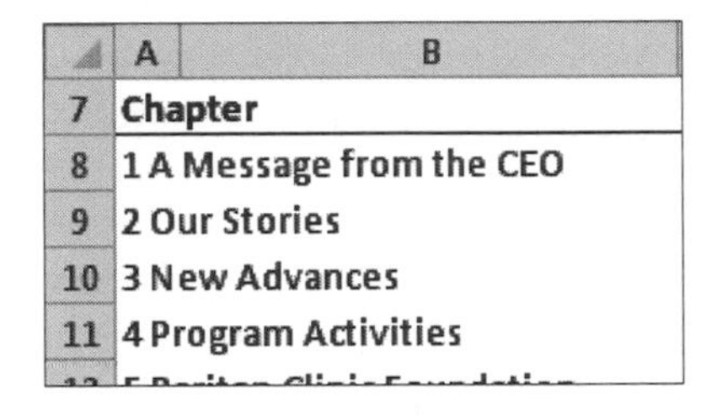

...may be split into multiple columns.

QUICK REFERENCE | **CONVERTING TEXT TO COLUMNS**

Task	Procedure
Split text in a single column to multiple columns	■ Select the text in one column to be converted. ■ Choose Data→Data Tools→Text to Columns from the Ribbon. ■ Follow the instructions in the Convert Text to Columns Wizard, and click Finish.

DEVELOP YOUR SKILLS 18.6.3

Convert Text to Columns

In this exercise, you will split the chapter data in column A to two columns. Currently, the chapter number and chapter name are in a single cell.

Before You Begin: You must have completed Develop Your Skills 18.6.2, and the AR Production Schedule workbook should be open. If you reopened the file and a Data Connections Have Been Disabled warning appears, click the Enable Content button.

Add a Delimiter Character to Text

1. Insert a blank column at **column B**.
   The blank column will receive the chapter names from the split text.
2. Select **cell A7** in the Editing Schedule worksheet.

3. Follow these steps to add a space before the word *Chapter*:

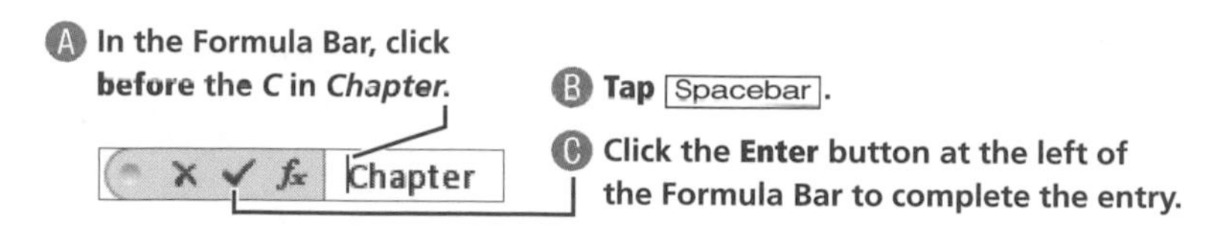

A In the Formula Bar, click before the C in *Chapter*.
B Tap Spacebar.
C Click the **Enter** button at the left of the Formula Bar to complete the entry.
Chapter

The space you just added will become a delimiter for that cell as you split text in the next few steps.

Split Text into Two Columns

4. Select the **range A7:A14**.
5. Choose **Data→Data Tools→Text to Columns** from the Ribbon.
   The Convert Text to Columns Wizard – Step 1 of 3 dialog box opens. In the upper half of the dialog box, notice that Fixed Width is selected because the data contains a space between the chapter number and chapter name.
6. Click **Next**.
   Step 2 of the wizard contains instructions to break the text at the desired location.
7. **Scroll down** in the Data Preview section until **row 5** is visible.
   Notice that the chapter numbers are in one column and the chapter titles are in a second column. Some text extends to the right of the column break line and would be placed in a third column. You will adjust the text to be placed in the second column in the next step.
8. **Drag** the column break line from 20 to the right until it displays just to the right of *Foundation*.
9. Click **Next** to continue with step 3 of the wizard.
10. Leave the column data format set to General, and notice that the destination cell is **A7** in the dialog box.

```
        10        20        30
1 A Message from the CEO
2 Our Stories
3 New Advances
4 Program Activities
5 Raritan Clinic Foundation
```

11. Click **Finish**; click **OK** when asked if you wish to replace the contents of the destination cell.
    Notice that the text originally after the space in each cell of column A has been moved to the new column B.

Adjust Column Widths

12. Point at the border between the column headings for **columns A and B**, and drag to the left to decrease the **column A** width.

	A	B	C	D
7		Chapter	Due Date	Status
8	1	A Message from the CEO	1-Aug	Done
9	2	Our Stories	2-Aug	Done
10	3	New Advances	2-Aug	Done
11	4	Program Activities	7-Aug	On schedule
12	5	Raritan Clinic Foundation	8-Aug	On schedule
13	6	Financials	16-Aug	Late 1 day
14	7	Board of Directors	17-Aug	Late 2 days

13. **Double-click** the border between the column headings for **columns B and C** to autofit the column B width.
Rows 7–14 should look similar to the illustration.

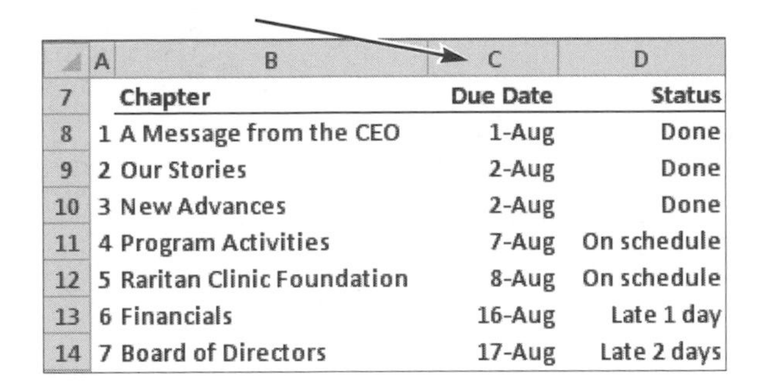

	A	B	C	D
7		Chapter	Due Date	Status
8	1	A Message from the CEO	1-Aug	Done
9	2	Our Stories	2-Aug	Done
10	3	New Advances	2-Aug	Done
11	4	Program Activities	7-Aug	On schedule
12	5	Raritan Clinic Foundation	8-Aug	On schedule
13	6	Financials	16-Aug	Late 1 day
14	7	Board of Directors	17-Aug	Late 2 days

14. **Save** the changes, and **close** the workbook.

18.7 Saving Workbook Elements as a Web Page

Video Lesson labyrinthelab.com/videos

You may save a worksheet range, an entire worksheet, or a workbook with multiple sheets as a page that users may view on the web or your organization's intranet. They cannot edit the Excel data or view formulas, and some formatting may be lost when you save as a web page. You may save as either a web page with components stored in separate files or as a single web page.

For best results, the workbook upon which the web page is based should have no spaces in the filename. You may use the underscore (_) character to connect words, if desired.

Saving as a Web Page

The Web Page option in the Save As Type list creates a main document with the filename extension .htm in the HTML (Hypertext Markup Language) format. Excel also creates a destination folder and saves workbook elements as files in that folder. You then can access individual items. For example, you may wish to replace one picture file in the folder rather than revise and republish the entire web page. You must copy both the main document and the folder to your web server.

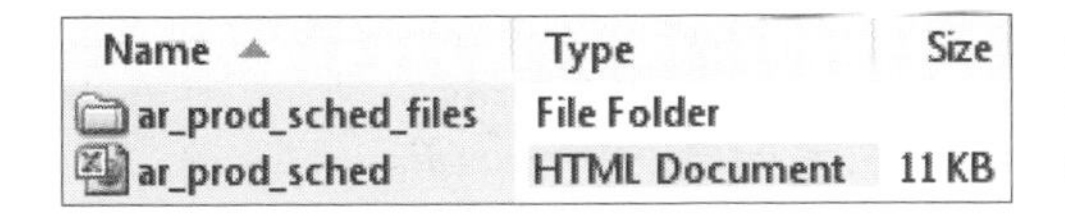

Name	Type	Size
ar_prod_sched_files	File Folder	
ar_prod_sched	HTML Document	11 KB

Saving an Excel workbook as a web page results in one main document and a folder containing files necessary to display the web page.

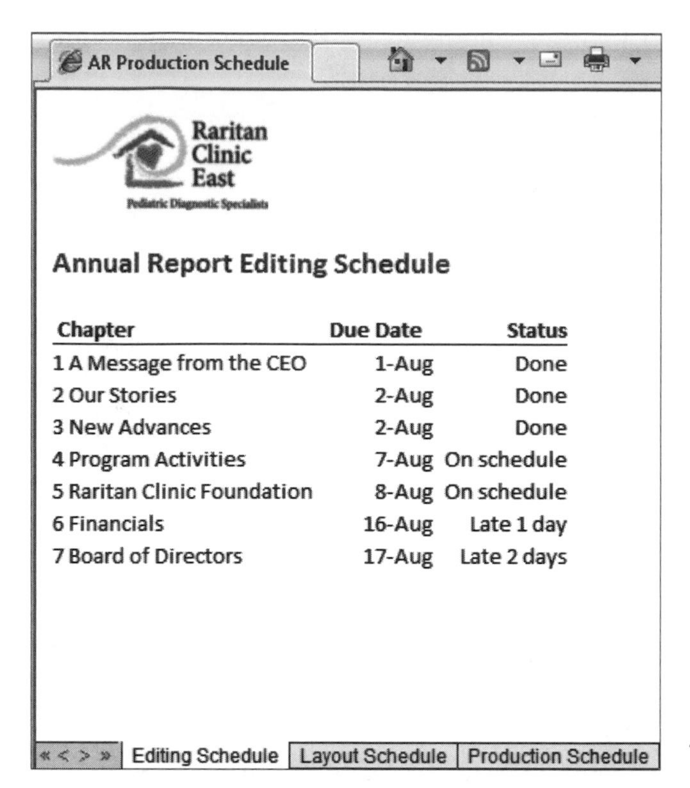

The web page as viewed in a browser

Saving as a Single File Web Page

The Single File Web Page option in the Save As Type list is used to save all the web page elements in one file. The file is created with the filename extension .mht using the Web Archive file format. This method is useful for sending a web page as an email attachment for collaboration with others. The Web Archive file format has several limitations. A significantly larger file size results because all elements are embedded in a single file. Also, a web developer cannot edit the HTML code to update the page, and not all web browsers can open an MHT file.

Publishing the Web Page

You must publish, or upload, your document to a web server. Your network administrator may set up a destination folder on the server for you. You may publish the web page as you save it, or you may upload it later. The Save As dialog box contains options to select the workbook portion to be saved and publish the web page. You may add a page title that would be displayed in the tab of the user's web browser. You may publish first to a drive on your computer and preview how the web page looks before uploading to a web server.

QUICK REFERENCE	SAVING WORKBOOK ELEMENTS AS A WEB PAGE
Task	**Procedure**
Add the Web Page Preview button to the Quick Access toolbar	■ Right-click the Quick Access toolbar, and choose Customize Quick Access Toolbar from the context menu. ■ In the Excel Options dialog box, choose Commands Not in the Ribbon from the Choose Commands From list. ■ Choose Web Page Preview from the commands list, and click Add.
Save a range, worksheet, or entire workbook as a web page	■ Save the workbook with a filename containing no spaces. ■ Select the range or display the desired worksheet if the entire workbook is not to be saved. ■ Choose File→Save As. ■ In the Save As dialog box, choose one of the following from the Save As Type list: ◆ Web Page (creates a main document and a folder containing page elements) ◆ Single File Web Page (saves all page elements in a single file) ■ Choose an option for the workbook portion to be saved, and choose other options, as desired. ■ Click Save. ■ If a Microsoft Excel message about web page compatibility displays, read the message and choose Yes. ■ Open the web page file in a web browser, or click the Web Page Preview button on the Quick Access toolbar to check the page content.

DEVELOP YOUR SKILLS 18.7.1

Save a Worksheet as a Single File Web Page

In this exercise, you will save one worksheet from a workbook as a single web page. Then, you will preview the web page in your browser.

Before You Begin: A web browser, such as Internet Explorer, must be installed on your computer to view the saved web page.

Set the Single File Web Page Option

1. **Open** the ar_prod_sched workbook from the Lesson 18 folder.
   Notice that the workbook name contains underscore (_) characters between words. Filenames and folder names containing spaces often do not display well in a web browser.
2. Display the **Production Schedule** worksheet.
3. Choose **File→Save As**.
4. In the Save As dialog box, choose **Single File Web Page** from the Save As Type list.
   Other options now appear in the bottom section of the dialog box.

Set Web Page Options

5. For the **Save** option, choose **Selection: Sheet**.
6. Click the **Change Title** button in the bottom-right corner of the Save As dialog box.
   The Enter Text dialog displays.

7. In the Enter Text dialog box, type **AR Production Schedule** and click **OK**.
   The Save As dialog box reappears. The Title box displays the text you just typed. Your dialog box should resemble the one below except for the Authors.

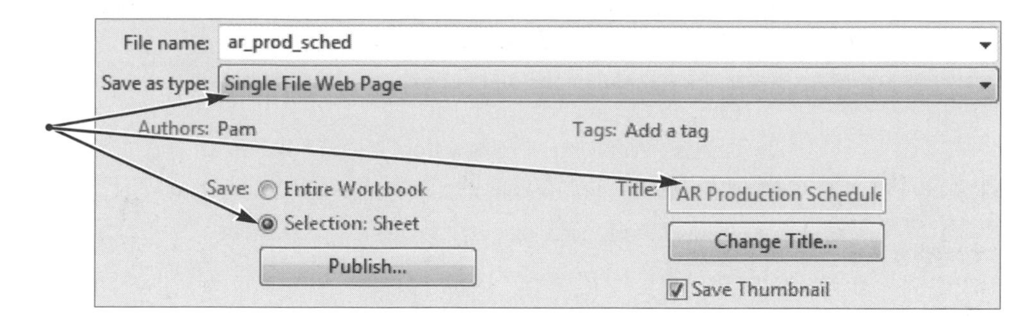

Save and View the Web Page in a Browser

8. Click **Save**.
   The Publish as Web Page dialog box appears. Notice that the options you selected are summarized in the dialog box.
9. Place a checkmark next to **Open Published Web Page in Browser**.
   Skip this step if your computer does not have a web browser installed.
10. Click **Publish**.
    The web page opens in your browser. Your browser may be different than shown. The page title you specified shows in the tab and at the top of the web page.

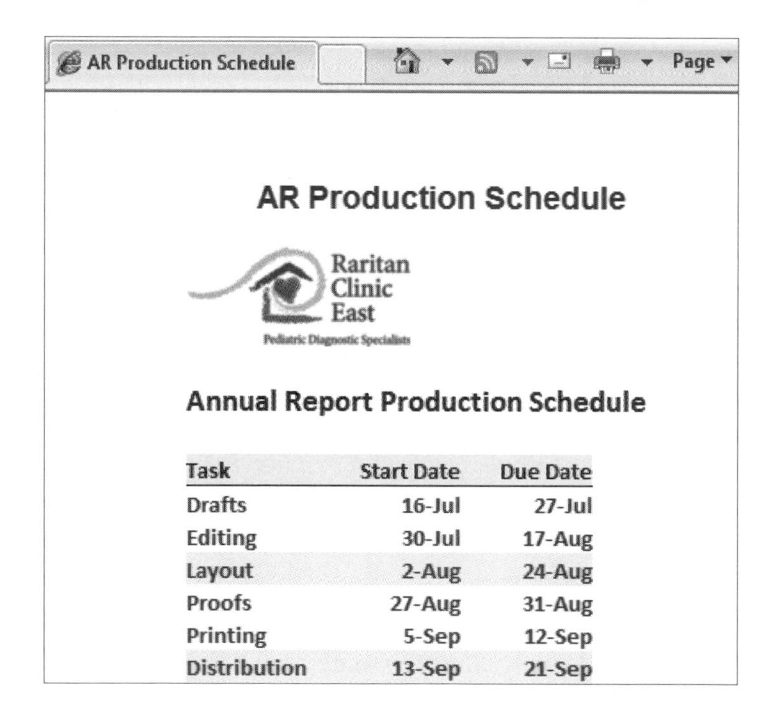

11. **Close** the browser window.
12. **Close** the workbook without saving, and **exit** Excel.

18.8 Concepts Review

Concepts Review labyrinthelab.com/excel10

To check your knowledge of the key concepts introduced in this lesson, complete the Concepts Review quiz by going to the URL listed above. If your classroom is using Labyrinth eLab, you may complete the Concepts Review quiz from within your eLab course.

Reinforce Your Skills

REINFORCE YOUR SKILLS 18.1

Save a Worksheet in Comma Delimited Format

In this exercise, you will save a workbook in a nonnative file format. Then you will open the newly converted file in Excel and Notepad.

Save the Worksheet

1. **Open** the rs-TyncoLabs Q1 Sales workbook from the Lesson 18 workbook in your file storage location.
2. Choose **File→Save As** from the Ribbon.
3. Display the **Save As Type** list and choose **CSV (Comma Delimited)**.
4. Change the filename to **`rs-TyncoLabs Comma Delimited`**.
5. Click **Save**.
   Excel warns you that you may lose some features if you convert the data to this new file format.
6. Choose **Yes** to continue saving in the new file format.
   Excel saves the worksheet to the new file but continues displaying the normal Excel workbook file. To see the file in its newly converted format, you must open it.
7. Use Ctrl+W to **close** the workbook and leave Excel **open**. Choose **not** to save when you are asked to save any changes to the file.

Open the Converted File in Excel

8. Choose **File→Open** from the Ribbon.
   Notice that the newly converted file is not listed. That's because the conversion changed it from an Excel file to a text file.
9. Display the Files of Type list and choose **Text Files**.
   Now the converted filename should be visible.
10. **Open** the rs-TyncoLabs Comma Delimited file.
    Although the layout of data in specific cells is preserved, the table formatting and cell border formatting have been lost.
11. Select **cell D5**, and then read its data in the Formula Bar.
    Since the entire date is entered, Excel determined that this data should be displayed in Date format.
12. Use Ctrl+W to **close** the workbook and leave Excel **open**. Choose **not** to save if you are asked to save any changes.

Open the Converted File in Notepad

Now you will open the converted file in a different program. The Notepad applet is a simple text editor program that comes with Windows. It will allow you to view exactly what the data in your converted file looks like.

13. Choose **Start→All Programs→Accessories→Notepad**. (The path may be different on your computer.)
14. In the Notepad window, choose **File→Open**.
    The Open dialog box appears. Once again, the converted file is not listed.
15. Display the **Files of Type** list, and choose **All Files**.
16. **Open** the rs-TyncoLabs Comma Delimited file.
    Notepad displays the data in the file. Notice the commas that separate data items. Each comma represents a column when you open the file in Excel.
17. **Exit** Notepad. Choose **not** to save if you are asked to save any changes.

REINFORCE YOUR SKILLS 18.2

Import Data from Access

In this exercise, you will bring data into Excel from an Access database table.

Import an Access Database

1. **Start** a new workbook in Excel and save it as **`rs-Shelter Summary`** in the Lesson 18 folder.
2. Rename the **Sheet1** tab as **`Occupancy`**.
3. Select **cell A1**, if not already selected.
4. Choose **Data→Get External Data→From Access** from the Ribbon.
5. In the **Select Data Source** dialog box, navigate to the Lesson 18 folder in your file storage location.
   Excel displays only Access files in the folder.
6. Choose the rs-Shelter Occupancy database file and click **Open**.
   Excel displays the three tables in the database file and asks you to select the one to be imported. In this case, you will import the Year 1 occupancy data.
7. In the **Select Table** dialog box, choose **Shelter Occupancy – Year 1** and click **OK**.
8. In the **Import Data** dialog box, make certain that the options appear as shown in the illustration at right and click **OK**.
   You may view data as a table, PivotTable, or PivotTable with PivotChart. You may place the imported data on the existing worksheet or a new worksheet.

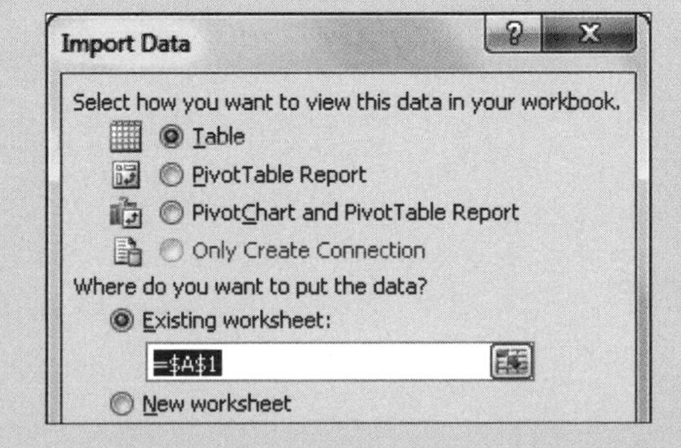

Your imported database table should look like the following illustration. You set the data to start in cell A1 on the currently displayed worksheet.

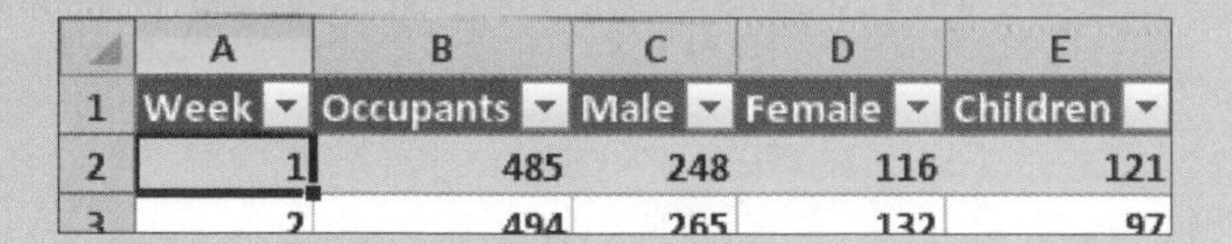

	A	B	C	D	E
1	Week	Occupants	Male	Female	Children
2	1	485	248	116	121
3	2	494	265	132	97

9. **Save** the changes, and leave the workbook **open** for the next exercise.

REINFORCE YOUR SKILLS 18.3

Import Data from Word

In this exercise, you will bring data into Excel from a Word table.

***Before You Begin:** The rs-Shelter Summary workbook should be open from Reinforce Your Skills 18.2. If your instructor directed you to skip that exercise, start a new workbook and save as rs-Shelter Summary in the Lesson 18 folder.*

Import from a Word Document

1. Rename the **Sheet2** tab as `Q1 Budget Summary`.
2. Start **Word** and then **open** the rs-Quarter 1 Budget document from the Lesson 18 folder.
   You will use the Copy and Paste commands to import data from a Word table.
3. If necessary, **scroll down** the document and then select the **Q1 Budget Summary** heading row and all the other rows of the budget table shown. (Do not include the title Cypress Shelter in the selection.)

Q1 Budget Summary

	January	February	March	Totals
Mortgage & Insurance	$ 3,779	$ 3,779	$ 3,779	$ 11,337
Utilities	720	678	623	2,021
Food	1,860	1,900	1,720	5,480
Staff Salaries	5,895	5,895	5,895	17,685
Maintenance & Repairs	325	370	1,493	2,188
Outreach & Fundraising	280	280	260	820
Grand Total	**$ 12,859**	**$ 12,902**	**$ 13,770**	**$ 39,531**

4. Choose **Home→Clipboard→Copy** from the Ribbon.
5. Close **Word**. Choose **not** to save if asked to save any changes.
   The data you copied to the Clipboard remains there even after you close the application from which you made the copy.
6. Select **cell A1** in the Q1 Budget Summary worksheet and choose **Home→Clipboard→Paste** from the Ribbon.
   Excel pastes the heading and table, including the text formatting that was set in the Word document.

Clean Up the Pasted Data

The column widths and row heights may need to be adjusted.

7. Adjust **column widths** as necessary.
8. Reset the **row 1** height to 18.75.
9. Select **rows 2 through 11** and reset the row height to 15.00.
10. Select the **range B4:E4. Hold down** [Ctrl] and select the **range B11:E11**.
    Both ranges are highlighted.
11. Format the selected cells as **Accounting format with no decimal places**.
    Your worksheet should look like the following illustration.

	A	B	C	D	E
1	Q1 Budget Summary				
2					
3		January	February	March	Totals
4	**Mortgage & Insurance**	$ 3,779	$ 3,779	$ 3,779	$ 11,337
5	**Utilities**	720	678	623	2,021
6	**Food**	1,860	1,900	1,720	5,480
7	**Staff Salaries**	5,895	5,895	5,895	17,685
8	**Maintenance & Repairs**	325	370	1,493	2,188
9	**Outreach & Fundraising**	280	280	260	820
10					
11	**Grand Total**	**$ 12,859**	**$ 12,902**	**$ 13,770**	**$ 39,531**

As you can see, some formatting was necessary after pasting the table from Word. Also, the numbers in the Grand Total row pasted as values, not formulas.

12. Select **cell B11** and create a formula that sums the **range B4:B9**.
13. Copy the formula in **cell B11** to the other grand total cells.
14. **Save** the changes and leave the workbook **open** for the next exercise.

REINFORCE YOUR SKILLS 18.4

Check Compatibility and Save a Workbook

In this exercise, you will check a workbook's compatibility with prior Excel versions and then save for a prior version.

Before You Begin: *You must have completed Reinforce Your Skills 18.2 and Reinforce Your Skills 18.3, and the rs-Shelter Summary workbook should be open.*

Run the Compatibility Checker

1. Choose **File→Info→Check for Issues→Check Compatibility.**
   After a few moments, the Microsoft Office Excel – Compatibility Checker window appears with its report of three issues causing a minor loss of fidelity.
2. Click the **Copy to New Sheet** button in the lower-right area of the dialog box.
3. Read the report in the new worksheet that appears.
   Two issues relate to the table in the first worksheet, and another general formatting issue is reported with three occurrences. Because these issues are reported as minor, you will not correct them.
4. **Save** the workbook with the Compatibility Report worksheet included.

Use Save As

Next you will give the Save As command to save the file for an earlier Excel version.

5. Choose **File→Save As**, and choose **Excel 97-2003 Workbook** from the Save as Type list.

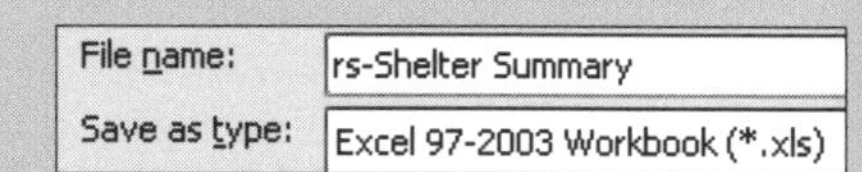

6. Click **Save**.
   The Compatibility Checker window reappears to report the same issues as it did previously.
7. Click the **Continue** button to save the file with the issues unresolved.
   This save creates a separate workbook with the Excel 97-2003 file format. If that workbook is opened in Excel 2003, the table in the first worksheet is converted to a normal list and loses its font colors and shading, but the data is not altered.
8. **Close** the workbook.

REINFORCE YOUR SKILLS 18.5

Save a Workbook as a Single File Web Page

In this exercise, you will save an Excel workbook as a single file web page.

Before You Begin: A web browser capable of displaying files with the .mht file extension, such as Internet Explorer, must be installed to view the published web page.

Save a Workbook as a Web Page

1. **Open** the rs-Budget Summary workbook from the Lesson 18 folder.
2. Choose **File→Save As** .
3. In the **Save As** dialog box, change the file name to **`rs-Web Summary`**.

Set Web Page Options

4. Drop down the **Save as Type** list and choose **Single File Web Page**.
5. Click the **Change Title** button in the lower-right corner of the Save As dialog box.
6. In the **Enter Text** dialog box, type **`Shelter Summary`**, and click **OK**.
   This descriptive title will display in the page tab when you open the web page in your browser.
7. In the lower-left corner of the **Save As** dialog box, make certain the Save option is set to **Entire Workbook**.
   Your dialog box should resemble the following illustration.

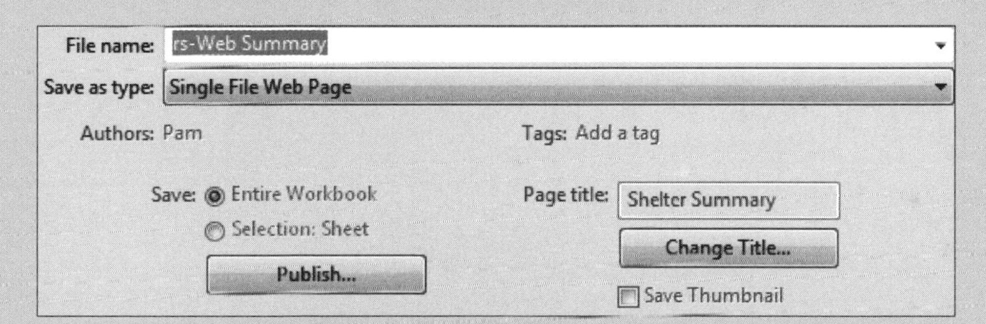

8. Click **Save**, and click **Yes** to continue saving when the Microsoft Excel compatibility message displays.
   The workbook is saved with the filename extension .mht using the Web Archive file format. The workbook appearance does not change in Excel.
9. **Close** the workbook file, and leave Excel **open**.

View the Web Page

10. **Open** your web browser, such as Internet Explorer.
11. Choose **File→Open**, navigate to the Lesson 18 folder, and **open** rs-Web Summary.
    The single file web page displays in the browser. The page title Shelter Summary displays in the page tab above the workbook data. Tabs for two worksheets display at the bottom of the browser window because you chose the Entire Workbook option while saving the web page.
12. View the worksheets by clicking tabs at the bottom of the browser window.

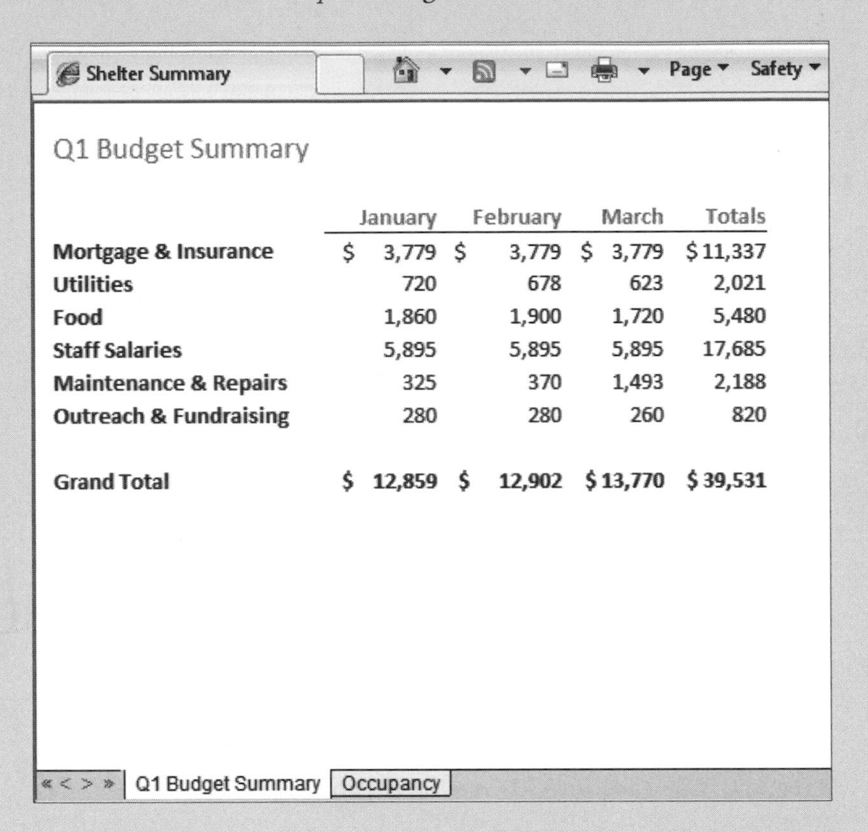

Q1 Budget Summary

	January	February	March	Totals
Mortgage & Insurance	$ 3,779	$ 3,779	$ 3,779	$ 11,337
Utilities	720	678	623	2,021
Food	1,860	1,900	1,720	5,480
Staff Salaries	5,895	5,895	5,895	17,685
Maintenance & Repairs	325	370	1,493	2,188
Outreach & Fundraising	280	280	260	820
Grand Total	**$ 12,859**	**$ 12,902**	**$ 13,770**	**$ 39,531**

13. **Close** [X] the browser window when you are finished.

Apply Your Skills

APPLY YOUR SKILLS 18.1

Save a Worksheet in Tab Delimited File Format

In this exercise, you will save a workbook in a different (nonnative) file format. Then you will open the converted file in Excel and print it.

1. **Open** the as-Cypress Budget workbook from the Lesson 18 folder in your file storage location.
2. Save the Budget worksheet in the **Text (Tab Delimited)** file format with the name **`as-Cypress Budget Tab Delimited`**.
   This step saves the data to a separate file, but the original workbook still appears.
3. **Close** the workbook, and choose **not** to save when asked if you want to save changes.
   Remember that the newly converted workbook is a text file.
4. **Start** a new workbook.
5. **Import** the as-Cypress Budget Tab Delimited file. Start the import with **row 3** of the data (the column headings Q1, Q2 and so on). Use the General column data format for all columns. Import to **cell A1** of the worksheet.
6. After completing the import command, adjust **column widths**, if necessary, to make all text visible.
7. **Print** the worksheet.
   Your tab delimited data should look like the following illustration.

	A	B	C	D	E	F
1		Q1	Q2	Q3	Q4	Totals
2	Mortgage & Insurance	11,337	11,337	11,337	11,337	45,348
3	Utilities	2,021	1,464	1,504	1,809	6,798
4	Staff Salaries	13,093	17,685	17,685	17,685	66,148
5	Maintenance and Repairs	845	951	3,113	724	5,633
6	Outreach & Fundraising	820	2,006	576	712	4,114
7	Grand Totals	28,116	33,443	34,215	32,267	128,041

8. **Save** the workbook with the name **`as-Delimited Import`** and **close** the workbook.

APPLY YOUR SKILLS 18.2

Import Data from Comma Delimited File Format

In this exercise, you will import data into Excel from a comma delimited file and then format the data.

1. **Start** a new workbook and save it with the name **as-Data Import** in the Lesson 18 folder.
2. Rename the **Sheet1** tab as **Imported Data**.
3. **Import** all the data (including titles) from the as-Comma Delimited Data file in the Lesson 18 folder. In the wizard, choose **Comma** as the delimiter type and make certain to preview the data. The first column will contain both animal and age data, which you will separate in a later step. Place the imported data at **cell A1** on the Imported Data worksheet.
4. After importing the data, insert a **blank column** before the **Health** column.
5. **Split** the text currently located in the **range A4:A23** into two columns for Animal and Age. Choose **Space** as the delimiter type. Preview the data to ensure that Total Costs in **cell A24** will not be split.
6. Adjust the **column widths** and add other **formatting** so that the data are easy to read.
7. Make certain that the totals in the bottom row are formulas.
   Your formatting may vary from the following illustrations.

	A	B	C	D	E	F	G
1	Triangle Animal Shelter						
2	March Expense Report						
3							
4	Animal	Age	Health	Date Arrived	Shelter Cost	Veterinary Care	Total Costs
5	Cat	Adult	Healthy	1-Mar	$82.50	$10.00	$92.50
6	Dog	Adult	Healthy	2-Mar	$79.75	$10.00	$89.75
23	Dog	Adult	Healthy	30-Mar	$2.75	$10.00	$12.75
24	Total Costs				$888.25	$340.00	$1,228.25

8. **Save** the changes, and **close** the workbook.

APPLY YOUR SKILLS 18.3

Import Data from Word

In this exercise, you will copy and paste text and an image into Excel from a Word document and then format the data.

1. **Start** a new workbook and save it with the name **as-EduCare Fiscal Summary** in the Lesson 18 folder.
2. Rename the **Sheet1** tab as **Year-End Report**.
3. Start **Word** and then **open** the as-EduCare Year-End Report document from the Lesson 18 folder.
4. **Drag and drop** the text Year-End Report from the Word document to **cell A1** of the Year-End Report worksheet.
5. **Copy** the Q1 through Q4 headings, data rows, and the Total row from the Word document. **Paste** them into an appropriate row of the Excel worksheet.
6. **Close** the Word document without saving.
7. **Format** the data in the worksheet, such as column widths and row heights, as necessary to make the data easy to read.
8. Do whatever is necessary to have the Total row contain **formulas**, not values.
   Your worksheet may vary slightly from the following illustration.

	A	B	C	D	E
1	Year-End Report				
2					
3		Q1	Q2	Q3	Q4
4	Mortgage and Insurance	$6,779	$6,750	$6,750	$6,846
5	Utilities	2,120	1,678	1,728	1,893
6	Food	4,860	4,900	4,720	5,720
7	Staff Salaries	8,695	8,695	8,895	8,895
8	Maintenance and Repairs	3,325	1,370	1,493	1,493
9	Outreach and Fundraising	1,280	1,280	1,260	1,260
10					
11	Total	$27,059	$24,673	$24,846	$26,107

9. **Save** the changes, and keep the workbook **open**.

APPLY YOUR SKILLS 18.4

Save a Worksheet as a Single File Web Page

In this exercise, you will save a worksheet from an Excel workbook in the Single File Web Page file format.

Before You Begin: *You should have completed Apply Your Skills 18.3, and the as-EduCare Fiscal Summary workbook should be open. A web browser capable of displaying files with the .mht file extension, such as Internet Explorer, must be installed to view the published web page.*

1. Check the as-EduCare Fiscal Summary workbook for **compatibility issues**. After reviewing the compatibility report, determine whether you need to take any action.
2. **Save** the Year-End Report worksheet as a single file web page. (Do not save the entire workbook as a web page.)
3. **Open** the saved web page file in your browser, and check that it displays correctly.
4. **Close** the browser.
5. **Save** the workbook, and then **close** it.

Critical Thinking & Work-Readiness Skills

In the course of working through the following Microsoft Office-based Critical Thinking exercises, you will also be utilizing various work-readiness skills, some of which are listed next to each exercise. Go to labyrinthelab.com/workreadiness *to learn more about the work-readiness skills.*

18.1 Import Data from Access

Raritan Clinic East provides special services to families with newborn infants. You will help coordinate the data for several projects. To gather information efficiently, you have asked for the Access database source file. You have received this file and now need to import it into Microsoft Excel. Open a new Excel workbook. Import the external Access data file ct-Newborn Weights (Lesson 18 folder) as an Excel table. Delete the ID column, and sort the table by birth date in oldest to newest order. Save your workbook with the name **ct-Newborn Weights [Your Last Name]** in the Lesson 18 folder. Keep the file open.

WORK-READINESS SKILLS APPLIED

- Serving clients/customers
- Organizing and maintaining information
- Applying technology to a task

18.2 Save a Worksheet in Tab Delimited Format

Volunteers deliver congratulatory cards to each family with a newborn, and employee Jessica Allen coordinates this activity. She needs you to create a text list of patients, their newborns' birth dates, and the birth weights. The volunteers will use this information to individualize the cards. Open ct-Newborn Weights [Your Last Name], if necessary. Save the worksheet data as a text file in tab delimited format. Close the text file.

WORK-READINESS SKILLS APPLIED

- Serving clients/customers
- Organizing and maintaining information
- Applying technology to a task

18.3 Save a Worksheet as a Single File Web Page

Raritan East Clinic also supplies the local newspaper with infant birth statistics. The information is to remain static (no opportunity for anyone to change data), so you will save the data as a single file web page. You will provide this information by emailing it to the local newspaper. Open ct-Newborn Weights [Your Last Name]. Enable content if a security warning displays. Remove any personal information that could identify the patients. Then, save the worksheet as a single file web page, and enter a web page title. Open the published web page in a web browser to check the data before submitting it. Close your browser window, and close the Excel file without saving.

WORK-READINESS SKILLS APPLIED

- Serving clients/customers
- Organizing and maintaining information
- Applying technology to a task

Index

G

H

I

K

L

M

N

O

P

R

S

T

U

V

W

X

Notes

Notes